# The Wendell Smith Reader

# The Wendell Smith Reader

*Selected Writings on Sports, Civil Rights and Black History*

WENDELL SMITH

*Edited by* Michael Scott Pifer

*Introduction by* Michael Marsh

McFarland & Company, Inc., Publishers

*Jefferson, North Carolina*

LIBRARY OF CONGRESS CATALOGUING-IN-PUBLICATION DATA

Names: Smith, Wendell, 1914–1972 author. | Pifer, Michael Scott, 1961– editor.
Title: The Wendell Smith reader : selected writings on sports, civil rights and
    Black history / Wendell Smith ; edited by Michael Scott Pifer ; introduction
    by Michael Marsh.
Description: Jefferson, North Carolina : McFarland & Company, Inc.,
    Publishers, 2023 | Includes bibliographical references and index.
Identifiers: LCCN 2023007490 | ISBN 9781476691756 (print) ∞
    ISBN 9781476649412 (ebook)
Subjects: LCSH: Smith, Wendell, 1914-1972. | Sportswriters—United States—
    Biography. | Sportscasters—United States—Biography. | Sports—United States. |
    African Americans—History. | Racism.
Classification: LCC GV742.42.S5 S65 2023 | DDC 796.092 [B]—dc23/eng/20230306
LC record available at https://lccn.loc.gov/2023007490

BRITISH LIBRARY CATALOGUING DATA ARE AVAILABLE

ISBN (print) 978-1-4766-9175-6
ISBN (ebook) 978-1-4766-4941-2

Front cover: J. G. Taylor Spink Award winner Wendell Smith
(National Baseball Hall of Fame Library, Cooperstown, New York)

Printed in the United States of America

McFarland & Company, Inc., Publishers
    Box 611, Jefferson, North Carolina 28640
    www.mcfarlandpub.com

For Paulette Christine Hahn,
the Prime Mover behind the Wendell Smith Project

# Table of Contents

# Table of Contents

# Acknowledgments

*The Wendell Smith Reader* is my first book and I needed help every step of the way. Fortunately, many people provided help. Jerry Reinsdorf, owner of the Chicago White Sox, responded to my request by asking Scott Reifert, the team's vice president of communications, to give me leads. Ron Rapoport was one of the names Scott gave to me. This book would not have been written without Ron's guidance and encouragement. Kyle Weaver is a friend from childhood and an editor by trade. Like Ron, he provided practical advice about a variety of issues. Michael Marsh and the Society of American Baseball Research (SABR) provided important biographical information that I could find in no other source. Michael has researched Wendell's life for more than two decades and contributed the introduction to this book. Sarah Cary, Dave Gerdes, Dave Daegling, Geoff Good and Tom Pifer read various sections of the book and provided valuable criticism. Ethan Magoc introduced me to newspapers.com, which provided access to the *Pittsburgh Courier* and other newspapers. Hilary Mac Austin performed the research on the Chicago papers that I could not access from home. She promptly and thoroughly did what I asked and then did a bit more. Hilary found four columns that Wendell wrote for the *Chicago Defender* despite my insistence that there was no way Wendell wrote for the *Defender* while he was writing for the *Courier.* Hilary's was a significant find.

Growing up in the 1960s and 70s, I could not have imagined that I would one day interview some of the professional athletes I was watching. This book gave me those opportunities and every athlete was friendly and generous with his time. Thank you to George Altman, Gary Brokaw, Vida Blue, Don Buford, Al Downing, Carl Erskine, Ferguson Jenkins, Jerry Harkness, Ken Holtzman, and Billy Williams. Blue, Downing, Erskine, Jenkins and Holtzman would also be a formidable starting pitching rotation. Bill Haller, former American League umpire, provided valuable insight on several matters, not least among them Emmett Ashford.

Two recipients of the Sam Lacy–Wendell Smith Award also were generous with their time. Claire Smith and I spent about half of our time talking Big Five basketball. If you get a chance to see a basketball game at the Palestra, do it; you'll be glad you did. Bob Costas was the only interview that made me nervous. Turned out he is a nice guy and there was no need to be nervous.

Roger Valdiserri, longtime sports information director at Notre Dame University and arguably the women's basketball team's biggest fan, provided much needed information regarding what Wendell was like in person. I thoroughly enjoyed speaking with Roger. Apparently everyone else does as well.

The Henry Ford Organization, West Virginia State University (Wendell's alma mater), and the National Baseball Hall of Fame were a pleasure to deal with and provided valuable information for my research.

I am eternally grateful to Tom Barton, Henry Libhart and Louise Black, three English teachers who made me a better writer. More important, they made me a better reader. They ignited my imagination. Reading has always been a joy.

And finally, thank you to Ray Pifer, Henry Albright, Bob Davis, Bill Murtha and Albert Kashmere. I love baseball because of these men.

Thanks to the Sporting News and Real Times Media for permission to use columns from *The Sporting News*, *Pittsburgh Courier* and *Chicago Defender*. I made multiple efforts to identify rightsholders for the defunct magazine *Tuesday Morning at Home*, and the few columns used from the *Chicago Tribune* and *Chicago Sun-Times*, all to no avail.

# Preface

To the extent Wendell Smith is known by the public, it is likely as the journalist Branch Rickey hired to shadow Jackie Robinson, as depicted in the movie *42*. While he might be remembered for that significant work, there is far too much that is forgotten. My primary objective in presenting this collection of Wendell Smith's writing is to introduce the reader to the full scope of his work, with representative selections from across his career in journalism (1937–72), the various publications in which his work appeared, the topics about which he wrote, and the forms in which the work appeared (e.g., columns, book reviews, etc.). Determining which writings to include in which chapters is as much art as science, and many could be included as easily in chapters other than the ones in which I've placed them. The entries in the chapters that follow were culled from more than 1,500 pieces that spanned thirty-five years. This book contains only his written work: There are to be found within no transcriptions, for instance, from Smith's twenty-five-year career in broadcast journalism.

This volume is aimed primarily at the sports-loving lay reader and for those interested in civil rights, sports history, African American history, or advocacy journalism. It is also intended for use as a supportive text, at both the undergraduate and graduate level, in courses related to those topics.

Much of Wendell's writing is in fact advocacy journalism. He wrote mainly, but not exclusively, about sports. Wendell was a pioneer for Black journalists in radio and television. He also produced a documentary about Blacks in Chicago and narrated an educational film strip/album about Dr. Martin Luther King, Jr., for young people. While I seek to broaden the reader's appreciation for Wendell's work beyond the boundaries of his relationship with Jackie Robinson, there is a crucial parallel throughout their lives: They were on a mission. Jackie was paid for playing baseball; Wendell, to be a journalist. But playing a sport and writing about a sport were merely vehicles to transport their people to the Promised Land of racial equality. Most of what these two men said and did in some way related to obtaining and securing the rights of Black people in America.

Although Smith's writings could be organized in a number of ways, including chronologically or by sport, I chose to categorize them under the cause to which he was dedicated: expanding opportunities for Black people. Fighting racism was of primary importance, but Wendell wrote about progress at every opportunity, so there is a chapter for those more optimistic pieces. He traveled much and cared about the welfare of Black people throughout the world, thus the chapter "Foreign Affairs." Because there were no Black studies classes and Black individuals were slighted in the history books, Wendell wrote about Black history often, so it seems appropriate to devote a chapter to those articles as well.

There was no "eureka" moment for me over the course of compiling this volume. I respected Jackie and Wendell when I began and I respect them now, having completed it. What has changed is the level of respect. We know how the story ends. They succeeded in improving opportunities for Black individuals in America and to a lesser extent the world. They did not eliminate racism from the face of the earth. This book can be read in hours and the story proceeds efficiently. It is difficult to communicate drudgery and uncertainty. Waiting. Disappointment. Waiting. Humiliation. More waiting. And there was the constant risk that it would all be in vain. There was no guarantee that they would not be murdered. That was a constant risk to "uppity negroes." No amount of money or fame could compensate for enduring the disappointments and humiliations. Only men on a mission could have persevered. I was energized by the spiritual aspect of their journey. They were incessantly, relentlessly, tirelessly advocating for opportunity.

I have taken the liberty to correct misspellings and obvious errors that might divert the reader's attention from the point Wendell is making. He was a reporter and a columnist. I focus on the writings that appear in the *Pittsburgh Courier* (1937–67), *Defender* (1964), *The Sporting News*, *Tuesday at Home* (1971–72), and the *Chicago Tribune* and *Chicago Sun-Times* (1969–72) because he expressed his opinions in those pieces. He was hired by the *Chicago Herald-American* as a boxing reporter, later serving as the paper's beat writer for the Chicago White Sox. There were few Black baseball writers covering Major League Baseball (MLB) at that time. By working for a daily newspaper, Wendell became the second Black member of the Baseball Writers Association of America, with which (as the reader will see) he had an acrimonious relationship.

I did not include any of Smith's *Herald-American* writings in this book, however. The reader should not perceive this to mean those writings and his time with the paper are not important. The *Herald-American* allowed Wendell to transition to Chicago and pursue opportunities in broadcast journalism that were not available to him in Pittsburgh. But he was writing a column for the *Pittsburgh Courier* during that period as well, and the pieces from the *Herald-American* that I sought to republish in this volume also appeared (in slightly altered form) in the *Courier*, from which I was able to secure permission.

More than a half century after Wendell's death, we are still struggling with racism and pursuing racial justice. But what does that mean? Individuals perceive it differently. The case of Al Dark (Chapter 5) provides insight to how Wendell struggled with this issue. Wendell had no doubt that his cause was just. He did not think that gave him the right to skew his reporting, however. He was concerned about process and outcome. Advocacy journalism does not mean misrepresenting the facts.

To fully appreciate Smith's work the reader also would benefit from seeing the world through the eyes of a *Pittsburgh Courier* journalist. I would have liked to include a column about Isaiah Nixon, but Wendell did not write one. Smith was involved in raising money for the Nixon family and Evelyn Cunningham, the *Courier* reporter who covered this story, identifies Wendell as the individual to whom money should be sent for the benefit of the Nixon family. In 1948 Isaiah Nixon, a Black farmer in Georgia, defied the threats of some white neighbors (the sheriff-elect) and voted. He was shot and killed in front of his family. Killing him took care of one Black voter. Killing him in front of his family was perhaps intended to dissuade Isaiah's children from voting. The family left their home, and no one seemed to know what happened to them. They had family in Jacksonville, Florida, and that is where they eventually turned up. The *Courier* covered the story and raised money for Sallie Nixon, Isaiah's widow, and their six children. Hubert Nixon was age seven and a sports fan. I wondered if Hubert and Wendell interacted. Hank Klibanoff of Emory University won a Peabody Award for his podcast *Buried Truths*. In the podcast, Klibanoff investigates unresolved murders involving civil rights issues. I contacted him in hopes of speaking with any surviving Nixon children about Wendell. None of the surviving children knew Wendell and Hubert had passed away. The Nixon family confirmed that Hubert was a lifelong sports fan. One final point, and this is important: When the Nixon children became adults, they voted. Why bring this up?

Each week the *Courier* brought news of more atrocities committed against Black citizens across the nation. Rapes, lynchings, broken contracts, etc.; these stories were on the front page of almost every issue of the *Pittsburgh Courier*. Wendell did not live in a cocoon. He not only knew the Nixons' story but, sadly, he also knew many equally horrific stories. Wendell's friends appreciated his sense of humor. He liked to laugh. He was a warm and friendly man. But he had looked into the eyes of children who had recently watched their father be executed because he had exercised his constitutional right to vote. Still, Wendell insisted on being fair. He was many things; vengeful was not one of them. Determined was. He understood what "We shall overcome!" required.

Whenever possible in this book I have tried to demonstrate how Black athletic accomplishments related to the civil rights movement. For example, the East-West Classic (Negro League All-Star Game) does not compare in historical significance to the Montgomery Bus Boycott. There are, however, similarities. It was a logistical accomplishment to organize the Classic, played at Comiskey Park in Chicago, which drew more than 50,000 fans during the World War II years. This was not just an accomplishment on the part of the team owners. The fans had to travel to Chicago. Conventional (white) opinion held that Black people could not congregate in an orderly manner. Most of those 50,000 fans were Black. They congregated, had a good time, and left Comiskey Park in good order. The Montgomery Bus Boycott was largely a year-long movement that required more from the rank and file than the leaders of the movement. The East-West Classic foreshadowed the Montgomery Bus Boycott. Logistical genius. Disciplined individuals. Wendell wrote several columns that were directed to the Black baseball fan concerning how to behave during a game. Every individual had a role to play.

The EW Classic and the Montgomery Bus Boycott were organized without the Internet. The *Pittsburgh Courier* and other Black newspapers played a crucial role in uniting Black people across America. Radios, phones, television and churches contributed to organizing the civil rights movement as well. But newspapers could be read and passed on to others. Sports were important to Smith, but they were a means of advancing the civil rights movement. His style of writing changed during his career. What did not change was the brand of journalism he practiced: advocacy journalism in the proud tradition of Wells, Du Bois, Douglass, and a host of other Black journalists who preceded him.

# Introduction

## Wendell Smith's "Life of Splendor and Excitement"

### BY MICHAEL MARSH

On April 15, 1947, Wendell Smith arrived at the Brooklyn Dodgers' Ebbets Field for one of the most important assignments of his career. As usual, Smith wore a fedora and a suit which covered his tall, athletic build. Smith had traveled from Pittsburgh to cover the team's season opener, which was also Jackie Robinson's debut with the team. Smith was well prepared for the occasion given he was the sports editor for the *Pittsburgh Courier*, the leading Black weekly in the United States. The 32-year-old Smith had displayed both savvy and persistence as he evolved from cub reporter to veteran journalist.

For Smith, the occasion was important both professionally and personally. When Robinson took the field on that sunny day, he became the first Black man to play in the modern era of major league baseball. The debut remains an important story in sports history and civil rights history. Smith had a special interest in Robinson. Smith had campaigned to end baseball's color line, had recommended Robinson to Dodgers president Branch Rickey two years earlier and had traveled with Robinson over the previous year.

Smith deployed his skills before and after the game. While 25,623 fans filed into the stadium, Smith watched Robinson pose for pictures in his white uniform and shake hands with well-wishers. Afterward, Smith took notes as the Dodgers beat the Boston Braves 5–3. Robinson didn't get a hit, but he scored one run and played first base without an error. Smith produced four game-related articles for the April 19, 1947, issue of the *Courier's* New York edition. He wrote a piece about Robinson sparking a key rally with a bunt, a feature about the pomp and circumstance of Robinson's debut, a play-by-play account of the game and a recounting of

5

Robinson's at-bats and fielding plays.[1] He dictated his articles to a Western Union telegraph operator, who sent them to the weekly's office in Pittsburgh. Smith's coworkers, mobilized in an all-hands-on-deck effort to beat a deadline, typed his stories, selected photographs and designed page layouts.

In one article, Smith noted the game's importance. He wrote: "There was more significance to this opening day tilt than usual. It was of more historical significance than any other opening day game in the majors.... It was a great day. It was a great day for Brooklyn. It was a great day for baseball, and above all, a great day for JACKIE ROBINSON!"[2]

The day epitomized a career that he later called "a life of splendor and excitement." Smith lived such a life. His career, marked by excellent reporting abilities, strong interpersonal skills, and pioneering career advances, represents a special chapter of media history and Black history.

Smith used advocacy journalism, which presents news and facts of a story as part of a social or political agenda, to advance Black people. Smith capped his fight to integrate major league baseball when he helped Robinson join the Dodgers. Smith also helped desegregate Spring Training housing accommodations in Florida and Arizona by writing articles about the issue in both the *Courier* and *Chicago's American* (formerly known as the *Chicago Herald-American* and the *Chicago American*) during the early 1960s. Both campaigns boosted the cause of Black baseball players.

He established a notable record in the Black press and the mainstream media, paving a path for future Black sportswriters. He extensively covered Negro League baseball and other sports for the *Courier*, helping to preserve the exploits of Black athletes. He especially became adept at covering boxing, earning recognition as a top writer in the field. When he started work at the *Chicago Herald-American* in 1947, he became the first Black sportswriter to work for a daily newspaper. Smith established another first for Black sports journalists when he provided radio commentary for a championship boxing match in 1958. He later became one of the first Black sportswriters to work as a beat writer for a major league baseball team. During the 1960s, he became one of the first Blacks to work for a television news show in Chicago. He won election as the first Black president of the Chicago Journalism Club. His career is a model of achievement.

Smith was more than an advocate during his 35-year career. Smith evolved into a well-rounded newsman. He mastered the basics of journalism, displaying solid skills as a gatherer of facts, as an excellent interviewer, and as a passionate and insightful writer. Occasionally, he wrote light, slice-of-life pieces. He also toughened his prose for opinion pieces whenever he wanted to make a point. Furthermore, Smith never turned into a racial demagogue. Smith was an equal opportunity critic willing to rebuke anyone regardless of race.

Smith turned to journalism after major league baseball's color line kept him from signing a contract with a team. Born in 1914 to a club steward and a homemaker, Smith played baseball and basketball while he grew up in Detroit. But after a Detroit Tigers scout would not sign Smith, Smith played both sports at West Virginia State College (now West Virginia State University) and prepared for a journalism career. The rejection fueled Smith's determination to help Black athletes.

Although Smith experienced occasional controversies during his career, Smith gained the friendship and respect of many of his contemporaries. He displayed much personal warmth, humor, modesty and kindness toward coworkers. After he passed away in 1972, reporters across the country wrote tributes about him. Since his death, he has received many posthumous honors, including the J.G. Taylor Spink Award given by the Baseball Writers' Association of America (now called the BBWAA Career Excellence Award). The Spink awards are displayed in the Scribes and Mikemen exhibit area at the National Baseball Hall of Fame and Museum in Cooperstown, New York.

## Wendy

The little boy struggled to keep up with his father as the pair walked in the Canadian wilderness. The father gripped his son's hand with one hand and a rifle in the other. He sometimes stopped and scanned the trees for game. The two then trudged forward, hearing a bird's squeal. Finally, the father stopped and fired. A squirrel fell dead, and the pair retrieved it. The child admired the man he would later call the first great athlete he knew. "I swelled with pride and adulation," he wrote. "The Huntsman beside me was a hero greater than all the heroes I had ever known. He was taller, stronger and more fearless."[3]

The boy was John Wendell Smith, the future sportswriter. The hunter was his father, John Henry Smith. They had traveled from their home in Detroit, Michigan.

John Henry Smith, born on May 10, 1887, grew up in Dresden, Ontario, Canada. Dresden, named after a city in Germany, is a farming community in southwestern Ontario. Before the Civil War erupted in the United States in 1861, the Dresden area served as a stopping point for the Underground Railroad. The Underground Railroad consisted of a network of secret routes and safe houses which abolitionists used to assist Black slaves who fled plantations in the United States. One notable former slave, Josiah Henson, settled near the city. Henson's life inspired Harriet Beecher Stowe to write the novel *Uncle Tom's Cabin.*

Despite Dresden's role in the abolitionist movement, white residents there discriminated against Blacks. One of Wendell Smith's cousins, Hugh Burnett, campaigned against racial discrimination in the city during the 1950s.[4]

John Henry Smith had roots in Canada. His maternal grandfather, a farmer named Robert Burnett, appeared in the country's 1861 census. Smith's immediate family worked on a farm. One of his cousins, Jim Dudley, told a reporter that life didn't suit Smith. At the time, farmhands worked from sunrise to sunset for a dollar a day, plus half a hog per year and some eggs.[5] Instead Smith cooked for Canadian and American railroads and Great Lakes ships. He migrated to Detroit in 1911. Smith later served as head steward at the city's Yondotega Club, an exclusive social organization. He also worked as a chef on Henry Ford's private rail car. He also joined the Nacirema Club, a Black social organization.[6]

During the Great Depression, reporters from both the *Detroit News* and the *Detroit Free Press* mentioned him while they covered a court case involving the Yondotega Club. Arguing that Yondotega merely provided a place to eat and didn't exist as a club, the members sued the federal government to get a refund of $10,913 paid in taxes on membership dues, assessments, and initiation fees.

Both papers recounted Smith's testimony during the trial. The *News* reported: "Well, it seemed that Steward Smith was close to tears when he told the court that the place is not what it used to be. The paint, he said, is coming off the walls. The 'sitting room' should be all done over. All through the house the plaster is coming off, the woodwork is decaying, the floors sway under foot and the jousting January breezes whiz right through the cracks in the windows.... He went into a detailed account of the special dishes for which the club's cuisine is world famous: Clam chowder, ox tail soup, lobster newberg, deviled pigs' feet, Warfield steak, deviled turkey legs, creamed potatoes, not to mention apple, pumpkin and mince pies. My, my, you could scarcely believe your digestion!... Steward Smith rather disappointed his audience, once off the general subject of the cooking art. His memory of special parties was obscure. He recalled in a vague sort of way that Frederick M. Alger, Jr., gave one such. It was in honor of Azucar, but Steward Smith confessed he didn't know that Azucar is quite a famous horse."[7]

The testimony from Smith and several Yondotega members did not sway the judge. He ruled against the club.[8]

Along with career success, John Henry Smith found love in the Motor City. In 1912, he married Detroit native Lena Gertrude Thompson.

Thompson, born on September 1, 1882, was a member of a family prominent in local Black society.[9] Her parents, Henry and Josephine Thompson, were born in Kentucky and New York, respectively. According to the 1910 Census, Lena Gertrude Thompson was employed as a garment worker. After her marriage, she was a homemaker. She attended St. Matthew's Episcopal Church (now St. Matthew's and St. Joseph's Episcopal Church) and worked with three volunteer groups connected with it—Willing Workers, King's Daughters, and the Dorcas Society.[10]

Lena Smith gave birth to the couple's only child, John Wendell Smith, on June 27, 1914.[11] Wendell Smith grew up in a Detroit emerging as a manufacturing center. Car builders, led by Ford, were firmly established in the Detroit area. Detroit produced other goods as well. The 1914 city directory bragged about the Motor City's production of condiments, freight cars, soap, furniture, and twist drills.[12]

Detroit had to contend with serious racial problems during Smith's childhood. The city's Black population increased from 5,741 in 1910 to 40,838 in 1920 during the Great Migration of Blacks from the south to the north. Racial tensions, partly fueled by police brutality against Blacks and economic competition, rose as a result.

One especially notable incident took place in 1925. A Black doctor named Ossian Sweet and his family moved into a house in an all-white neighborhood on the city's east side. A crowd of white protestors moved toward his house. Someone inside the house shot into the crowd. The gunfire killed one man and wounded another. The prosecutor charged Sweet and other defendants. Sweet's brother was tried for the incident and acquitted. The prosecutor dropped the charges against the rest of the defendants.

Smith avoided much of the racial drama. He spent a pleasant childhood socializing with relatives and friends while growing up on Lemay Avenue. The street was located in a predominately white, working-class neighborhood on the city's east side. His friends called him Wendy. He pitched during sandlot baseball games with youths on his block, including future major league catcher Mike Tresh.[13] Tresh later spent 12 seasons in the major leagues, playing for the Chicago White Sox and Cleveland Indians. Tresh's son, Tom, also enjoyed a major league career. The younger Tresh spent most of his nine seasons with the New York Yankees, playing left field, shortstop and third base.

Another cousin of Wendell Smith, Herb Jeffries, grew up in the city. Jeffries, also known as Herbert Jeffrey, earned renown as a singer and an actor. He became cinema's first Black singing cowboy during the 1930s, starring in *The Bronze Buckaroo* and other Westerns. Jeffries also sang with Duke Ellington in the 1940s.

Jeffries spent time around Smith and his parents. He said Lena Smith kept the family's home immaculate and cooked well. Jeffries attended Sunday school and Nacirema club events with Smith and others at the Graystone Ballroom on Woodward Avenue. Their group also enjoyed outings at Vernor's Ginger Ale shop on Woodward Avenue, picnics and ice-skating outings at Belle Isle and Sugar Island and swims in the Detroit River. Jeffrey described Smith as a popular youth and a collegiate-looking dresser. "He was well-liked by the young ladies," he said. "He was a physically attractive young man."[14]

According to Smith's childhood friend and former next door neighbor, Martin Hogan, Smith's parents displayed friendliness and kindness. John Henry Smith paid Hogan a nickel on Sunday mornings for buying cigars for him at a store. Smith often smoked them while sitting on his porch and reading a newspaper. "A nickel was big in those days," Hogan said. "I do know that the family had a social life, because there were times on Sunday afternoon, they would have a group over and they were all very nice people."

Hogan recalled that the boys in the area often played touch football, baseball and basketball in the alley behind his family's house, known as Hogan's Alley. Kids cleaned up the alley to play sports because neighbors dumped ashes there. Hogan said Wendell Smith demonstrated strong athletic abilities. "Wendell could really throw a football," he recalled. "He had a spiral in those days like very few people have. He had a good arm, he could throw it a long distance," he said. "At one point, he and I used to spar a lot with open hands. We were whacking at one another's heads. It would sting a little bit, but that was about all. A little later he got hold of one of those big sand bags. He hung it in his garage. We had some boxing gloves at our house so some of us would go over there and do some boxing with Wendell. He had a pretty good sized garage. The bag was there so we could punch the bag and we would have some boxing matches. Nobody ever got mad. We had a lot of fun with it."

Sometimes Smith avoided his mother while he played with his friends. Hogan said: "There were times she'd come out calling Wendell wanting him to come home for something. He would duck someplace. He wanted to keep playing sports."

According to Hogan, Smith saw Negro League baseball in the Motor City.[15] A Negro National League squad, the Detroit Stars, achieved some success in the city. The Stars, led by outfielder Norman "Turkey" Stearnes, played at Mack Park.[16] Smith and Hogan walked to the single-decked, wooden stadium without money. Often the gatekeepers let them in after a few innings or another visitor brought them inside the park.

Smith also played basketball for the Detroit Athletic Association team at the Central Community Center.[17] Sportswriter Russell J. Cowans described Smith's team-oriented approach while he wrote about one of Smith's basketball games in 1932.

With Wendell Smith, 17-year-old Eastern high school forward pacing the way with seven baskets and three foul shots, the Detroit Athletic Association basketball team crushed the highly-touted Cincinnati Lion Tamers Saturday night 62 to 22, at the Central Community center gymnasium.
Smith was a thorn in the sides of the Cincinnati outfit. He was all over the court raimming [*sic*] the hoop with most of his shots. He might have increased his total but numerous times he passed to a teammate with an easy shot near the basket.[18]

During his time at the center, Smith met another Black up-and-comer: future heavyweight boxing champion Joe Louis.[19] Smith would write many pieces about Louis, including one early in his time at the *Courier*.[20]

Despite these good times, Smith experienced some discrimination. Hogan recalled that he was not allowed to join the sports teams when he attended predominantly white Southeastern High School. "I know it was hard for him," Hogan said. "He was not permitted to play sports. I don't know whose policy it was."[21]

Smith played American Legion baseball, but officials removed him from the team. Henry Ford interceded on Smith's behalf and he was reinstated.[22]

Smith suffered a crushing blow as a teenager. During an interview with longtime friend Jerome Holtzman, he said he had won an American Legion baseball championship game. After the game, Tigers scout Wish Egan told Smith he could not sign him because he was Black. Egan signed the losing pitcher and Mike Tresh, Smith's teammate.[23] According to Smith's widow, Wyonella, he cried.[24] Years later, Wendell Smith told sportswriter Bill Gleason the rejection marked the first time he understood baseball had a color line.[25]

## Smitty

After high school, Smith enrolled in West Virginia State College in 1933 as a physical education major. The school, located in Institute, West Virginia, was predominately Black. It was founded to provide training for Blacks in agriculture and the mechanical arts.

Years later, Smith explained his choice of colleges to Mort Edelstein, a co-worker at the *Chicago American*. Edelstein recalled Smith told him: "'In the 30s a Negro really was a second class citizen. So I chose a Negro school so that I would not have to suffer the frustrations and anxieties that so many of my friends did who went to white colleges.'"[26]

He, however, could not escape prejudice. During rides on the Chesapeake & Ohio railroad between his home and school, he had to sit in a segregated car part of the way.[27] Hogan said: "I know my brother John told me that he got a letter from him in which Wendell said that when he was living on Lemay Avenue, he didn't know that it was a little dream world compared to what it was outside so far discrimination is concerned. He never really felt it that much other than at school."[28]

At West Virginia State College, Smith acquired the nickname "Smitty" and established long-term friendships with school president John W. Davis and Will Robinson. Davis served as president from 1919 to 1953, expanded the school's academic program and oversaw the construction of new buildings on the campus. Robinson had roomed with Smith at the school's Gore Hall. Robinson lettered in baseball, basketball, football and gymnastics, graduating in 1937. Robinson later coached basketball at Pershing High School in Detroit. There, he won the state title in 1967 with a team led by future National Basketball Association star Spencer Haywood and another in 1970. Robinson achieved firsts in the National Football League and the National Collegiate Athletic Association. The NFL's Detroit Lions hired him as the league's first Black scout. An NCAA Division I school, Illinois State University, hired him as the first black head coach at that level. At ISU, Robinson coached future NBA player and head coach Doug Collins.

Smith met his first wife, the former Sara Mae Wright, at the school. Wright was born in Kinston, North Carolina, on March 23, 1915. Her family eventually settled in Norfolk, Virginia. She majored in biology and minored in music. Smith and Wright married in 1939.

Smith played guard and forward for the school's basketball team. On Christmas Day, 1933, the WVSC Yellow Jackets faced Smith's old squad, which had changed its name from Detroit Athletic Association to the Central Big Five, in Detroit. Smith scored nine points, but West Virginia State lost, 28–19.[29]

One of Smith's college schoolmates, Calvin "Sweaty" Banks, discussed Smith's skill on the court. "He had a stutter step dribble which threw people off and he would make layups," Banks said. "He was a terrific basketball player, but his real heart was in baseball. That was why he liked Jackie Robinson so much. He represented something he [Smith] was unable to do."[30]

According to West Virginia State's sports information department, Smith competed for the school's baseball team. According to a listing of team members published by the student newspaper, Smith had recorded nine hits in 12 at-bats at one point during a Yellow Jackets season.[31]

Smith began to develop his media skills in college. As the football team's publicist, he kept sportswriters informed about the squad's progress with press releases and photographs. Occasionally, the *Courier* and the *Norfolk Journal and Guide* reprinted his releases with his byline. In a 1936 letter to Davis, Smith listed his accomplishments.

> When I undertook this job, I fully realized the work it required and the possibilities it offered in the way of advertising West Virginia State College. Thus, I succeeded in living up to my adapted motto which was "Headlines for West Virginia in some paper throughout the country every single week." I, surprisingly, succeeded in having pictures printed in both Charleston papers—a feat that I was urged, by many, to drop, as efforts in the past to have pictures in the Charleston papers had been futile.
>
> My greatest satisfaction came when the All American Team was chosen and Roderick Price was on the first team. The fact that Price was chosen by many Sport's Editors in the distant parts of the country, although they had never had the pleasure of seeing him play, convinced me that my work was bringing results. It convinced me that West Virginia State College was being heard of in the line of athletics.[32]

Smith gained another benefit by publicizing the team. According to former *Courier* writer Frank Bolden, he established friendships with *Courier* sportswriters Ches Washington and Bill Nunn, Sr., when they covered events at the school.[33] These two men would help him in the future.

He wrote sports columns for the campus newspaper, the *Yellow Jacket*. In one column, he praised Washington for his coverage of the school's football team.[34] Smith told students to be grateful for Washington's work. Washington, in turn, respected Smith. He called Smith "one of the best collegiate correspondents in the business."[35]

Shortly before he graduated in 1937, Smith applied for a sportswriting job at the *Courier*. Smith took a train to Pittsburgh and met with Washington, the paper's sports editor, and *Courier* publisher Robert Vann in the former's office. Afterward, Smith wrote Vann a letter. "Although I have a little experience in this type of work I realize that I have a great deal to learn. If given the opportunity I will work diligently to become a success."[36]

The interview worked for Smith. He began writing for the paper as an assistant to Washington in that fall. His starting salary was $17 per week.[37]

Davis congratulated him in a letter. "I shall expect most excellent work from you as a worker with the Pittsburgh Courier. We shall be delighted to send football materials and other articles to you. Work hard. Be amenable to suggestion. Study always. If I can be of assistance feel free to call on me."[38]

# A Way of Life

Smith joined the *Courier* the same year that its circulation briefly rose to 250,000, earning status as the nation's leading Black weekly.[39] The paper had come a long way from humble beginnings. The *Courier* was started as a literary outlet in 1907 by Edwin Harleston, a security guard and aspiring writer.[40] Vann, an attorney, drafted incorporation papers and took over as the newspaper's editor-publisher, treasurer, and legal counsel in 1910.[41] Under his leadership, the *Courier* evolved into a journalistic enterprise that crusaded on behalf of African Americans. Along with news, it provided coverage of society, entertainment and sports. It advocated for improvements in housing, health and education and sought to empower Blacks politically. In the early 1930s, the paper launched a campaign against the *Amos 'n' Andy* daily radio program due to the program's stereotypical portrayals of Black people.[42] Between 1942 and 1943, the *Courier* conducted its "Double V" campaign. The campaign demanded a double victory: African Americans who contributed to victory in World War II should receive full citizenship rights at home.[43] The *Courier* occupied a three-story building in the predominantly Black Hill district, which was located east of Pittsburgh's downtown area.

To build circulation, the *Courier* published both national and local editions. Vann promoted the *Courier* as a national newspaper partly because Pittsburgh's Black population was smaller than the Black populations of other cities. During the 1940s, the *Courier* printed editions in Chicago, New York and other cities with large Black populations.[44]

Years after retiring from the *Courier*, former executive editor P.L. Prattis stated that the *Courier* strove to provide "the best and most accurate news." Prattis wrote: "It was a mission appointed by Robert Lee Vann from the founding of the paper in 1910, carried out in his lifetime and extended through the lives of Ira F. Lewis [business manager, executive editor, and president] and finally Mrs. Robert Lee Vann. All three themselves traveled to fulfill this tradition. It was a way of life at the *Courier* for the reporters too, for Bill Nunn, for Ches Washington, for Wendell Smith and George Schuyler; and, for all those great Negro journalists who sometime or other worked for the paper billed as 'America's Best Weekly.'"[45]

The paper provided a valuable service to the city's African American population, according to Andrew Buni's biography of Vann. Buni wrote: "Pittsburgh's black community, which numbered twenty-five thousand by 1910, had a real need for its own newspaper. Of the six white newspapers, only the *Pittsburgh Press* had ever carried any black news regularly, and its Jim-Crowed 'Afro-American News' column was discontinued in 1914. When news of blacks did find its way into the Pittsburgh newspapers, it consisted mainly of sensational criminal cases or other lurid details of Black life."[46]

The sports coverage was especially important to Pittsburgh's Black residents. Two of the Negro Leagues' greatest teams, the Pittsburgh Crawfords and the Homestead Grays, were based in Pittsburgh. In the book *Sandlot Seasons*, Rob Ruck wrote: "In the 1920s, 1930s, and 1940s, sport offered Black Pittsburgh a cultural counterpoint to its collective lot, one that promoted internal cohesion and brought together both the Pittsburgh-born residents and the southern migrants in the context of a changing Black consciousness. Moreover, sport helped the scattered Black Pittsburgh community to gain a sense of itself as part of a national Black community."[47]

Smith worked hard at the paper. Both Bolden and Bill Nunn, Jr., who eventually succeeded Smith as sports editor, confirmed he developed into a fast typist. Smith also learned the business from the ground up. "I did a little bit of everything," Smith told Holtzman. "I wrote fillers and high school sports. I didn't cover anything big but I learned the mechanics of the business: makeup, how to write captions, a basic journalism education."[48]

According to Bolden, Washington and Nunn Sr. trained Smith. "He improved fast," Bolden said. "Reporters usually don't mature fast unless they have a lot on the ball. He had a knack for talking with players, could make friends with them."[49]

Nunn Jr. said Smith had a desk on the second floor along with the other editors. Smith's desk often had a stack of papers on it. Vann and Lewis occupied offices on the third floor. The advertising department worked on the first floor.[50]

Smith proved he could handle other assignments besides sports. In 1940, the paper promoted him to city editor.[51] Following the promotion, he wrote a letter to Davis: "Because I feel that you are interested in whatever progress I am making I take this means to inform you that I have been promoted to the position of City Editor of the Pittsburgh Courier. Of course I am pleased over my good fortune and feel that my four years at West Virginia State are now bearing fruit. (Even if Mr. Thorne did flunk me in English one year.)"[52]

Former *Courier* reporter Edna Chappell McKenzie told the author in 1997 that Smith exercised good judgment while he ran the city desk. "He was sharp about what would make a good story," McKenzie said. "It was his outgoing personality that drew people to him. You were always cooperative because he was not arrogant or vain or dogmatic. Everybody had a sense of loyalty. You wouldn't let him down. That probably describes the relationship.... Nobody was going to jump on you about anything while he was the city editor. He might criticize, but never in a mean-spirited way. We felt a pride in the city desk. During the time he was city editor, there was such a spirit of camaraderie."

McKenzie benefited from Smith's leadership. She got her start with the *Courier* by assisting the paper's society columnist but wanted to cover news. In friendly conversations with Smith, he said he would love to have her work with him. Thus, she became the first female reporter on the city news staff. McKenzie said: "Wendell was especially encouraging and kind. So I became a real newspaper writer, not a society reporter. Because he gave me a lot of responsibility and I handled it well, I think it helped me to develop as a writer. I did reporting, but I also did editing. In those days, you had to go to the pressroom. And they worked with metal. I'd do it right there on the spot. The guys down there used to call me 'Second Look.' Wendell did not ever want to send the paper down unless I saw it too."

That same year, he got good news at home. On February 3, 1940, Sara Smith gave birth to their only child, John Wendell Smith, Jr. The proud father sent a letter to Davis months later. He wrote: "P.S.—Have a twenty pound quarterback up here for you! He can really call signals, too!"[53]

A year later, the *Courier* promoted Smith to sports editor and made Washington an assistant business manager.[54]

During Smith's time at the *Courier*, he extensively covered Negro League baseball. One especially notable article by him reaffirmed the humanity of Black athletes. Smith interviewed shortstop Willie Wells during a trip to Mexico City, Mexico. Wells had played in the Mexican League rather than return to the Newark Eagles. Wells told Smith he experienced excellent treatment south of the border.

"One of the reasons I came back to Mexico," he said, "is because I've found freedom and democracy here, something I never found in the United States. I was branded a Negro in the States and had to act accordingly. Everything, including playing ball, was regulated by my color. They wouldn't even give me a chance in the big leagues because I was a Negro, yet they accepted every other nationality under the sun."

"Well," the famed shortstop said, "here I am a man. I can go as far in baseball as I am capable of going. I can live where I please and will encounter no restrictions of any kind because of my race. So, you see, that also had a lot to do with my decision to return here."[55]

## Challenge to Conscience

Smith's efforts to integrate baseball represented part of a 63-year struggle.

Blacks had competed in major league baseball before Jackie Robinson.

The first Black player in the major leagues before Robinson, Moses Fleetwood Walker, played catcher for the Toledo Blue Stockings in the American Association in 1884. At the time, the American Association was considered a major league. An unwritten agreement among baseball owners and officials kept Blacks out of the major leagues until 1947.[56]

Black writers advocated for integration. Negro league pioneer Sol White wrote in his 1907 book *Sol White's Official Base Ball Guide*: "Base ball [*sic*] is a legitimate profession…. It should be taken seriously by the colored player, as honest efforts with his great ability will open an avenue in the near future wherein he may walk hand-in-hand with the opposite race in the greatest of all American games—base ball."[57] Washington started a series of articles on the subject in the February 25, 1933, issue of the *Courier*.[58]

Black sportswriters continued to push for integration in the late 1930s and 1940s. That group included Smith, Joe Bostic of the Harlem-based *People's Voice*, and Sam Lacy of the Baltimore–based *Afro-American*. Some white writers, including Dave Egan and Lester Rodney, also wrote about the issue. Egan was a columnist for the *Boston Record*. Rodney was the sports editor for the *Daily Worker*. The *Daily Worker* and the *Courier* had an informal agreement to print stories from the other paper related to the integration issue.[59]

Lacy described the passion he and Smith had for the fight. He wrote: "We talked deep into the nights in ghetto hotels, at his house in Pittsburgh and in my home in Washington, at dimly-lit ballparks where our paths would cross while covering Negro National League games, in lunchrooms in Harlem and in greasy spoon hogmaw joints of Memphis, St. Louis, Baltimore and Philadelphia."[60]

In 1938, Smith entered the fray with his column "A Strange Tribe," which criticized Blacks for supporting major league baseball when it barred Black players. Smith wrote: "They're real troopers, these guys who risk their money and devote their lives to Negro baseball. We Black folk offer no encouragement and don't seem to care if they make a go of it or not. We literally ignore them completely. With our noses high and our hands deep in our pockets, squeezing the same dollar that we hand out to the white players, we walk past their ball parks and go to the major league game. Nuts—that's what we are. Just plain nuts!"[61]

The following year, Smith made a significant advance in his crusade. He surveyed major league players about their attitudes toward Black players. He wanted to disprove the idea that the players opposed Blacks in the majors. He talked to 40 players and eight managers at the Pittsburgh Pirates' Forbes Field and the Schenley Hotel, located near the park. Most of the interviewees said they did not oppose integration.[62]

Rodney praised Smith's effort during a conference about the 50th anniversary of Robinson's debut held at Long Island University. He told the audience: "Give a little thought to the courage and initiative of the Black man 'intruding' into the comfortable old boys white baseball establishment with his challenge to conscience."[63]

Smith later told Holtzman the *Courier* management liked the survey and gave him a raise.[64]

On December 3, 1943, a group of leaders from Black newspapers, along with actor Paul Robeson, met with major league commissioner Kenesaw Mountain Landis and other baseball officials to present the case for integration. The meeting took place at the Hotel Roosevelt in New York City. The group included Lewis, John Sengstacke, the publisher of the *Chicago Defender*, and Howard Murphy of the Afro-American newspaper chain.

Smith attended the meeting. He described it to Holtzman. "The reaction, frankly, it was silence. We went in, made the presentation, came out and the meeting continued. Later, a letter was written to Landis thanking him for the privilege. There was no reply. But I do recall that the man who seemed the most interested was Branch Rickey. Mr. Rickey didn't say anything during the meeting but he was very gracious."[65]

By that time, Rickey had extensive baseball experience. He, however, had not been a crusader. He was born in Scioto County, Ohio, on December 20, 1881. During a brief major league career, Rickey had played catcher, outfield and first base for the St. Louis Browns and New York Highlanders, later called the Yankees. He earned a bachelor's degree at Ohio Wesleyan University and coached the school's baseball team. He later earned a law degree at the University of Michigan. Afterward he joined the St. Louis Browns, later known as the Baltimore Orioles, as an executive in 1913. He had managed the Browns and the St. Louis Cardinals before he joined the Brooklyn Dodgers in 1942. Before the meeting, Rickey had not made any attempts to integrate major league baseball.

Rickey may have been gracious due to a combination of idealism and business reality. An incident Rickey experienced during his time at Ohio Wesleyan may have sparked the former. When the baseball team traveled out of town for a game, its only Black player, Charles Thomas, was denied entry at the hotel where the team stayed because of his race. The denial upset Thomas. The latter surfaced when Rickey joined the Dodgers. The team had a roster packed with older players. In order to boost the team's fortunes, he had considered recruiting Black players.[66]

Two developments took place in 1945. Bostic took two Negro League players, pitcher Terris McDuffie and outfielder Dave "Showboat" Thomas, to the Dodgers' Spring Training camp in Bear Mountain, New York, unannounced to demand a tryout in early April 1945. An angry Rickey allowed the tryout but did not sign the players.

Meanwhile, the push to integrate baseball heated up in Boston. A white city councilman who represented a predominantly Black neighborhood, Isadore Muchnick, got involved in the issue. He told the Boston Red Sox and Boston Braves (who eventually moved to Milwaukee and Atlanta) that he would back demands from religious groups in the city to ban Sunday baseball games if the teams didn't make efforts to integrate their teams. Smith read about Muchnick's efforts and called him. Smith told Muchnick he could bring Black players to tryouts with the two Boston teams. Muchnick agreed with Smith's plan.[67]

## *Jackie Robinson*

That same month, Smith called Robinson and asked him to participate in a tryout in Boston. Robinson had recently joined the Kansas City Monarchs as a shortstop and expressed reluctance to ask the management for time off. Smith persuaded him to ask for it anyway. The Monarchs' management denied permission. Robinson told Smith, who called team officials and said he'd tell the public that they were blocking efforts to integrate major league baseball. The owners gave Robinson permission.[68]

Smith took three Negro League players to Boston: Robinson, Marvin Williams, a second baseman for the Philadelphia Stars, and Sam Jethroe, a center fielder for the Cleveland Buckeyes.[69] At the time of the trip, Williams and Jethroe were competing in their third and fourth seasons, respectively, in the Negro Leagues. Both had earned all-star honors. Robinson was a rookie.

He had taken a circuitous route to professional baseball. Robinson was born on January 31, 1919, in Cairo, Georgia. He was the youngest of five children. After Robinson's father left the family in 1920, the family moved to Pasadena, California. Robinson's mother worked as a maid to support the family, but it suffered from poverty.

Robinson's older brother, Mack, became a sports star. He won a silver medal in the 200 meter race during the 1936 Summer Olympics in Berlin, Germany. He finished behind Jesse Owens.

Jackie Robinson attended Pasadena Junior College before he enrolled in the University of California, Los Angeles. At UCLA, he became the school's first athlete to win varsity letters in four sports: baseball, basketball, football, and track. The *Courier* occasionally wrote about Robinson's football exploits.[70]

During his college career, Robinson met a UCLA nursing student named Rachel Isum. They eventually married. In 1941, Robinson left school before graduation. He found a job as an assistant athletic director with the National Youth Administration.[71]

In March 1942, Robinson and Negro League pitcher Nate Moreland had a tryout with the Chicago White Sox during Spring Training in Pasadena.[72] Later that month, the U.S. Army drafted him and assigned him to a Black cavalry unit in Fort Riley, Kansas. He earned a commission as a second lieutenant there the following year. Afterward, the Army transferred Robinson to Fort Hood, Texas, where he joined a Black tank battalion. Robinson's military career nearly ended when the Army court martialed him in 1944 following a false accusation of insubordination. The Army acquitted him and later transferred him to Camp Breckinridge in Kentucky. There, he served as an athletics coach. A former Monarchs pitcher stationed at the camp encouraged Robinson to write to the team and ask for a tryout. Robinson followed the advice. He received an honorable discharge in November 1944 and joined the Monarchs the following year.[73]

After a delay, the Red Sox gave the three players a sham tryout on April 16, 1945. The players performed well and completed application cards.[74] That tryout generated little publicity in the mainstream media, most likely because the newspapers were covering the recent death of President Franklin Roosevelt.

On the way home afterward, Smith attended a press conference conducted by Rickey in New York City. Rickey announced plans to establish a Black baseball league called the United States League. He claimed the Negro Leagues were "rackets."[75]

Rickey's words disappointed Smith, but he kept his cool. After the press conference, Rickey asked Smith if any of the players he took to Boston could succeed in the majors. Smith recommended Robinson.[76]

Smith later told sportswriter Shirley Povich why he had touted Robinson. Smith recalled:

> He wasn't the best Negro ballplayer I could have named. There were others with more ability but to have recommended them would have been a disservice to the cause of the Negroes.
>
> I recommended Robinson because he wouldn't make Negro baseball look bad either on the field or off it. Jackie got my vote because of many factors. He was a college boy. I knew he would understand the great responsibilities of being the first Negro invited to play in organized baseball in more than 60 years. He was a mannerly fellow. At UCLA he had played before big crowds. I gambled that he wouldn't freeze up under pressure. And he had an honorable discharge from the Army as a lieutenant.[77]

Rickey followed up on the recommendation by sending scouts to watch Robinson's games. The scouts gave favorable reports to Rickey. Satisfied,

Rickey met with Robinson at the Dodgers' office in August 1945. Two months later, Rickey signed him to a minor league contract. To assist Robinson, Rickey paid Smith to serve as Robinson's mentor and arrange for his lodging and travel in segregated areas during 1946 and 1947. *Courier* photographer and entertainment writer Billy Rowe accompanied them.

Lacy said Rowe provided valuable assistance to Smith during the search for accommodations. He recalled: "Wendell had the advantage because he and Billy Rowe were traveling together. Billy was also an entertainment writer and he had friends all over the country."[78]

During the 1946 season, Robinson played for the Montreal Royals, the Dodgers' Triple-A affiliate. Robinson led the Royals to the championship of the International League and victory in the Little World Series. Smith wrote stories about his progress.

Smith and Robinson encountered difficulties when they traveled together in the South. Smith told the *Chicago Tribune* about a tense incident.

> I remember a night when Jackie and I were staying in this motel in a southern town. Some "southern gentlemen" broke into our room and said, "don't let the sun set on you."
>
> We stayed and nothing happened. Another time in a town in Florida, Jackie was up at bat. The pitcher kept throwing balls and the umpire kept yelling strikes. He went "one, two, three. You're out." Then he looked up at the press box and waved his arms. He yelled at me, "And you're out too. Get out of this ballpark." I don't think he liked us much.[79]

By early 1947, Smith suspected his fight for integration would succeed. On February 4, 1947, he sent a positive letter to Robinson. Smith wrote: "You should not worry about the plans they have for you. As I see it you are definitely going to get a chance. All you have to do is keep a cool head, play the kind of ball you are capable of playing and don't worry about anything. As you know, Rickey is no dummy. He is a very methodical man and will see to it that you are treated right. All you have to do is take care of Jackie Robinson on the playing field and he will do the rest.... The fact that you came through last year so well, means you can go through anything now. Personally, I don't see how you can miss."[80]

Rickey proved Smith correct two months later. On April 10, 1947, the Dodgers hosted the Royals in an exhibition game at Ebbets Field. Smith covered the game in the press box. During the game, Arthur Mann, assistant to Rickey, gave each reporter a press release announcing that the team had purchased Robinson's contract from the Royals. Five days later, Robinson debuted with the Dodgers.

During 1947, Smith ghosted a *Courier* column for Robinson. The columns were generally positive pieces designed to avoid controversy. In one,

Robinson downplayed the racist heckling he received from the Philadelphia Phillies and their manager, Ben Chapman, one week after his debut.[81] Years later, Smith called the Phillies one of the most racist teams in the National League in an article for *Ebony*.[82] He mentioned Robinson's trouble with Chapman.

One magazine, *Sport*, mentioned Smith's assistance to Robinson during the 1947 season. In the piece, Roscoe McGowan wrote a sympathetic portrait of Robinson and his occasional isolation from his teammates. He wrote:

> When the team detrained in these two cities [St. Louis and Philadelphia], groups of three or four of your teammates would barge into taxicabs and ride to the hotel. But you would ride alone to the place that you or your friend Wendell Smith, sportswriter on the Pittsburgh Courier, had arranged for you. Smith, incidentally, travels with the club all around the National League circuit.
>
> In St. Louis, it would be the De Luxe Hotel, a hostelry operated exclusively for a Black clientele.... Smith, incidentally, is a sort of unofficial guide and companion for Robinson.[83]

## *Sweet Home, Chicago*

In August 1947, Smith joined the *Herald-American*, an afternoon newspaper known for aggressive investigative reporters.[84] He became the first Black sportswriter to work for a daily newspaper.[85] According to the paper's sports editor Leo Fischer, Walter Howey, the paper's editor, brought Smith to Fischer and said, "with his customary abruptness, 'I want you to meet Wendell Smith. He's going to help you on sports coverage.'"[86]

Smith had some familiarity with the city and Fischer. He had previously covered the annual Negro League all-star game held at the White Sox' Comiskey Park. Two years earlier, Fischer had told Smith that the paper's national professional basketball tournament did not discriminate against Black teams.[87]

Smith initially split time between the *Courier* and the *Herald-American* before he eventually left the sports editor position at the *Courier* in 1952. Bill Nunn, Jr., succeeded Smith and later joined the Pittsburgh Steelers football team as an assistant personnel director and scout. Smith began writing full time for the *Herald-American* and settled in Chicago. He continued to write columns for the *Courier* until 1967.

Smith began his career with the *Herald-American* by writing a series of articles about Robinson's rise to the major leagues. He contended Robinson's signing proved anyone could succeed in this country. "It's a story of this great country and proves beyond every doubt that a man can soar to lofty heights in the United States if he has the ability," he wrote. "True enough, the struggle may be more difficult for some more than others, but Jackie Robinson, a Negro and first baseman for the Brooklyn Dodgers, is proof enough that it can happen."[88]

Smith took issue with the *Daily Worker* that same year. He blasted the paper in a *Courier* column.

> When Allan B. Tine writes in the *Daily Worker* that his paper went to bat for Satch [Satchel Paige] and all the other great Negro players by polling the most popular managers and players in the big leagues, he sounds like a Russian diplomat trying to sell Communistic propaganda to someone Stalin had just kicked in the seat of the pants. The *Daily Worker* did not personally interview those big league players and managers. The *Pittsburgh Courier* made those interviews and ran a series of articles on their views and re-actions. That was way back in 1939. The *Daily Worker* then picked the stories up and published them. In the main, the Communist paper tried to take credit at that time for those stories. Now its [sic] trying to take credit for getting Negroes into the majors.
>
> So, for a matter of record and so that our kids won't come up with ideas that the "great" Communist party is responsible for Negroes playing in our national pastime ... let me assure you that the Reds had nothing to do with it at all. The most they did was bungle the campaign up at times when it appeared that some headway was being made. Like a bad penny, they always turned up when least wanted.[89]

Rodney discussed the controversy in a letter to the author. Rodney wrote:

> I was quite hot about it at the time, not about his anti-communist views, to which I had no right to object, but to his allegation that we falsely took credit for his interviews, and that it was obscene for us to say that we went to bat for Satchel Paige. I responded at the time with a letter to Smith telling him that our attorney said the column was libelous, that I had decided not to pursue it because of our past cooperation and good relations, but that if he ever repeated those falsehoods, all bets were off. He never responded to my letter, and to my knowledge never repeated those charges, at least not in print.
>
> Now I am not going to say that there were never any articles in the Daily Worker which sounded too boastful about our role, or even may have given the impression that WE did it, without mentioning the pioneering work of Smith and the Negro press. I could certainly understand Wendell being irritated by that. But it is another thing to then make the silly assertion that we secretly hoped to sabotage the campaign, that we pirated his stories without permission or attribution, had "nothing to do with the case," did not do our own interviews, and did nothing about Paige.

Rodney's letter mentioned Rickey, a staunch anti–Communist. He wrote:

I can't analyze his violent change in this regard, though I suppose it is worth noting that he was in the employ of Branch Rickey when he wrote that column. Whatever, I prefer to remember Wendell Smith as the courageous reporter who started the campaign, and as the person who generously wrote his congratulations to us in the letter we published Sunday, Aug. 20, 1939 when the campaign was in full swing.[90]

Smith had to overcome a major barrier. When he attempted to cover a Dodgers game at Forbes Field in 1947, he was denied entrance into the press box. A white sportswriter, Vince Johnson of the *Pittsburgh Post-Gazette*, noted: "But Smith had to cover the game from the grandstand."[91] At the time, only members of the BBWAA were admitted into the press box. Smith was not a member. Smith had applied for membership in the Pittsburgh and Chicago chapters of the BBWAA. Both rejected him. Johnson claimed the rejection by the Pittsburgh chapter was racially motivated. "The association's constitution restricts full membership to those actively engaged in reporting games for a daily newspaper. This clause, strictly interpreted, has the effect of barring Negro writers, who for the most part, work for weekly publications. But it seems to me that when a constitution of any sort works undemocratically, it should be modified.... While barring a Courier representative from the press box at Forbes Field, the Pittsburgh chapter has frequently admitted all sort of dead-heads. The only qualification of these men, as far as admittance to the press box is concerned, is that their skin is white."[92]

The Chicago chapter eventually admitted Smith. He became the second Black journalist, after Lacy, to gain admission into a BBWAA chapter. Both men were listed as members in the BBWAA directory as of November 1, 1959.

Smith notched two achievements in 1948. He wrote the first biography of Robinson, titled *Jackie Robinson: My Own Story*. The book has one embarrassing error: it lists Robinson's full name as "John Roosevelt Robinson." The correct name is Jack Roosevelt Robinson.[93] He also covered the Summer Olympics in London for the *Courier*.

Smith's personal life changed during the late 1940s. He and Sara Smith divorced. She retained custody of their son and eventually returned to Norfolk. According to Bolden, the time Wendell Smith spent away from home covering sports was partly responsible for the breakup. "Good sportswriters are poor husbands and fathers," Bolden said. "They are never home."[94]

Sara Smith eventually remarried and obtained a Broadcast Music, Inc., composer's license. She managed about 30 recording acts.[95] A granddaughter of John Wendell Smith, Jr., Ryan Cuffee Caston, told the author: "Sara was a proud woman and there were things she wasn't willing to do to get ahead musically. Eventually she started her own music publishing company."[96] John Wendell Smith, Jr., followed his mother into the music business. He sang and taught himself to play the piano and the guitar. He released several songs, including a high tempo rocker called "Puddin' Pie."[97] Sara Smith helped manage her son's music career.[98] John Wendell Smith, Jr., also served as a minister and worked as a welder at the U.S. Naval Shipyard in Norfolk. Cuffee Caston said: "When my grandfather worked in the shipyard as a welder, he was nicknamed 'Flash' because he was so fast."[99]

Smith experienced major events in 1949.

Early that year, he participated in a *Courier* campaign to raise money for the family of Isaiah Nixon. Nixon was shot to death after he voted in Montgomery County, Georgia, in 1948. The paper raised money toward the purchase of a new home for Nixon's family. Smith solicited money from his contacts in the athletic community.[100]

That March, Smith's previously warm relationship with Robinson began to change in a very public manner. Smith slammed Robinson in the *Courier* for hinting that some sports reporters were treating him unfairly after a confrontation between Robinson and a teammate. Smith alleged Robinson "isn't as popular in the press box as he once was."[101]

Late that year, Wendell Smith found some personal happiness. He married the former Wyonella Hicks Creft on November 25, 1949.[102] She was born in Oxford, North Carolina, on July 14, 1921, and graduated from North Carolina College (now North Carolina Central University) in Durham. Her nephew, James "Biff" Henderson, later worked as the stage manager for *The Late Show with David Letterman*.[103] The ceremony took place in Detroit. The marriage did not produce any children.

For Wyonella Smith, the marriage was her second. The couple had met while they worked at the *Courier*. Creft helped retype the stories Smith had dictated during Robinson's debut with the Dodgers.[104] Years later, longtime WGN television sportscaster Jack Brickhouse wrote about the couple's first meeting. "It seems they were crossing the street in front of the Courier one wintry day, and while Wendell was looking at traffic in one direction, Wyonella was looking the other way, and slipped and fell. Wendell helped her to her feet and the rest is history."[105]

After they moved to Chicago, Wyonella Smith worked as a secretary for Harlem Globetrotters owner Abe Saperstein.[106] She also volunteered for the following charitable organizations: Women's Board of the United Negro College Fund, Friends of New Provident Hospital, the Board of Directors of Chicago Maternity Center and the Board of Managers for the YMCA of Metropolitan Chicago.[107]

The Smiths shared a deep love and partnership. They occasionally traveled together on Wendell Smith's out of town assignments. Once, they went to Grossinger's Camp in New York to watch Rocky Marciano prepare for his second fight against Ezzard Charles.[108] Bolden said Wyonella Smith supported her husband. "She understood him. She encouraged him," he said.[109] A longtime friend of Wendell Smith and former head of the International Boxing Club, Truman Gibson, Jr., praised Wyonella Smith. Gibson said: "He was fortunate in his choice of wives. She knew everybody who was anybody in the sports world. This was extremely helpful to him. She was beautiful, brainy and devoted to Wendell."[110]

Smith continued his pattern of befriending younger coworkers. One such colleague, Mort Edelstein, met Smith during the early 1950s. Edelstein wrote:

> With three years in World War II behind me, and armed with a college degree, I joined the sports department of the old Chicago American in 1951. But the greats who worked there at that time didn't hold it against me, particularly Wendell Smith, then the boxing writer.
>
> While the legendary figures of our sports staff—Warren Brown (who gave TV personality Ed Sullivan his first job on a newspaper), Harry McNamara, and Davis Walsh—were great guys, it was Wendell who treated me like a son. When I told him I had two weeks vacation coming and planned to go to Texas, he shouted at me: "Why Texas? Go to New York City and see what life is all about."
>
> I protested I didn't have that kind of money.
>
> He quickly wrote some names on a piece of paper, and said, "After you find a reasonable hotel, look up these guys, and you won't have any problems." He had written the names of New York's best sports writers and restaurant owner Toots Shor.
>
> "And if you should run out of money," he said, smiling, "I'll send you some more." He winked, adding: "But don't ask for too much."[111]

Smith notched a special achievement as a boxing writer in 1953. He won election as president of the Chicago Boxing Writers and Broadcasters' Association.

Noted Chicago boxing promoter Ben Bentley met Smith in 1954 when he started publicizing fights. Bentley recalled:

> When I was at the [Chicago] Stadium, I used to come to his home. He used to kid me. "You're riding out on the south side. When you get out of the car, be very careful. Tell them you know Wendell Smith."
>
> He would tell me, "You know, this manager you introduced me to is not telling the truth. He is trying to fancy himself up as one of the top boxing managers." He could talk to you and he would reach an opinion midway. "He told me a bunch of lies and I was sitting there and I had to nod to him, be very polite and then I said I got a deadline to make." That was his favorite expression when he wanted to get rid of you.

He would talk to fighters who were training for a major fight and get information that some of the other writers could not get. He had a way of talking and making them feel like they were world champions and they weren't but he just had a knack of being able to get into you real good.

Wendell was able to put his arm around a fighter. Both were Black and remember there was strong feeling at that time. Wendell was able to get things that everybody else was looking for. The fighters would trust him. He wouldn't say don't talk to anyone that's white. The fighters, the managers would have a feeling for Wendell as opposed to any of the white writers. They used to say to me, "They're always in a hurry." But Wendell was like one of them. He'd rib them, kid them. They'd talk family.

He's so sweet and nice and ask you all these questions. The next thing you know, you're blabbering all over the place and you can't wait to get rid of him. How could I tell when he was looking for a column? When he's sitting down with whoever he wants to do a column about. He'll talk about a new car and the guy says, "No kidding. You got that kind of a car. Tell me. I like that car. How much was it?" He'd get them on that. And then he'd get on vacations. "Where do you go for vacations?" "Oh I take my family here and there." He would imbed himself so deeply with the individual that the guy wanted to give him all personal secrets. We'd get into the car and Wendell would say, "He gave me a hell of a column."[112]

Smith displayed some humor during the 1950s, according to Gleason. Gleason, then working as a sports writer at the *American*, recalled the day following a boxing match at the Chicago Stadium, Smith held court at the paper. He told his coworkers about the famous reporters who covered the fight. Smith listed the names and concluded: "There was Red Smith, and then there was Black Smith."[113]

Smith sparked a minor controversy in 1957 with a negative *Courier* column about Althea Gibson, the first Black to win the women's singles title at England's Wimbledon tennis tournament. Smith criticized Gibson for allegedly acting rudely toward reporters after she competed in a tournament in Chicago. He wrote: "Her curt manner and insulting responses to friendly writers of all papers in Chicago justifiably won her the dubious title of 'Tennis Queen and Bum of the Court.' It might be wise for Althea to take stock at this time and realize that while she wields a mighty racket, she is still only a tennis player and nothing more."[114]

Along with the column, the *Courier* ran an editor's note which stated Gibson told *Courier* reporter Evelyn Cunningham she feared that the friends she gained after she became famous would keep her from the friends who had helped her achieve success. Smith complained to Prattis about the note. Prattis respected Smith but had to contend with falling circulation that would cause the paper's eventual purchase by Sengstacke.

Prattis replied with a letter. He wrote:

Althea is on top. She won at Wimbledon. She won at Chicago. She won in the Wightman Cup matches. She won the Essex tournament. She's riding the crest of victory, so what are you gonna do? She's an IDOL. When your article came in, I had to say to myself: "Well, Wendell is smattering one of our idols. Our readers won't like that, no matter how true what he writes is." So I dutifully turn to my typewriter and peck out an editor's note, designed to soften (just a wee bit), the blow you were delivering. Please believe me when I write you that the next week, we were bombarded with letters—against your article. We used the one from New York to symbolize the avalanche.

As a personality, I think the gal is lousy. I went to a dinner and cocktail party where she was. I introduced myself and tried to start a conversation. I got exactly nowhere. But I did meet a very lovely girl at the party, Darlene Hard. She and I had a long conversation. Some of the things she told ME, I wrote into the story I did and signed Nunn Junior's name to. So if you're hot about the story, blame me—and Darlene. Nunn Junior was able to get very little out of Althea. I had told him to try to get her to tell him what other colored players, male and female, might be able to make the grade in big-time tennis. She bluntly told him there weren't any. That sounds silly to me. As great as Jackie Robinson was, Willie Mays and Hank Aaron came along, both of whom are as great or better than Jackie. Althea ought to be helping others make the big time like she was helped.

She was just as ungracious to reporters here as she was in Chicago. I know that. I talked to one of the white guys (Pittsburgh Press) whom she brushed off. But he sagely commented, "What are you going to do as long as she's winning?"

In this letter, I'm not suggesting that you lay off the IDOLS. What I am suggesting is that you recognize their existence and the fact that we may have to give them special treatment—inasmuch as we are trying to make the public like us."[115]

Smith established another first for Black sports journalists in 1958. That March, he provided radio commentary, along with Dr. Joyce Brothers and Jack Drees, for the middleweight championship fight between Sugar Ray Robinson and Carmen Basilio at the Chicago Stadium. Wyonella Smith sat about ten rows behind Smith at the arena while she listened on the radio. His parents entertained friends at their home in Detroit after the fight.[116]

Smith took stock of his own career two years later. In a column for the *Courier*, he thanked the paper's previous sports editors for blazing a trail for his own career. He wrote:

This has been a life of splendor and excitement—baseball training camps, fight camps, the Olympics and other arenas of excitement for the younger ones that the older ones, by their dedication and perseverance made possible.

Thus those who sit in the press box at the World Series, or ringside at the big fights, or in "typewriter row" at similar classics, should remember that they are there because of the ceaseless campaigns waged by those before them, particularly by those representing this newspaper.[117]

## The Last Crusade

Smith conducted his final media crusade in 1961. At the time, Black major leaguers whose teams held Spring Training in the southern states still had to stay in segregated accommodations. The lodgings and dining available to them were less desirable than those their white teammates enjoyed. Smith covered the issue in both the *Chicago's American*, which had evolved from the *Herald-American*, and the *Courier*.

In the January 23, 1961, issue of the *American*, Smith wrote:

Beneath the apparently tranquil surface of baseball there is a growing feeling of resentment among Negro major leaguers who still experience embarrassment, humiliation, and even indignities during spring training in the south. This stature of respectability the Negro has attained since [Jackie] Robinson's spectacular appearance on the major league scene has given him a new sense of dignity and pride, and he wants the same treatment in the south during spring training that he has earned in the north.

The Negro player resents the fact that he is not permitted to stay in the same hotels with his teammates during spring training, and is protesting the fact that they cannot eat in the same restaurants, nor enjoy other privileges.[118]

During the campaign, Smith deployed blunt prose. After Birdie Tebbetts, then vice president of the Milwaukee Braves, said the team's Black players were satisfied with segregated accommodations, an angry Smith wrote the following for the *Courier*:

When Mr. Birdie Tebbets [sic] was a major league catcher, he was acknowledged as a competent receiver but never considered dangerous at the plate in a crucial situation.

On the basis of his reception to the nationwide protests over the deplorable conditions which Negro players—particularly his own—must tolerate in the South during spring training season, one can only conclude that Mr. Tebbets [sic] is still a weakling when the chips are down.[119]

Shortly after the start of the campaign, several major league teams made plans to provide integrated accommodations for their players. The White Sox bought a hotel to house all of their players.

Full integration throughout Spring Training accommodations in Florida and Arizona took place within the next two years.[120]

Smith earned recognition for the desegregation campaign. The magazine *Editor & Publisher* called him a reporter with "a built-in social conscience." The same article noted Smith enjoyed golfing and reading and reading books about the Civil War.[121] Smith received a second prize among Chicago sports reporters from the Associated Press.[122]

That year, Smith's relationship with Robinson took another negative turn. He privately expressed irritation with Robinson, who was recently fired from his job as a columnist for the *New York Post*. In January 1961, Prattis wrote a *Courier* column which criticized Robinson for his endorsement of Republican candidate Richard Nixon in the 1960 presidential election. "One cannot help but wonder if headlines go to the head of celebrities. Jackie has been exploited and has permitted himself to be exploited in many different ways—usually for some good purpose. He certainly deserves credit for giving his name to good causes. But popularity does not make a good leader. And celebrities, whether of the stage, diamond or gridiron, should be cautioned against taking leadership roles. By doing so, they often spoil their public image. I think Jackie Robinson had a perfect right in the last campaign to support Vice President Nixon. I hope he voted for him. But, in justice to himself, he should not have split his following by publicly taking sides and changing thousands of admirers into critics. In spite of Jackie's heroic effort for Nixon, between 70 and 80 per cent of all voting Negroes voted for Kennedy. They did not follow Jackie's advice, and some were downright angry with Jackie for trying to tell them how they should vote. His reception as a political partisan was far different from the acclaim he received as a baseball hero."[123]

Smith complimented Prattis in a letter.

> Just a quick note to say I enjoyed your column on Jackie Robinson and his political manipulations.
>
> I am in full accord with your views relative to Jackie and others in the sports and entertainment world projecting themselves into an area where they are obviously unqualified.
>
> Some day the big politicians are going to realize that the adulation Negroes heap upon their sports and entertainment celebrities is wisely confined to the playing fields and theatrical stages.
>
> History has shown that when those public idols (Jackie, Joe Louis, Jesse Owens, etc.) have attempted to extend their popularity and influence into the complicated world of politics, they have been consistently repudiated.[124]

Prattis wrote back to Smith. "Thanks for your note. It came at a good time. I am enclosing a letter from Jackie. I have written him that his letter is rude and impudent. The guy you used to nurse has ideas these days."[125]

Smith replied:

> I am returning the letter you sent me from YOUR boy, Robinson. It is very typical and very insulting. I am not surprised, however, I am sure you have never received a letter from him thanking you for a story praising him. In fact, I do not know of any writer who has.

Incidentally, I had a telephone conversation the other day with Arch Murray of the N.Y. Post. He confirms your impression that Robinson was fired by the Post because of his political affiliations.[126]

The historical record contradicts Smith. Robinson complimented Smith's writing and thanked him and the *Courier* in a 1945 letter.

During this period, Smith made another pioneering career advance. He became one of the first Blacks to work as beat writer for a major league baseball team when the *American* assigned him to cover the White Sox during the late 1950s and early 1960s. Smith also covered the Cubs during the 1958 season. He often traveled with Holtzman, who covered baseball for the *Chicago Sun-Times*. Once Holtzman bought Smith a sandwich at a restaurant in Tampa, Florida, during Spring Training. That establishment would not serve Smith due to his skin color.[127]

## Broadcast News

Two years later, Smith left the *American*. He became one of the first Black journalists to work for a television news broadcast in Chicago when he joined WBBM to cover news and sports in February 1963. Smith's hiring was part of a wave of Blacks advancing into radio and television jobs in the city.[128]

The *American* printed a story about Smith's departure. "I'm certainly sorry to leave Chicago's American where I've had so many pleasant associations." he said. "This is an opportunity, tho, which I could hardly afford to pass up.... The American afforded me a wonderful opportunity. It was gratifying to be accepted as one of the staff right from the start—and that acceptance has never wavered thru all the years I've been on the paper."[129]

Fischer paid tribute to Smith in the same paper. He wrote: "No metropolitan daily had ever hired a Negro sports writer before and it's no secret that one matter of concern was the kind of acceptance he'd get on assignments. Actually it turned out to be no problem. Not for Wendell Smith. Not for us."[130]

A reporter for the Associated Negro Press news service, Charles J. Livingston, praised Smith in an article.

In his own way, Wendell, a big fellow with an infectious smile, also is kind and willing to give a struggling scribe a helping hand.... But because he is a serious and hard taskmaster, his intentions and actions are sometimes misinterpreted.... There are those who say Smitty is a trifle snobbish.... I've even heard the opinion that he got his "break" with the American as a result of his past close contact and friendship with Robinson.... I wouldn't know about all that.... I only know that Smitty is an outstanding newspaperman; a writer who is qualified enough to make any newspaper on his ability.... He combines a sharp mind with an uncanny ability to "get behind the news." What Smitty writes is always fresh and informative because he always manages to come up with a new and interesting angle.... One dull day last season when the Chicago White Sox were getting whacked around Comiskey Park, Smitty found a fine alternate subject to treat.... He wrote an interesting article about the hundreds of yards of bandages used by trainer Ed Froelick on injured Sox players.

I remember quite well the first time I met Smitty.... I was a rookie reporter working my first fight alone and trying to beat the wire service deadline for filing.... I had no trouble writing the articles, but I was being crowded out the "service" by veteran reporters.... Wendell was then (the first Negro) president of the Chicago Boxing Writers Assn., and the hint had been dropped by other jealous sports writers not to expect too much help from him.... But Smitty, sensing my dilemma, came over on his own and offered several helpful suggestions.... He has since remained warm and friendly towards me.[131]

In February 1964, Smith again demonstrated his professionalism. He interviewed Alabama governor George Wallace for a WBBM panel show called *Target: News*. Wallace had gained infamy in 1963. He declared "segregation now, segregation tomorrow, segregation forever" during his inauguration speech. Later that year, he stood in front of the University of Alabama's Foster Auditorium in a failed attempt to stop the enrollment of two Black students. Smith managed to maintain his professional demeanor while he interviewed Wallace. After the show, Wallace shook Smith's hand and said, "When you come to Alabama, be sure to stop in and see me!"[132]

Four months later, he switched to WGN. Smith initially split his time between the news division and a sports team led by Brickhouse.[133] "Wendell was really the ideal addition to the staff at the time," Brickhouse wrote for *Overset*, the newsletter of the Chicago Press Club. "The rest of us, it seemed, were always on the road with the Cubs, the Hawks, the Bears, or covering college football, or a basketball game. We needed someone who wasn't traveling to cover the sports scene in Chicago, someone who knew sports and knew how to communicate. At the same time, the WGN News staff needed about 'half' a reporter. So, initially, Wendell was shared between the sports and news departments."[134]

At times, Smith did not appear on camera during his assignments. He simply posed a question to a subject and positioned the microphone to record the answer.[135] He spent much time at Wrigley Field, home of the Chicago Cubs. He interviewed both Cubs players and opponents, including Pittsburgh Pirates third baseman Richie Hebner and St. Louis Cardinals pitcher Bob Gibson.

Two former WGN staffers, John Hogan (no relation to Martin Hogan) and Chuck Shriver, provided more insight about Smith's time at the station.

Hogan spent 16 years as a WGN reporter before he joined Commonwealth Edison as director of communications. Hogan recalled: "He was a gentleman through and through. A very classy, friendly, soft spoken sort of guy."[136]

Shriver, who worked five years at WGN and spent eight years as manager of information and services for the Cubs, said Smith successfully made the adjustment to writing for television news. Shriver noted the script has to match the images broadcast on the television. "He wrote most of his own scripts," Shriver said about Smith. "He was an excellent writer. He picked it up very quickly."

Shriver also said Jack Brickhouse and WGN producer Jack Rosenberg helped Smith learn how to speak in front of a live camera. "It took him a little bit of time to get comfortable," Shriver said.[137]

Smith helped the news division by covering stories and working on special projects.

Shortly after Smith arrived at WGN, the station sent him to the federal courthouse in Chicago's downtown to cover jury deliberations for the trial of Jimmy Hoffa. Hoffa, then the president of the International Brotherhood of Teamsters, was on trial for misuse of the union's pension fund. The jury eventually convicted Hoffa in July 1964.

On March 13, 1965, WGN broadcast a show produced by Smith called *Let Freedom Ring: The Negro in Chicago*. The show presented the social and economic gains made by Blacks in Chicago. The show included footage of two predominantly black institutions: Provident Hospital and the Supreme Life Insurance Company. Smith conducted interviews with Sengstacke and Chicago Urban League director Edwin C. "Bill" Berry. The program broadcast footage of blacks working at Sears, Illinois Bell and O'Hare Airport, as well as Black players for the city's professional sports teams and Black members of the city council, including Ralph Metcalfe. The show also included footage of Wyonella Smith typing at the Globetrotters' office.

A month later, WGN broadcast another show in which Smith participated. On April 19, 1965, the station broadcast a special called *Decade with Daley*. The show commemorated the tenth anniversary of Chicago mayor Richard J. Daley's first election to the office. The program functioned more as a tribute to Daley rather than a critical review of his job performance. It included interviews with Daley's childhood friends and footage of Daley at a city council meeting, a mayoral press conference and a high school basketball game.

As part of the program, Smith interviewed Daley and his wife Eleanor "Sis" Daley at their house and accompanied the mayor on a helicopter tour of the city. The program marked the first time the couple allowed television cameras into their home.

A former news director at WGN, Bob Manewith, named a few reasons why the station picked Smith to interview Daley. "There was more than one reason. I list them in no order of importance. Our City Hall reporter, Don Harris, did not get along with Mayor Daley. Wendell could put him at ease by talking sports, particularly White Sox baseball. Daley was a devoted fan.... The mayor had a reputation for being no friend of African Americans and disdaining their abilities. Sending Wendell was sending a message."[138]

In 1966, Smith displayed his ability to cover hard news. According to Hogan, Smith was the first WGN reporter to cover the infamous Richard Speck murder story. Between July 13 and July 14, 1966, Speck killed eight student nurses in their dormitory on Chicago's south side. A jury convicted Speck of murder the following year. He eventually died in prison.

In early 1967, Smith became the sports anchor for the station's 10:00 p.m. news broadcast. He became the first Black sports anchor on a television news show in the city. WGN had hired John Drury to anchor the newscast and expanded it from 15 minutes to 25 minutes. Smith's sports coverage helped fill the extra time. The coverage included highlights of Cubs games in color, a revolutionary development.[139]

A columnist for The Herald, Paul Logan, called Smith a terrible announcer.

> Wendell seems to mispronounce at least one sports name each night. And many times he repeats the mistake on the same show which is uncalled for.
> Even if he gets the name right, his voice is atrocious. His style is as ragged as the day he began announcing, nearly seven years ago!
> The only good part of the show are the taped highlights, but he butchers them sometimes, too.[140]

Brickhouse had a different take on Smith's skills. "He didn't have the most professional broadcasting voice in history. You paid attention to the editorial content of what he was saying. And he was an excellent reporter. He knew how to report. If he said that 39 runs batted in, go to the bank and get a loan on it."[141]

Smith's status as a television personality made him a valued participant in community activities. Smith narrated a sound filmstrip about the Rev. Dr. Martin Luther King, Jr., which was produced by the Chicago-based Society for Visual Education, Inc.[142] Smith served as master of ceremonies at a dinner honoring Chicago area high school basketball stars. One honoree, Hales Franciscan's Sam Puckett, led the Chicago Catholic league in scoring.[143] Hales was an all–Black, all–male school located on Chicago's south side. Smith served as a board member for a small service center for children on Chicago's south side.[144] He presented tips about interviewing politicians at Roosevelt University, located in downtown Chicago.[145] Smith participated in a journalism workshop for high school students held at Chicago State University.[146] Smith, along with other local media figures, participated in a seminar with coaches from the Chicago public schools. During the meeting, participants discussed ways to improve media coverage of the city's public high school sports teams.[147]

Smith started participating on another WGN show in 1969. The station began broadcasting *People to People*, an urban affairs television program hosted by Berry. Smith posed questions to guests on the show. The show presented topics of importance to Blacks, including "Federal Employment and Black Americans," "From Protest to Politics," and "Blacks in Sports." Will Robinson appeared as a guest for the discussion about sports.[148]

Smith returned to his journalistic roots that same year. He started writing a weekly sports column for the *Chicago Sun-Times*. He continued to write the column until shortly before his death.

Three *Sun-Times* columns he wrote in 1971, two about Robinson and one about Ali, are especially noteworthy.

In January 1971, Smith interviewed Robinson during Robinson's visit to Chicago. Robinson had spent a day campaigning with the Rev. Jesse Jackson, head of Operation Breadbasket (later the Rainbow Push Coalition), ahead of that year's municipal elections. Robinson had supportive words for beleaguered Cubs manager Leo Durocher. The two had clashed when Durocher managed the Dodgers during Robinson's time with the team. During another interview with Smith, Robinson said Black baseball stars Frank Robinson and Maury Wills would make good managers in the major leagues.[149] The interviews may have represented a reconciliation between Smith and Robinson. According to a *Chicago Tribune* article written by Holtzman in 1993, Smith had told him he and Robinson had fallen out and hadn't spoken in nearly ten years. In the same article, Holtzman reported Wyonella Smith's insistence that the two men had remained friends.[150]

That March, Smith wrote a sensitive piece about the scene in Muhammad Ali's locker room after Joe Frazier defeated him in the first of their three bouts.[151] Smith empathetically depicted a battered Ali comforting a sobbing Diana Ross, the famous singer, and his mother, Odessa Ali, watching over the boxer. The column is especially remarkable given that Smith had criticized Ali several years earlier for his boasts in a *Courier* column. Smith wrote: "He shouts to the house tops that he's the greatest, ignoring the fact that modesty is the mark of a champion and that public esteem is a desirable goal for all athletes."[152]

Smith notched another achievement that year. He was named to the

Special Committee on the Negro Leagues for the Baseball Hall of Fame. That committee made Satchel Paige its first choice for induction in the Hall of Fame. The Smiths traveled to the Hall of Fame, located in Cooperstown, New York, for the ceremony.

In 1972, Smith gained more recognition as a leader in his field. That January, he was installed as the first Black president of the Chicago Press Club. He succeeded *Chicago Tribune* financial editor Nick Poulos. Smith could not attend the annual President's Dinner at the Pick-Congress Hotel, during which new officers were installed, because he was hospitalized due to his battle with cancer.

As the year progressed, Smith's illness grew worse and forced him back to the hospital. Brickhouse recalled his visit with Smith. "When I saw that skeleton of a man lying there and realized what he had been compared to what he was, it grabbed you right in the heart."[153]

During that year, Robinson and Smith appeared together in Chicago and recounted Robinson's tryout with the Red Sox.[154] That same year, Robinson, along with co-author Al Duckett, completed an autobiography, *I Never Had It Made: An Autobiography of Jackie Robinson.* In the book, he acknowledged his debt to Smith for his recommendation to Rickey.[155]

On October 15, 1972, Robinson appeared at Game 2 of the World Series between the Oakland A's and Cincinnati Reds. Robinson threw out the first pitch. Afterward, he said he wanted to live to see a Black manager in the major leagues.

When Robinson passed away from a heart attack nine days later, Smith memorialized him in what would be his final column for the *Sun-Times.* Smith wrote: "He never backed down from a fight, never quit agitating for equality. He demanded respect, too. Those who tangled with him always admitted afterward that he was a man's man, a person who would not compromise his convictions."

Robinson's remarks at the World Series did not surprise Smith. In the column, he wrote: "As I sat there and listened and watched, I just knew that Jackie Robinson was going to say something like that."[156]

Sometime following the World Series, Smith returned to the hospital. Duckett visited him. They discussed the autobiography. Smith told Duckett he was thrilled about Robinson's acknowledgment.[157] Shortly afterward, on Sunday, November 26, 1972, Smith passed away.

Smith's wake took place at the Griffin Funeral Home, located near Comiskey Park, on the following Tuesday. Chicago media figures Russ Ewing, Walter Jacobson and Fahey Flynn attended the wake. At the wake, Mayor Daley said: "We have lost a very great citizen, who was interested in the city and most of all the city's children."[158]

The funeral took place the next day at Griffin Funeral Home. A crowd of 200 people packed the facility. Attendees included Metcalfe, Chicago Bears owner George Halas, Cook County commissioner John Stroger, and sports stars Billy Williams, Gale Sayers and Johnny Morris. *Courier* columnist Hazel Garland, Bill Nunn, Jr., Will Robinson, and Hogan and his brother, John, flew into town to attend the funeral. *Sun-Times* columnist Jack Griffin battled tears while he spoke about Smith during the service.[159]

Wyonella Smith asked the Rev. Dr. Kenneth B. Smith, pastor of the Church of the Good Shepherd Congregational Church, to officiate the service.[160] The Rev. Smith told the mourners: "We are here today to thank Wendell for what he has given and for what he was. We gather to thank God for Wendell's life and the gift of Wendell's spirit. We praise God and we say amen and amen."[161]

Years later, the Rev. Smith noted that many well-known people attended the funeral. "It was a virtual who's who," he said. "That tells you the man was highly respected."[162]

After the service, Smith was buried at Burr Oak Cemetery in Alsip, Illinois. Alsip is a suburb located fifteen miles southwest of Chicago.

Gleason drove the Hogans to nearby Midway Airport. Along the way, they surprised him by calling Smith "Wendy."[163]

For about three weeks after Smith died, journalists in Chicago and other parts of the country wrote tributes about Smith.

"The death of Wendell Smith, Sun Times sports columnist and WGN broadcaster, cast a pall over the Soldier Field press box Sunday [the Chicago Bears lost to the visiting Cincinnati Bengals 13–3 at the stadium]. All knew that Mr. Smith's days were numbered because of a lingering illness, but his death still had a numbing effect. He was an able newsman, but more, a respected gentleman in his profession and a dear friend," Irv Kupcinet wrote for the *Sun-Times*.[164]

"There was a soft humor about Wendell, never anything vicious," Griffin wrote for the *Sun-Times*.

> He was a fairly big man. He walked with a sort of a shuffle, a limp left over from his athletic days at West Virginia State.
> I knew the part he had played in bringing Jackie Robinson in the major leagues as baseball's first Black player. I knew because other people told me. Wendell never mentioned it. He never operated with the bugles playing.[165]

"Wendell was neither a Black bigot nor an Uncle Tom," Robert Cromie wrote for the *Chicago Tribune*. "He was a beautiful guy who liked all good people and was, in turn, liked by everyone worth bothering about. He could lose his temper. I once saw him shove a burly guard aside in Yankee Stadium after an altercation—with an ease that made me suddenly realize how very strong he was. But laughter was more his style. I always think of him as laughing because he had so delightful a sense of humor."[166]

Another *Tribune* columnist, Vernon Jarrett, referred to Smith's column about Black jockeys who competed at the Kentucky Derby. The column, included in this collection, was published in the May 7, 1949, issue of the *Courier*. Jarrett wrote: "It was nearly 30 years ago that I read a piece under his byline about the Kentucky Derby. It was Wendell Smith telling his readers that a Black jockey was the winner of the first Kentucky Derby at Churchill Downs in 1875, and that a Black rider named Ike Murphy, who had won 49 of 50 races at Saratoga, won the Kentucky Derby three times before the turn of the 20th century.... Wendell was a great one for doing his homework. He was forever demonstrating in both his writing style and his research the kind of Black pride that so many of our school teachers were stressing at the time."[167]

Garland recalled that Smith had encouraged her during his stint as the *Courier*'s city editor. One day in 1944, Garland had stopped by the *Courier* offices with an article. Smith read it, then brought her to Bill Nunn, Sr. Smith told Nunn, the managing editor, that Garland had potential as a journalist. Afterward, the paper used Garland as a freelance substitute for reporters on vacation. She advanced to staff writer, assistant women's editor, women's editor, entertainment editor and city editor. Garland wrote: "But if Wendell Smith hadn't noticed I had some talent and was willing to give an inexperienced writer a chance to develop it, where would I be now?"[168]

Recalling Smith's efforts on behalf of Robinson, Lillian S. Calhoun wrote for the *Chicago Journalism Review*: "In those old days, Wendell lived advocacy journalism but unlike today's form which usually expresses a journalist's pet ideological bent. Wendell's advocacy and that of many who worked for the black press was unselfish. He fought with his typewriter to gain equality for all but he never curved a sports story he wrote."[169]

A columnist for the *Los Angeles Sentinel*, Brad Pye, Jr., wrote: "Like old soldiers, sportswriters never die, they just fade away, and Black baseball players of the Negro Leagues, as well as Black major leaguers of the present and the past, should never let his memory die."[170]

## Sportswriters Never Die

The memory of Smith has not died. Within a month after his death, the Chicago Press Club renamed its scholarship fund the Wendell Smith–Chicago Press Club Scholarship Fund. Around the same time, the *Chicago*

*Sun-Times* donated $1,000 for a scholarship in Smith's memory to be awarded through the National Merit Scholarship Fund.

Smith received more posthumous recognition in 1973.

The University of Notre Dame, with the cooperation of DePaul University, established the Wendell Smith Award that year. Notre Dame sports information director Roger Valdiserri had pondered his nice working relationship with Smith. Valdiserri originated the idea of giving an award in honor of him to the most valuable player of the school's annual game against DePaul.[171]

Valdiserri got permission from Wyonella Smith to put her husband's name on the award. "He died much too young," he said. "And when he did die, I thought it would be a good thing to have an award named after him. Basically, I thought we could use him as a role model for the ethnic youngsters who were involved in athletics."

The award was first given on January 11, 1973. Notre Dame beat DePaul at the latter's Alumni Hall 72–67. Reporters at the game voted Notre Dame guard Gary Brokaw the first recipient of the award. Brokaw led the Fighting Irish with 21 points. Wyonella Smith presented the award at midcourt after the game.

Valdiserri said: "I was rather proud to see the thing being presented for the first time and to have Wendell's wife make the presentation. Everybody that knew him I think was rather moved including all the media from Chicago. I remember telling our players who he was [before the game in the locker room] and why the award was named after him, that he was somebody they could emulate and look up to and take pride in."[172]

Shortly after the game, the Chicago Press Club honored Smith. On January 20, 1973, about 500 people trekked to Chicago's downtown to attend the organization's President's Dinner at the Pick-Congress Hotel. The event started with an invocation by Father John S. Banahan. During the invocation, Fr. Banahan said: "Well Lord, here we are again, this peculiar group of the good and the bad ... and the misinterpreted ... called the Press Club.... May we humbly remind You of a great blunder for which You were responsible ... for whoever made the decision to take Wendell Smith from among us was not of this number."[173] During the event, Wyonella Smith handed the gavel of office to Robert G. Schultz, the new club president. At the time, Schultz was the city editor of the *Chicago Daily News*.

That same year, the Chicago Board of Education named an elementary school in his honor and WGN created the Wendell Smith Memorial Award for baseball figures considered ambassadors of goodwill and presented by the Chicago chapter of the Baseball Writers of America at its annual dinner.

The Wendell Smith Elementary School, located on the city's far South Side, held a dedication ceremony in 1974. Brickhouse, Jarrett and Wyonella Smith spoke at the event.[174] Brickhouse recalled: "I couldn't think of anything more appropriate than to dedicate a school in his name to little kids like that. One of the most appropriate dedications I ever saw."[175]

Smith received more honors during the 1970s and 1980s. In 1975, the Chicago Park District named a park after him. In 1982, he was elected to the Chicago Journalism Hall of Fame. He was elected to the Chicagoland Sports Hall of Fame in 1983.[176]

Wyonella Smith continued working for the Harlem Globetrotters after her husband's death. The team was sold in 1976 to Metromedia, which eventually moved it to Los Angeles.[177] Smith remained in Chicago. She found work in the public information office for the City of Chicago's Department of Aging.[178] She confided to Garland that she had finally gotten over her husband's death. She eventually moved into a senior residence facility located on the city's South Side.[179] The same facility housed Mary Frances Veeck, the widow of former White Sox owner Bill Veeck. The Smiths and Veecks had been good friends. The two women maintained a strong relationship after the deaths of their husbands.[180] Wyonella Smith died on Thanksgiving Day, November 26, 2020, at the age of 99. She was buried at Burr Oak next to her husband. Coincidentally, the Smiths were married during the month of November and died during that month.

Smith remained a role model for Jarrett. In 1986, New York Giants linebacker Laurence Taylor received treatment for drug addiction. Jarrett thought of Smith while he denounced Taylor in a column for the *Sun-Times*.

> If the late sportswriter Wendell Smith were alive today, he would be a man enraged. Just as I am enraged over the use of dope by professional athletes.
>
> Even though the flow of narcotics crossed the boundaries of race, Smith would have been particularly sickened over the thought of Black athletes sniffing cocaine.... Smith angrily would have ripped into all athlete-addicts. However, he would have reminded the black users that black crusaders of previous generations such as the great athlete-scholar-performer Paul Robeson, did not march in picket lines around ball parks just to make it easy for ingrates to make a big buck and sniff cocaine.[181]

Public interest in Wendell Smith gradually faded for more than 20 years after his death. The attention increased during the 1990s. The BBWAA's Spink Award committee nominated Smith in 1993. The full membership voted for it, making him the first Black writer to receive the honor. Holtzman, himself a Spink honoree, had campaigned on Smith's behalf.[182] The announcement of the award sparked a revival of interest in Smith.

On February 20, 1994, WGN aired a segment about Smith as part of a broadcast of *People to People*. The broadcast, hosted by Allison Payne, included reporting by Rich King and interviews with Holtzman and Wyonella Smith. King visited Wendell Smith Elementary School. Wyonella Smith praised her late husband. She said: "He was a champion for civil rights and for everything that stood for equality for everyone." The show featured a shot of the den of Smith's home. The den, where Smith wrote articles, included a desk, mounted bookshelves, a file cabinet and a Royal typewriter. A portrait of Smith hung above the desk.

On July 31, 1994, Wyonella Smith accepted the Spink award on her late husband's behalf at the Baseball Hall of Fame's annual ceremony. She told the crowd:

> Twenty-three years ago on August 8th, 1971, Wendell and I were here in Cooperstown on the occasion of the establishment of the wing for players in the Negro Baseball Leagues and to honor those fine years.
>
> Because he was a very modest man, I am quite sure that it never occurred to Wendell that someday he would be honored as he is here today. It was baseball and his love of the game that started him on a career as a sports writer. This is a very happy day for me and there are many who also wish that he could be here to accept this wonderful award in person.
>
> It has occurred to me that 22 years after his death his peers remember his work and dedication to making the game of baseball a favorite pastime for every American.
>
> Those of you who knew Wendell remember that he was a really swell, gentle man with a terrific sense of humor, that you the members of Baseball Writers' Association have selected him for induction into the writers' wing of the Baseball Hall of Fame, fills me with tremendous pride and deep appreciation, and so for Wendell I say, Thank you.[183]

Wyonella Smith later donated her husband's papers to the Hall of Fame. The papers consisted of many of Wendell Smith's columns from the *Courier* and part of his correspondence.

West Virginia State University inducted him into its hall of fame the same year. The following year, Holtzman included his interview with Smith in an updated edition of his book, *No Cheering in the Press Box*. The book is a collection of interviews with sportswriters who worked between World War I and World War II.

In 2013, Smith received more posthumous recognition. The film *42*, which took its title from Robinson's jersey number, was released in theaters. The film focused primarily on Robinson's first two years with the Dodgers organization and depicted his relationship with Smith. *Sun-Times* reporter Dave Hoekstra drove Wyonella Smith to a screening of the movie.[184] The National Association of Black Journalists inducted Smith into its Hall of Fame.[185] The Shirley Povich Center for Sports Journalism at the University of Maryland's Philip Merrill College of Journalism created the Sam Lacy–Wendell Smith Award. The award recognizes a sports journalist or broadcaster who has made significant contributions to racial and gender equality in sport.[186]

A year later, in 2014, the Associated Press Sports Editors honored Smith with its Red Smith Award.[187]

Smith had gained wide admiration and respect, but did not escape criticism. Fay Young claimed Smith was "anxious to grab off some glory" when he took players to the tryout with the Red Sox.[188] *Michigan Chronicle* sportswriter Bill Matney claimed that Smith recommended a high school player to Rickey without observing the player in person. That player flopped in the minor leagues.[189] When a Black Los Angeles Dodgers player stayed in a Black-owned hotel instead of housing with the rest of the team in a white-owned hotel, Smith wrote an angry letter to the player. The player gave the letter to a team official, who tried to chastise Smith.[190]

Author Mark Ribowsky attacked Smith in his book, *A Complete History of the Negro Leagues, 1884 to 1955*. Ribowsky alleged Smith and other writers for the Black press helped destroy the Negro Leagues. He argued writers cut back on coverage of Black baseball in favor of the major leagues after Robinson joined the Dodgers.[191]

Smith's actions contradict that claim. In May 1947, Smith reminded readers to continue to support Black baseball.[192] In a 1949 letter to Rickey, Smith suggested that the Dodgers sponsor a Black baseball team.[193] Smith continued to cover the Negro Leagues' East-West All-Star game.[194]

Despite the occasional criticism, most observers recognized Smith's achievements and modest personality.

Smith demonstrated that modesty on April 15, 1947. He did not write about his role in Robinson's ascent to the Dodgers nor the realization of his dream to integrate major league baseball. Instead, he wrote a description of Rickey that he could have written about himself.

Smith wrote:

> When Jackie galloped out to his position at first base, attired in a snow white uniform with Brooklyn scrolled across the chest, it marked the highlight of Branch Rickey's campaign to put a Negro player on the Dodgers.
>
> It took a lot of hard work on the part of the Brooklyn owner to make this ambition a reality. He fought many forces in the inner circle of baseball as well as handling the difficult task of putting ROBINSON on his team without affecting its morale. But he did it. And here Tuesday afternoon, he saw his dream come true.[195]

*Michael Marsh is a paralegal and a freelance writer based in Chicago, Illinois. A former staff writer for the Chicago Reader, he is a member of the Society for American Baseball Research.*

## Acknowledgments

The author wishes to thank all of the interviewees as well as the following individuals: Bill Adee, Christina Banks, Estela Beltran, Glen Bleske, Gloria Brown, Michelle Carver, George Castle, Ryan Cuffee Caston, Delores Comeaux-Taylor, Rory Costello, Marian Crawford, Mary Dempsey, Mary Dillon, Diana Dionisio, Bruce DuMont, Gene Farris, Robert Feder, Rich Gannon, James Griffin, Donna L. Halper, Elise Harding-Davis, Elliot Harris, Fr. Glendon Heath, James "Biff" Henderson, James Henderson III, Sarah Henry, Carol Rodgers Hill, Dave Hoekstra, John Jeansonne, Margarite Jenkins, Idella Johnson, Michael Kolleth, Robert Kurson, Kevin Larkin, Adam Lechnir, Cassidy Lent, Joseph J. Leonard, Larry Lester, Eleanor Archer Lofton, Norman Macht, Bob Mazzoni, John Montgomery, the late Archie Motley, the late Edgar Munzel, Bill Nowlin, Andrew O'Toole, George Pappas, Humberto Perez, Scott Pifer, Norm Potash, Ron Rapoport, Jim Reisler, the late Edmund J. Rooney, the late Jack Rosenberg, The Honorable Roy Roulhac, Corey Seeman, the late Burl Sellers, Scott C. Smith, Lillian Stefano, the late Tom Tresh, Deborah Tucker, the late Jules Tygiel, James Robert Walker, Shawn Williams, the late A.S. "Doc" Young, Janice Young, and the late Jack Zerby. Finally, the author wishes to thank his late parents, Michael and Peggy Marsh, and his late sister, Rhonda Banks.

The author also wishes to thank the following institutions: the Center for Research Libraries Chatham-Kent Public Library, the Chicago History Museum, the Chicago Public Library's Special Collections and Preservation Division, the Chicago Public Library's Vivian G. Harsh Research Collection, the Chicago Public Library's Newspapers and Periodicals Division, DePaul University's Sports Information Department, the Detroit Public Library's Burton Historical Collection, the Museum of Broadcast Communications, the National Baseball Hall of Fame and Museum, Inc., the Newberry Library, the Society for American Baseball Research, the University of Illinois–Chicago's Special Collections & University Archives, the University of Pittsburgh's Hillman Library, Wendell Smith Elementary School, the West Virginia State University Archives and Special Collections Department, and the West Virginia State University's Sports Information Department.

## Notes

1. Wendell Smith, "Robbie's Bunt Turns Tide," *Pittsburgh Courier* (New York edition), April 19, 1947: 1; Wendell Smith, "Robinson Mobbed by Cameramen and Fans at Historic Opener," *Pittsburgh Courier* (New York edition), April 19, 1947: 1; Wendell Smith, "Jackie Romps Homes from Second Base as 26,000 Cheer," *Pittsburgh Courier* (New York edition), April 19, 1947: 1; Wendell Smith, "Robinson's Game Record," *Pittsburgh Courier* (New York edition), April 19, 1947: 1.

2. Wendell Smith, "Robinson Mobbed by Cameramen and Fans at Historic Opener," *Pittsburgh Courier* (New York edition), April 19, 1947: 1; Benedict Cosgrove, *Covering the Bases: The Most Unforgettable Moments in Baseball in the Words of the Writers and Broadcasters Who Were There* (San Francisco: Chronicle Books, 1997), 74.

3. Wendell Smith, "The Sports Beat," *Pittsburgh Courier*, May 12, 1945: 12.

4. Hugh Burnett's efforts are noted in John Cooper's book, *Season of Rage: Hugh Burnett and the Struggle for Civil Rights*, published in 2005.

5. Mark Malone, "Journalist with Chatham Ties Wrote Robinson's Story," *Chatham Daily News*, July 19, 2013.

6. "John H. Smith, Chef to Fords, Dies Saturday," *Michigan Chronicle*, July 9, 1966, A-1. The same article identifies Herb Jeffries as a cousin of Wendell Smith.

7. George W Stark, "Food at Yondotega Club Is Extolled, but Its Lore Remains Veiled in Court," *Detroit News*, January 27, 1938; "Yondotega Is an Ugly Spot, but Yum, Yum—That Steak!," *Detroit Free Press*, January 27, 1938: 1, 2.

8. "Judge Says Yondotega Club Is Not Too Humble to Tax," *Detroit Free Press*, January 29, 1938: 1.

9. Gladys M. Johnson, "The 'Elite' of Yesterday: Where Are They Today," *Michigan Chronicle*, April 22, 1961: A12.

10. "Mrs. Lena Smith, Detroit Resident," *Detroit Free Press*, October 11, 1970: 17-C.

11. The date of birth was stated on the draft card Smith completed during World War II. Another date, March 23, 1914, has been listed as Smith's date of birth.

12. Detroit City Directory, R.L. Polk & Co., 1914.

13. Wendell Smith, Smitty's Sport Spurts, *Pittsburgh Courier*, January 27, 1940: 16.

14. Herb Jeffries telephone interview with the author, April 30, 1997.

15. Martin Hogan telephone interview with the author, June 10, 1996.

16. Richard Bak, *Turkey Stearnes and The Detroit Stars: The Negro Leagues in Detroit, 1919–1933* (Detroit: Wayne State University Press, 1995), 58.

17. The Central Community Center was eventually renamed the Brewster-Wheeler Recreation Center. It was closed in 2006.

18. Russell J. Cowans, "Detroit Nips Cincinnati 5," *Chicago Defender*, January 16, 1932: 9.

19. Wendell Smith, "The Tragic Saga of Joe Louis ... FIGHTER," *Pittsburgh Courier*, August 4, 1956: 28.

20. Wendell Smith, Smitty's Sport Spurts, *Pittsburgh Courier*, January 15, 1938: 16.

21. Martin Hogan telephone interview with the author, June 10, 1996. The yearbook from Smith's senior year does not list any extracurricular activities for him.

22. "Sports Writer Champions Desegregation in Baseball," *Editor & Publisher*, April 1, 1960.

23. Jerome Holtzman, *No Cheering in the Press Box* (New York: Henry Holt, 1995), 323.

24. Dave Hoekstra, "Jackie Robinson and Sportswriter Wendell Smith: A Team for the Ages," *Chicago Sun-Times*, April 7, 2013, Sunday Show section, 2.

25. Bill Gleason telephone interview with the author, July 22, 1995.

26. Mort Edelstein, *Chicago Daily News*, November 28, 1972: 21.

27. Will Leonard, *Chicago Tribune*, December 2, 1972: Section 2, 11.

28. Martin Hogan telephone interview with the author, June 10, 1996.

29. Russell J. Cowans, "Detroit Team Defeats West Virginia 28–19, "*The Tribune Independent*, December 30, 1933: 7.

30. Calvin "Sweaty" Banks interview with the author, June 8, 1995.

31. Undated clipping in *The Yellow Jacket*. Courtesy of West Virginia State University's sports information department.

32. Wendell Smith letter to John W. Davis, dated May 15, 1936. Courtesy of West Virginia State University Archives and Special Collections Department.

33. Frank Bolden interview with the author, June 28, 1995.

34. Wendell Smith, "Sportiana," *Yellow Jacket* (student newspaper). Courtesy of West Virginia State University's sports information department.

35. Chester L. Washington, "Sez Ches," *Pittsburgh Courier*, October 3, 1936: 4.

36. Wendell Smith letter to Robert Vann, dated August 3, 1937. The letter is part of the Wendell Smith file, courtesy of the National Baseball Hall of Fame and Museum.

37. Jerome Holtzman, *No Cheering in the Press Box* (New York: Henry Holt, 1995), 314.

38. John W. Davis letter to Wendell Smith, dated September 28, 1937. Courtesy of West Virginia State University's Archives and Special Collections Department.

39. Andrew Buni, *Robert L. Vann of the Pittsburgh Courier: Politics and Black Journalism* (Pittsburgh: University of Pittsburgh Press, 1974), 257.

40. Buni, 42.

41. Buni, 47.

42. Buni, 228–230.

43. Buni, 325.

44. Mabel M. Smythe, ed., *The Black American Reference Book* (Englewood Cliffs, NJ: Prentice-Hall, 1976), 859.

45. P.L. Prattis, "Days of the 'Courier' Past' ...," *Perspectives of the Black Press: 1974*, edited by Henry La Brie, III (Kennebunkport, ME: Mercer House Press, 1975), 73.

46. Buni, *Robert L. Vann*, 45.

47. Rob Ruck, *Sandlot Seasons: Sport in Black Pittsburgh* (Urbana: University of Illinois Press, 1993), 14.

48. Jerome Holtzman, *No Cheering*, 314.

49. Frank Bolden interview with the author, June 28, 1995.

50. Bill Nunn, Jr., interview with the author, July 30, 1995.

51. The *Courier's* masthead published on December 7, 1940, lists Smith as the city editor.

52. Wendell Smith letter to John W. Davis, dated November 8, 1940. Courtesy of West Virginia State University's Archives and Special Collections Department.

53. Wendell Smith letter to John W. Davis, dated October 1, 1940. Courtesy of West Virginia State University Archives and Special Collections Department.

54. "Smith New Sports Editor," *Pittsburgh Courier*, September 27, 1941: 16.

55. Wendell Smith, Smitty's Sport Spurts, *Pittsburgh Courier*, May 6, 1934: 12.

56. David W. Zang, *Fleet Walker's Divided Heart: The Life of Baseball's First Black Major Leaguer* (Lincoln: University of Nebraska Press, 1995), 47.

57. Sol White, *Sol White's Official Base Ball Guide*, edited by H. Walter Schlichter, Philadelphia, 1907, reprinted in *Sol White's History of Colored Base Ball* (Lincoln: University of Nebraska Press, 1995), 67.

58. Ches Washington, "Sez Chez," *Pittsburgh Courier*, February 25, 1933: Section 2, 5.

59. Irwin Silber, *Press Box Red: The Story of Lester Rodney, the Communist Who Helped Break the Color Line in American Sports* (Philadelphia: Temple University Press, 2003), 67.

60. Sam Lacy, "Opening Much More Than Pandora's Box," *The Afro-American*, March 13, 1973: 15.

61. Wendell Smith, Smitty's Sport Spurts, *Pittsburgh Courier*, May 14, 1938: 17.

62. Wendell Smith, "Cincinnati Reds' Manager, Players Laud Negro Stars," *Pittsburgh Courier*, July 15, 1939: 13, 16.

63. Lester Rodney presentation, April 1997. Courtesy of Lester Rodney.

64. Holtzman, *No Cheering*, 315.

65. Holtzman, 316.

66. Andy McCue, "Branch Rickey," SABR Biography Project, https://sabr.org/bioproj/person/branch-rickey; Arnold Rampersad, *Jackie Robinson: A Biography* (New York: Knopf, 1997): 121–122; 89; Jules Tygiel, *Baseball's Great Experiment: Jackie Robinson*

*and His Legacy* (New York: Oxford University Press, 1983): 48–52; https://www.baseball-reference.com/players/r/rickebr01.shtml.

67. Carl Rowan with Jackie Robinson, *Wait Till Next Year: The Life Story of Jackie Robinson* (New York: Random House, 1960), 96–98.

68. Rowan, 97.

69. Jethroe eventually played in the major leagues. He won Rookie of the Year honors after his debut with the Boston Braves in 1950.

70. Wendell Smith, "Washington All American—Smith," *Pittsburgh Courier*, November 18, 1939: 17; "Robinson Sparkles for All-Stars Against Chicago Bears," *Pittsburgh Courier*, September 6, 1941: 17.

71. Rampersad, *Jackie Robinson*, 101–113, Tygiel, *Great Experiment*, 60–61, 64.

72. Rampersad, *Jackie Robinson*, 89; William Hageman, "Chicago's 55-Year-Old Secret: Jackie Robinson's Tryout with the White Sox," *Chicago Tribune*, March 26, 1997: Section 5, 1.

73. Rampersad, *Jackie Robinson*, 99, 109–111, 113.

74. Rowan, *Next Year*, 99–100.

75. Rowan, 104.

76. Rowan, 106–107.

77. Shirley Povich, *All These Mornings* (Englewood Cliffs, NJ: Prentice-Hall, 1969), 13.

78. Sam Lacy telephone interview with the author, August 16, 1995.

79. Stephanie Fuller, "Talent, Wit Help Wendell Score," *Chicago Tribune*, December 5, 1970: 16.

80. Wendell Smith letter to Jackie Robinson, dated February 4, 1947, from the Wendell Smith file, National Baseball Hall of Fame.

81. Jackie Robinson, "Jackie Robinson Says," *Pittsburgh Courier*, May 17, 1947: 14.

82. Wendell Smith, "The Most Prejudiced Teams in Baseball," *Ebony*, May 1953, 111–114, 117–118, 120.

83. Roscoe McGowan, "If You Were Jackie Robinson," *Sport*, September 1947: 41, 78–79.

84. The *Chicago Herald-American*, like other afternoon papers, gradually lost circulation after World War II as people moved from the city to the suburbs and television news attracted viewers. In 1953, the *Herald-American* became the *Chicago American*. The *American* was bought by the *Chicago Tribune* in 1956 and was renamed *Chicago's American*. The paper continued as a broadsheet until 1969 when the *Tribune* converted the paper from a broadsheet to a tabloid and renamed it *Chicago Today*. Circulation continued to decline and *Chicago Today* ceased publication in 1974.

85. Smith continued to write a sports column for the *Pittsburgh Courier* on a freelance basis until 1967.

86. Leo Fischer, *Chicago's American*, February 18, 1963: 15.

87. "'No Racial Bars In Tourney—Fischer,'" *Pittsburgh Courier*, January 6, 1945: 11.

88. Wendell Smith, "Jackie Robinson's Story the Saga of a New America," *Chicago Herald-American*, August 20, 1940: 25.

89. Wendell Smith, "Wendell Smith's Sports Beat," *Pittsburgh Courier*, August 23, 1947: 14.

90. Lester Rodney letter to the author, April 26, 1997.

91. Vince Johnson, "Once Over Lightly," *Pittsburgh Post-Gazette*, November 29, 1948: 21.

92. Vince Johnson, "Once Over Lightly," *Pittsburgh Post-Gazette*, July 22, 1949: 17. The same article noted that the 1948 membership roster of BBWAA listed Sam Lacy as an associate member of the Baltimore chapter.

93. Jackie Robinson as told to Wendell Smith, *Jackie Robinson: My Own Story* (New York: Greenberg, 1948), 7.

94. Frank Bolden interview with the author, June 28, 1995.

95. "Son of Sports Scribe Disrs 'Puddin' Pie,'" *Chicago Defender*, July 12, 1960: 21.

96. Ryan Cuffee Caston Facebook message to the author, March 8, 2022.

97. "Son of Sports Scribe Disrs 'Puddin' Pie,'" *Chicago Defender*, July 12, 1960: 21.

98. John Wendell Smith, Jr., died in 1988. Sara Smith, later Sara Bembry, died in 1992.

99. Ryan Cuffee Caston Facebook message to the author, March 8, 2022.

100. Evelyn Cunningham, "Sports, Theatrical Worlds Join Nixon Fund Campaign," *Pittsburgh Courier*, January 22, 1949: 1, 4.

101. Wendell Smith, "Wendell Smith's Sports Beat," *Pittsburgh Courier*, March 19, 1949: 10.

102. "Wyonella Creft Weds Wendell Smith," *Michigan Chronicle*, December 3, 1949: 15.

103. "Woman Celebrates 100th Year-Julia Henderson," *The Herald Sun* (Durham, North Carolina), February 6, 2006: B6.

104. "How Courier Went to Press With Jackie Robinson on Opening Day," *Pittsburgh Courier*, April 26, 1947: 13.

105. Jack Brickhouse, "Wendell Smith Rates a 'Hey Hey!' as a Natural for Newscaster," *Overset: News Bulletin of the Chicago Press Club* (January-February 1972): 1, 3. From the Chicago Public Library's Special Collections Division.

106. "Personalities in the News: TV Newsman produces 'Negro in Chicago,'" *Chicago Defender*, March 16, 1965: 11.

107. Wyonella Smith's volunteer activities are listed in the *Wendell Smith Journal*, May 28, 1974. The *Wendell Smith Journal* was produced by the students of Wendell Smith Elementary School.

108. Toki Schalk Johnson, "Toki Types," *Pittsburgh Courier*, July 15, 1954: 8.

109. Bolden interview with the author, June 28, 1995.

110. Truman Gibson, Jr., interview with the author, August 4, 1995.

111. Mort Edelstein, "Mort," *Chicago Daily News*, November 28, 1972: 21.

112. Ben Bentley interview with the author, May 15, 1996.

113. Bill Gleason interview with the author, July 22, 1995.

114. Wendell Smith, "Has Net Queen Althea Gibson Gone High Hat?" *Pittsburgh Courier*, July 27, 1957: 24.

115. P.L. Prattis letter to Wendell Smith, dated August 20, 1957. The letter is part of the Wendell Smith file, courtesy of the National Baseball Hall of Fame and Museum.

116. Robert M. Ratcliffe, "Behind the Headlines!" *Pittsburgh Courier*, April 5, 1958: 7.

117. Wendell Smith, "Wendell Smith's Sports Beat," *Pittsburgh Courier*, September 17, 1960: 17.

118. Wendell Smith, "Negro Ball Players Want Rights in South," *Chicago's American*, January 23, 1961: 1.

119. Wendell Smith, "Wendell Smith's Sports Beat," *Pittsburgh Courier*, February 18, 1961: 27.

120. Brian Carroll, "Wendell Smith's Last Crusade: The Desegregation of Spring Training, 1961," in *The Cooperstown Symposium on Baseball and American Culture, 2001*, edited by William Simons, 123–137 (Jefferson, NC: McFarland, 2002).

121. "Sports Writer Champions Desegregation in Baseball," *Editor & Publisher*, April 1, 1960.

122. "Newswriting Winners Named," *Chicago's American*, October 15, 1961.

123. P.L. Prattis, "Horizon," *Pittsburgh Courier*, January 7, 1961: 11.

124. Wendell Smith letter to P.L. Prattis, dated January 9, 1961. The letter is part of the Wendell Smith file, courtesy of the National Baseball Hall of Fame and Museum.

125. P.L. Prattis letter to Wendell Smith, dated January 16, 1961. The letter is part of the Wendell Smith file, courtesy of the National Baseball Hall of Fame and Museum.

126. Wendell Smith letter to P.L. Prattis, dated January 30, 1961; Jackie Robinson letter to Wendell Smith dated October 31, 1945. Both letters are part of the Wendell Smith file, courtesy of the National Baseball Hall of Fame and Museum.

127. Holtzman mentioned the story during the February 20, 1994 broadcast of the WGN show *People to People*.

128. Bob Hunter, "Local TV Stations Getting Into Race Act," *Chicago Defender*, July 30, 1963: 16.

129. "Smith to Enter TV, Radio Field," *Chicago's American*, February 9, 1963.

130. Leo Fischer, *Chicago's American*, February 18, 1963: 15.

131. Charles J. Livingston, "Tribute to a Fellow Scribe—Smitty," Associated Negro Press, March 18, 1963.

132. Herb Lyons, "Tower Ticker," *Chicago Tribune*, February 21, 1964: 16.

133. George Castle, "Brickhouse top on-air salesman for both sports, racial tolerance," Chicago Baseball Museum (https://chicagobaseballmuseum.org/) The article includes a recording of part of Smith's broadcast from June 11, 1967.

134. Jack Brickhouse, "Wendell Smith Rates a 'Hey Hey!' as a Natural for Newscaster," *Overset: News Bulletin of the Chicago Press Club* (January-February 1972): 1, 3. Courtesy of the Chicago Public Library's Special Collections Division.

135. Clay Gowran, "A Story of 4 TV Men You Will Seldom See," *Chicago Tribune*, August 8, 1966: Section 1A, 2.

136. John Hogan interview with the author, May 26, 2022.

137. Chuck Shriver telephone interview with the author, May 23, 2022.

138. Bob Manewith email to the author, May 24, 2022.

139. John Owens and David J. Fletcher, *Chili Dog MVP: Dick Allen, the '72 White Sox and a Transforming Chicago*, edited by George Castle (Chicago: Eckhartz Press, 2021), 290.

140. Paul Logan, *The Herald*, April 22, 1971: Section Two, 8.

141. Jack Brickhouse interview with the author, March 3, 1996.

142. "Documentary Filmstrip of Life On Dr. King Available to Schools," *Chicago Defender*, September 21, 1968: 34.

143. John Leusch, "Honor Prep Basket Stars: Glittering Dinner Event Draws Over 400," *Chicago Tribune*, April 3, 1969: D1.

144. Judy Roberts, "Red Schoolhouse Pre-Teen Center Lures Youngsters," *Chicago Tribune*, March 18, 1971: Section 3C, 6.

145. "Wendell Smith Speaks on WGN," *Chicago Defender*, October 27, 1964: 9.

146. *Chicago Defender*, June 21, 1969: 36.

147. Bill Gleason, "City Coaches Seek New Status," *Chicago Sun-Times*, February 11, 1970: 110.

148. *Chicago Defender* photograph, May 30, 1970, 25.

149. Wendell Smith, "Jackie Robinson Discusses Old Adversary Leo," *Chicago Sun-Times*, January 26, 1971: 72; Wendell Smith, "Jackie Robinson Tabs Black Managers," *Chicago Sun-Times*, October 5, 1971: 75.

150. Jerome Holtzman, "Jackie Robinson and the Great American Pastime: And the Man Behind Him," *Chicago Tribune*, April 11, 1993: B-4, 5, 15.

151. Wendell Smith, "Ali Tells Diana Ross: I Ain't No Champ," *Chicago Sun-Times*, March 9, 1971: 83.

152. Wendell Smith, "Wendell Smith's Sports Beat," *Pittsburgh Courier*, January 16, 1965: 15.

153. Jack Brickhouse interview with the author, March 3, 1996.

154. David Condon, "Jackie Robinson: A Man of Summer," *Chicago Tribune*, June 25, 1972: S-3, 3.

155. Jackie Robinson and Al Duckett, *I Never Had It Made: An Autobiography of Jackie Robinson* (New York: HarperCollins, 1972), 41.

156. Wendell Smith, "The Jackie Robinson I Knew...," *Chicago Sun-Times*, October 25, 1972: 98, 100.

157. "Sportswriter Who Aided Jackie Robinson's Entry Into Baseball Dies at 58," *Jet*, December 14, 1970, 30.

158. "Daley: He Loved Our City and its Children," *Chicago Defender*, November 29, 1972: 4.

159. James M. Stephens, "Funeral for Wendell Smith," *Chicago Defender*, November 30, 1972: 4.

160. Rev. Dr. Kenneth Smith interview with the author, August 10, 1995.

161. Stephens, "Funeral for Wendell Smith."

162. Reverend Dr. Kenneth Smith interview with the author, August 10, 1995.

163. Bill Gleason telephone interview with the author, June 22, 1995.

164. Irv Kupcinet, "Kup's Column," *Chicago Sun-Times*, November 27, 1972: 40.

165. Jack Griffin, "Wendell Smith: Courage, Dignity, Fun," *Chicago Sun-Times*, November 27, 1972: 82.

166. Bob Cromie, "Warm Memories of Wendell Smith," *Chicago Tribune*, November 29, 1972: 26.

167. Vernon Jarrett, "Farewell to an Old Friend," *Chicago Tribune*, November 29, 1972: 26.

168. Hazel Garland, "Thing to Talk About," *Pittsburgh Courier*, December 9, 1972: 13.

169. Lillian Calhoun, "Black and White," *Chicago Journalism Review*, January 1973: 22.

170. Brad Pye, Jr., "A Giant Is Dead," *Los Angeles Sentinel*, December 7, 1972: B-5.

171. John Leusch, "Notre Dame Nips DePaul by 72–67," *Chicago Tribune*, January 12, 1973, C-1.

172. Roger Valdiserri telephone interview with the author, May 7, 1996.

173. "Dinner Invocation Tells It Like It Is," *Overset: News Bulletin of the Chicago Press Club* (January-February 1973): 4. Courtesy of the Chicago Public Library's Special Collections Division. "Bob Schultz Takes President's Gavel from 'Gallant Lady,'" *Overset: News Bulletin of the Chicago Press Club* (January-February 1973): 1, 4. Courtesy of the Chicago Public Library's Special Collections Division.

174. The attendees are listed in the *Wendell Smith Journal*, May 28, 1974. The *Wendell Smith Journal* was produced by the students of Wendell Smith Elementary School.

175. Jack Brickhouse interview with the author, March 3, 1996.

176. "Notes," *Chicago Tribune*, September 17, 1983, A-5.

177. Ben Green, *Spinning the Globe: The Rise, Fall, and Return to Greatness of the Harlem Globetrotters* (New York: Amistad, 2005), 352.

178. David Schneidman, "Worker, 79, to City: I Do My Job Well," *Chicago Tribune*, May 18, 1984: B-7.

179. Hazel Garland, "Hazel Garland's Things to Talk About," *Pittsburgh Courier*, January 15, 1977: 13.

180. Ben Strauss, "Friendship as Priceless as the National Pastime," *New York Times*, August 22, 2012.

181. Vernon Jarrett, "Drugs Blur Black Gains in Sports," *Chicago Sun-Times*, February 21, 1986, 31.

182. Larry Gross, "Smith: A Trailblazing Sportswriter," *Chicago Defender*, February 19, 1994: 46.

183. Transcript courtesy of the National Baseball Hall of Fame and Museum.

184. Hoekstra, Sunday Show section, 2.

185. "NABJ Selects Six Journalists to Be Inducted into NABJ's Hall of Fame," October 1, 2012, NABJ press release, 20.

186. "Povich Center Announces Sam Lacy—Wendell Smith Award," July 2013, Povich Center press release.

187. Rhiannon Walker, "Wendell Smith Honored with Red Smith Award," University of Maryland Sports Journalism Institute, May 21, 2014.

188. Fay Young, "Through the Years," *Chicago Defender*, May 26, 1945: 7.

189. Bill Matney, "Jumpin' the Gun," *Michigan Chronicle*, July 19, 1947: 15.

190. A.S. "Doc" Young, "The Black Athlete in the Golden Age of Sports: Stereotypes, Prejudices, and Other Unfunny Hilarities," *Ebony*, June 1969: 114–122.

191. Mark Ribowsky, *A Complete History of the Negro Leagues, 1884 to 1955* (New York: Birch Lane Press, 1995), 288.

192. Wendell Smith, "The Sports Beat," *Pittsburgh Courier*, May 3, 1947: 14.

193. Wendell Smith letter to Branch Rickey dated July 5, 1949, from the Wendell Smith file, National Baseball Hall of Fame.

194. Wendell Smith, "Wendell Smith's Sports Beat," *Pittsburgh Courier*, August 20, 1949: 22; Wendell Smith, "Wendell Smith's Sports Beat," *Pittsburgh Courier*, August 11, 1951: 14.

195. Wendell Smith, "Robinson Mobbed by Cameramen and Fans at Historic Opener," *Pittsburgh Courier* (New York edition), April 19, 1947: 1, 4.

## Further Reading

Bleske, Glen L. "Agenda for Equality: Heavy Hitting Sportswriter Wendell Smith." *Media History Digest* (Fall-Winter 1993): 38–42.

Buni, Andrew. *Robert L. Vann of the Pittsburgh Courier: Politics and Black Journalism* (Pittsburgh: University of Pittsburgh Press, 1974).

Cooper, John. *Season of Rage: Hugh Burnett and the Struggle for Civil Rights* (Toronto: Tundra Books, 2005).

Manley, Effa, and Leon Herbert Hardwick. *Negro Baseball.... Before Integration* (Chicago: Adams Press, Chicago, 1976).

Owens, John, and David J. Fletcher. *Chili Dog MVP: Dick Allen, the '72 White Sox and a Transforming Chicago*, edited by George Castle (Chicago: Eckhartz Press, 2021).

Peterson, Robert. *Only the Ball Was White: A History of Legendary Black Players and All-Black Professional Teams* (New York: Oxford University Press, 1970).

Rampersad, Arnold. *Jackie Robinson: A Biography* (New York: Knopf, 1997).

Reisler, Jim. *Black Writers, Black Baseball* (Jefferson, NC: McFarland, 1994).

Robinson, Jackie. *Baseball Has Done It* (Philadelphia: Lippincott, 1964).

Rowan, Carl, with Jackie Robinson. *Wait Till Next Year: The Life Story of Jackie Robinson* (New York: Random House, 1960).

Ruck, Rob. *Sandlot Seasons: Sport in Black Pittsburgh* (Urbana: University of Illinois Press, 1993).

Silber, Irwin. *Press Box Red: The Story of Lester Rodney, the Communist Who Helped Break the Color Line in American Sports* (Philadelphia: Temple University Press, 2003).

Tygiel, Jules. *Baseball's Great Experiment: Jackie Robinson and His Legacy* (New York: Oxford University Press, 1983).

Weaver, Bill L. "The Black Press and the Assault on Professional Baseball's 'Color Line,' October 1945–April 1947." *Phylon* XL, no. 4 (Fourth Quarter, 1979).

Wiggins, David K. "Wendell Smith, the Pittsburgh Courier-Journal and the Campaign to Include Blacks in Organized Baseball, 1933–1945." *The Journal of Sports History* (1983): 5–29.

Ancestry.com, Baseball-Reference.com, ChicagoBaseballMuseum.org, Newspapers.com, PaperofRecord.com, SABR.org, YouTube.com.

# 1

# Remembering Wendell

*One of the challenges of writing a book about an individual who passed more than a half century ago is that there are not many people to speak with who knew him. Many of his contemporaries have passed as well. If I could have interviewed those individuals, I would have asked them what made Wendell Smith unique. Why do they miss him? Fortunately, some of his colleagues wrote columns answering these questions.*

## *December 9, 1972*

### Hazel Garland's Things to Talk About, *Pittsburgh Courier*, p. 13

This may not be the way it was originally stated, but there is a saying that "in the midst of life, there is death." How true. One can be having a very gay time one minute and in the next second, all happiness is swept aside by the news of the death of a dear friend. And so it was with me a few days ago.

I had just arrived home from St. Louis where I had a most enjoyable time participating in the installation of the St. Louisiennes into the 29th chapter of Girl Friends, Inc., when I learned of the death of Wendell Smith. A mutual friend, Mrs. Harry (Mildred) Gibson called to say she had Wyonella (Wendell's pretty wife) on the phone. Hearing "Wyonnie's" voice convinced me to hop a plane for Chicago the next day.

There has been so much written in the press; said on radio and television about Wendell that has been heart-warming just to read and hear. Like every professional athlete who has to give credit to the late newsmen for helping to improve his status in the world of sports, I, too owe a debt of gratitude to Wendell for being where I am today. Wendell and the late William G. Nunn, Sr., gave me my first newspaper job.

I will never forget my first meeting with Wendell Smith. It was back

51

in 1944 at the old *Pittsburgh Courier* plant up on Centre Avenue. Although he was officially the paper's sport's editor, Wendell was also holding down the city editor's desk where I was directed with my first journalistic effort.

After reading my story, Wendell hurriedly ushered me into Managing Editor Bill Nunn, Sr.'s, office. Wendell told Nunn that he thought I showed some talent as a writer and with a little help might develop into a pretty good reporter. Nunn explained that while there was no opening on the editorial staff at the time, they could use me as a "stringer" with the option of being hired first chance given.

During the vacation season, I subbed for various reporters. Then in 1947 I became a full-time staff reporter and six-months later was named assistant woman's editor to Toki Schalk Johnson. Ten years ago I was promoted to women's editor and six years later took on the additional job of entertainment editor. This past September, I was elevated to city editor of the *New Pittsburgh Courier*. But if Wendell Smith hadn't noticed that I had some talent and was willing to give an inexperienced writer a chance to develop it, where would I be now?

Good friends are like rare jewels ... treasured. Two of my best friends in Chicago are June and Vernon Rhinehart. June is a former McKeesporter who used to ride with me to work each day when she too worked at the old *Courier*. She now holds the position of vice president and assistant to publisher John H. Johnson. Her husband is a rising young attorney and they reside in a gorgeous 10-room (with three baths) apartment in a beautiful residential section of the "windy city."

Their home is always open to me so naturally I called them as soon as I hung up after talking with Wyonella. Before I could ask them, Vernon said of course you are staying with us, and that made asking unnecessary.

Wendell and Wyonella's many friends were on hand for the Memorial Services conducted from the Griffin Funeral Home on S. Martin Luther King Jr. Drive. The Rev. Dr. Kenneth B. Smith of the Church of the Good Shepherd delivered a beautiful eulogy. He was assisted by the Rev. H. Lynn McDowell with Richard Fullman as soloist.

Television co-workers and friends of long standing served as pall bearers. Included were Jack Brickhouse, Jack Cole, Harry H.C. Gibson, George Gillett, Benjamin C. Johnson, Theodore Jones, Jim Mullen, Robert Schultz, George Denison and Arthur Turnbull. Because Wendell loved and spent his life serving people of all ages and walks of life, the family acknowledged as honorary pallbearers all friends and all organizations with which Wendell had been associated.

Bill Nunn, Jr., who cut his teeth on the sport's desk working with Wendell during the summer while at West Virginia State College, flew in from Pittsburgh for the services Wednesday morning. Young Nunn now holds an executive position with the Pittsburgh Steelers. Former *Courier* theatrical editor Billy Rowe came down from New York and Will Robinson of Detroit was another ex-Courierite at the services.

Although the occasion was a sad one, it was good seeing still another former Courierite Ted Coleman and his pretty wife Frances. Ted is one of Chicago Mayor Richard Daley's "Right-hand" men. Saw ex-Pittsburgher Malcolm Scipio at the receiving (the casket was unopened). It has been about 20 years since we last met. Although a little grayer, he looks just the same.

## December 9, 1972

### Louis Martin's The Big Parade: "We Mourn a notable friend," *The Pittsburgh Courier*, p. 3

Whenever one recalls the sports heroes of a decade or two ago, Jackie Robinson, Joe Louis, et al., the pictures that come to my mind are never complete until I can see the bespectacled, smiling face of Wendell Smith. For me and thousands more, he was the expert who foretold the triumphs and explained, clearly enough for us squares, how and why the prediction hit or missed the mark.

Wendell was buried Wednesday. The news of his death hit many of us like a short-circuit in a packed stadium that knocked out all the lights. The tributes are pouring into the newsroom and it seems nobody ever had more friends. Somewhat belatedly, it seems, everyone is telling how Wendell helped pave the way for Jackie Robinson in breaking the color bar in baseball, telling of the time he gave a stumbling guy a helping hand or counseled a wavering superstar. The stories are all true too.

There is an interesting thread running through all the tributes almost without exception. In these times I think it is worthy of special notice. The point upon which all agree is that Wendell was every man's friend. As one commentator inferred, there was not a malicious bone in his body. Sensitive to all the ugly implications of the American color line, Wendell drew no color lines when it came to winning friends. We are in a period when some blacks seem to feel that the race is being betrayed when a brother wears a smile. Wendell was a natural born smiler, if there is any such person.

The menacing frown is the popular mien for many blacks now who seem so anxious to tell all whites how much they hold them in contempt. Wendell knew that whites, like blacks, come in all shapes, sizes and characters. Men were smart, stupid, good or evil irrespective of skin color in the world of Wendell Smith. He took the measure of each individual and judged every person on his own merit. He knew there were Branch Rickeys as well as Jim Eastlands and knew the difference between them. His freedom from malice and prejudice made him doubly-strong in the struggle he led to abolish the racial barriers in the world of sports. Earnest, honest and selfless, Wendell developed the kind of personality that was hard for any man to hate. Yet no angry civil rights leader nor fiery freedom fighter every did more to open the doors of opportunity to black youth.

Aside from his life style and the warmth of his personality, Wendell was fortified by his early experiences as a member of the black press. He shared the sensibilities and something of the spirit of the pioneers, beginning with the first black newsman, John B. Russwurm, who started *Freedom's Journal* in 1872. He was a journalist and an advocate. Advocacy journalism, as the pioneers knew it, was based on the assumption that the truth would make you free.

This tradition of advocacy journalism is not fully understood nor always appreciated but it can count up some notable victories in the endless war against racial injustice in our society. It was no accident that Frederick Douglass with his *North Star* and Dr. W.E.B. DuBois with his first literary efforts followed this tradition.

Perhaps the single most significant principle that has dominated the minds of black newsmen has been equality of opportunity. It is the keystone of our constitutional arch and one of the basic blessings of the democratic promise. Wendell Smith, in his own gentle but exciting way, fought for its realization. All of us shared the thrill he felt when Jackie Robinson first walked out of the Dodger dugout in Ebbets Field. Wendell deserves the tributes of this sad hour and every American, black and white, is a little taller because he passed this way.

## December 16, 1972

### Dick Young, *The Sporting News*, p. 16

Wendell Smith was a gentleman, a reporter of discernment. When a ballplayer, black or white, was good, he praised him. When a ballplayer was wrong, black or white, he ripped him. He was there with us, from the beginning of the Robinson days, and did his job with dignity. Wendell Smith, in a difficult time, was a good one. The newspaper business owes him.

*Wendell's colleagues in Chicago expressed their admiration and affection for him in the tribute columns they wrote after his passing as well.*

*Many noted his sense of humor. Occasionally he would attempt humor in his columns, but his colleagues seemed to be referring to his private behavior. Wendell was not rowdy, but he enjoyed people and life.*

*While attending West Virginia State College, Wendell regularly rode the train to and from Detroit. The train would pass briefly through Kentucky and the conductor would enforce the segregated seating laws of that state. Wendell would have to move to the segregated car and could return to his original seat after the train exited Kentucky. He befriended a conductor and told Will Leonard, "There was nothing wrong with that man. He was doing something stupid that he'd been ordered to do"* (Chicago Tribune, December 2, 1972, p. 207). *Wendell told this story to Leonard as a grown man. But Smith was a young man when the incident occurred. It takes a perceptive young man to be able to separate the conductor's behavior from his soul. By rising above the fray, Wendell was able to build a bridge to a reasonable white man. He consistently repeated that behavior throughout his career.*

*Bob Cromie wrote, "Wendell viewed people as people, not symbols, and if that isn't the way it should be done, let me know and I'll drop you from my sensible list"* (Chicago Tribune, November 29, 1972, p. 26). *Wendell would criticize friends when he thought they were wrong and compliment those he thought less of if they did something right. He saw individuals, not stereotypes. He valued fairness and was willing to reconsider his views and even change his mind.*

*In the chapter "Black History," you will see that Wendell was not only writing about sports but was also often teaching Black history to readers. As Vernon Jarrett wrote, "He was forever demonstrating in both his writing style and his research the kind of black pride that so many of our school teachers were stressing at the time"* (Chicago Tribune, November 29, 1972, p. 26). *Wendell and the schoolteachers about which Jarrett writes were the forebears of the Black history courses of today. But Wendell made history as well.*

*Jackie Robinson played his first game as a Dodger in 1947.* Brown v Board *was decided in 1954. And MLB Spring Training facilities remained segregated into the 1960s. After unsuccessfully attempting to work behind the scenes to desegregate those facilities, Wendell decided to go it alone. He wrote column after column demanding that Black MLB stars speak up and team owners threaten to leave localities that refused to change. Dave Condon opined, "Wendell accomplished in my time something that should have won him the Pulitzer Prize, and yet it has been almost forgotten in this modern age"* (Chicago Tribune, November 29, 1972, p. 75). *Almost forgotten.*

*Albert Dunmore was Wendell's colleague at the* Pittsburgh Courier *and Lacy J. Banks quoted Dunmore in his tribute column: "Black progress was his life.... Smith was a fighter, but was also a gentleman. He got things done in a quiet orderly way"* (Chicago Sun-Times, *November 28, 1972, p. 37). Sounds like something that could have been said about Hank Aaron as well. Aaron and Smith were plodders. It is easy to underestimate the plodders. They are not sensational. Aaron hit 755 career home runs, but never had a 50 home run season. Much of Wendell's contribution to the progress of Black people required consistent effort throughout his life. His willingness to celebrate small victories along the way contributed to his capacity to persevere. He remained relevant his entire career.*

*Wendell's relationship with Muhammad Ali deserves and receives an entire chapter in this book. Jack Griffin makes an additional point: "He was the only fighter Ali would allow in his dressing room after Frazier had lumped him up. Wendell never made a big thing out of it, but then he never did when he had a major news break"* (Chicago Sun-Times, *November 27, 1972, p. 83). Wyonella Smith told me Wendell did not bring his work home with him. She was glad I was doing a book on him but a bit perplexed. She noted that it's not like he was George Washington or Abraham Lincoln. Wendell did not brag about his accomplishments and neither did his widow. He was too busy plodding along. There was always more that needed to be done.*

*Tom Fitzpatrick wrote a particularly moving column about visiting Wyonella and listening to a tape-recording Wendell made of his career. He wrote simply, "Far and away, Wendell Smith was the most decent human being I've ever known.... He had a genuine sense of humor, and he was able to laugh at himself"* (Chicago Sun-Times, *November 27, 1972, pp. 8, 47). Wendell received a few awards, but not as many as he deserved. He was a minor celebrity but did not have the notoriety of the athletes he covered. He is not as well remembered as he should be, but we are doing something about that here, aren't we?*

*Ken Holtzman knew and liked Wendell when Ken pitched for the Chicago Cubs. In fact, Wendell participated in games of pepper with Cubs players. While in Chicago, Ken played for manager Leo Durocher. After the 1971 season, he was traded to the Oakland Athletics where he pitched in the 1972 World Series and met Jackie Robinson, who advised him to "keep your hopes up and the ball down and you'll do just fine." Holtzman played for manager Al Dark in Oakland as well. He interacted with many of the individuals Wendell wrote about and he provided an interesting perspective on those individuals.*

*Ken is Jewish, and while he experienced anti–Semitism, he emphasizes that his experiences were not comparable to those of Black ball players. I want to share his response to my request for feedback on work he has done in the community. Ken wrote: "As far as my experiences as an educator; I was supervisor at our region's JCC (Jewish Community Center) for over 8 years. One of my duties was to allocate resources and oversee programming for both our membership and the community at large. One of these groups were special needs kids between the ages of 10–18 and involved the setting up of weekly sports and games activities with appropriate facility and format modifications in order to enhance participation and achievement (lowered baskets, softer equipment, eye protection, etc.). One day I was overseeing a basketball game between kids with Down's syndrome and one little girl was having a hard time getting in the flow of the game. After talking to her for a while she was able to insert herself into the activity and when she made her first shot, this big old ex-jock broke down and lost it. I have 3 daughters and 3 granddaughters and winning game 7 of the '73 World Series could not compete with the overwhelming sense of triumph I got watching that little girl make that shot. I think people like Wendell would know what I was feeling."*

Ken Holtzman nailed it. He is not talking about participation ribbons here. He is addressing opportunity and achievement. Wendell Smith did not have the opportunity of seeing how far his pitching ability could take him in Major League Baseball. He worked tirelessly to provide future Black athletes with an opportunity he did not have. The little girl Ken describes was neither his daughter nor his granddaughter. She was not "his responsibility." But she was something in relation to him. Wendell was helping to pave the way for future Black individuals he did not know. They were not his family. But they were something in relation to him. Carl Erskine argues in What I Learned from Jackie Robinson *that Jackie's efforts opened doors for individuals with disabilities as well as racial minorities. Wendell would know exactly what Holtzman and Erskine meant. And Wendell was not shy about sharing with readers what he was thinking and feeling either, as you are about to discover.*

# 2

# Black History

*Wendell was a journalist, not a historian. He was also a history buff who used his columns to communicate Black history to his readers. There were no Black Studies programs in white colleges and most of his Black readers did not attend Black colleges. For many, Wendell's columns served as Black history classes. Wendell does not limit himself to listing the achievements of these athletes in their respective sports. He delves into the personal side of the story as well. Willie Mays might have made playing baseball look easy, but what kind of pressure was he under that might not be the same for his white teammates? And what was it like to be a Black baseball player in the South during Spring Training? Read on and find out.*

## July 30, 1938

### Smitty's Sport Spurts,
### *Pittsburgh Courier,* p. 16

The history of the Negro in boxing is one that is filled with chapters of brilliant and amazing feats. It is a history that every Negro in the world should know something about, should study and make note of the men who have played such an important part in the world's oldest sport.

We are proud of the three great champions we have today. No race in the world can point to three better men than [Joe] Louis, [John Henry] Lewis and [Henry] Armstrong. Besides the fact that they are great fighters, they are also regarded as gentlemen and the type of men who portray the real characteristics of a race that has never been understood since the days of the biblical Ham.

However, we are glad to know that these men are not the first Negro athletes who were looked upon as gentlemen by the world. If these three champions were the first, we would be forced to admit that as a race we have been rather slow in becoming civilized with the rest of the world.

Thus, we point out with a great deal of pride, that the first man to ever represent America in the prize ring was not only a gentleman, but a black man … a Negro.

His name was Bill Richmond and he was known throughout the world as "The Black Terror." He was born on August 5, 1763, of slave parents in the little town of Cuckhold, Staten Island, New York. The story of this black gladiator is one of the most romantic and colorful in all history. It is probably even more thrilling than that of Joe Louis, due to the fact that Richmond was not only the first Negro fighter to gain fame and fortune, but because he left his homeland and won laurels in another country.

While the country was in the midst of a fight for liberty against the British, Richmond was a mere boy living on Staten Island. When the English captured the Island, Earl Percy, head of the British army, took a fancy to the little black boy and made him his private valet. When the English soldier went back to England. He took Richmond with him.

In 1775 Earl Percy, who by that time had become a Duke, sent the thirteen-year-old Negro boy to one of the finest schools in all England. It caused a great deal of comment at the time, in view of the fact that it had not been the policy to educate people of black pigment. At first, the students snubbed the boy and resented his presence. Several years later, however, he was one of the most famous personalities in England and his once dicey schoolmates were only too glad to say that they went to school with him.

Bill Richmond became a fighter more by accident than by intentions. Like many of us, he liked loud, flashy clothes, and as a result attracted a great deal of attention wherever he appeared. His first fight resulted after he had been insulted by the town bully who cracked about Bill's clothes and color one day. Although the man was twice as large as the American Negro boy, he received a terrific lacing.

After a number of fights, all of which were precipitated by insults, Bill turned professional. He became a professional fighter because his friends desired it and not because he liked to fight. By nature he was quiet, courteous and very friendly. He only fought when it was absolutely necessary.

Bill's fistic career was studded with brilliant victories. He fought the famous Tom Cribb, the champion of England at that time, and lost after twenty-four rounds of brutal combat. Richmond weighed 168, Cribb 196.

After his fighting career ended, Bill became the owner of a tavern. All of the greats of England including Lord Byron, frequented his place. He was hailed throughout England as a great athlete and intelligent individual and a gentleman.

We received a great deal of satisfaction in reading about Bill Richmond, "The Black Terror." It disproves the theory often offered by prejudiced people that we Negroes are not really civilized. It also proves that the first real fighter from America was a gentleman ... and a Negro.

EDITOR'S NOTE—The historical background of Bill Richmond for this article was taken from Nat Fleischer's book: "Black Dynamite."

## March 6, 1943

### Sports Beat, "Young Frank Dixon Refutes Old Myth About Durability of Negro Runners," *Pittsburgh Courier*, p. 19

It has long been a contention in certain quarters that Negroes are not durable and therefore not adapted to distance running. The myth that the black man lacks durability has continued to live despite the fact that it was proven a fallacy long before Dixon came bounding along the boards. Dixon's victory in the AAU meet in New York last Saturday night, however, should put the lid on that myth and salt it away in moth balls forever more.

Because of his brilliant record in the mile, and by virtue of his triumph last Saturday, 20-year-old Frank Dixon is being hailed as the boy wonder. There has been a tendency to establish the New York University galloper as the first great Negro miler, but the truth of the matter is that the trail of the mile was blazed by one of Frankie's brothers some time ago.

According to the mechanical stop-watch, Dixon is our greatest miler. But I cannot go along with those who contend he is our first great miler. In my little book of outstanding cinder diggers the name of Phil Edwards, who was a miler, stands out conspicuously. Edwards never picked 'em up and laid 'em down with the rapidity that Frankie does, but he wasn't any turtle, either. Phil, without a doubt, was a great miler. He never finished worse than third in two Olympic races at the metric mile. Most recall him as a great half-miler, but his Olympic record as a miler speaks for itself.

### When Fate Stepped In, John Borican Was on His Way to Become an Outstanding Miler

On the record books of immortality you will also find the name of John Borican, who died recently. Had not fate stepped in and dealt Big John a fatal blow, he might have been as great in the mile as he was in the shorter distances. Borican's ambition was to be a great miler. He had all the qualifications a miler needs, plus the heart and will to win. Borican held all the indoor marks for every distance from 600 yards to three-quarters of a mile. He was an outstanding hurdler, and a national decathlon champion. He had everything necessary to become a great miler. Death was the only thing that stopped him.

Frank Dixon had a big load on his young shoulders last Friday night when he came galloping down the stretch to win that thrilling mile race from the experienced Gil Dodds. He proved once again that Negroes are durable and have the stamina necessary to run a mile race at top speed. He disproved all the old myths and theories established long ago by so-called experts of the track world. Still a boy, standing at the threshold of manhood, Frankie did a man's job, and did it well.

Frankie's all right. So were Edwards, Borican, Woodruff, Earl Johnson and the rest who blazed the trail in prior years.

*It was conceded that Black athletes could run fast. But could they run faster farther? Distance running was more tactical. It required strategy. Sprints were technique. Wendell documents that Frank Dixon was no fluke. Stereotypes, even those associated with positive attributes, had to be discredited.*

## *August 31, 1946*

### Sports Beat, "Marshall Bowling King," *Pittsburgh Courier*, p. 16

Not too many years ago Jack Marshall was a ball player of national repute and playing the outfield for some of the best teams in the country. After he quit the horsehide business, he started bowling and today is the nation's outstanding Negro bowler. Not only is he the national match game champion and holder of the highest combined league averages in the land, but also recently he signed a contract with the Balk-Collender Company to give a series of exhibitions. That is a distinctive achievement because it marks the first time in bowling history that any Negro player has been so honored.

Marshall's new job calls for him to tour around the country, giving exhibitions and showing people how to bowl strikes. It's nice work if you can get it, and he has it for sixteen weeks. After he completes his tour the Balk-Collender Company will probably renew his contract because Jack is a personable athlete and he's going to spread a lot of goodwill for his employers.

Marshall has won the national doubles championship with his partner, Bob Robinson for the past two years. He has also copped the singles crown with the highest average ever compiled in any NBA tournament. He is the captain of Chicago's famous Sewell Brothers team, which holds the national team championship, and he has held the Chicago singles crown for the past four years. During the past year Marshall was awarded the "Joe Blue Award" for his outstanding achievements on the alleys and also for his keen sense of sportsmanship.

Bowling and golf are the fastest growing sports among Negroes in the country. Both games have "caught on" like wild fire during the past four years. In Detroit, Chicago, Cleveland and Indianapolis bowling has already become a major sport with thousands of people blasting away at the maples regularly.

Jack Marshall is now in an excellent spot to help advance the game even more rapidly. Clubs and organizations should take advantage of the opportunity to have him put on exhibitions for them. They will be in for a great treat and will certainly get some valuable advice from him. His appointment as a representative of the largest bowling supply company in the world is definitely a great achievement and worthy of more than just passing notice. His address is 339 East Garfield Boulevard, Chicago 37, Ill., and he's available and ready to show you bowling enthusiasts how to bowl those pins over like a champion.

*While bowling might not be perceived to be an elitist sport, it had a racist history. Wendell wrote several columns noting that Blacks were interested in bowling but met racial barriers in bowling alleys no less often than in other, less surprising venues (e.g., golf courses). Wendell occasionally would provide an address to which interested parties could address correspondence. It was a different era.*

## August 16, 1947

### Sports Beat, "Louis Amateur King; Rhodes Tops Pros in Courier Meet," *Pittsburgh Courier*, p. 14

Heavyweight Champion Joe Louis came into his own as a golfer here in Pittsburgh last week by blasting his way through a tough field of golfers from every section of the country and winning the Eastern Golf Association Amateur Championship. Louis defeated the "Bearded Wonder," Jacques Isler, a New York attorney, 4 and 3, in the final round to win his first major golf title. The king of the heavyweights got a great wallop out of winning. He has been trying for a number of years to win a tournament and when he finally struck pay dirt on the fifteenth hole of the tricky South Park course he was all smiles.

In coming through to the finals, Louis had to beat Willie Adams of Baltimore and Judson Grant of Los Angeles. The victory over Adams was won with comparative ease, but Grant provided him plenty of anxious moments. In fact, Louis had to birdie the seventeenth and eighteenth holes to tie the fifty-one-year-old veteran, and then play two extra holes before he qualified for the championship round with Isler. After it was all over Louis said: "I got a great kick out of winning this tournament. It's the first one I ever won and I'm going to take good care of the big trophy they gave me for winning." Louis and Isler proved to be a picturesque twosome in the finals, if nothing else. The heavyweight champion towered above the short, sprightly New York lawyer. Bronzed by the summer sun and apparently in the pink of condition, Joe showed a large gallery that he is just as cool on the links as he is in the ring. On the other hand, Isler looked like a man who had just returned from the depths of the jungles. He sported a flourishing beard, wore a battered turned-down hat and smoked a pipe.

The contestants Isler defeated to reach the finals complained that he beat them by taking too much time and being too technical about the rules. They charged that he won only because he tried their nerves throughout the matches and not because he was the better golfer.

"That guy works on your nerves," one of the players Isler beat said. "He stalls around and gets you unnerved. Then when you're upset he goes ahead and wins."

When Louis went out on the tee to face the beard-wearing New Yorker, he had been well coached by friends. "I'm not going to let him get me down," Joe said. "I'm going to take my time, too. I'll get on his nerves."

It is questionable whether Louis wore down Isler or vice versa. Both took their time and did just about as they pleased. But this much is certain—Louis had a definite psychological advantage over the "Bearded Wonder." He gained that advantage by standing on the tee and poking out drives that averaged 250 yards. Isler is small and, naturally, didn't pack the wallop that Joe did. Joe was always far out in front on his drives and Isler found himself pressing time and again on long holes.

As the old saying goes, Isler was never really in the ball game. Going into the thirteenth he was five holes down. They halved the thirteenth and Isler won the fourteenth with a four against Joe's five. The fifteenth was the final hole. Isler found himself in a position where he had to win the last four holes to gain a tie. Louis got a par three and when Isler tried for a birdie and missed, after landing on the green about fifteen feet from the cup, Louis emerged victorious. The gallery swarmed around him and shook his hand, pounded him on his broad back and begged for the ball he was using. The heavyweight champion was his usual gracious self and went stalking off with the championship in the bag and a broad smile on his deeply tanned face.

Not since the days when Pat Ball of Chicago was going around winning everybody's tournaments has a golfer come along like Ted Rhodes, winner of the professional tourney. Several years ago, Joe Louis picked Rhodes up in Nashville, Tenn., and hired him as his personal golf tutor. Not only did he get Joe off to a good start in the game, but he kept improving himself. Today he is probably the No. 1 Negro golfer in the country. He has played in three tournaments this year—the Texas Open, Miami View Open in Dayton, Ohio, and the Courier-Yorkshire tourney here in Pittsburgh. He won all three tournaments and now is gunning for top money in Cleveland's Sixth City tournament and the Joe Louis Open.

Here in Pittsburgh he shot a sizzling 283, five under par. The nearest player to him was Howard Wheeler, whose 292 total was nine strokes over Rhodes. If Rhodes comes through in the Cleveland and Detroit tourneys, he will have won approximately $2,500 in five meets. By the time the season ends he has a chance to reach the $4,000 mark, which isn't exactly chicken feed for a year of golf.

Rhodes is a stylist on the links. He plays par golf—or close to it—consistently. He hits a long ball and plays his irons like a champion. At one time he had a tendency to grumble and fret when things went wrong. But he has conquered his temper and consequently his game has improved considerably. In another year he should be able to compete in the big tournaments against the best white golfers and hold his own. He completely dominates the Negro field now. He had practically no competition in the Courier tournament. It was just a matter of completing seventy-two holes and collecting $750 in prize money.

*Joe Louis' son, Joe Louis Barrow, Jr., would go on to play an active role in the First Tee Foundation making golf more accessible to disadvantaged young people.*

## May 7, 1949

### Sports Beat, *Pittsburgh Courier*, p. 22

*They're Gone But Not Forgotten...*

Those little brown boys with the colorful uniforms and long-peak caps are, unfortunately, no longer in the saddle on Derby Day. There is no evidence that they have been victimized by the color line or racial barriers.

It seems, however, that Negro youngsters are no longer fascinated by horses to the extent that they yearn for a jockey career.

That is regrettable because at one time they were outstanding in the Kentucky Derby and responsible for some of the most thrilling, glorious chapters in the history book of the Mint Julep classic.

The first time they ever held the Derby, May 17, 1875, a Negro jockey by the name of O. Lewis rode the winner. He was on Aristides and beat Volcano by one length to win the prize money, which amounted to $2,850.

In that initial race the horses got off to a good start with Volcano in front, Verdigris second and Lewis' horse a close third. The Negro jockey moved Aristides into second place along the back stretch and soon afterward was in the lead.

At the head of the stretch, H.P. McGrath, owner of Aristides, waved to Lewis and instructed the jockey to let the horse go all the way from that point on. Lewis obeyed instructions by loosing the pull on the bridle. Meantime, Volcano came with a final desperate rush, but Aristides stalled off the challenge in great style and went over the winner. He was the first horse to win the Kentucky Derby and Lewis the first victorious jockey in the big race. The time was 2:37¾ for the two-mile distance.

## They Scored Thirteen Derby Victories...

Nine Negro jockeys have booted home winners in the Derby and their combined total of triumphs amounts to thirteen. After Lewis won that first race, eight others duplicated his feat. They were: Billy Walker, 1877; Babe Hurd, 1882; Isaac Murphy, 1884, 1890, 1891; Erskine Henderson, 1885; Isaac Lewis, 1887; Alonzo Clayton, 1892; Willie Simms, 1896, 1898; and Jimmy Winkfield, 1901 and 1902.

Only two jockeys have ever won consecutive Derbies and they are both Negroes, Murphy and Winkfield. On May 14, 1890, Murphy rode the horse, Riley, to victory by two lengths over Bill Latcher in 2:45. The following year he came through again on Kingman, winning by one length over High Tariff in 2:52¼. In the 1890 classic, Riley went to the post a 4 to 1 shot and going into the backstretch was dead last. But the great Murphy brought him home in front by two lengths to win $5,460.

Winkfield piloted His Eminence home by two lengths in 1901 and repeated the following year on Alan-a-Dale, beating out Inventor by a nose. In the latter race both Jockey Winkfield and his horse displayed raw courage and racing fortitude. Alan-a-Dale was four lengths in front in the stretch. In the final eighth he suddenly went lame but displayed a thoroughbred's heart when he virtually limped the rest of the way home to win by a nose.

*Babe Hurd Won with 10 to 1 Shot...*

In the eighth running of the Derby, May 16, 1882, Jockey Babe Hurd took a 10 to 1 shot by the name of Apollo and rode one of the most thrilling races in the history of the great classic. At no time during the first part of the race was Apollo in it. Runnymede and Bengal led the pack with Apollo as far back as eighth at one point. When they were an eighth of a mile from home, with Runnymede appearing to have sewed the race up, Apollo came with a cyclonic rush, caught Runnymede a few yards from the wire, and then won by half a length.

Another Negro jockey who came through with a sensational ride was Willie Simms who zoomed home on Ben Brush in the 1896 Derby. In those days they did not have starting gates and it took twenty minutes to get the horses in order and away. Simms' horse failed to get off well, stumbling and almost throwing the Negro rider. Those who had bet on Ben Brush gave up hope as he trailed the pack. He began to move in the backstretch, however, and caught the leaders in the stretch. With Simms riding masterfully, Ben Brush did what seemed was the impossible, beating Ben Eder by a nose in a great race.

These nine Negro jockeys won a grand total of $52,320 in first place money. Murphy pulled down the biggest purse when he rode Riley to victory in 1890, a total of $5,460. He won three Derbies and his total earnings amounted to $14,000. If he were riding in the Derby Saturday he could win more than $90,000.

But he won't be riding, nor will any other Negro jockey. They will be conspicuous by their absence, a fact which blemishes the sport of kings and taints some of the glory of the famous Kentucky Derby.

*In Vernon Jarrett's tribute column cited in Chapter 1, he compliments Wendell on a column Wendell wrote about Black jockeys' success in the early years of the Kentucky Derby. Jarrett mentions that the jockeys were victims of Jim Crow and did not appear in later Derby races. Yet, Wendell specifically writes that it was not racism but choice that led Black jockeys away from the sport. I think it likely that Wendell was wrong and Jarrett was right.*

## January 7, 1950

### Sports Beat, *Pittsburgh Courier*, p. 20

*They're Amazing, Those Globetrotters...*

The most sensational basketball team in the world, pro or amateur, is that band of slick-passing, sharp-shooting, fun-loving, bronze wizards who play under the name of the Harlem Globetrotters.

Last Sunday night they reached the pinnacle of twenty-three years of rollicking and rolling around the basket-ball world by showing a terrific crowd at Madison Square Garden how basketball should be played. It was the first time these merry madcaps of the court had ever displayed their amazing talents in basketball's big palace. It was the first time New York had ever seen anything like it, too. Everyone agreed, too, that there isn't a better show on Broadway, including *South Pacific*, than the hilarious skit the Trotters put on.

For some unexplainable reason professional basketball has never reached the financial heights that its promoters hoped it would. There are numerous leagues scattered around the country and all of them are operating in the red. The largest and most pretentious is the National Basketball Association. It stretches from Boston all the way to Denver. Some of the wealthiest promoters in the country have money invested in this basketball octopus and practically all are fighting off the wolf, who is one of their few loyal and regular customers. But despite the obvious apathy of the public toward the play-for-pay game, the Globetrotters continue to roll merrily along, packing the arenas and gymnasiums in which they play every night in the week.

The owners of the teams in basketball's biggest league, the NBA, are amazed, to say the least. They want to know, of course, how they do it. "How can the Globetrotters," they wonder, "make so much money and draw such terrific crowds?"

The only way to get an answer to such a query is to go to the source, find the man provoking the question. In this instance, it's a man whose physical features resemble a basketball. He's short and fat and sorta' bloated. He's running around the country all the time, bouncing into one town and then another, keeping his Globetrotters trotting down the road to unprecedented success. His name is Abe Saperstein and he smugly refers to Chicago as his home, but the world knows better.

"Well, you see," said Mr. Saperstein, pointing a stubby finger at us, "you have to have something else besides just a basketball team. You know what I mean—you must have more than just a ball and five players to please the fans."

Mr. Saperstein's lecture on how to promote basketball successfully was interrupted momentarily by a long distance telephone call. It was from Kamloops, British Columbia. Now, if anyone in the class can tell us where in the universe that is, they automatically win a fur-coated cookie duster and a double barreled cap pistol with real bullets. Anyway, it seems that out there in Kamloops things get awfully slow around dog-sled time and the folks in the town want the Globetrotters to bring their basketball up there and use it. The man talking from Kamloops said they would declare a holiday and close the school for that day if Mr. Saperstein would be so kind. Being a great lover of children, especially children who have a school with a gymnasium in it, Mr. Saperstein said he would be so kind. So, basketball's on its way to Kamloops as soon as Mr. Saperstein finds his compass.

"Now," said the little Barnum of basketball as he resumed his lecture, "we give the fans something extra. We give them the best basketball possible and we put on the best show possible at the same time. The fans love it, too. We go into towns where they have topnotch professional clubs that can't spark up enough interest to attract more than a thousand people to a game. When we play, between five and ten thousand turn out. That's why they call us the most amazing outfit in the business. But it's not amazing to me. We give the fans what they want."

Last week, for instance, the Globetrotters gave the fans in seven towns on successive nights what they wanted and every game was played before a capacity crowd. When they departed from each town they took a bundle of rave notices from the press and an even bigger bundle of cash. More than 75,000 fans have seen them play already this season. By the end of their journeys they will have gone well over the million mark, a feat no basketball team in history has ever accomplished. The Globetrotters combine basketball magic with a hilarious show to make the turnstiles sing a profitable tune.

"Now you take Goose Tatum," said Mr. Saperstein. We interrupted abruptly to point out that we realized he was only joking when he commanded us to take "the Goose." After all, Mr. Tatum is not only a great player but one of the funniest performers in the entertainment world. He's the key man in the Trotters comedy routine and he never fails to click. We knew Mr. Saperstein had no intentions of giving away "Mr. Goose," the guy who ganders so well up and down the court.

"Well," said 'Honest Abe,' with sincere honesty, "I wouldn't give any of my boys away. They're all fine fellows and have developed into the greatest unit in basketball. There's Nat (Sweetwater) Clifton, Babe Pressley, Elmer Robinson, Marques Haynes and Tatum, plus three rookies, Johnny Wilson, Bobby Milton and Clarence Wilson. Once the fans see them play and put on their show, they never fail to come back. That's the way to promote basketball, put on such a show that when you return they can't resist coming back to see you perform."

That's where the lecture ended. Mr. Saperstein didn't have time to give a whole course in basketball promotion. But it would do other promoters well to take a leaf from his little book. The page titled, "Put on a Great Show," is hereby recommended.

Obviously, basketball promoters aren't born, they're made. Sometimes they have to cavort in the sticks until they grow up. Before Mr. Saperstein grew up, for instance, he nursed the whistle-stops and hamlets along the way. He had many harrowing and exciting experiences, too.

One of the most exciting was the time the team was playing in Wheatland, Iowa. "We were playing in a hayloft upstairs in a barn," he recalls. "The big door at the end of the barn where they load the hay was boarded up. There was some pretty fair body contact in those days and somebody hit one of our boys, Lester Johnson, and Lester crashed right through the boards and disappeared into the night. We thought Lester was killed for sure. We all ran outside. He wasn't hurt, much to our surprise, but he certainly wasn't happy. You see, the farmer had his fertilizer heap right under the door."

Brother, the Globetrotters will do anything to draw a crowd, won't they?

*The Harlem Globetrotters were formed in Chicago, but it was 23 years before they played Madison Square Garden. Given the success of the National Basketball Association, it is difficult for the reader to appreciate that the NBA's history is brief relative to other professional sports leagues (e.g., MLB). Professional basketball was not a lucrative venture during much of Wendell's career. The Globetrotters attracted larger crowds than professional basketball teams and were often the feature game of a double header when paired with a professional game. They became pioneers through their world travels as well. They represented America to the rest of the world. They were Black ambassadors.*

## January 3, 1959

### Sports Beat, *Pittsburgh Courier,* p. 25

The late Harry Wills was one of those fine Negro athletes who had the unfortunate experience of being born just a little too soon. Like such immortals as Josh Gibson, one of baseball's greatest hitters; Smokey Joe Williams, the magnificent pitcher; big Ben Stevens and Tank Conrad of football fame; and many other illustrious Negro performers, Wills was a victim of the white man's intolerance.

In a sense, Wills' position in the fight industry was vaguely similar to that of George Selkirk, the outfielder who succeeded Babe Ruth as the Yankees' right fielder. The baseball public always compared Selkirk with the mighty Bambino. Such a comparison was unfair to Selkirk, of course, because Ruth was a legend and probably the most dramatic ballplayer of all time. Thus, there was nothing his successor could do to establish himself as a player of acceptable quality, although Selkirk was one of the best of his day.

Whereas Selkirk suffered as a result of Ruth's magnificence, Wills was unable to overcome the wrath of the whites who resented the fact that his Negro heavyweight predecessor, Jack Johnson, committed the "unpardonable sin" of crossing the racial lines in marriage. Johnson's "grievous error" was Wills' burden throughout his career.

As Warren Brown, famed columnist of the *Chicago American,* pointed out a few days after Wills died last week, Harry was a victim of the era in which he lived. "At his best," Brown commented, "Wills belongs with the great heavyweights. His misfortune was that he came along at a time when in all competitive sports there was as little tolerance for men of his race as there now is for football coaches who do not win 'em all." (The simile was inspired by the dismissal of Terry Brennan as Notre Dame's football coach.)

Throughout the last half of his career Wills stalked Jack Dempsey, trying vainly to lure the heavyweight champion into the ring and a title fight. He once collected $50,000 after signing a contract for a title fight with Dempsey when the latter found it "inconvenient" to live up to the obligations of the pact.

A few years ago, the nation's boxing writers named Dempsey "The Fighter of the Century." There are a few of us, however, who will always frown upon that selection because the Manassa Mauler never did match punches with the outstanding challenger of his time—Wills. How can any fighter be designated as "the greatest" if he fails to accept the challenge of the No 1 contender? There are those who contend that Dempsey did not fight Wills because of the racial complications such a fight would have created. They insist Dempsey would have defended against Wills, the most capable challenger around during Jack's reign until Gene Tunney came along, had it not been for the potential racial strife. There may be a degree of merit in that argument, but it does not settle the controversy once and for all by any means. There is still a shadow of doubt hanging over that explanation by Dempsey's supporters.

There is reason to believe, also, that the fighter who was voted "the greatest heavyweight champion" wasn't overly anxious to fight Wills because the latter was likely to beat him. Nat Loubet, a recognized boxing authority and writer for the Bible of boxing—*Ring Magazine*—said as much in that publication, in the issue of March 1958. Here is what he wrote:

"Harry Wills, one of the world's best heavyweights during the 'White Hope' era, was caught in the tide of the times and although he was a perfect example of virtuous living, he never got a chance at the crown held by Jack Dempsey.

"Tex Rickard, Garden promoter, and Jack Kearns, Dempsey's manager, used the feeling that was prevalent to deprive Wills of the chance he deserved.

"They believed that Wills was a dangerous opponent, that easier contenders could be picked for Dempsey and they gave 'racial prejudice' as their Excuse for keeping Wills from fighting for the crown."

The capitalization of the word—"excuse"—is ours. But everything else is as Loubet wrote it. Thus, there is good reason to believe Dempsey used "racial prejudice" as a convenient means not to give the deserving Wills a shot at the title.

In contrast, Joe Louis fought everyone and anybody when he was champion. He ducked no one, offered no excuses.

Louis, not Dempsey, is the greatest in this book.

Wills may have been … but he never got the chance.

*During the many years that separated Bill Richmond and Joe Louis, there was only one Black heavyweight champion: Jack Johnson. Johnson was not concerned about being a role model. Johnson suffered for his actions. Sadly, so did Harry Wills. Jack Johnson was not the primary reason Wills did not have a chance to fight Jack Dempsey for the heavyweight championship. But he was useful to those who argued that a Black man could not be counted on to maintain the dignity of the heavyweight championship. Joe Louis was given that opportunity and became one of the most popular champions in boxing history.*

## March 25, 1961

### Sports Beat, *Pittsburgh Courier*, p. 38

*Spring Training Bias Is Humiliating Experience*

Sarasota, Fla.—It is impossible for anyone, unless they have actually experienced it, to visualize what it is like to be a Negro baseball player in Florida during the spring training season.

Therefore, in view of the fact that the season is now at its height, there could be no more appropriate time than this to describe it. Actually it is an impossible chore but, nevertheless, even a feeble attempt is better than none at all.

Suppose, for example, you are one of the seven Negro Chicago White Sox—Minnie Minoso, Al Smith, Juan Pizzaro, Frank Barnes, Floyd Robinson, Stan Johnson and Winston Brown—training here for the coming season. Their experiences are typical of what most other Negro players must tolerate.

Three are established major leaguers, Minoso, Smith and Pizzaro, whose combined salaries exceed $100,000. The other four are on the fringe of the majors. Maybe they will make it, maybe they won't. Regardless, you are one of them, highly skilled in your chosen profession and respected in your Northern community.

If you are Minoso, Smith or Pizzaro, you do not, for example, make less than $25,000 each a year because of your skill. Whomever you are, you possess a talent that only a few among millions own. Like a great artist, musician, physician or scientist ... your talent sets you apart from the crowd.

You are a man of great pride and perseverance.... Otherwise you would not be where you are today, training with a major league team in Sarasota, Fla.

Yet, despite all your achievements and fame, the vicious system of racial segregation and discrimination in Florida's hick towns condemns you to a life of humiliation and ostracism.

If you are one of these unfortunate men in Florida at this time of the year these are some of the indignities you must suffer:

You cannot live with your teammates.

You cannot eat the type of food that your athletic body requires.

You cannot get a cab in the mornings to take you to the ball park, unless it happens to be Negro-driven.

You cannot enter the hotel in which your manager lives without first receiving special permission.

You cannot go to a movie or night club in the heart of town, nor enjoy any of the other normal recreational facilities your white teammates enjoy so matter-of-factly.

You cannot bring your wife and children to the town where you are training because accommodations are not available where you are imprisoned.

You cannot, even if there are facilities, take them to the town's sprawling beaches or parks; unless, of course, they are designated as "Negro."

You cannot do anything that you would normally do in any of the major league cities where you make your living during the summer. You are quartered in a neighborhood that ordinarily you would be ashamed to be seen in.

You are horribly embarrassed each day when the bus returning the players from the ball park, stops on "this side of the railroad tracks" and deposits you in "Colored Town," and then proceeds on to the plush hotel where your white teammates live in splendor and luxury.

You suffered a bruised leg sliding into second base, but you cannot receive immediate treatment from the club trainer because he is living in the "white" hotel. If he can get away during the night and come to your segregated quarters, he will, of course; but, for obvious reasons, he prefers to wait until daylight.

Your wife cannot call you in case of an emergency from your home because the place where you are incarcerated does not have telephone facilities available at all times.

That is what it is like to be a Negro big leaguer in Florida during spring training.... And the story has been only half told.

*Wendell is descriptive here. He is writing from the player's perspective. Willie Mays and an unknown rookie suffered the same treatment during Spring Training. Wendell too suffered those indignities. But he does not write about himself.*

## January 20, 1962

### Sports Beat, *Pittsburgh Courier,* p. 45

The complexities of the coaching profession are difficult to bear under the most favorable conditions and certainly reprehensible in situations where an individual is constantly subjected to petty coercion and compelled to work under duress. Many a basketball and football coach has thrown up his hands in utter despair and fled an ideal job simply because he could not tolerate the nerve-wracking pressures and nightmarish tensions. Others have been able to accept those liabilities and managed to live a comparatively normal life. Any coach who can retain his equilibrium, especially in professional sports, and maintain a reasonable degree of sanity deserves all possible commendation, especially if he is harassed and tormented by cantankerous and insipid employers or owners. He who succeeds in spite of such circumstances is nothing less than a genius.

Johnny McLendon, the quiet perfectionist who led the Cleveland Pipers to the first-half championship of the American Basketball League's Eastern division, is such a wondrous man. Those who are aware of the almost intolerable conditions under which he has been forced to labor since the recent inception of the country's newest professional basketball circuit view his success with awesome curiosity.

The fact that he was able to keep his team on top while all around him nothing but confusion and turbulence existed substantiates unequivocally the contention of the most respected basketball authorities that he is a coach who has few, if any, equals. If Johnny McLendon can produce a winner in Cleveland under the torture inflicted upon him by his tyrannical boss, George Steinbrenner, he must go down in history as one of the greatest coaches of all time.

It is unfortunate, indeed, that McLendon should be subjected to the rattle-brained intrusions of Steinbrenner at this stage of his illustrious career. When Steinbrenner selected McLendon to coach the Pipers three years ago the selection was hailed by knowledgeable basketball men as one of rare wisdom. McLendon had previously established himself as one of the great college coaches by producing superbly coached championship teams at Tennessee State. When he resigned that secure post to take over the Pipers, who were then in the National Industrial League, he gave up what could have been a lifetime job and a highly enjoyable existence in Nashville, Tenn.

He retained his magical touch in Cleveland, however, and proceeded to produce more championship teams. When the NIL disbanded, the Pipers Steinbrenner wisely retained McLendon's services and at the start of the season Abe Saperstein, commissioner of the ABL and shrewdest of all basketball authorities, commended the Cleveland owner for doing so.

"With McLendon as coach," said Saperstein, who also owns the internationally famous Harlem Globetrotters, "Cleveland is the team to beat for the championship. He is without a doubt one of the smartest and most dedicated coaches in the business. Steinbrenner has made a wise decision and will reap the benefits from it."

This was an ideal basketball situation at that time. McLendon had a talented squad composed of the key players from his championship NIL team, including several stars he had developed at Tennessee State.

Had he left well enough alone, Steinbrenner could easily have had the most prosperous franchise in professional basketball. He had a squad of outstanding players and a coach who was superbly equipped to handle them.

But the Cleveland owner has not been able to resist the temptation to project himself into the coaching picture. His constant meddling has reached the obnoxious stage. It is a wonder, indeed, that the Pipers have been able to win any games.

Approximately a week before the first-half of the ABL schedule was concluded, the Pipers were fighting Pittsburgh for first place in the Eastern Division. Cleveland was trailing by the slim margin of half a game when the pompous Steinbrenner declared:

"McLendon must win the championship. I will not accept anything less than a winner."

That comment startled everyone interested in the ABL race. It was a threat that was in no way appropriate. It also cast a new light on Steinbrenner and forced those who had respected him as a highly capable executive to conclude that he is something far less.

It must be said in his behalf, however, that his attitude toward his talented coach is not based on any racial antipathy. The fact that he hired McLendon as his coach refutes any such allegation. He is, in fact, a very tolerant and unbiased individual in that respect. However, he is an individual who apparently takes a sadistic delight in sticking his nose where it doesn't belong. McLendon has forgotten more basketball than Steinbrenner will be able to absorb in the next one hundred years. Why he persists in second-guessing the best coach in the league and making life miserable for everyone associated with the team is one of the great mysteries of professional basketball. He should get wise ... before it is too late. He is about to ruin what can be the best franchise in the sport. He also is about to drive away the finest coach in the game.

*In summation, Steinbrenner was petty, coercive, cantankerous, insipid, tyrannical, rattle-brained, meddling, obnoxious, pompous, and sadistic. But he was not a racist. Many Yankee fans, and Billy Martin, would have agreed.*

## June 22, 1963

### Sports Beat, *Pittsburgh Courier*, p. 15

The anniversary of Joe Louis' ascension to the heavyweight title is June 22. It has been 26 years since young Joe, a perfect fighting machine, knocked out James J. Braddock in the eighth round to win the championship. It was a balmy, exciting night in Chicago. Comiskey Park was the scene of the battle.

Louis, his smooth muscles rippling under the bright ring lights, won the fight after getting off the floor. Braddock, an aging but clever veteran sent him to the canvas in the first round as a capacity crowd gasped with astonishment. Louis, also surprised, got up, dusted the resin off his trunks, and then proceeded to perform a surgeon's job on the champion. Joe terrorized Braddock with the stiffest left jab in history for five rounds, and then took nine more minutes to put over the finishing touches.

"He'll be a great champion," Braddock predicted afterward. "He'll be good for boxing both in and out of the ring."

Those were prophetic words. Louis went on to defend his title 25 times, more than any champion in boxing history, and also conducted himself in such a manner that no one could point an accusing finger in his direction. When Joe won the title, he was only 23. He was exciting, modest, and above reproach. The fight game was the same then as now, full of scheming, notorious personalities. There were "dumped" fights and crooked deals. There were "dive" fighters and referees who could be propositioned. It was a sordid business. But Louis, by his conduct, brought respectability to what sportswriter Jimmy Cannon so vividly describes as the "red light district of sports."

Joe was managed by John Roxborough and Julian Black, shrewd businessmen whose sole purpose in life was to give the new champion honest advice and direction. They were an asset, indeed. They tolerated no foolishness from boxing's wise guys. When they took Joe to New York for his first major fight, two years before Braddock, they were propositioned by the mob.

"The public won't stand for another Negro heavyweight champion yet," the calculating mobsters told Roxborough and Black. They were Primo Carnera's spokesmen. "Let Carnera win this one," they advised, "and then, when he wins the title again, we'll give you a shot at it."

"The only shot Carnera will get at Louis," Roxborough and Black said, in essence, "is in this fight. If he can whip Joe, okay. If he can't, forget it. There will be no deals."

Louis, fighting superbly, knocked out Carnera. He was well on his way to the top. Max Schmeling interrupted his journey momentarily in one of the biggest upsets of all time. But Louis got his shot at Braddock in spite of that loss, and then knocked out Max in the first round of a return bout.

Riches came to Louis, of course, as he battered down opponent after opponent. Most of his treasure disappeared in the twilight of his long career due to unfortunate financial deals. But his image as the most influential and respected heavyweight champion of them all remained intact. In his way, Louis did as much for Negro advancement—particularly in sports—as the Rev. Martin Luther King and the late Medgar Evers of Mississippi accomplished in the field of civil rights.

It is reasonable to assume, for example, that the entrance of the Negro player into major-league baseball would have delayed beyond 1947 if Louis had not, in his inimitable way, paved the way for more tolerance.

Joe was never an orator. He was straightforward and candidly brief when facing the racial issue. His stature took him to areas that were off-limits to other Negroes. On more than one occasion, he needled a major-league baseball owner with this question: "How come you don't have any Negro players on your team?" Usually they were too embarrassed to answer. Some gave meek replies and promised that they would see what could be done about it. Eventually, Jackie Robinson came along. Branch Rickey hired him and the door of the majors was opened. Robinson, and those who followed, made the grade on sheer ability, of course, but nevertheless it was Louis who set the stage for baseball's racial revolution by virtue of his conduct and impact on the American public.

Yes, it has been 26 years since young Joe Louis knocked out Jim Braddock and won the heavyweight title. It occurred on June 22, 1937.

It's a date nobody in this turbulent, strife-torn nation should forget.

*To Wendell, Joe Louis would always be The Guy. Louis was not the reason that Major League Baseball was integrated, but he played a role in it being integrated in 1946–47. Had integration been delayed a few years, Jackie Robinson would have been too old to be the first.*

*Joe Louis Barrow, Jr., Joe Louis' son, tells of meeting Nelson Mandela. Mandela related to Barrow the significance of Joe Louis to a young Mandela growing up in Africa. Louis represented pride and hope to Black individuals throughout the world. MLB has publicized the date of Jackie Robinson's first game with the Brooklyn Dodgers. We have largely forgotten June 22, 1937. Wendell never did.*

## September 21, 1963

### Sports Beat, *Pittsburgh Courier*, p. 15

Willie Mays, a robust young man who plays centerfield for the San Francisco Giants better than anyone ever played it for them before, passed out on a two-and-two pitch. He collapsed from physical—and mental—exhaustion at the plate. They carried him off the field. This startling development was the second time that Willie, one of the greatest competitors in baseball history, succumbed to the tensions and agonizing pressures of the game.

Last season he was stricken similarly during a game against Cincinnati. He was standing in the dugout on that occasion. Suddenly he fainted dead-away and had to be carried to the club house. His teammates were terrified. But Willie was back in action in a few days and led the Giants to the 1962 National League pennant.

Willie's collapses are significant. They refute the contention of those who argue that today's ballplayers do not perform with the zest and fervor that the old timers demonstrated. Willie's condition dramatically symbolizes the fortitude and competitive spirit of most contemporary players. They play just as hard today as they did back in the era of Ty Cobb, who was the Willie Mays of his day.

There are those, of course, who take the easy way out, contributing only a minimum of effort. But it has always been that way. In Cobb's days, for example, there were those who loafed and procrastinated too. However, nobody has ever played the game harder, with more concentration and determination than the likes of Mays, Hank Aaron, Ernie Banks and other modern players. And who played with more zeal and dash than Jackie Robinson, Roy Campanella and Larry Doby when they were active? Nobody—not even Cobb.

It is an acknowledged fact that Negro ballplayers, generally, exert themselves above and beyond normal expectations in their day to day performances. There have been, of course, some who favored the line of least resistance, but they were exceptions to the rule and in most instances disappeared from the major league scene. The point is, that the average Negro ballplayer is a furious competitor because of necessity or because of sheer instinct. Before his tragic accident, Campanella said:

"They'll have to tear this uniform off me; I'll never voluntarily take it off."

The Negro player, like Negroes in other fields of highly skilled endeavor, is acutely aware of the fact that he is expected to surpass the average performer. He acts and plays accordingly. He knows he must maintain a superior standard consistently, otherwise his security is in jeopardy. That is true even in such cases as Mays, who is obviously ill and physically exhausted. Owners and fans alike apparently are oblivious to the fact that some Negro players have physical and mental limitations like other players. The fact is however, that the juries in the front offices and stands are in most instances, intolerant. They expect too much.

"You know I'm not going to ask for a rest," Willie Mays said the day after he collapsed. "If the guys I'm playing for, if they don't see it, I'm not going to tell them how tired I am. I'm so tired," Willie continued, "that I don't want to move or anything else. I tried to make myself move and it just wasn't there. But the way the club needed me. I wasn't going to say anything."

At that time, the Giants were in the thick of the pennant race. Since then, however, they have dropped out of contention. Willie just wasn't physically able to carry them all the way again this year. Willie feels badly because he could not do the impossible. He has carried the Giants on his back for years. This season—with age taking its toll—he just couldn't do the job alone.

On the other hand, Maury Wills, the little shortstop of the Dodgers has voluntarily embraced the responsibility of spurring his team to first place and the 1963 pennant. Like other Negro players, Wills realized that more is expected of him in a crisis. Two other Negro stars on the Dodgers playing regularly—Tommy Davis and the veteran Jim Gilliam—know too that they have a similar responsibility. As they go, so go the Dodgers— Sandy Koufax and Don Drysdale to the contrary.

"This club is depending on me to do certain things, and I have a lot to live up to," says Maury Wills.

That is the story of all Negro players. They have "a lot to live up to," especially if their team is in contention. And it has ever been thus, since the day Jackie Robinson crashed the color barrier in the majors.

Negro players have always had "a lot to live up to."

In trying to live up to the almost inhumanely high standards set for them, some Negro players exert themselves into a state of complete mental and physical exhaustion.

That's what happened to Willie Mays.

His salary of $105,000 is the highest in the majors.

But even so ... you have to wonder if that amount of money is of any real value ... if you have to play yourself sick to earn it.

## March 28, 1964

### Sports Beat, *Pittsburgh Courier*, p. 19

*National Hockey League Is Still Looking for*
*Negro Good Enough to Make Grade*

With the Stanley Cup playoffs coming up, it suddenly struck us that professional hockey is the one major sport in which Negro performers are conspicuous by their absence.

It is particularly true of major-league hockey. There are Negro players in the minors, but none in the National Hockey League. There must be some prospects in Canada, the cradle of hockey.

"Yes, there must be," agreed Reggie Fleming, the fiery star of the Chicago Blackhawks, on the eve of the Stanley Cup classic. "But you must remember that Canada is a small country in comparison to the United States, and therefore you are going to find only a small number of players, regardless of color, good enough for the National Hockey League.

"I am sure that any team in the NHL would sign a Negro player if he could make it. There is no discrimination in hockey. You're either good enough, or you're not. It's strictly a case of ability."

A few years ago, the Boston Bruins gave Willie O'Ree, a Negro forward, a tryout. He is, in fact listed in hockey's history books as the first Negro player in the NHL.

The Bruins brought him up from Kingston, Ontario, of the Eastern Professional League, in December 1961.

At that time, the Boston coach, Milt Schmidt, called him "a nice kid and an excellent prospect."

"He has all the potential a big-league hockey player needs," said

Coach Schmidt, when O'Ree joined the Bruins. O'Ree was 25 years old then. He broke into professional hockey with Quebec City of the Quebec League, in 1956–57. A native of Fredericton, New Brunswick, Willie was outstanding in the minors.

"I'll never understand why O'Ree never made the grade," Reggie Fleming said during our discussion of Negro hockey players. "He was big and fast as lightning on skates. He could do everything from a technical standpoint that is expected of a big-league hockey player."

O'Ree is now playing with the Los Angeles Blades on the West Coast.

"I played with him at Kingston, Ontario," Reggie continued, "and he was one of the best players in that league. I don't know what happened at Boston. All I do know is that they wanted him and would have kept him if he had been good enough.

"I was told, but can't vouch for it, that Willie didn't dig very hard in the corners."

In hockey parlance, that means that Willie may have been a little timid in certain areas on the rink where the slamming and banging go on. That doesn't mean, of course, that he lacked courage, simply that he was not adept at that sort of warfare.

"There is a trick to it, and also," explained Reggie, "a knack some players never acquire. But Willie was tough and strong. He wasn't a coward, far from it.

"There also was another Negro player, by the name of Stan Maxwell. I remember him, too. He was plenty good, exceptionally fast. I thought he would make it some day, but understand that he is also playing on the Coast."

Back in 1948, the New York Rangers gave Herb Carnegie, a fast-skating Negro, a tryout. At the time, he was 26, married and the father of three children. He also was an outstanding baseball player and for a time was in the Dodgers' farm system. However, he, too, vanished from the major-league-hockey scene.

Fleming, a native of Montreal, predicts that there will be Negro players in major-league hockey before very long.

"The kids play hockey in Montreal," he said, "just like American kids play sandlot baseball. Wherever there is a vacant lot they play. I see colored kids all the time when I'm home, playing hockey. They also play in high school and college. Some day one of those kids is going to make it. It's bound to happen eventually.

"The main thing is that there is nothing to stop them from making it. There is no color barrier, no discrimination. It's like I said—there just aren't many Negroes in Canada, at least up in the regions where hockey is played most of the year. But some day there will be a Negro in big-league hockey. How soon that will be, I just can't say."

*In the final game of the 2021 National Hockey League season, the Tampa Bay Lightning played a Black line (center and two wings). It did not receive much attention outside of the hockey world. But Daniel Walcott, Mathieu Joseph and Gemel Smith comprised the first Black line in NHL history. About 3 to 6 percent of NHL players are Black. Ferguson Jenkins, Hall of Fame pitcher for the Chicago Cubs, is Canadian. He played organized hockey in Canada and remembers his father taking him to see Willie O'Ree. Jenkins also played basketball with the Harlem Globetrotters. He chose baseball and that turned out reasonably well for him.*

## July 4, 1964

### Sports Beat, *Pittsburgh Courier*, p. 15

*Elston Howard Now the Man Who Leads New York Yankees*

Elston Howard, the best catcher in baseball and the American League's Most Valuable Player last season, has progressively developed to the place where he is indispensable to the success of the New York Yankees.

This year he is the Yankees' workhorse, the sparkplug, the take-charge-guy. With Mickey Mantle struggling along under a chronic leg injury, Roger Maris playing below his usual form and Tony Kubek ailing frequently, Howard is the new leader of the fabulous Bronx Bombers.

"Yes, he's the boss out there on the playing field," declared Manager Yogi Berra, the old catcher who once sparked the Yanks. "Elston has all the qualities of leadership and this year he has come into his own. We couldn't win without him."

As though to prove his point, Berra called on Howard to catch a Sunday doubleheader in Chicago. The first game went the regulation nine innings, but the second was a 17-inning marathon.

The Yankees won them both. In the first game, Elston drove in the only run of the contest. His homer in the second was the first of the two runs New York scored in a 2–1 triumph. At the end of the 17 innings, the big, powerful catcher, who first played baseball as a boy in his native St. Louis, was tired, naturally. "All I want to do is to relax and get a little sleep," he said wearily while sitting in front of his locker in the clubhouse. "It's been a long day." Yogi Berra peered around the corner from his little office and smiled knowingly, "You'll get some rest tomorrow, Elli," he promised. "You did a helluva job for us today."

Howard, of course, will be the American League's starting catcher in the All-Star game next week. He has missed only one All-Star classic since 1955.

To say that Elston owns a distinguished major league career is putting it mildly. Since his rookie year with the Yankees in 1955, the 35-year-old, 6-2 star has been in eight World Series. He is one of the many who will testify that "it's great to be a Yankee."

His finest year was 1961 when he hit .348, dividing his time between first base and as relief for Berra behind the plate. Despite that fat average and over-all success, he didn't enjoy that season as much as he did last year's.

Casey Stengel managed the Yankees in '61. "I had a great year at the plate." Ellie recalled, "but I was switched around in the field too much. One day I'd be playing first, then the next Casey would stick me behind the plate. I didn't have a chance to concentrate on any one position.

"When Ralph Houk took over the club, he kept me behind the plate. Yogi has done the same thing, and I'm really happy, probably the happiest player in the majors these days."

Howard has developed into a master receiver. He knows how to handle pitchers. His predecessor, Berra, was equally as skillful in the art of "managing" pitchers from behind the iron mask.

Berra now places a great deal of responsibility on Howard when it comes to handling pitchers. "He knows the pitchers and hitters," Berra explained. "They're ordered to throw what Howard orders."

Even Whitey Ford, the leagues' winningest pitcher, acknowledges that Howard is in top command. This is a high tribute when you consider the fact that Whitey is the Yankees' pitching coach.

"We've never had any problems," Whitey said. "Ellie gives me the sign and I throw what he calls for. He doesn't make any mistakes. If they hit what I throw, it's my fault. It's not his 'call,' it's my pitch.

"Once in awhile, maybe twice a game, I'll shake him off. But that's just because I feel like throwing a certain pitch, not that he is wrong."

Ford is the only Yankee pitcher who can shake off Howard's call and get away with it. A youngster like Al Downing, for example, wouldn't dare shake him off. "He can if he wants to," said Ellie, "but he doesn't."

Downing had a brilliant 13–5 record his rookie season. In this, his sophomore year, Al has started slowly. His control has been off. Howard is getting him straightened out.

"His arm came up sore during spring training," Elston said, "and then after it got well, he hurt his back. Those two things hampered him, hurt his control.

"Al has looked good in the last few games," he continued, "and

I'm sure he'll be as good as ever in a few weeks. His control has been off because he has been compensating for his bad back. In doing so, he has had a tendency to get the ball too high. He's a great low ball pitcher, but he's been throwing them 'up' on the hitters.

"He's starting to come around now. His pitches are getting down where they are most effective. He'll be all right soon."

What about the Yankees? They've been having trouble getting in front.

"Don't worry," he answered with a wink and smile. "When we get to the end of the road, everybody else will be trying to catch us. We're going to win it again."

Then the leader of the Yankees set aside his glove ... put away his mask ... and headed for the showers.

*Al Downing told me a story about Elston Howard. On the evening of July 31, 1964, in Minneapolis, Downing took a 3–2 lead into the bottom of the ninth inning against the Twins. With a runner on base and two outs Downing caught Harmon Killebrew looking at a pitch that appeared to have caught the inside corner of the plate for strike three. Umpire Ed Hurley called it a ball. Neither Howard nor Downing questioned the call. Howard did not argue with umpires, and he did not want his pitchers arguing, either. Killebrew drove the next pitch off the foul pole for a walk-off home run and the Twins won 4–3. Howard and Downing were having their traditional post-game bowl of soup at a restaurant and in walks Ed Hurley. The umpire made his way to their table and said, "It may have been a ball; it may have been a strike. But I like the way you handled it." Sometimes it is more important what is not said than what is said.*

## September 5, 1964

### Sports Beat, *Pittsburgh Courier*, p. 14

*Ashe a Player with Too Many Strokes*

Arthur Ashe, Jr., the 21-year-old tennis star from Richmond, Va., is unique in sports if for no other reason than that he is going to try to duplicate something a girl has already achieved.

Moments after he won the recent Eastern Grass Court Championships at South Orange, N.J., the 6-foot, 150-pound youngster, who plays under the colors of UCLA, the university Jackie Robinson "made famous," said his ambition is to win the Wimbledon Championship.

Just in case you're not a tennis buff.... The Wimbledon championship is comparable to the Masters tournament in golf, or baseball's World Series and football's Rose Bowl.

Significantly, the path to Wimbledon has been paved for the young man. Back in 1957, a tall, sometimes temperamental, young lady from Harlem by the name of Althea Gibson won the women's singles championship at Wimbledon, England, and in so doing made history.

Ashe will be gunning for the men's singles championship, if he makes the grade, of course.

Althea celebrated her 37th birthday last week. She no longer plays competitive tennis but, instead, is now slamming golf balls with the same vicious determination that she smashed tennis balls. There are respected golf judges who contend that she is also going to be a champion golfer before long. Althea, who was born in a sharecropper's shack in Silver, S.C. and raised in the teeming streets of New York's Harlem, makes no predictions about her golf career. All she says is that if she is ever going to be a golf champion, it better happen soon because she isn't getting any younger.

Althea won the Wimbledon singles title on June 6, 1957, beating Darlene Hard, a blonde waitress from Montebello, Calif., 6–3, 6–2, on the famed center court steaming in 100-degree heat. Later she teamed with Miss Hard to add the women's doubles crown, beating a pair of Australia's women champions.

Queen Elizabeth II, attending Wimbledon for the first time in her life, presented the trophy. The previous year, Althea had performed at Wimbledon, but lost in the quarter-finals to Shirley Fry, who won the championship. But the tall, bronze girl from Harlem made good the second time she journeyed to England. If Arthur Ashe gets to Wimbledon next year, he will have something in common with Althea. It will be his third appearance there.

He competed at Wimbledon last year and this year, but each time was eliminated in the quarter-finals. He won the Eastern Grass Court tournament by defeating Clark Graebner of Beachwood, Ohio, after upsetting Dennis Ralston in the quarter-finals and Gene Scott, the defending champion, in the semi-finals.

Thus, he became the first male of his race to win a major grass court tournament. Althea, who was the female Athlete of the Year in 1957 and 1958, was the first Negro ever to do so.

Ashe first hit the headlines in 1961 by winning the National Interscholastic Championship. He was ranked 28th nationally that year. He was No. 10 in 1962 and moved up to sixth last year. He also became the first Negro named to the U.S. Davis Cup team.

"I'd like to win at Wimbledon," he said after winning the Eastern Grass Court title. "I'm California state champ now. However, I'd rather be

Pennsylvania state champion because that tournament has more prestige. It's the same thing with Wimbledon. If you're the Wimbledon champ they think you are the best."

Pancho Gonzales says young Arthur will probably be unbeatable when he stops experimenting with his shots.

Ashe offers no argument. "I guess I hit my backhand shots 70 different ways. In my match against Scott, I figured out how to spin a lob with my backhand. The only trouble is that sometimes I have trouble making up my mind which way to hit—there are so many, you understand. I also have another new shot, a forehand with too much top-spin. I'm trying to get my assortment of shots down. I don't need as many as I now have. When I do, I'll be a better player."

Well ... other tennis players would like to have such a problem. Even Althea Gibson, who was the greatest in her day, probably would have treasured such an assortment of shots.

*Ashe won at Wimbledon in 1975. He died at the age of 49 from AIDS-related pneumonia derived from a tainted blood transfusion. Being the first Black male tennis player to win Wimbledon is a significant accomplishment and would alone qualify him for inclusion in this chapter. The dignity and grace with which Arthur Ashe lived and died is another. Wendell gives us a glimpse of a great man before he became famous.*

## October 22, 1966

### Sports Beat, *Pittsburgh Courier*, p. 15

Bill Russell, the Monrovia rubber baron, finds himself burdened with the most unenviable responsibility in the world of professional sports as the new play-for-pay basketball season gets underway.

He is the new coach of the Boston Celtics, that glittering quintet which won eight consecutive National Basketball Association championships under the direction of ex-coach Red Auerbach.

The old coach built a basketball dynasty comparable to that which the Yankees once owned in baseball. Russell's job is to maintain it, and if he doesn't there are those in Boston and elsewhere who will say, "They shouldn't have put a Negro in charge of such a great team."

Also, owners of professional baseball and football teams will be watching Russell's efforts with intense interest. If he is a miserable failure, those who may be considering the employment of a Negro manager in baseball, or coach in football, may throw up their hands in despair and say, "Forget it!"

So Russell finds himself on the hottest seat in sports, not only because he has a winning tradition to uphold in Boston but, also, because no Negro has ever been where he is now—leader of a successful team in a major professional sport.

It is gratifying to point out, however, that Bill Russell has all the qualifications to do the job which has been heaped upon his broad, capable shoulders. And that is a fine testimony to Red Auerbach, the old coach who personally selected Bill to be his successor. Auerbach is giving Bill the opportunity he deserves.

Russell's rise to the top has not been easy. He was born in Monroe, La., 36 years ago. When he was eight years old his mother took him and his brother, Charlie, to Oakland, Cal., where their father had gone to work in a war plant. Russell grew up there.

In the eighth grade, he almost flunked and became a potential dropout. In the ninth, at Hoover Junior High, he couldn't even make the home room basketball team, which proves that he wasn't a "born" basketball player. At McClymonds High school he was nothing more than Charlie's kid brother. He had to share the 15th uniform with another boy, on the junior varsity.

But by the time he was a senior and 6-5, he was playing on the varsity and by working exceptionally hard developing into a fair basketball player. He went on from there to the University of San Francisco and stardom, to the Olympics in Australia and the Boston Celtics.

Russell is aware of the significance his "breakthru" means. He knows, too, he has attained his lofty position solely on merit. He has never, during the course of his advance, compromised on racial matters for the sake of expediency. He has never hid his bitterness at limitations on opportunities for Negroes, has never hesitated to voice his opinions while attempting to extend them. He is a staunch member of the militant corps, but not a Stokely Carmichael henchman.

As the *New York Times* pointed out after he was named the Celtics' coach, his main characteristics are "pride, intelligence, an active and appreciative sense of humor, a preoccupation with dignity, moodiness, a capacity for consideration once his friendship or sympathy has been aroused, and an unwillingness to compromise whatever truths he has accepted."

Bill Russell is a man who definitely knows where he intends to go … on the basketball court and off. As far back as 1959 he decided to risk his money in a business venture in Monrovia, Africa. In this distant country, infested with elephants, snakes, hyenas, leopards and many primitive people, he invested in a rubber plantation. The land was in Salala, about 80 miles from Monrovia, the capital. He and two Boston friends paid 50 cents an acre and 50 cents for surveying. They hired about 95 people at eight cents an hour. Bill and his associates planted 85,000 rubber trees on 1,500 acres of land. The rubber plantation is now paying off and Bill Russell is well on his way to becoming a wealthy man.

*Wendell was comfortable with Dr. Martin Luther King's approach to advancing the civil rights movement through integration. He was not comfortable with leaders such as Malcolm X (while with the Nation of Islam) and Stokely Carmichael who argued that a Black individual in America had more in common with a Black individual in Africa than with a white individual in the United States. Russell was somewhere in between the two approaches. He intended to eventually live in Liberia, but he was succeeding in the United States. Russell was intelligent, articulate, and respected throughout the NBA. He did not relocate to Africa but was an effective participant in the civil rights movement. Wendell was able to respect individuals without agreeing entirely with what they said.*

## December 17, 1966

### Sports Beat, *Pittsburgh Courier*, p. 14

*Alcindor Rated All-Time Soph Cager*

They were talking about Lew Alcindor, UCLA's new super-star with Don Haskins, coach of Texas Western's national collegiate champions, and he said that he had seen the 19-year-old giant play as a freshman and has never forgotten it.

"Why," exclaimed Haskins, "he could do everything as a freshman that Wilt Chamberlain did as a senior when he was playing for Kansas."

When Alcindor graduated from Power Memorial Academy in New York City, he had 100 offers from colleges across the country. As a high school performer Lew broke every scoring record in New York history.

Coach Haskins, whose starting five last season were all Negroes, was among those who tried to recruit Alcindor with an enticing scholarship. "I wonder," Haskins said during the bull session, which included such other top college coaches as Johnny Dee of Notre Dame, "how in the world UCLA ever got him? After all, that's a long way from home for him."

No one bothered to mention that Texas Western is almost as far. Instead, someone offered an explanation, saying that they understood that Ralph Bunche, the great American diplomat and a UCLA alumnus, had convinced Lew he should attend UCLA.

"Yes," the man said, "I understand that Mr. Bunche sold Lew on UCLA."

Haskins, who obviously is not familiar with politics or diplomacy, looked puzzled. "Who," he asked, "is Ralph Bunche?"

Somebody in the crowd laughed. "You're kidding. Come on, now, you know who Ralph Bunche is!"

The Texas Western coach wasn't pretending. "Who," he demanded, "is this guy Bunche? Does he scout for UCLA?"

When told of Ralph Bunche's accomplishments as an American statesman, Haskins simply shrugged his shoulders and drawled "I wish somebody had told me about this Bunche fellow," he said forlornly, "I'd appealed to him, too. I sure wanted the boy to play for me at Texas Western."

The fact that Haskins didn't know who Ralph Bunche is isn't at all flattering to the celebrated diplomat. But, on the other hand, it is highly complimentary to Lew Alcindor, the 7 foot 1-1/2 inch sophomore sensation who is expected to lead UCLA to the national championship that Coach Haskins is trying to retain this season.

According to all the experts who have seen or heard about Lew, Texas Western can forget it!... UCLA, they say, can't miss with Alcindor in the lineup. Lew and his coach, Johnny Wooden, aren't saying anything.

But in his first game Lew gave everyone an idea of what to expect when he scored 56 points against Southern California and led the Uclans to victory.

One of the reasons so many colleges hounded Lew when he graduated from high school was the fact that his scholarship credentials were far superior to the average athlete's. He came out of prep school with a "B" average and a reputation that marked him as a fine student and a youngster with a level head.

Although he is living within a stone's throw of Hollywood as a UCLA student he has not allowed the glitter of that movie metropolis to rub off on him. He doesn't want a star stamped on his door ... even though he's the most talked about college basketball player in the world. He's modest, quiet and as inconspicuous as any 7 foot 1-1/2 individual can be.

Lew comes from a good, substantial home. His father, Ferdinand Lewis, Sr., is a transit policeman who studied at the famed Juilliard School of Music in New York. He has appeared as a musician at Carnegie Hall. His mother, Cora Douglas Alcindor, once sang in the Hall Johnson Chorus. Lew's father is 6 feet 3, his mother is 5-11. His grandfather, however, was 6 feet 8.

One of the amazing things about Lew is that despite his tremendous height, he is not a towering, stumbling goon. Rafer Johnson, the former Olympic decathlon champion from UCLA, believes he would make a fine track man.

"He has the coordination of a man 5 foot 8," says Rafer.

Lew could be a sensational high jumper. On the basketball court he can jump from a standing position and touch the top of the back board, at least 13 feet above the floor. "With a running start," someone said, "he could jump out of sight."

And he's just a kid. Sometimes he practices shooting with a lollipop in his mouth. When Coach Wooden thinks about that his eyes light up and his face beams.

"Just wait until Lew grows up," he says, "he'll really be something!"

*Lew Alcindor converted to Islam and became Kareem Abdul-Jabbar. He is in the conversation about who is the greatest player in NBA history. He is the greatest English major to play in the NBA.*

## July 20, 1971

### "Golfing riches still elude Sifford" by Wendell Smith, *Chicago Sun-Times*, p. 81

Australian Bruce Crampton turned in a total score at the Western Open of 279 and collected $30,000 prize money.

Charley Sifford of Charlotte, N.C., and Los Angeles registered a total score in the same tournament at Olympia Fields of 291 and collected a paltry $870.

It has ever been thus for Charley Sifford, a black golf pro who never had a big chance at the big money until he had turned the back nine of his mediocre career.

Bruce Crampton has been on the pro tour since he was 21 years old. He is now 25. Charley Sifford started on the same circuit, but he had to wait until he was 33.

"If I had been given a chance to play at 21," he said after his final round Sunday, "I guess I would have been rich today. But back in those days, when I was young and really able to play this game, they wouldn't let me join the Professional Golfers Assn., and I couldn't even play in the qualifying rounds of the major tournaments. I had to play in Negro tournaments, where $500 was considered big money."

Charley Sifford is now 49 years old. He's on the tour, playing for the lucrative purses that now evade him because of his age.

Now and then he plays well enough to earn a substantial amount of money, but it's still a hard life because the established players usually finish in the top brackets and the young golfers are taking the leavings.

"I've been in 20 tournaments this year so far," he said, "and have made only $10,000. That doesn't take care of my expenses.

"Most of the other players have sponsors, golf companies that supply them with equipment and also pay them fees. I don't have that kind of backing. I have to make it on my own. I had a deal with one company (Dunlap) but they said they couldn't sponsor me any more because they hired Gary Player, the South African golfer, and they wanted to deduct $1,500 from my salary.

"I wouldn't agree to that much of a cut and they decided they didn't need me anyway."

On the tour last year Charley Sifford won only $23,000. "That wasn't a lot of money," he said, "I had expenses that exceeded that."

Why, then, does he continue to play golf? He thought about the question for a moment or two and said:

"Because I love the game of golf. It's all I know. I started caddying in Charlotte, N.C. All I've ever done is play golf. You just don't walk away from the only thing you know."

Most professional golfers add to their income as tutors at various private and public golf clubs around the country.

"I have tried to get one of those jobs," he said, "but no club will hire me. In Los Angeles, for example, I have made an effort to get a pro job at two clubs and they've turned me down. So, I have to keep playing and do the best I can in various tournaments. It's not an easy life."

Charley Sifford's biggest golf year was 1967 when he surprised everyone by winning the Hartford Open. He collected $58,000 that year.

"I haven't had one like that since," he confessed. "But I keep hoping and trying for another year like that."

Time is now running out on him, and he knows it. "I don't know how long I can stand the pace of the tour," he said with a weary sigh. "This is a tough life, even if you're making big money.

"But I'm not going to quit. Some day, perhaps, I'll get a job as a pro at a good golf club and then I'll have enough security to quit the game."

Until that happens Charley Sifford is going to keep trying for the big purses.... The $870 he wins in tournaments like the Western Open, however, is only gas money for the two-year-old car he drives from city to city on the tour.

*Charley Sifford died in 2015. He was inducted into the World Golf Hall of Fame in 2004. He paved the way for Black professional golfers like Lee Elder (the first Black golfer to play at Augusta in the Masters) and ultimately Tiger Woods. Charley won the Greater Hartford Open in 1967 and the Los Angeles Open in 1969. He also attained success in Senior golf tournaments.*

*May 9, 1972*

## "Pressure hasn't bothered
## Aaron in push for Ruth's homer mark"
## by Wendell Smith, *Chicago Sun-Times*, p. 98

Henry Aaron of the Atlanta Braves is so nonchalant at the plate that Robin Roberts, then pitching for the Phillies, once said of him: "He's the only hitter I know who catches up on his sleep between pitches."

That's very true. Nothing seems to disturb the Braves veteran slugger, not even the fact that he is methodically moving closer and closer to Babe Ruth's home run record of 714.

Only two others have slugged more career homers than the soft-spoken, genteel gentleman from Atlanta, the great Bambino of the Yankees and Willie Mays of the Giants.

Aaron came into this season with 639 homers, seven less than Mays and 75 short of Ruth's. Any day now he will pass Willie's mark. Ruth's record is still more than a mere stone's throw away.

But Henry's gunning at the Babe's total and there are those, including Paul Richards, the Braves general manager, who predict he'll reach it by the 1974 season.

"If he stays healthy," says Richards, "Henry is going to set a new record in total homers sometime during the 1974 season." At the age of 38 Hank Aaron personifies power and co-ordination. He looks 10 years younger, weighing 180 solid pounds and his reflexes at the plate are as quick as they were back in 1954, his rookie season.

Slowly the tension and pressure is building around Henry as he pursues Ruth's record but it will not become intense until he hits No. 700. From that time on the pressure and intensity may stifle him. It may make him lose his nonchalance and cool. Roger Maris of the Yankees, for example, lost his as he approached Ruth's season record of 60 homers. In fact, there are those who say the pressure drove Roger out of the majors before his time.

### Still Relaxing

Henry's disposition is such, however, that his home run mission is not likely to have the same devastating effect on him. He is acutely aware of the magnitude of his effort but not smothered by it emotionally.

"I believe I can live with it," said the composed slugger while passing through town with the Braves. "I suppose I'll become more aware of what I'm trying to do the closer I get to the record but right now I'm as relaxed as ever and not pressing."

Hank Aaron's $200,000-plus salary is the highest in baseball history. That figure is a long way from the starting salary of $7,000 he was paid his first season. The Braves purchased his contract in 1953 for $10,000 from the Indianapolis Clowns of the old, defunct Negro American League. He received no bonus for signing.

"I'm just catching up with what I missed when they signed me," he says. "I was a second baseman then. I didn't care whether I received a bonus or not. All I wanted to do was play baseball. If I were coming up today I guess I could demand at least $50,000 to sign. However, I have no regrets. Baseball's been very good to me and my family."

## Never Been Spectacular

Unlike Willie Mays, who has played the game with a dash and flair that excited everyone, Aaron goes about his business on the field with an almost dull perfection. He has never been spectacular. Some have suggested he should project himself and his talent more.

"I'll never change," he says. "I've been told I should be more of a leader, more aggressive, more outspoken. But I can't lead any other way than by my actions. I'm no chatter guy. I've never been thrown out of a game. I've never called a clubhouse meeting, and I don't expect I ever will. I'll just keep doing my thing and hope that my teammates and fans will appreciate what I'm trying to do—play the best I possibly can.

"I play my own natural way," he continued. "I know I'm not particularly spectacular. I don't try to be. I dress well, but not flashy. I want to be remembered as just plain Henry Aaron."

When it's all over it's quite likely that he will be remembered that way. However, there is the distinct possibility that there will be an asterisk beside his name in the record book, saying:

"Most career home runs."

That will surely make him different.

*As he approached Babe Ruth's career home run record, Hank Aaron was treated worse than Roger Maris was treated while Maris pursued the Babe's single season home run record. Aaron received death threats to himself and family that were related to his race. The worst Maris heard was his own fan base telling him he was not worthy of breaking Ruth's record. However, both men received this abuse for largely the same reason: They were about to rewrite the record books in a way that would diminish the standing of a beloved figure. There were ways in which Aaron was treated better than Maris as well. Ford Frick, commissioner of baseball in 1961, ruled that if Maris did not reach Ruth's total of 60 by game 154, there would be an asterisk in the record book noting it (the asterisk was not added). That was the first season that the schedule expanded from 154 to 162 games. Maris did not catch Ruth by game 154 and hit his 61st home run off Tracy Stallard of Boston in the fourth inning at Yankee Stadium in the last game of the season in front of 23,154 fans. It was not difficult to get a ticket.*

*Commissioner Bowie Kuhn and MLB enthusiastically supported Aaron when he broke Ruth's all-time home run record in 1974. The record-breaking home run was seen on a national television broadcast. It was a celebration. Fulton County Stadium hosted 53,775 fans. It was not easy to get a ticket.*

*Two years later, Hank Aaron was playing his final season with the Milwaukee Brewers. My friend Joe Kashmere's father took us to Baltimore to see him. After the game we waited outside the Brewers' locker room to get Hank's autograph. We were two among many waiting for Aaron. Henry Aaron walked past us, got on the bus, and did not sign one autograph. We were disappointed. Then he opened a window and signed every autograph. He signed those autographs the same way he played: with a quiet dignity. He accepted his responsibility to the fan but fulfilled that responsibility in his understated style. A belated "thank you" to the late Mr. Aaron from a then-14-year-old kid who remembers a 42-year-old Aaron methodically signing each item. Joe and I cherish our autographs and the memory.*

# 3

# Jackie Robinson

*Jackie Robinson is an icon. He was a man. Wendell wrote about Jackie the athlete and Jackie the person. He respected Jackie always. He liked Jackie sometimes. Long after men like Jackie, Dr. King, and Abraham Lincoln pass, we cease to remember them as men and recall only what they represent to us. It is understandable but it distorts and is incomplete. Wendell is not trying to bring down the hero in these columns. He is describing the man.*

## April 27, 1946

### The Sports Beat, *Pittsburgh Courier*, p. 16

*It Was a Great Day in Jersey*

Jersey City, N.J.—The sun smiled down brilliantly in picturesque Roosevelt Stadium here Thursday afternoon and an air of excitement prevailed throughout the spacious park, which was jammed to capacity with 25,000 jabbering, chattering opening day fans.... A seething mass of humanity, representing all segments of the crazy-quilt we call America, poured into the magnificent ball park they named after a man from Hyde Park—Franklin D. Roosevelt—to see Montreal play Jersey City and the first two Negroes in modern baseball history perform. Jackie Robinson and Johnny Wright.... There was the usual fanfare and color, with Mayor Frank Hague chucking out the first ball, the band music, kids from Jersey City schools putting on an exhibition of running, jumping and acrobatics.... There was also the hot dogs, peanuts and soda pop.... And some guys in the distant bleachers whistled merrily: "Take Me Out to the Ball Game" ... Wendell Willkie's "one World" was right here on the banks of the Passaic River.

The outfield was dressed in a gaudy green, and the infield was as smooth and clean as a new-born babe.... And everyone sensed the significance of the occasion as Robinson and Wright marched with the Montreal team to deep centerfield for the raising of the Stars and Stripes and the "Star-Spangled Banner"... Mayor Hague strutted proudly with his henchmen flanking him on the right and left.... While the two teams, spread across the field, marched side by side with military precision and the band played on.... We all stood up—25,000 of us—when the band struck up the National Anthem.... And we sang lustily and freely, for this was a great day.... Robinson and Wright stood out there with the rest of the players and dignitaries, clutching their blue-crowned baseball caps, standing erect and as still as West Point cadets of dress parade.

## What Were They Thinking About?

No one will ever know what they were thinking right then, but I have traveled more than 2,000 miles with these courageous pioneers during the past nine weeks—from Sanford, Fla. to Daytona Beach to Jersey City—and I feel that I know them probably better than any newspaperman in the business.... I know that their hearts throbbed heavily and thumped a steady tempo with the big drum that was pounding out the rhythm as the flag slowly crawled up the centerfield mast.

And then there was a tremendous roar as the flag reached its crest and unfurled gloriously in the brilliant April sunlight.... The 25,000 fans settled back in their seats, ready for the ball game as the Jersey City Giants jogged out to their position.... Robinson was the second batter and as he strolled to the plate the crowd gave him an enthusiastic reception.... They were for him.... They all knew how he had overcome many obstacles in the deep South, how he had been barred from playing in Sanford, Fla., Jacksonville, Savannah and Richmond.... And yet, through it all, he was standing at the plate as the second baseman of the Montreal team.... The applause they gave so willingly was a salute of appreciation and admiration.... Robinson then socked a sizzler to the shortstop and was thrown out by an eyelash at first base. The second time he appeared at the plate marked the beginning of what can develop into a great career. He got his first hit as a member of the Montreal Royals.... It was a mighty home run over the left field fence.... With two mates on the base paths, he walloped the first pitch that came his way and there was an explosive "crack" as bat and ball met.... The ball glistened brilliantly in the afternoon sun as it went hurtling high and far over the leftfield fence.... And, the white flag on the foul-line pole in left fluttered lazily as the ball whistled by.

## He Got a Great Ovation from Team, Fans

Robinson jogged around the bases—his heart singing, a broad smile on his beaming bronze face as his two teammates trotted homeward ahead of him…. When he rounded third, Manager Clay Hopper, who was coaching there, gave him a heavy pat on the back and shouted: "That's the way to hit that ball!"… Between third and home—plate he received another ovation from the stands, and then the entire Montreal team stood up and welcomed him to the bench…. White hands slapping him on his broad back…. Deep Southern voices from the bench shouted, "Yo abo' hit 'at one, Robbie, nice goin' kid!"… Another said: "Them folks 'at wouldn't let you play down in Jacksonville should be hee'ah now. Whoopee!"… And still another: "They cain't stop ya now, Jackie, you're really goin' places, and we're going to be right there with ya!" Jackie Robinson laughed softly and smiled…. Johnny Wright wearing a big, blue pitcher's jacket, laughed and smiled. And, high up in the press box, Joe Bostic of the *Amsterdam News* and I looked at each other knowingly, and, we, too, laughed and smiled…. Our hearts beat just a bit faster, and the thrill ran through us like champagne bubbles…. It was a great day in Jersey…. It was a great day in baseball!

But he didn't stop there, this whirlwind from California's gold coast…. He ran the bases like a wild colt from the Western plains. He laid down two perfect bunts and slashed a hit into right field…. He befuddled the pitchers, made them balk when he was roaring up and down the base paths, and demoralized the entire Jersey City team…. He was a hitting demon and a base-running maniac…. The crowd gasped in amazement…. The opposing pitchers shook their heads in helpless agony…. His understanding teammates cheered him on with unrivaled enthusiasm…. And Branch Rickey, the man who had the fortitude and courage to sign him, heard the phenomenal news via telephone in the offices of the Brooklyn Dodgers at Ebbets Field and said admiringly—"He's a wonderful boy, that Jackie Robinson—a wonderful boy!"

### They Mobbed Him After the Game

When the game ended and Montreal had chalked up a 14 to 1 triumph, Robinson dashed for the club house and the showers…. But before he could get there he was surrounded by a howling mob of kids, who came streaming out of the bleachers and stands…. They swept down upon him like a great ocean wave and he was drowned in a sea of adolescent enthusiasm…. There he was—this Pied Piper of the diamond—perspiration rolling off his bronze brow, idolizing kids swirling all around him, autograph hounds tugging at him…. And big cops riding prancing steeds trying unsuccessfully to disperse the mob that had cornered the hero of the day…. One of his own teammates fought his way through the howling mob and finally "saved" Robinson…. It was Red Barrett, who was a hero in his own right because he had pounded out two prodigious home runs himself, who came to the "rescue." He grabbed Robinson by the arm and pulled him through the crowd. "Come on," Barrett demanded, "you'll be here all night if you don't fight them off. They'll mob you. You can't possibly sign autographs for all those kids."

So, Jackie Robinson, escorted by the red-head outfielder, finally made his way to the dressing room. Bedlam broke loose in there too.... Photographers, reporters, kibitzers and hangers-on fenced him in.... It was a virtual madhouse.... His teammates, George Shuba, Stan Breard, Herman Franks, Tom Tatum, Marvin Backley and all the others, were showering congratulations on him.... They followed him into the showers, back to his locker and all over the dressing room.... Flash bulbs flashed and reporters fired questions with machine-gun like rapidity.... And Jackie Robinson smiled through it all.

As he left the park and walked out onto the street, the once brilliant sun was fading slowly in the distant western skies.... His petite and dainty little wife greeted him warmly and kindly. "You've had quite a day, little man," she said sweetly.

"Yes," he said softly and pleasantly, "God has been good to us today!"

*When America was fulfilling its promise to Black citizens, Wendell was a patriotic man. He writes that they sang "lustily and freely" because it was a great day. America was making good on its promise. When he thought America was reneging on its promise, Wendell could be harshly critical for he knew the country could be better ... which is also patriotic.*

*This piece contains some of his best descriptive writing. The reader can sense that something momentous is taking place. Wendell asks, "What were they thinking?" Note that it is "they," not "he." Johnny Wright endured the hardships as well.*

*That Jackie Robinson could play that well that day was an omen of what was to come. Jackie could handle intense pressure. Although Wendell did not know that for certain, he does note that he smiled at Joe Bostic "knowingly." Wendell concludes with Rachel and Jackie reunited after the game. Rachel Robinson was essential to Jackie Robinson's success. They were a team. And it would be that way until Jackie's death.*

# June 7, 1947

## The Sports Beat, *Pittsburgh Courier*, p. 14

*In the "Cradle of Democracy" Again!...*

Boston—This is Boston ... where in '75 a rugged band of tattered and torn Americans fought off the British ... and, where Crispus Attucks, a black man, was shot down by the Red Coats as he defied their deadly muskets in the cobble-stoned streets near the old North Church.

This is Boston ... where Paul Revere hung his lantern—"one, if by land, two, if by sea"—and thereby erected the first Statue of Liberty in America.... The place where tyranny died a horrible death and the Torch of Democracy first cast its brilliant glow across the face of a confused and battered world.

All that happened in April of 1775 ... and, as the old patriotic poem puts it: "Hardly a man is now alive who remembers that famous day and year."

But there are those of us who remember well what happened here in April of '45 ... 1945, that is. For it was at that time that Jackie Robinson first leaned against the sturdy barrier which barred Negroes from the major leagues and left an indelible impression.

*Courier Sent Three Players...*

In April of 1945, the *Pittsburgh Courier* paid the expenses of three players to Boston in order that they might get a trial with the Boston Red Sox or Boston Braves. Those three players were Jackie Robinson, shortstop, Kansas City Monarchs; Sammy Jethroe, outfielder, Cleveland Buckeyes, and Marvin Williams, second baseman of the Philadelphia Stars: The managements of the two clubs had promised a Boston councilman, Isadore Muchnick, that they would give Negro players a tryout. On the basis of that promise, the *Courier* sent these three young players to Boston. The Braves were playing away from home, so we approached the management of the Red Sox and they consented to "look them over." We went to Fenway Park, and with Manager Joe Cronin and Eddie Collins, general manager, looking on, Robinson, Jethroe and Williams worked out with a group of Red Sox recruits. After the workout, the three Negro players met Cronin and Collins and were told: "You'll probably hear from us soon." The fact that they never did hear from the Sox again is not important. What is important is that the "experiment" was splashed in papers throughout the Nation and caught the eye of Branch Rickey, who later signed Robinson.

This column is being written on Memorial Day. And, it marks the second memorable day we've spent here in Boston. The first was that day in '45 when we, under the sponsorship of the *Pittsburgh Courier*, brought Jackie Robinson and the two other Negro players here for that "historic" tryout with the Red Sox. That was a memorable day for two reasons: (1) It was Robinson's first step in the direction of the major leagues. He went from here on to the Brooklyn Dodgers, signifying the end of the color-line in organized baseball. (2) The "experiment" here in Boston happened on the same day that Franklin D. Roosevelt, a great President, died with a suddenness that shocked the entire world. Ironically, the President, whom Robinson admired greatly, died the day that Jackie was "born," insofar as his baseball future was concerned.

We left Boston the next day and went our respective ways, never dreaming that sometime in the near future we'd return and Robinson would be an established big leaguer. He returned to the Kansas City Monarchs and we went back to Pittsburgh. But, as I pointed out above, this is the second memorable day for us in Boston. It is memorable because we have returned!...

Not on an experimental basis as we did before, but because Robinson is now a big leaguer and is here with the Dodgers to play against the Boston Braves. In a sense, that first visit was a failure because nothing solid came of it. We came, we saw, but we never conquered.

## Robbie Now a Big Leaguer...

This time, however, it's different. Robinson has conquered! He's a big leaguer and some forty thousand fans will turn out on this particular Memorial Day to pay tribute to him and Branch Rickey, the man who gave him a chance. His appearance here is also somewhat of a slap in the face of the Sox and Braves, because either of them could have grabbed him before Rickey. But the managements of those two clubs had neither the intestinal fortitude nor the foresight of Rickey. They were afraid to buck tradition— an undemocratic one at that—and consequently lost the best drawing card in the sports world today.

Time and tide wait for no man, they say. The whole world can change in two years. In fact, it has changed. The last time we were here the world was locked in a death struggle and the sun was beginning to set on Hitler and the bloody soil of Germany. We came in the regalia of outcasts, seeking a chance to prove that Negro players could make the grade in the big leagues if only given the chance. We were received with an abrupt coolness and tolerated just long enough to go through with an experiment that the baseball world wanted no part of then.

We were treated as "freaks" from a strange and distant world. Meantime, men died on the battle fields of Europe so that others might live and enjoy the fruits of life ... which includes playing baseball, among many other things.

But the owners of the Braves and Sox, didn't understand that.... They couldn't comprehend that a new day had come: that the rumblings of guns from across the Atlantic were changing the entire world, even baseball and its staid old custom of barring men on the basis of their God-given color.

*Color Line Is No More...*

Now all that they couldn't see then is clearly visible. So are those trying and uncertain days. Hitler and his Nazis are gone. Robinson and his bat have arrived. The color-line is no more in big league baseball and the American public is glad, because it never approved of it and wanted it wiped out a long time ago.

There is a great contrast between today and the day we came here in '45. Where there was hostility then, there is hospitality now. Where Robinson was once looked upon as an intruder and an unwelcomed guest, he now is accepted like anyone else.

So this is the most memorable Memorial Day we've experienced in our time. Robinson is playing first base for the Dodgers against the Braves and the whole world is just a bit better off because of it.

Yes, this is Boston, where this whole thing actually started. This is Boston ... where Revere went on his ride and Attucks died, and the patriots came from every village, Middlesex and farm to fight those who would deny them the rights of America.

This is Boston, where democracy loomed and still flourishes, even though at times it rocks and reels with uncertainty.

This is where Jackie Robinson first struck a smashing blow at big league hypocrisy.

This is the "Cradle of Democracy" ... where both America and the Negro ball player came into their own and first saw the light of day.

*Imagine how Wendell and Jackie felt returning to Boston with the Dodgers two years after the staged tryout. For Red Sox fans it is a painful reminder that they could have signed Jackie Robinson in 1945. For the American public it is joyous, for it did not support the color ban. Wendell consistently made this argument. MLB apartheid was not popular among baseball fans. It was a construct of MLB owners and the powers that be. Like Dr. King, Wendell believed that most white people did not want segregation. Racism was not going to disappear all at once. Advance. Persuade more people. Advance some more. The struggle was and is ongoing.*

# March 19, 1949

## Sports Beat, *Pittsburgh Courier,* p. 10

According to the usually reliable Associated Press, Commissioner A.B. (Happy) Chandler, boss of baseball's empire, found it necessary to call Jackie Robinson on the carpet and warn him against such outbursts as he exhibited last week during an intra-squad game at Vero Beach, Fla.

It seems that a Brooklyn pitcher, Chris Van Cuyk, objected to some of Mr. Robinson's bench-jockeying and retaliated by throwing at the Negro star when he came to bat.

According to newspaper reports, Mr. Robinson objected to Van Cuyk throwing at him. That is understandable. It is also reported that Mr. Robinson approached the pitcher after the incident and allegedly said: "If you had hit me, I would have punched you in the nose."

The Associated Press further stated that Mr. Robinson made light of the affair when called before the commissioner and said the newspapers blew the affair up beyond ordinary proportions. He said it wasn't anywhere as serious as the newspapers made it appear.

Now that may be true, but it seems that Mr. Robinson and some other ball players usually take pot shots at the press when they find themselves in such embarrassing positions.

Last year, for instance, Mr. Robinson reported to training camp no less than fifteen pounds overweight. His physical condition was displeasing to both Manager Leo Durocher and owner Branch Rickey. They exhibited their displeasure and the newspapermen covering the camp reported the objections. Mr. Robinson violently objected to such reportings and in one instance let it be known in no uncertain terms that he resented the reports of a writer of the *New York Post*. He said, in effect, that the writer didn't tell the truth; that he was "blowing up" a story as a favor to Durocher and Rickey.

That, we assure you, was not the truth. Rickey and Durocher did not like Robinson reporting overweight. They said as much to the writer in question and he quoted them.

We point out this particular situation because it merely substantiates the latest incident. Mr. Robinson is called on the carpet and in defending himself once again attempts to imply that the press has been unjust and unfair to him.

This, it seems, is time for someone to remind Mr. Robinson that the press has been especially fair to him throughout his career. Not only since he made his debut in organized baseball but all the time he was in college. If it had not been for the press, Mr. Robinson would have been just another athlete insofar as the public is concerned. If it had not been for the press, Mr. Robinson would not have been in the majors today. If it had not been for the press—the sympathetic press—Mr. Robinson would probably still be tramping around the country with Negro teams, living under what he has called "intolerable conditions."

We do not know whether he was right or wrong in the conflict with Chris Van Cuyk. We hope he was justified in saying the things he is reported to have said.

We do know, however, that Mr. Robinson's memory, it seems, is getting shorter and shorter. That is especially true in the case of the many newspapermen who have befriended him throughout his career.

*Mr. Robinson? Wendell became particularly aggravated when players resorted to claiming they were misquoted whenever they got in trouble (see Al Dark). In his much praised (deservedly) book* Baseball's Great Experiment, *Jules Tygiel writes: "Unlike other ballplayers, he [Jackie Robinson] never avoided adverse repercussions by denying a controversial statement" (p. 324). In this column written during Spring Training 1949, Wendell complains of Jackie doing that very thing.*

## May 19, 1951

## Sports Beat, *Pittsburgh Courier*, p. 14

*Flaherty Spanks Jackie with a Typewriter...*

Vincent X. Flaherty, one of the most highly regarded sports columnists in the business and the ace of the Los Angeles Examiner's sports staff, has taken Jackie Robinson to task for his recent outbursts.

It appears that Robinson, who rode to the majors atop the most favorable wave of publicity any player ever enjoyed, isn't as popular in the press box as he once was.

If that observation is correct, then Robinson had better take inventory. When such highly respected writers as Flaherty turn against him, it is something to be concerned about.

Here is what Flaherty wrote in a recent column:

"Sooner or later Jackie will realize the real stars of baseball never are umpire-baiters, nor do they hustle into the middle of disputes between other players and umpires.

"It is all right for a player to be aggressive, but there is such a thing as overdoing it. Nobody admires a mug in any walk of life. The enduring figures of sports were all real gentlemen—like Mathewson and Johnson and Dempsey and Tunney and Louis and many others.

"Jackie will some day learn that tolerance and understanding are things that work both ways.

"I was rooting for the fellow before he got into organized baseball and I have been rooting for him ever since, but that doesn't mean I do not become discouraged by his attitude.

"It's fine to be a great ball player but baseball contributes very little to the world. Robinson can be anything he wants to be if he overcomes his churlishness. He can be elected to Congress, or he can follow the illustrious trail of Ralph Bunche, one of the important people of our times."

Flaherty then reveals that he had a slight skirmish with Robinson via the mails. He wrote:

"Robinson resents criticism. Year before last, when he got into a skirmish in St. Louis I wrote a column about Jackie, telling him to pattern himself after Joe Louis and encouraging him to be one of the real gentlemen of sports.

"I was astonished when I got a letter from him telling me that he thought I was a friend of the Negro—but that he had to change his mind because of the contents of my column. Instead of explaining his side of the incident in question, Jackie took stern issue with me. It was the kind of letter one doesn't answer."

Flaherty's concluding shot was this:

"Robinson will read this and when he does, instead of smoldering into a rage, I hope he digests a little of it and looks to the future. I hope, in days to come, people won't point and say: 'There goes Jackie Robinson ... what a guy he might have been!'"

*Jackie Robinson excelled under pressure few other athletes have faced. He was able to block out everything, including good advice. This column illustrates a divide between men based not on race but by profession: journalists vs. athletes. Wendell is a Black man. He is also a journalist. He has more in common with Vince Flaherty than Jackie Robinson for purposes of this discussion.*

## *February 26, 1955*

### Sports Beat, *Pittsburgh Courier*, p. 12

*Would Robinson Like to Manage Some Day?*

Jackie Robinson predicted the other day that eventually a Negro will be selected to manage a major league team.

"We will have a Negro manager eventually," he said, "and it will be the finest thing that could happen to baseball when it comes. But I don't know if there is anyone ready to do the job right now."

He stressed the fact that he is not a candidate for the job and at the same time hinted he might consider such an offer in the future. In other words, he gave out with some double talk.

"It would take an awful lot of persuasion to get me to take the job," Robinson stated. "However, the way the fans have responded to Negro players is an indication they will accept a Negro manager.

"The appointment of a Negro manager would be a wise thing and would prove to people who use racial propaganda against our country that we are making strides and are sincere about freedom and equality."

The Brooklyn star, who will start his ninth season as a Dodger this year, confessed that he has never given the possibility of becoming a major league manager serious consideration. He, apparently, has been too busy trying to help the Dodgers win pennants.

"I haven't given the idea of managing much thought," he said. "My wife and I have talked it over a few times, of course. I guess it's the aim and ambition of every ball player to manage at some time, but I worry too much.

"I worry about myself, the crowds, the other guys. Managing would give me ulcers." One of the most fiery players in baseball history, Robinson worries because he is a great competitor, a man who fights to win every ball game played during the long season. If he had his way, Brooklyn would never lose a single game.

## "You Don't Play Ball for the Manager"—Jackie

Commenting further on the managerial situation, Robinson said: "I don't really know if there is a man ready to become the first Negro manager.

"Of the ball players in the majors now that I know, I would say Roy Campanella would be a candidate. Roy knows the game and men like him. Campy loves the game, too. That's a big point.

"I doubt that there would be any conflict with the players if a club management hired a Negro manager. I don't think there would be any trouble about playing for a Negro. You don't actually play for the manager. You play for yourself, with direction, of course.

"This man would have to be an exceptional manager. It takes a certain amount of drive and tact and skill in handling twenty-five men. Unless there was a real necessity, I wouldn't ever manage."

Robinson's views on this important subject indicate that he has one foot in the door and one foot out. He says he wouldn't manage a big league club but also adds, "Unless there was a real necessity."

He sounds, more or less, like a potential presidential candidate. They always say: "I do not plan to run for the presidency of the United States. That's the farthest thing from my mind. However, if the people express a desire for me to do so, I probably would."

Is Robinson being coy? Considering everything he has said on the subject the only conclusion that can be drawn is that he is. If the opportunity presented itself the odds are overwhelmingly on the side of his acceptance. It would be a great honor, and no one likes honors more than he does.

There is little possibility, however, that Jack will ever have such an opportunity. The general feeling in baseball is that he lacks the necessary leadership qualities to manage a team of twenty-five big leaguers.

Of all the Negro players in the big leagues today, Campanella, they say, possesses the best qualities for a manager's job. As Robinson says himself, Campanella knows the game and men like him.

The bulky Brooklyn catcher has a more even disposition than Robinson. His genial personality is contagious and he has a keen sense of humor. He is particularly liked by the sportswriters who follow the Dodgers, whereas Robinson's relations with the press have been strained to the breaking point many times.

It is quite likely that Campanella will remain in the Brooklyn organization after his playing days. If they have managerial plans mapped out for him, they probably call for Roy to start in a league of low classification and move up gradually.

Robinson, on the other hand, will probably leave baseball forever when he hangs up his glove and spikes. There is no indication that the Brooklyn club has any particular spot set aside for him within the organization.

His future, in fact, is so uncertain, insofar as the Dodgers are concerned, that Robinson went so far a few months ago to state that he would not be surprised if Brooklyn traded him to another club. That comment, however, probably erupted on one of his "grouchy" days, any number of which he has been afflicted with during a year's span.

Because of his temperament, it isn't likely that he'll ever boss a big league, nor top minor league, team. Right now, Campanella is the No. 1 candidate to become the first Negro major league pilot. Roy has all the qualities ... all he needs is the chance.

*Roy Campanella likely would have been the first Black manager in MLB had he not suffered the car accident that left him paralyzed. Had the accident occurred today, he likely would have been given the opportunity despite the disability. Granted, that is speculation, but it is not unfounded.*

*Wendell gets a couple of digs in at Jackie. He states that no one likes honors more than Jackie. And he notes that Jackie discussed a potential trade on one of his "grouchy days." Conclusion: Jackie has a big ego and is moody, neither of which contributes to managing a baseball club effectively nor endears one to Wendell Smith.*

*Wendell correctly forecasts that Robinson will leave baseball after he retires and Campy will remain in the Dodger organization. Correct on both predictions. It would be almost two decades before Frank Robinson would become the first Black manager in MLB. During Jackie's last public appearance at the 1972 World Series Jackie would again call for someone to hire a Black manager. Neither Jackie nor Wendell would live to see it.*

## January 19, 1957

### Sports Beat, *Pittsburgh Courier*, p. 25

*Jackie's Gone, But Doby's Still Around*

Jackie Robinson's exit as a big leaguer was almost as controversial as his entrance.

When he made his debut as the first Negro in the majors in 1947, following a year of stellar play at Montreal, there were all kinds of explosive vibrations. The St. Louis Cardinals threatened to strike, rather than play against him; National League officials feared that riots would flare, and baseball in general was sitting on a barrel of dynamite.

Because of those various turbulent ingredients—plus many more—Robinson's presence in those early days was of historical significance and, understandably, he received world-wide publicity.

Then, when he bowed out last week, via an exclusive story in *Look* magazine, a great cry of protest went up. There were those who charged that he betrayed the daily press generally, and the New York press in particular, for a gratuity of a "mere" $50,000. And, Buzzy Bavasi, the Dodger official, heaped words of wrath upon him because Robinson's decision nullified his (Jackie's) trade from Brooklyn to the Giants.

Thus, they screamed when he came into the majors ... and they screamed when he went out.

Meantime, while all this was boiling and sizzling, the first Negro in the American League and second in the majors—Larry Doby—signed his 1957 contract to play with the Chicago White Sox unceremoniously.

As Warren Brown of the *Chicago-American* pointed out so pointedly, many have forgotten that Doby was the first of his race to crash the once all-white American League. Robinson and Doby, significantly, came up the same year, 1947. Jackie set a racial precedent by only a few months. Whereas he came up in a stormy atmosphere, Doby's arrival was comparatively quiet and reasonably normal.

There was a vast difference between these two ball players. Robinson was fiery, dramatic and brash as he fought to establish himself in the majors.

Doby, on the other hand, was quiet, conservative and rather shy. Yet, both made the grade and history, each in his own way.

Reviewing Doby's contributions to the national pastime, Brown, who incidentally, is one of baseball's most informed, seasoned and prolific writers, points [out] that Robinson was, indeed, the stormier figure of the two.

Perhaps that was all for the best. What would have happened had both Robinson and Doby been the "stormy" type, or if both had been the docile, subservient type? Had they been exactly the same—either way—perhaps baseball history would have been entirely different on this particular phase of the game. Commenting in his widely read column on Doby, Brown writes:

"In his first year with the Indians Doby was cast, off and on, as a first baseman, as a second baseman and as a shortstop. It was another year before the Indians thought of exploring his possibilities as a center fielder.

"In that capacity he became—and still is—one of its foremost exponents.

"As has been the case with Robinson, though not as often in such a vocally expressive way, Doby has had an immense pride in his accomplishments. This has been, not as much, I think, for what they have done for him as an individual, as for what they have meant for the team with which he has been associated.

"Last season, Doby's first with the White Sox, was one that found him leading the club in runs batted in, with a 102 figure. He led it in home runs with 24. This latter figure, even though 77 games were played in a park not as conducive to homers as the Cleveland Stadium with its trick contours, left Doby but five behind the existing White Sox standard of 29, a figure which Gus Zernial and Eddie Robinson share jointly."

When Doby sent in his signed contract last week, he also expressed the hope that he will do even better this coming season than he did last.

"I shall be greatly surprised if he doesn't have his wish come true," Brown writes, "for that's the kind of competitor Larry Doby is.

"His entire attitude and outlook on the profession he follows have been lasting proof that as the American League's pioneer of his race Larry Doby, in his own emotionally restrained way, was as wise a choice as Jackie Robinson."

All of which is so true. Robinson's gone now ... never to be forgotten.

But, thank goodness, Larry Doby's still around.

*Wendell and Wyonella Smith were the godparents of one of Larry Doby's daughters. Wendell and Doby were friends in a way Jackie would have not permitted.*

*Between 1947 and 1964, the New York Yankees won the American League pennant every year except 1948, 1954, and 1959. Larry Doby was a member of all three teams. Doby would become the second Black manager in MLB and eventually be enshrined in the Hall of Fame.*

## February 9, 1957

### Sports Beat, *Pittsburgh Courier*, p. 25

Salvatore Maglie was visiting around and about town, and had a few thousand or more words to say about baseball in general, and the Roy Campanella–Jackie Robinson verbal battle in general.

Herewith is presented what Mr. Maglie said. If it doesn't come out like he put it, it's because someone among the copy desk butchers chopped it up to their liking. But, as best as we can remember from our notes, and casual conversation with the 40-year-old "comeback pitcher of the year," this is a reasonably precise account of what he had to say:

"We'll have the best pitching in the league, and a strong bench without Jackie Robinson.

"I saw Roy Campanella the other day and he's determined to make up for the rather poor season he had last year.

"He's down to 210 pounds, looks great, and the bad finger that has bothered him so much has healed completely. This will surely be another good year for Roy, it that's true.

"If we could win with Campy so much off form, watch out for us with him in good shape. With him physically able to catch more than 100 games next season, Brooklyn should win again."

Then, of course, the subject of Robinson came up. Is Jackie really a "pop off" ball player, a man who likes to keep things steaming, and a locker room lawyer? Was he justified in saying that Campy is at the end of the road; that Roy is old and decrepit?

"No," declared Maglie. "What's Robinson think he is, a doctor, too? I've had a long talk with Campanella. He tells me that the operation on his hand was successful. He says he can grip a bat again, that the pain is gone; that he can throw now with the same accuracy he did before the trouble, and that he's rearin' to go. That's what Campy says, and I believe him. What does Robinson know?"

Then Maglie voluntarily jumped, headlong, into the controversial issue about Robinson and his tendency to "pop off," or, say the wrong thing at the expedient time. He said:

"Robby has always been like that. He says a lot of things, like he said about the Milwaukee ball club (Robinson said Milwaukee lost the pennant because a number of their key players hit the high spots in the early morning during baseball season) and then when a lot of people get mad, he sits down and writes a letter saying he was sorry they didn't like what he said.

"Now, I'm Italian, and I have been told how my people had to fight to get recognition in this country when a generation of them came over here from Italy. So, I'm, naturally, conscious about what goes on. But, you have to be considerate. Everytime one of my people yells 'foul' that doesn't mean the fellow is right.

"Robinson, I think gets the idea that if he isn't given the best of everything, then it's because of his race. Maybe he's right, I don't know. All I know is that he put a bad rap on Campy, who, incidentally, is the son of an Italian father and Negro mother. Maybe that is why I'm leaning a little in Campy's direction."

Robinson has retired from baseball. Earlier in the week he said he'd only come back to the game as a manager. Would he make a competent boss of a big league club?

"I don't think he'd make a good manager," said Maglie. "I doubt if the players would go all-out for him. He was always very cold in the club house. He'd congratulate me if I pitched a good game, but he never took part in the general kidding and joking around the club house after a game.

"Maybe, if he got into shape, he would have been able to play another year. But he knew—and all of us did—that it would be a real struggle. So, he accepted the $50,000 offer from *Look* magazine and the $30,000 job from that other firm in New York.

"I don't blame him for that. I think I'd have done the same thing, had the opportunity presented itself. But I still say he will never be a manager of a big league ball club."

What about Campanella? Will he ever get the chance?

"I think he will," said the ancient pitcher. "Roy's got the touch, can handle men. I don't think Jackie can."

Behind all this, however, you must remember that Maglie was Campy's battery mate. Robinson was a part-time third baseman and leftfielder last season.

Roy caught Maglie's stunning no-hitter near the end of the season. Robinson was just another player on the field that day!

So, take this for what it's worth.

*The Brooklyn Dodgers finished third in 1957. The Milwaukee Braves stayed away from the night life enough to win the National League pennant. Roy Campanella appeared in 103 games and had a subpar season. Sal Maglie appeared in only 19 games but pitched well for a 40-year-old hurler. Jackie's assessment was accurate.*

*May 20, 1959*

## The Sporting News, p. 4

*Robbie Was Rip-Roarer—Banks Big Breeze*

By Wendell Smith, Chicago, ILL

EDITOR'S NOTE: Wendell Smith, then sports editor of the *Pittsburgh Courier*, was the first to recommend Jackie Robinson to Branch Rickey as a Dodger prospect in April 1945. Smith served as liaison between Rickey and Robinson in their secret negotiations in the summer of 1945. In the spring of 1946 he was employed by Rickey to travel with and arrange lodgings for Robinson and Pitcher John Wright, also a Negro, in Florida and other Southern communities. Smith served on the Dodger scouting staff from the spring of 1947 until Rickey moved to the Pirates. In August 1947, Smith joined the *Chicago American* sports staff but he continues to write a column for the *Pittsburgh Courier*.

A graduate of West Virginia State College, where he captained the baseball and basketball teams, Smith has been writing baseball since 1937. Besides Robinson, he recommended a number of other Negro players who were signed by the Dodgers or other major league clubs.

*Ex-Dodger Great, Cub Star Alike in Their Many Ways,
But Different Temperaments*

Whenever a Negro player reaches the pinnacle of stardom in the major leagues, such as the Cubs Ernie Banks has done, the natural inclination is to compare him with the pioneer and trail blazer of the race—Jackie Robinson. The retired Brooklyn Dodger immortal, who is almost a cinch to be the first Negro to win Hall of Fame recognition, will exist forever as the yardstick by which such players are measured.

Robinson was not only the first Negro, but also one of the greatest players in major league history. That is why all present and future members of his race who attain distinction will be scrutinized by historians on the basis of Jackie's magnificent and historical achievements.

Statistically and performance-wise, Banks compares favorably with Jackie. Both were former shortstops of the Kansas City Monarchs. Robinson was the first Negro in the majors and Ernie the first to play in a Cub game, although he and Gene Baker came up on the same day, September 14, 1953.

*Each Won Most Valuable Award*

Each won the coveted Most Valuable Player award in the National League. Their selection for the annual All-Star Game was almost automatic.

Robinson was one of the game's most feared line-drive clutch hitters. Banks is equally dangerous as a slugger and home-run hitter. Robinson won the 1949 National League batting title with a .342 average. Last season Banks hit 47 homers, chalked up 129 RBIs and accounted for 379 total bases, all tops in the majors. He holds the record for most home runs hit by a shortstop. Defensively, Jackie was one of the game's superior second basemen. He made only seven errors in 1951, a record which still stands for second basemen. He also holds the season record for most double plays by a second baseman, 137.

## Thomson's Tribute to Ernie

Bobby Thomson, the veteran Cub outfielder who has seen the best of the game's shortstops over the past 14 years, saluted Ernie with this comment soon after he was traded by Milwaukee to Chicago in 1957:

"The one thing that surprised me when I had a chance to see Ernie play every day was the fact that he does so well in the field. People think of him only as a hitter. I think he's an outstanding shortstop, too. He'd even be valuable if he were just another hitter."

Manager Bob Scheffing agrees. "He does a great job for us in a business-like manner," the Bruin boss said recently. "There are few shortstops anywhere as dependable and consistent as Ernie."

Thus, it is not far-fetched to stand the Cub star alongside Robinson, whom the experts have justifiably selected as the model by which Negro players are to be judged, and say:

"There is a similarity between them. Both have distinguished themselves on the field and under fire. When you compare their statistical records, you'll find that each was particularly outstanding in numerous, if different, aspects of the game." When the record book is put down, however, and the personalities of the two players are analyzed on and off the field, the similarity between Robinson and Banks come to an abrupt, almost astonishing, end. Although cut from the same ebony texture, they are as different as night and day.

Banks' most striking characteristic and virtue is his humility and natural modesty. Ernie wears his badge of fame and distinction with a quiet, unassuming elegance. His disposition is warm, contagious and instinctively calm. If there is one criticism that can be directed at this 28-year-old Cub clouter, it is the fact that he shrugs off the leadership qualities and "take charge" responsibilities that managers inevitably offer a star of his magnitude.

"He's almost too quiet out there on the field," Scheffing says. "I'd like to get more holler out of him."

Banks, who speaks softly and cautiously, understands what the boss wants and at times actually tries to spur his teammates with inspirational chatter.

"I holler," Ernie commented recently, "I holler a lot. But I don't have any growl in my voice and they don't hear me."

Banks is one of the best-liked and most admired players in the major leagues. The opposing players take great delight in ribbing him, in the same manner they do popular Willie Mays of the Giants. There is nothing vicious about their jibes. They never hurl the stinging epithets at Ernie that riled Robinson in his day. Ernie, on the other hand, can dish it right back in his gentle, undemonstrative way. He has a keen sense of humor.

He demonstrated that fact a few years ago when he was hit on the nose by a pitched ball. The whole Cub team rushed from the dugout when he went down, fearing the worst. They were all relieved when they discovered he wasn't seriously injured.

Hank Sauer, then with the Cubs, eased the tension when he said jokingly to Ernie:

"Why didn't you get out of the way? Don't you know you can't hit a fast ball with your nose?"

## Retains His Sense of Humor

There was a devilish glint in Ernie's eyes when he looked at Sauer, who definitely has one of the largest, most prominent schnozzles in the baseball world. "You're right," Ernie replied, grinning. "But if that pitch had hit your nose it would have gone for a solid single."

Ernie is an introvert more or less. Very few events stimulate him outwardly. It takes a very crucial and explosive situation to compel him to walk to the mound and communicate with a pitcher in trouble.

"Whenever I see Banks walk to the mound and say something to the pitcher," a Cub fan said recently, "I know it's time for the manager to take the pitcher out. When Ernie does that, things are really bad."

When a newspaperman asked Ernie to explain his reticence, he explained that it does not mean he is immune to impending disaster, then added:

"I didn't come up here to talk. I came to play ball."

In comparison, Robinson was a roaring extrovert and perhaps the most controversial figure in the game's recent history. He was a stormy petrel throughout his career, although he managed to restrain his violent emotions at the outset. Robinson was an enigma. He could converse with the President of the United States and curse Sal Maglie with equal intensity and skill. He was a fearless knight riding a dashing white steed, on his way to fight and destroy evil, in the eyes of millions. To others, he represented evil and was viewed as a swashbuckling, notorious villain.

### Jackie Rugged Individualist as Player

Robinson was a spectacular, rugged individualist as a player. If the other players on the team were dilatory about winning, he wouldn't wait.... He'd go ahead and win by himself. He was the most exciting player since Ty Cobb.

It was not as a Dodger star but rather as a man that Jackie aroused controversy. He fought individuals and issues, friend and foe; wherever he went, whenever he spoke, storm clouds gathered and a tumult resulted. His entrance into Organized Ball created a furor and throughout his exciting career a turbulence of major proportions existed. He battled umpires, opposing players, his own teammates, rival managers and pilots who were supposed to manage him. He accused the Yankees and Red Sox of racial prejudice.

He said the 1956 Braves lost the pennant in night clubs; he accused Walter O'Malley of forcing his savior, Branch Rickey, out of Brooklyn; he insisted on staying in restricted hotels; and when he retired, he invited the wrath of the daily press by giving the story exclusively to a national, bi-monthly magazine.

Summing it all up, the only conclusion one can reach in comparing the current star of the Cubs with the once-great Dodger is this:

Jackie Robinson stormed his way through the major leagues.... Ernie Banks is breezing his way through.

*But there would have been no Ernie Banks without Jackie Robinson. Wendell describes Jackie as divisive. Is Robinson a divisive figure today? Obviously not. When was the last time you heard anyone criticize Jackie Robinson? While he lived, however, he was divisive. Being divisive is not a sin. Jackie paid a price in popularity while he lived that made it easier for those Black players who followed to be themselves. In a couple of years Wendell would be writing articles demanding that guys like Ernie Banks should be more like Jackie and take a more aggressive stance in integrating Spring Training facilities.*

## June 3, 1961

### Sports Beat, *Pittsburgh Courier,* p. 34

*What a Difference a Name Makes!*

Baltimore—You walk into the Baltimore Orioles clubhouse and see Earl Robinson sitting there all by himself in front of his locker.

He looks so lonely ... so apart from the ball club. He's an outfielder, the only Negro on the team. He looks like Jackie Robinson, the courageous player who was the pioneer of all Negroes in the majors today.

But there the similarity dies. Jackie Robinson was a fighter.... Earl Robinson is not.

Jackie Robinson was strictly on his own, nobody paved the way for him, for example, to receive a $50,000 bonus, which is what Earl Robinson received for signing with the Dodgers, the same team for which Jackie played.

Jackie Robinson fought for everything ... not only equality on the field, but also in hotels and restaurants, on the trains and planes ... everything.

His namesake, Earl Robinson fights for nothing. He submits to segregation and discrimination willingly. The Dodgers signed him and gave him that fat bonus because Buzzie Bavasi, the general manager of Los Angeles, visualized another Jackie Robinson in the making. But Earl didn't have it. They sent him to Baltimore last December.

There is a striking similarity between the two Robinsons—Jackie and Earl. They were cut from the same cloth, and apparently, from a physical standpoint. They talk alike and walk alike and come from the same college, UCLA.

But that's where it ends. Obviously, Bavasi didn't recognize the difference in the two when he laid out all that money in 1958, eleven years after Jackie Robinson.

He thought this Robinson, like the other, would be a fighter. Branch Rickey signed Jackie in 1947 to play for the Dodgers, when they were in Brooklyn. Ever since then the club has been looking for another like him. Jackie was a star from the start, and he was also a problem, because he fought for his basic rights. He protested against segregated training quarters, against inadequate hotel accommodations and everything else that was not equivalent to that which the white players enjoyed.

Naturally, he was censored for his "aggressiveness." They said he wanted "too much, too soon." Even Rickey, who agreed with his attitude, tried to harness his energy, tried feebly to quell Jackie's zest for equal treatment.

But Jackie Robinson refused to be detoured.... And when he went out of baseball, he had earned the respect and admiration of every single person in the country, even those dedicated to segregation and discrimination.

"He was a fighter," they admitted, "a real ball player and a real fighter for his people."

Unfortunately, Earl Robinson is different. He is the Negro player who voluntarily requested segregation this past spring, when the Baltimore front office asked him if he wanted to stay in the same hotel with the white players on the club.

He said he didn't. He wanted to stay in Miami's Negro hotel, where he would be "more comfortable." When he was asked by this reporter if he didn't realize the consequences of his decision, if he didn't recognize what people like Martin Luther King, and hundreds of Negro college students, were trying to do, he replied:

"All I want to do is make the Baltimore team, nothing else matters."

Well, he has "made" the team. At last look he was hitting a "magnificent" .190, and the night this observer saw him play against the Chicago White Sox recently he went to bat three times and struck out three times in succession.

What a difference a name makes.... What a difference between Jackie Robinson and Earl Robinson. Earl Robinson—you can have!

*This column was written while Wendell was fighting fiercely to integrate Spring Training facilities. What would Ernie Banks have done if he were asked to make the same decision that Earl Robinson had to make? Earl probably should have moved to the integrated facility. But his biggest faults were that he was in the wrong place at the wrong time and he was not Jackie Robinson. Wendell's anger is understandable. It just might not be entirely fair. Wendell's perspective on Jackie Robinson has changed from the prior column, has it not?*

## May 17, 1964

### "Changing Times in the U.S. and England," *Chicago Tribune*, p. 190

*Baseball Has Done It by Jackie Robinson*

A review by Wendell Smith

Jackie Robinson, in collaboration with Charles Dexter, has added a new dimension to baseball literature in this book, his third since he leaped the game's color barrier in 1947. The first two, written in collaboration with this reviewer and Carl T. Rowan, respectively, were biographies of his exciting and spectacular career on the baseball diamond. This one, however, veers from the technicalities of the game and plunges headlong into all the racial aspects of integration and the current civil rights storm.

It is calculated to demonstrate and to prove that Negroes and whites can live and work together in harmony. It does not prove its point conclusively but does illustrate that sports generally, and baseball in particular, has accomplished more in that area over a span of 17 years than many groups dedicated to human relations on a full time basis.

The book's strength lies in the series of interviews Robinson obtained from other Negro major leaguers. Outstanding players such as Hank Aaron, Ernie Banks, and Bill Bruton, and many former stars examine the American problem of prejudice and national hate. They reveal some of their startling almost unbelievable experiences with prejudice and the impact they have had on their lives.

Robinson and his Negro colleagues resent those traumatic experiences, most of which occurred off the playing field, and their protestations have a familiar ring. They echo the demands of the Rev. Martin Luther King, James Meredith, the NAACP, CORE and all the others involved in the fight for civil rights. They demand democracy now.

Baseball's commissioner, Ford Frick, says it can be achieved in other segments of American life just as it has been accomplished in baseball. But he calls for patience and understanding.

"It's going to take time in a great sociological upheaval like this before all the problems are solved, all the dissenters silenced," he says. "There will be disappointments, disillusionment, dissatisfaction. It will take a lot of years before all the people demand for all the people can be had."

Branch Rickey, the man who introduced Robinson to the big leagues, is more aggressive. Rickey censures the Negro who would rather be segregated than go to restaurants and other public places where the evidences of discrimination are so patent.

"This Negro moderate," he comments, "is hurting his people a very great deal. There should be no compromise on the part of the Negro people in this country. The big challenge to the Negro body today is to fight for the right to be equal and then to qualify as an equal. And no less important is the challenge not to compromise for less than equality."

Alvin Dark, the manager who depends on Willie Mays' speed for his bread and butter, wants Negroes to go slowly off the playing field.

"The majority of people in the south like colored people," says Dark, who is from Louisiana. "They consider them as human beings, but right now it's [integration] being rushed too fast. Being a Christian, I feel this will be solved one day in the south. But they're rushing it a little too quickly right now."

The book is important and provocative. It is full of fury and controversy. As Robinson says, "It's a book not so much about hits, runs, and errors on the diamond as about hits, runs, and errors in real life."

This is not only Robinson's finest writing contribution, it is one of the best books on human relations in a long time. Baseball, as such, is nothing more than a by-product.

(Lippincott, 226 pages, $2.95)

Wendell Smith, a former sports writer now with WBBM, arranged for Robinson's major league tryout.

*Willie Mays and Maury Wills did not respond to Jackie's request for a written contribution to the book and he lets them know he noticed. Branch Rickey criticizes the Black moderate in a manner similar to the way Wendell criticized Earl Robinson in the prior entry. Al Dark will be addressed in Chapter 5.*

## January 26, 1971

### "Jackie Robinson discusses old adversary Leo," *Chicago Sun-Times*, p. 72

Jackie Robinson came into this place on 75th street, walking pigeon-toed and wearing an expression of utter fatigue. He had been politicking all day with the South Side's Rev. Jesse Jackson and now it was 7:15 in the evening and when he saw all the people assembled there, waiting patiently for his words of wisdom, he slumped down in a chair as exhaustion seemed to overwhelm him.

"Been doing this ever since I got off the plane this morning," he said softly, running his dark hand over a head of gray-thatched hair. "It's starting to get me down. I'm not young anymore, you know."

Jackie Robinson will be 52 on the last day of this month and he has already lived at least two lives, one as a Hall of Fame baseball player and the other as a civil rights missionary. The intensity with which he has participated in those two areas has had its effect. He appears older than his years and there seems to be an urgency about his mission which accentuates the heavy toll of his involvement.

Jackie Robinson and Leo Durocher of the Cubs were never compatible during their Brooklyn Dodger days, perhaps because of the similarity in disposition. Leo was the abusive manager, Jackie the resolute crusader. Their personality collisions were constant and enduring.

Despite their hostility, however, each respected the other grudgingly. Neither has changed since they first collided 25 years ago. The weariness of Jackie Robinson vanished at the mention of Leo Durocher's name. While signing autographs for a group of Little Leaguers, he was asked for an analysis of Durocher, the manager.

"Well," he said, "I believe he was too confident in 1969, when he should have won the pennant in a walk. But he blew it when he failed to keep the Cubs' momentum up. When he left the club and went to that boy scout camp, or whatever it was he invited disaster. For a time, the Cubs had everything going for them but when he took off the way he did, that was the turning point. They were never the same after that, never.

"As for last season, he shouldn't be blamed, in my opinion. The Cubs just didn't have it to go all the way. Durocher had problems in the bullpen and he lost Randy Hundley, his No. 1 catcher, for a major portion of the season because of injuries.

"So, I don't think people are fair when they blame him for the Cubs failure in 1970."

There is a theory among baseball people that Leo Durocher cannot build a winning team. You have to give him a winner, they say, because he does not have the patience to nurse and develop young players into stardom.

"I don't believe that," said Jackie Robinson, reluctantly displaying his respect for Leo as a boss and tutor. "In 1951, he was fantastic with the Giants and he developed young guys like Willie Mays, Monte Irvin and others. He made that club a winner. Going into the last month of the season, we (Brooklyn) were 13 games in front of the Giants, and he caught us and passed us. He was a great manager that year."

"Durocher is the best manager I've ever seen with a winner. Give him a club loaded with talent and he'll direct it with perfection. On the other hand, he has a tendency to panic when things don't go right.

"Leo is very independent and self-centered. But, he is as intense about winning as any manager I've ever known. When he managed the Dodgers in '48, the players liked him because he fought for them. They knew he was for them all the way.

"I think the Cub players, with the exception of one or two, feel the same way about him, despite the camp incident. They know he's all for them, especially when things go wrong.

"I wouldn't say he's the best manager in the big leagues, but he's not the worst, either. In fact, you'd have to put him very high on the list when you rate managers. He knows baseball, despite his personality problems."

Now Jackie Robinson was through signing autographs. He got to his feet wearily and there was that haggard look on his face again. He heaved a deep sigh and started talking.

"Ladies and gentlemen, and Little Leaguers," he said…

He urged them to register and vote, to respect law and order, and to support the politicians recommended by the Rev. Jesse Jackson.

On and on he went. Leo Durocher was no longer on his mind…

*The primary topic in this column is Leo Durocher. But there is an element of foreshadowing as well. It is doubtful that Wendell expected Jackie (or himself) to be dead within two years. However, the reader gets the sense that Wendell perceives that Jackie is not healthy. Jackie is almost*

*"Christ-like" as he pushes himself relentlessly as though he is running out of time and there is still so much to do.*

## November 4, 1972

### "The Jackie Robinson I Knew,"
### *Pittsburgh Courier*, p. 9

(Editor's Note: Wendell Smith served for many years as sports editor of the *Pittsburgh Courier*. It was he who was largely responsible for Jackie Robinson getting into the major leagues. The following article was written for the *Chicago Sun Times* and it is with that newspaper's permission that the story appears here. Smith is a *Sun Times* columnist and popular TV sports personality.)

The Jackie Robinson I knew was a man around whom the winds of controversy swirled and blew during most of his spectacular lifetime.

From his boyhood days in Pasadena throughout his adulthood he was a constant source of worry and agitation to those who resented his black aggressiveness. They declared he was too "Pushy, wanted too much too soon."

But nobody could tell him that and smother his quest for racial equality in American life.

I first met Jackie Robinson in 1945. He was playing shortstop for the Kansas City Monarchs of the Negro American League. He believed then that he was a player of major league quality and was determined to break the barrier which had been erected to keep black players out.

That determination was easily discernable that season, two years before he reached his goal. As sports editor of the Pittsburgh Courier, I was taking Jackie and two other black players, Sam Jethroe of the Cleveland Buckeyes and Marvin Williams of the Philadelphia Stars, to Boston for what ostensibly was a tryout with the Boston Red Sox.

### Just a Gesture

We got to talking about this tryout—which turned out to be nothing more than a gesture—and Jackie said grimly, "I don't know what's going to come of this but if it means that the Negro player is a step closer to the major leagues then I'm all for it. I'll do my best to help make this project a success."

We were on a train going from New York, where the players had met me, to Boston.

The following day we went to Fenway Park. The Red Sox had not returned from spring training camp. Instead they went directly to New York where they were to open the season against the Yankees.

Duffy Lewis, the old-time Boston star, was looking over a group of sandlot and high school prospects. Robinson and the two other black players joined them. Jackie and his two colleagues were impressive, to say the least.

## A Small Step

Afterward, Duffy Lewis said good-by and assured the players, "You'll hear from us."

On the way back to New York, Robinson said, "We probably won't hear from him, but it may have put a crack in the dike."

It did. I stopped off in Brooklyn while Robinson and the other two players returned to their respective teams in Negro baseball. Branch Rickey of the Dodgers expressed an interest immediately and from that point on had scouts tailing Robinson, Jethroe and Williams.

Jackie didn't know it but he was on his way to the majors then. Instead of Boston, however, he was to end up in Brooklyn. In the spring of 1946 I accompanied Robinson and a pitcher, John Wright, to Sanford, Fla., the training site of the Montreal Royals and No. 1 Brooklyn farm club.

This event, which Rickey called "the great experiment," was the big training camp story that year. With Robinson and Wright in camp, Montreal, a minor league club, received more publicity than most big league teams.

The press paid more attention to Robinson because he was better known than Wright. Jackie had been an all-around star at UCLA. When World War II came he went into the service and became a first lieutenant.

Controversy followed him there. He became embroiled with some MP's because, according to Robinson, they had roughed up a Negro woman passenger on a bus trip while trying to force her to sit in the back.

## Louis Intervened

Jackie was almost court martialed for that incident. Only the intervention of Joe Louis then stationed at Fort Riley, Kan., saved Jackie from a long sentence. Louis appealed to Washington in Jackie's behalf and the matter was dropped.

During those spring training days in Florida, the townspeople in Sanford resented Jackie's presence in the camp. Controversy flared again when a spokesman for the chamber of commerce came to me and advised us to get out of town immediately.

When I told Jackie, he balked, saying he wasn't going to leave. Controversy again. I called Branch Rickey at his hotel and told him the problem. "Get Robinson out of this town immediately," he said. "We can't have any racial trouble now." We left with Robinson grumbling and protesting.

Robinson was making his Montreal bid as a shortstop. The regular shortstop was a French-Canadian and popular in the northland. When that was pointed out, Jackie said, "I don't care what he is, I intend to beat him out of the job because I believe I am better than he is." Controversy again. The French press fired its guns at Jackie for his "cockiness."

Wherever he went Jackie was in the midst of a racial controversy. After his first year at Montreal, where he was a sensation, and it became apparent that he was a cinch to play with the Dodgers, Dixie Walker asked to be traded. Even before that, during spring training in 1947, some Dodger players signed a petition against his eventual presence on the team.

And after the season started the St. Louis Cardinals threatened to strike rather than play against him.

He had a feud with manager Leo Durocher and never hesitated to shower an opposing pitcher he thought was throwing at him with a volley of obscenities. He slid into Roy Smalley of the Cubs here at Wrigley Field and they almost came to blows.

But through all this Jackie Robinson was always himself. He never backed down from a fight, never quit agitating for equality. He demanded respect, too. Those who tangled with him always admitted afterward that he was a man's man, a person who would not compromise his convictions.

In fact, in his last public appearance with death just around the corner, he was still fighting for his people and equality. Last week at the World Series, he threw out the first ball and thanked baseball for all it had done for him.

His final words were controversial. "I won't be satisfied," he told the capacity crowd and millions on television, "until I look over at the coach's box at third base and see a black manager there."

As I sat there and listened and watched, I just knew that Jackie Robinson was going to say something like that.

*Wendell was dying when he wrote this. Jackie and Wendell became estranged at some point after 1947. They eventually reconciled their differences. It was easy to respect Jackie Robinson. It was not always easy to like him. He was a man better equipped to handle the pressures of the big stage than the mundane and often trivial events of the average day in a common life. The last line in the column is telling. Wendell just knew that Jackie was going to say what he thought, not necessarily what people wanted to hear. That was the Jackie Wendell sometimes liked and always respected.*

*Wendell and Jackie were great men and for the most part good role models for the rest of us. But they were wrong to interrupt their friendship. It does not matter how significant the issue might have seemed to either at the time. In Willa Cather's short story "Two Friends" she writes of a beautiful friendship that was foolishly interrupted. Long after the participants had passed away, she observed: "When that old scar is occasionally touched by chance, it rouses the old uneasiness; the feeling of something broken that could have been mended; of something delightful that was senselessly wasted, of a truth that was accidentally distorted—one of the truths we want to keep"* (Obscure Destinies, p. 230).

*Jackie was 11 years old and living in Pasadena in 1931 when Cather wrote that while in Pasadena as well.*

# 4

# Foreign Affairs

*While following the Globetrotters through Mexico, Europe, and Russia, covering the Olympics in London, and traveling with Jackie Robinson through Latin America, Wendell saw the impact American foreign policy had on international relations. It would be difficult to separate the politics from sport when covering these events and Wendell did not pretend to do it. The Cold War is a constant theme. Wendell is consistently anti–Communist and usually pro–American, but he refuses to get boxed in on this issue. The Black Power movement, both domestically and internationally, is also a recurring topic. Wendell was an integrationist and was more interested in improving the lot of Black Americans in America than in establishing an international organization of Black people. That does not mean he was indifferent to discrimination against Black individuals outside of the United States. The reader will note that Wendell speaks out about the mistreatment of Blacks in England, Panama, and South Africa.*

*Foreign affairs discussed in the United States by Americans is often presented in binary terms. One is either "for us" or "against us." Wendell did not accept those limitations. His independence makes his views interesting and relevant more than 50 years after his passing. We are still struggling within this artificial binary perspective. America first? Global citizen?*

## *July 19, 1941*

### Smitty's Sports Spurts,
### *Pittsburgh Courier*, p. 16

Those of you who have joined the "All-Out for Britain" campaign may all be out on a limb before this war, presumably being waged for the preservation of democracy, in Europe is over. I understand that there are a great many of our darker-hued brethren digging down and dishing out for British relief because they believe that the English are fighting for the democratic way of life. The truth of the matter is that the British are fighting for their own way of life, and there is little of anything in that life for Negroes to try and preserve.

## The Martin Matter

Two weeks ago we reported the story of Tommy Martin, Negro heavyweight of England who has been denied the right to fight for the heavyweight championship of that "great and democratic" nation because he is a Negro. Despite the fact that Martin is the outstanding challenger for the title in England, the boxing lords refuse him the right to enter the ring with the champion. The only obvious reason is that they are afraid Martin, a black man, will rule the heavyweight throne of Britain.

Somewhere on the bloody battlefield of Europe Tommy Martin is fighting for the British and the British way of life. Any day he may die a horrible death, just as his father died recently in the line of duty. Martin is good enough to risk his life and his father good enough to die for the tricky, unscrupulous, treacherous, faithless English who are pleading with you to give them money, guns, ships and men, but neither Martin, nor his father, nor any of us black folk are good enough to wear the mythical crown symbolic of the heavyweight championship on our dusky brows.

## Another Story

And now comes another story of British deceit. Last week two of the greatest track stars in the United States were denied the right to sail with an American team to Jamaica, British West Indies because the officials of the British ship they were to sail on refused to grant them first class accommodations. All the white athletes were granted first class accommodations, but the two Negroes, John Borican and Barney Ewell, were denied this right. As a result, the two Negro stars were forced to stay home.

These two cases of British Negro-baiting are examples of the British attitude toward Negroes in general. The boxing game in England is under the supervision of the government and, of course, so are all ships flying the British flag on the high seas. If the English were so anxious to perpetuate democracy these incidents would not have happened. And, I wouldn't be forced to write this type of column this week.

Probably some people will ask if I would rather see the Nazis running things in Europe than the English. I can't say I would. The more I learn about the English, however, the more I hope this war will end in a deadlock with both sides just strong enough to lift their battered heads and lick the bleeding wounds they've inflicted upon each other.

*Keep in mind this was written four months before Pearl Harbor and long before Americans became aware of Nazi death camps. When the United States entered World War II, Black Americans faced the same issue. Why should a Black man die for a country that discriminates against him? Both England and the United States practiced hypocrisy and Wendell particularly disliked lofty statements coupled with unprincipled behavior. The Pittsburgh Courier adopted the Double V campaign. It did not view the struggle against totalitarianism abroad and discrimination at home as an either-or issue. Those battles could be waged simultaneously. Wendell harshly criticized England seven years later (as you will soon read), but he could tell the difference between an English hypocrite and a German Nazi.*

## January 10, 1948

### *Pittsburgh Courier, pp. 1, 4*

*"White" Problem, Not "Red," Held Cause of Panama's "No" to U.S.*

[EDITOR'S NOTE: Wendell Smith, author of the following article, is the sports editor of the *Pittsburgh Courier* and also a member of the sports staff of the *Chicago Herald-American*. His observations on the situation in Panama are authentic. Last year he went to Panama to cover the training camp activities of Jackie Robinson and the Brooklyn Dodgers. What he has written in the following article are true experiences.]

When the National Assembly of Panama voted 51 to 0 against the treaty providing for America to hold defense bases in that territory, a Senator stood up in the U.S. Congress and furiously denounced the legislators of the Latin-American country.

"I detect the Red hand of Moscow," he declared.

Since the war terminated it has become popular and "expedient" to smear and chastise any individual, group or country that fails to agree with the wishes, desires or ambitions of the American government.

But anyone who has been to Panama knows that it was not the "Red hand of Moscow" that influenced the National Assembly to cast a dissenting vote in the important matter. Instead it was the "White hand of the United States!"

Most Americans regard Panama as a small, isolated country in Central America.

In a sense that is true. But basically, Panama is the life line of this hemisphere, and because of its strategic position, one of the most influential small nations in the entire world.

The wave of anti–Americanism in Panama is not the result of diplomatic misunderstanding. Panamanians believe in capitalism, free enterprise, and everything else Americans regard as essential to "our way of life."

The real reason for discord, however, is racial discrimination and segregation. That is the issue. America's racial philosophy—"white is right"—or "white is might"—has created this most distasteful and irritating international problem.

The United States owns and controls the Panama Canal Zone. The word zone is exactly what it implies. It is a strip of land approximately ten miles wide and thirty miles long. The rest of the territory is a separate country in itself. It is a country whose inhabitants are essentially dark-skinned people. Their official language is Spanish and their views and attitudes are fundamentally Latin.

(Continued on Page 4, Col. 5)

END JIM CROW IN WASHINGTON

Any person, who is of Negro heritage or suspected of having Negro blood, suffers the same indignities, insults, humiliation and vicious restrictions that American Negroes experience in Mississippi when they are in the Canal Zone. The United States rules the Canal Zone just as the Rankinites operate Mississippi. Segregation and discrimination come first—democracy next!

Panamanians who live or work in the Zone, which is adjacent to the City of Panama, resent and deplore this segregation and discrimination.

On the other hand, the Americans assume an air of superiority ... treat the citizens of Panama like a master lords it over his chattel ... and never let them forget that while he is a visitor in the country, he can if he so desires, choke him to death with very little effort.

Consequently, Panamanians detest anything and everything remotely connected with the United States.

They hate discrimination!

They hate segregation!

They hate racial bias!

And they hate any one, or anybody who fosters it!

The only logical conclusion then is—they hate the United States!

Ambassadors, diplomats and men of State will, of course, deny that. They will, for diplomatic reasons tell you that "the people of Panama love the people of the United States."

But to learn the truth all you have to do is visit Panama. Walk down any street and ask any one you meet what they think of the "Good Neighbor Policy" and they'll go into convulsions laughing.

The Good Neighbor policy—publicized with intensity here—is a joke throughout South America and especially in Panama.

Ten months ago I was in Panama. I went there with Jackie Robinson and the Brooklyn Dodgers. While my major assignment was to cover the baseball fortunes of Robinson, I spent the majority of the time talking to the people about the United States Government.

I visited the Canal Zone. I saw the despicable "Gold" and "Silver" system. When I crossed the line from Panama City and went into the American territory, I automatically became "Silver." I glistened with inferiority. I went into the "Silver" wash rooms. I was only eligible to ride the "Silver" buses, attend the "Silver" schools, drink out of the "Silver" fountains and act as an humble "Silver" person!

I went to the biggest hotel there with Jackie Robinson to see Branch Rickey, owner of the Brooklyn Dodgers. We had an breakfast engagement. But we never had the privilege of enjoying such a repast.

Jackie Robinson and I were barred from eating in the dining room!

White Americans were "Gold" and human beings. They could do anything!

The dividing line between the Zone and Panama City is a railroad track. When you cross that track with a black face you automatically walk from Paradise into Mississippi!

There is no difference.

And, because the natives of Panama are generally of a swarthy color and definitely show strains of Negro blood there is constant tension. Thousands upon thousands of Panamanians are of Negro extraction. They range from black to white in color.

That is why there is so much anti–Americanism in Panama. That is probably the major reason the National Assembly voted against the United States keeping those important bases. The only way Panamanians can retaliate is by denying the United States something which is vitally important. Those bases are important!

Black Panamanians, brown Panamanians, yellow, beige, and white Panamanians are in the National Assembly. They unanimously voted against the United States. It was a protest vote against exploitation, racial discrimination and "white supremacy."

END JIM CROW IN WASHINGTON

*Not much about sports in this one. The United States government views the problem as being Panama's lack of support of U.S. government policy ... hence pro–Communist. Wendell sees the problem as being a racist U.S. government policy in Panama. Wendell rejects the binary straight jacket. This is a rare example of Wendell writing about discrimination he suffered. It is essential to the story and is included for that reason. The END JIM CROW lines were not part of Wendell's column. They were placed there by the*

Courier *and appeared often. There were also reminders to share the* Courier *with open-minded white people. H.L. Mencken, a well-known (and white) Baltimore Sun journalist, was a* Courier *subscriber. Most of the readership was Black, but there were regular white readers as well.*

## April 10, 1948

### Sports Beat, *Pittsburgh Courier,* p. 13

> "My Country 'tis of Thee
> Sweet Land of Liberty
> Of Thee I Sing…"

Miami, Fla.—The great battle for the preservation of democracy is now raging on all fronts and with particular intensity in countries to the south of the United States. The hairy claw of the Russian Bear has left the fatal marks on many of the pale, starving faces and there is every reason to believe it considers South/Central America a vulnerable spot in which to hibernate in the future.

We have just returned from the Dominican Republic with the Brooklyn Dodgers and have witnessed the technique the American Government is employing to combat the Red advance. The most common medium used by the United States, as we saw it, is the radio. Throughout the day programs are being beamed by the United States selling the virtues of the "last great Democracy" in the world today. These Government-sponsored radio programs were actually "sales talks" to the people of Latin America, hailing the virtues of the United States and its version of democracy. "This is the land of the free," the American announcers said in substance, "and the only true democracy left in the world today."

"'It is here,' the well-trained announcers told Latin-Americans, that life, liberty and the pursuit of democracy is not only a dream, but a reality. This is the country where every man owns the right to go where he wishes and work at the job he likes best."

Now, we don't know just how effective these programs are. We don't know whether or not they're worth the time and effort it takes to put them on the air. It does seem, however, that somebody is putting the cart before the horse. It seems to us that the programs should be reversed and we Americans should be listening to democratic talks from Latin America. Actually, we are more in need of such talks than the liberal and friendly people of Latin America.

We think, too, that we're only fooling ourselves when we fill the air with reports of flowing opportunities for all people in this land of the free. We believe that democracy is truly the best form of government and should be protected and preserved at any cost. But when we try to convince the Latins we are practicing true democracy here, we are only being asinine, because they know our boasts are nothing but outright falsehoods. The swarthy Latins know all about our discrimination and segregation policies; all about our lynchings and all about the denial of civil rights to one-tenth of the population.

They know—and won't hesitate to tell you—that the likes of Jackie Robinson are second-class citizens in the United States. They know that he enjoys more civil rights on Latin soil than he does at home; that he does not have to ride in the back of the bus or that of the train in their countries.... And they know, too, that his child can only get an equal education with other children in certain sections of his homeland. They know that when he travels with the Brooklyn ball club there are certain places he can't stay, certain places he can't eat and places where he can't even attempt to drink out of the same water fountains. They know that his life has been regimented ... that he must walk through doors marked "colored," live in neighborhoods marked "colored"... that his wife and mother must sit in "colored" sections at ball games if they want to see him play ... and they point out with a smirk on their faces that there are even churches—temples of God—where he cannot go and worship.

If you are in a Latin country and hear the American-beamed programs you are sure that the United States is a paradise for one and all. But when you get off the plane upon your return and slapped in the face with "colored" and "white" signs every place it is then you realize that something is wrong ... and it's not in Denmark!

Robinson and the rest of us are now back home. We've returned to this place we heard the American radio announcers speak of with deep affection when we were in the Dominican Republic last week. We left a land poor in resources but rich in democratic traditions and are now here in the "Sunny South," allegedly a part of the land where all men are free and equal.... At least that's what we heard over the radio in the Dominican Republic.

Is That Freedom?...

Where are that freedom and equality?

Is this the place they said exists as the last great bulwark of democracy?

If so then democracy is definitely half-dead, sickly and woefully weak. And, what inhuman beast—what vulture, if you please—has feasted upon the once strong and clean body of democracy and left it in a helpless state?

The answer is obvious. It is the men and women in this country who nail up the segregated signs, who mark off the separate doors to public buildings, who mob and lynch Negroes, who preach democracy but refuse to practice it ... and who worship the Almighty in pews marked "white only."

Let's not, in our desperation, heap the blame on those who are with the Russians. For their creeds and their ideas are inconsistent and absurd. They, too, are trying to deceive the Latin-Americans and all the others.... While we use "white" and "colored" signs in denying helpless people their rights, they use fodder and the cannon. If there is any mercy in our method it might be that ours is just a bit slower. But—the outcome is just as unbearable.

Communism can only survive on blood and thunder, on deceit and atheism. Democracy, on the other hand, is the offspring of liberty, freedom and equality. The Reds are feeding communism the evil foods it requires, but we are starving democracy.

So—let's quit kidding ourselves before it's too late. Let's quit sending such absurd radio programs to other people around the world and practice some democracy. For people all over the world America—the last great "bulwark of democracy" is terribly weak.... There are people who aren't concerned about saving anything so weak.

Let's take down those signs of color so that all Americans can ride the bus and the train as they please ... go where they want ... and enjoy a true democracy. In the meantime, why not have the Latin-Americans who believe in democracy beam some of the programs over here? Let them tell us how they make it work.

> "My Country 'tis of Thee
> Sweet Land of Liberty
> Of Thee I sing…" (Disgustedly)

*Only a patriot could write this column. He is furious at the contradiction between what he sees as America's promise and America's policy. Again, it is hypocrisy. This is the harsher version of "Come on, America, we're better than this." Wendell goes a bit too far, however, in asserting that America has much to learn from Latin American democracy. The track record of democracy in that region does not support Wendell's contention.*

## August 14, 1948

### Pittsburgh Courier, p. 7

*Fifty Negroes Arrested British Police Smash Riots*

Liverpool—Police here were mobilized at full strength last week with orders to smash racial riots which flared for four days and terrorized people living on the fringe of the city's "Little Harlem."

The rioting was between Negro and white seamen and it was necessary for mobile units equipped with radio and assisted by reserve forces to launch a major clean-up drive.

According to *The Daily Graphic,* "trouble raged between gangs of Negroes and a section of irresponsible white men and women."

## Fifty Arrested

More than fifty Negro men were arrested and charged with taking part in disorders. It was alleged that they carried swords, axes, daggers, clubs and broken bottles.

The chief constable of Liverpool, C.C. Martin, said, all the resources of the police service in the city were used to stamp out the disorders.

The *Manchester Guardian* reported: "Negroes were alleged to have attacked and stoned a number of white men who were walking peacefully along a road. Police officers were stoned, allegedly, and had bottles thrown at them from the windows of a Negro club where the windows were stacked with empty beer bottles for use as ammunition."

Bail was refused in cases where men were charged with being in possession of offensive weapons on the grounds that feeling was "running high" in the south end of the city between Negroes and whites, and there was a "grave danger of worse things happening" if the accused were allowed bail.

Among those arrested was Elsie Pink, a white woman, who was held for a week on a charge of disorderly conduct, and a Negro, Peter Dick, for disorderly conduct and being armed with a dagger.

Police charged that he was accompanied by four other Negroes and shouting: "We'll kill all white men in the streets of Liverpool."

Meantime, the English press has been giving considerable space to the case of Nat (King) Cole and the trouble he is having in Los Angeles getting into his new home.

*In 1948 Nat King Cole purchased a home in Hancock Park, a segregated and exclusive neighborhood in Los Angeles. The Klan burned a cross in his yard and the homeowners association informed him they did not want undesirables in the community. Cole agreed to let them know if he became aware of any undesirables moving into the neighborhood. Wendell reminds the English press that racism is alive and well in their homeland too. Those who live in glass houses...*

# November 7, 1953

## Sports Beat, *Pittsburgh Courier,* p. 14

*A Commie Paper Weeps for the "Poor Blacks"...*

The game of basketball, as played by the incredible Harlem Globetrotters, is a side-splitting, laugh-provoking piece of entertainment. But with all that, and despite the fact that the performers of this zealous band of basket-snipers are the best paid in the business, the owner of the team, Abe Saperstein, is a slave driver.

That, at least, is what the Communist newspaper, *L'Equipe*, in Paris calls him.

Following their recent appearance in Gay Paree this newspaper, which devotes its columns to sports, frankly admitted that the Globetrotters are no less than marvelous when it comes to basketball technique.

But it abhors the fact that the players on the team must sell their talent "for the profit of vile slave drivers, like M. Saperstein."

The writer of this amusing piece of Red propaganda constantly refers to the members of the Globetrotters as "The Blacks," or "The Basketeers Black," and displays great remorse over the fact that they operated under the lash of a "vile slave trader."

Those of us who do not have the time nor disposition, to concentrate on the international intrigue of the "Comrades," leaving such to better informed journalists, like George Schuyler and others, can detect in this so-called sports article the desperate frustrations of the Reds as they spread their venom and poison across the faces of Europe and the Orient.

Actually, a man with the capabilities of M. Saperstein needs no one to come to his defense. He stands on his twenty-seven-year record, and the salaries he pays out to "The Blacks" substantiate the fact that they are the best-paid in the business. There isn't a basketball team in the world, including the Minneapolis Lakers, whose payroll equals that of the Globetrotters. It is the highest paid basketball aggregation in the world, barring none.

## $40,000 Is Good Money for a "Slave"...

But the Reds portray M. Saperstein as a modern version of Simon Legree, an overseer who sports an over-sized plantation hat and holds in one hand a frosty glass containing a mint julep, and in the other a long, black whip, which he brings down on the weary backs of "The Blacks" at the slightest provocation. They are, in other words, nothing more than slaves whose talents are exploited by a vicious, greedy capitalist.

If the Reds wanted the authentic story about these "poor, downtrodden Blacks," all they had to do was to interview the players on the team when they were in Paris.

They could have asked Goose Tatum, for example, how he lives and survives as a member of the Globetrotters. His answer would have been something like this:

"I'm doing pretty good for what you people call a slave. I play less than forty minutes of basketball a night. My salary is better than $40,000 a year, which is more than most athletes make, including baseball players, and, also, much more than the ordinary businessman.

"I am not compelled to play basketball for M. Saperstein. I could play for other teams in professional basketball. But if I did, I couldn't make as much money as I do now.

"I make more money, for example, than George Mikan, who was voted the greatest player of the past fifty years. I also make more than such outstanding players as Andy Phillip, Bob Cousy, Jim Pollard and others who are college-trained and, as a result, must be paid well because they are equipped to do other things beside play basketball. If I wanted to I could play baseball, rather than basketball. But I wouldn't make as much money. As a basketball player, for example, I make more money than Roy Campanella, Mickey Mantle, Billy Martin, Larry Doby and other ball players in the top salary bracket."

## *They Travel All Over the World for Free...*

The Reds would prefer not to accept Tatum's word, of course, because it would be absurd to point out that here was a slave pulling down $40,000 a year.

But they could ask the captain of the team, Marques Haynes, one of the few "slaves" in history who has the distinction of owning a college degree. A graduate of Langston University, Haynes' salary is in the neighborhood of $30,000. It is probably above that figure. What, the Reds might ask, is a college graduate doing on a traveling professional team? His answer would, no doubt, be something like this:

"I have a degree to teach, but the salary I get playing basketball is four times as much as a teacher would get.

"Not only that, but as a member of this team I have traveled all over the world, to England, France, Italy, Belgium, Egypt, North Africa, Turkey, Greece, Brazil and many other places.

"These experiences have furthered my education. When I do quit playing basketball, I will be even better prepared to teach. We have other college men on the team and they feel the same way I do.

"We travel in the best style. We stay in the best hotels, get the best food and come in contact with the best people. And best of all, I get paid while all this is going on."

Granted that there are a lot of things wrong in the United States, particularly from a racial standpoint. There is still too much discrimination, segregation and bias. But the Harlem Globetrotters cannot be included among them. That organization must be listed on the credit side of the book.

Certainly no one can say that men whose salaries range from $5,000 to $40,000 a year for bouncing a basketball up and down the floor can be classified as slaves, nor can the man who pays them be guilty of slave-driving.

*Wendell and Abe Saperstein were close friends. Wendell's wife, Wyonella, worked for Saperstein. Wendell had access to the Globetrotter players anytime he wanted to interview them. So why would he write what they would say "if" they were asked? He could ask them and get a direct quotation. Ben Green in his book* Spinning the Globe *might have the answer. On page 253 Green writes that Marques Haynes quit the Globetrotters on October 31, 1953. Wendell's column appeared a week later. Perhaps Saperstein did not want Haynes' departure to be publicized. I do not know whether Wendell knowingly misrepresented the truth for Saperstein's benefit or made little effort to discover it in the dispute between Haynes and his friend. Goose Tatum too eventually left the Trotters in 1957. The Globetrotters were well paid and had jobs that most Americans would have envied. Characterizing them as slaves, as did the French newspaper, was ridiculous. However, putting words in players' mouths that misrepresent their opinions is not sound journalism.*

## July 25, 1959

### Sports Beat, *Pittsburgh Courier*, p. 25

Moscow—It takes more than a little bit to make a glum Russian laugh, even grin, but the Harlem Globetrotters have been rolling 'em in the aisles since they arrived here last week. Since Abe Saperstein's zany crew of basketeers came rollicking into this gigantic city behind the Iron Curtain, the crucial international situation has really become ticklish. Folks who haven't laughed here since the revolution are splitting their sides over the antics of such cage clowns as Meadowlark Lemon, Tex Harrison and the other Trotters teasers.

Everyone here, of course, gazes up at Wilt (The Stilt) Chamberlain, the seven-foot giant who first won fame and basketball glory at the University of Kansas, with a look of bewilderment on their faces.

Russians have seen big men like him before, but none so agile and nimble. He can move, this big boy, and he does so with an easy grace.

In the first game, against the San Francisco Chinese, Wilt dunked in 33 points with ridiculous ease. Naturally, the Globetrotters won. After the game, the fans swarmed around the tall, friendly Chamberlain, pleading for autographs.

The Russians appreciate his skills. They know basketball and admire an outstanding performer. Their team was second to the United States in the last Olympics, and there are some seasoned observers predicting that the Reds will cop it all next year in Rome.

The Russians would like nothing better than to beat the United States at its own game in the '60 Olympics. It would serve as excellent propaganda material to feed Asia and Africa, two theaters the Reds are now trying to bring within their sphere of influence.

Radio Moscow, for example, beams its programs to those areas daily. On the day the Globetrotters arrived here (July 6), Radio Moscow representatives were among the first to greet them at the airport.

"We want to interview Chamberlain and some of the other Globetrotters for a program we're beaming to Africa," a spokesman for Radio Moscow said.

Why Africa? Why not countries like Sweden, Denmark or perhaps Poland? The answer to the question was obvious. "We have nothing particularly in common with Africa, other than color," Clarence Wilson, captain of the Globetrotters, informed the man from Radio Moscow. "We're Americans in every sense of the word. We don't like the idea of you people trying to use us as propaganda pawns just because we happen to look like the people you are trying to win from the West."

Later, some of the Trotters did submit to an interview, but, in retrospect, it was not the most sensational Radio Moscow ever offered. The boys didn't echo the "party line."

Generally, however, the Globetrotters have been treated royally here. The Russians have gone out of their way to make their stay a pleasant one. This is the first all-Negro sports organization ever to perform in Moscow.

The team is quartered at the Ukraine Hotel, one of the newest here. Crowds follow the players down the streets and mobs gather in front of the stores and restaurants they patronize.

It is all very interesting and a little intriguing, too. The Russians trust them … but just so far. There is always someone making sure they go to the right places at the right time. There is something here the Russians don't want us to see. We haven't been able to figure out what it is.

There is one thing we definitely have not seen … other Negroes. There may be some here, but where they live and what they do remain a mystery. An African student turns up now and then in the hotel lobby, but, like we said before, we have nothing in common and, therefore, do not converse.

Converse?… Did you ever try to communicate with a Russian-speaking African? It's really a wild, crazy experience.

Meanwhile, the Globetrotters go their merry way … winning Russian friends and basketball games at the same time.

*Wendell reasserts his anti–Communist position. He also has no use for*

*Black internationalism. He sees it as a distraction from focusing on improving the status of Black Americans in America. He uses direct quotes in this column which would imply he is not telling us what the Globetrotters would have said if asked; these are their responses to questions that were asked. In another piece on Russia, Wendell describes Premier Khrushchev making an impromptu visit on a public street with the Globetrotters. It reminds us how popular the Trotters were. Khrushchev wanted to be seen with them.*

## May 12, 1962

### Sports Beat, *Pittsburgh Courier*, p. 45

*Big Bill Russell Sees Africa as Land of Hope*

Boston—They now call this area the Land of the Bean, the Cod, and Bill Russell.

The best defensive basketball player in the world, Big Bill recently led the Boston Celtics to their fifth title in six years. Before he came here from San Francisco, the Celtics had never won a championship. So everywhere in Boston you hear people paying homage to the goateed 6ft. 10in. strong man of professional basketball. Not even Ted Williams in his greatest baseball days was more popular.

Russell could settle down here for the rest of his life and live in comfort if he cared to. But Big Bill is getting ready to shake the dust of Boston from his shoes. He is an enterprising young man. He has decided that his future is in Africa, the land of his forefathers, and that is where he plans to eventually cast his lot.

He now lives in Reading, Mass., a suburb of Boston, with his wife, Rose, and their three children. Why is Bill giving up the comforts and fame he enjoys in this prosperous country for what may prove to be a perilous existence in distant Africa?

He wasn't home to answer the question but Mrs. Russell, a native of Austin, Tex., voluntarily gave us the reason.

"Bill became interested in Africa," she explained, "about three years ago. He went to Liberia on a State Department good will tour and what he saw opened his eyes. He saw opportunity there, a fine future for any young man who is willing to sacrifice and work."

When Bill returned home his mind was made up and his future was clearly before him. Not long after, he acquired a half interest in a rubber farm in the District of Salala, situated approximately 40 miles from Monrovia, the capital of Liberia.

Two years ago he took Mrs. Russell with him to Liberia. She liked what she saw too. What about living there?

"When Bill quits basketball in a few years," she answered, "we expect to make our home there. We'll take our three children (Bill Jr., 4; Jacob, 3, and Karen, three months old) with us. We'll build a home in Liberia and probably spend the rest of our lives there."

Like her husband, Mrs. Russell is fascinated by the new awakening they witnessed in Africa. It truly is the world's new frontier, she said, and they both want to participate in its exciting surge toward freedom and independence.

They realize that it is not going to be easy to forge a new destiny in a land so drastically different from the United States in customs and culture. But, like the fearless pioneers who opened up this country, Bill and Rose Russell happen to be the type of rugged individuals who can endure any type of hardship and eventually reach their goal.

They both were inspired by the progressive spirit which has inflamed all of Africa.

"The changes that are taking place there," said Mrs. Russell, "intrigued us. The most stimulating aspect of this new life in Africa was the feeling of complete freedom.

"There were no restrictions, no ugly racial complications, no segregation nor discrimination. It was like taking your coat off on a real hot day—We felt cool and comfortable, completely at ease for the first time in our lives.

"We experienced a feeling of great pride when we saw black men administering justice in the courts, others holding the highest positions in the government, and still others conducting major business enterprises successfully. We were proud of those people and decided we wanted to be a part of them and to live with them."

There, in essence, are the reasons why Bill Russell and his wife decided that their future is in Africa. They discovered complete freedom there … a rare, precious commodity in this turbulent world these days.

*As mentioned previously, Wendell did not share Bill Russell's feelings toward living in Africa. But he respected Bill Russell. He reports Russell's views and acknowledges that the world is a turbulent one. Russell remained in the United States, though. Intelligent individuals can disagree civilly.*

## April 27, 1963

### Sports Beat, *Pittsburgh Courier,* p. 11

*Union of South Africa Bars Door to Harlem Globetrotters*

The Harlem Globetrotters, who have played in every state in the Union and some 80 other countries across the world, have finally discovered a country where they cannot perform.

The country is that hell-hole of bigotry, prejudice and white supremacy ... the Union of South Africa.

Abe Saperstein, the owner of this most famous and beloved basketball aggregation, has been officially informed that he cannot take his magnificent quintet to the land of apartheid, which is a polite way of saying "white only" in that land of ignorance and cruelty.

South Africa is the country where a comparative handful of whites keep millions of black natives enslaved. It is a land of white greed, viciousness and intolerance. It is even worse than Ross Barnett's Mississippi.

Yet, it is a land that the United States and other so-called democracies willingly accept as a member of the "free world" we hear so much about.

In sports, for example, there is no loud cry to keep South Africa out of the Olympics. South Africa will have a team in Tokyo next year, even though it is a nation that still practices slavery and keeps the majority of its inhabitants in chains.

Saperstein's teams have played all over the world. This year, for example, the Globetrotters will invade the Iron Curtain again, playing in Poland and other Communist countries. A few years ago they invaded Russia and played ten games in Moscow.

Saperstein, who takes pride in the fact that the Globetrotters have won friends and represented the United States admirably every place they have visited, made a gallant, but futile, effort recently to penetrate South Africa.

He wrote to the Minister of Interior requesting permission to take the Globetrotters on tour through the Union of South Africa. The following is the reply he received:

"I write to acknowledge receipt of your letters dated 7th January, 1963, and 25th February, 1963, addressed to the Honorable Minister of the Interior in regard to a proposed visit to South Africa by the Harlem Globetrotters basketball team, and regret to inform you that the Department is unable to approve of the visit."

The reply was signed by the "Secretary for the Interior." The reason for refusing the Globetrotters permission is obvious. The natives in this hell-hole might see Saperstein's Team perform and get the idea that there are talented black people in the world after all.

"Sometimes it makes you wonder," Saperstein told us the other day. "The Globetrotters have been all over the world and nobody has regretted seeing them perform.

"We have played in Russia and other places behind the Iron Curtain, but when we try to enter the Union of South Africa, which is considered an ally of the democracies, we are barred.

"They have refused us permission to visit South Africa because they cannot afford to let the natives of the country see how much American Negroes have accomplished. They are afraid of such exposure."

Yet in countries where people are supposed to be denied the freedoms of which the West boasts so proudly, the Globetrotters are welcomed and permitted to demonstrate their basketball skills.

"We never get politically involved when we travel around the world," Saperstein explained. "All we do is play basketball, entertain the fans and then pack up and leave. We don't wave the American flag nor try to convince the people in the countries we visit that our way of life is better than that under which they live. It is none of our business how they live."

Well, this much is certain: The officials of the Union of South Africa are going to make sure that the Globetrotters do not have an opportunity to see how the black people there live. It is a country of hate ... and people who hate as the white South African does cannot afford to let others see how inhuman it is to other humans.

The whites in the Union of South Africa do not want the world to know, or see, how they perpetuate slavery, how they kill thousands of human beings each year with their brutality.... Not even Adolf Hitler and his crazed Nazis were as inhuman as the whites of South Africa.

Hitler and his henchmen killed six million Jews. The "Christian" whites of South Africa have killed that many black people without flinching. It's a game with them. It's great fun for them!

Upon thinking it over, perhaps the Globetrotters are lucky. Why take a chance with the murder-loving beasts of South Africa?

*Wendell refuses to see this in Cold War terms. South Africa was a U.S. ally. He views them as worse than the Soviet enemy. The enemy of an enemy is not necessarily a friend.*

## July 27, 1963

### Sports Beat, *Pittsburgh Courier*, p. 15

*Confiscation of Minoso's Nest Egg by Castro
Ends Retirement Dreams*

Minnie Minoso, the aging outfielder, has had better days in his time. He is now with the Washington Senators ... and that is as low as you can get in the American League. He is not playing regularly ... and the inactivity makes him feel that he's the low man on baseball's totem pole. And then—on top of that—there's Fidel Castro of Cuba...

"I've had a hard time getting back in the groove," Minnie admitted, putting on his Washington uniform in the Senators' clubhouse. "I was hurt last season and played in only 39 games. Since then, I've been trying to get back in the swing of things."

Over the years, Minnie has been one of the most colorful players in the majors. Ten years ago, Frank Lane called him "the most exciting player in the major leagues." That was when Lane was general manager of the White Sox and rebuilding the club. Frank Lured Minnie away from Cleveland. The first time he ever batted for the White Sox, the dashing Cuban clouted a long home run into the centerfield bullpen at Comiskey Park. From that day on, Minnie was a Chicago favorite. The fans liked his spirit and enthusiasm. Lane, a colorful character himself, affectionately referred to his dark outfielder as "My Cuban Son."

The time came when Lane pulled stakes and moved elsewhere, taking over at Cleveland and St. Louis. Minoso also went to St. Louis, but his "papa" was out of baseball when he arrived.

The White Sox traded him to the Cardinals for Joe Cunningham in the winter of '62. Minoso, playing with typical enthusiasm and hustle, got off to a good start, but soon after the season started was sidelined when he was hit on the right wrist with a pitch. When he returned to the lineup sometime later, he crashed into a wall, suffered a concussion and was no good to the team for the rest of the season. This year the Cardinals sent him to Washington.

"I'm sure I'll find myself," Minnie said with a note of determination in his voice. "It's just a matter of time. I'll hit if I can get in enough games."

Minoso is an itchy man on the bench. He wants to play every day. "I go crazy watching the others play," he said. "I want to get into the ball game."

When Minnie's wishes were conveyed to Manager Gil Hodges, who recently took the Senators' reins, he said:

"I want to use Minnie as much as possible. When I took over the club three weeks ago, he wasn't taking his customary good swing at the ball. He was merely waving at it. At first I thought perhaps the wrist he injured was bothering him but he assured me it wasn't. During the past four or five days, he has been swinging good, like he did in Chicago. So I guess I'll be using him quite a bit.

"I know how he feels about sitting on the bench. He hates it. That is one of the reasons Minnie is an asset to a club. He has plenty of competitive spirit, he gives a club added desire. That spirit is one of the reasons he's still in the major leagues. After all, Minnie is no kid. He's 41 years old, maybe a little more. But he plays like a teen-ager and that enthusiasm is the secret of his success. I'm sure he can help this club as soon as he finds himself and gets a chance to play more."

Although he admits he has slowed down the past few years, Minoso isn't thinking about quitting baseball. Over the years he has made big money. The White Sox paid him in the neighborhood of $50,000. Owner August Busch of the Cardinals paid him well, too. But most of his savings have disappeared. He must keep playing, even if he eventually has to go to the minors, or to Japan.

Blame that unfortunate condition on Castro…

"When Castro took over Cuba," Minnie explained forlornly, "I owned considerable real estate in Havana. I had invested most of my baseball earnings in property. I owned two large apartment buildings and some other property. I figured I was set for life, that after my baseball days I'd go back home and live the life of a gentleman.

"But Castro confiscated all that property, as well as the money I had in the bank. That happened to a lot of Cubans. He just took money and property as he pleased. That's why I must keep playing ball now. I don't mean that I'm completely broke, but I no longer can count on taking it easy. I must work, practically start my life all over again. I have lost much since Castro became the dictator of my homeland."

That's the way things are today with Minnie Minoso. At a time when he should be ready to retire with a full pot, the genial, personable performer must start all over again … saving and skimping for the future.

There have been better days … and better times … in the life of Minnie Minoso.

*Wendell focuses on the cost of Communism to an athlete he knows and likes. It is more than the conventional Cold War struggle. It is personal.*

## December 3, 1972

### Tuesday at Home Magazine, "Should the Olympic Games Be Continued," pp. 269–275

By Wendell Smith, Guest Editorial

[EDITOR'S NOTE: The author, who began his writing career with the *Pittsburgh Courier*, has been a sports journalist for over 30 years. He is well-known for his television commentary in Chicago, where he also writes a column for the *Sun-Times*. (*Tuesday Magazine*/December 1972)]

The Olympic Games are nothing less than an international athletic orgy in which the participating nations attempt to subdue each other under the guise of unswerving love and romanticism.

And among those who throw this Roman holiday every four years, the sponsors of the United States team have clearly demonstrated that they are the most perverse of those who attend the parties. The batch of stuffy old men comprising the U.S. Olympic Committee have, for years, capitalized on the vulnerability, innocence and immaturity of American athletes, leading them astray with the swaggering arrogance akin to that of a high-level wheeler-dealer who knows his crimes will be winked at by the authorities.

The promise of a piece of gold, a big party and a lot of fun is the lure the committee uses to hook and catch its athletes, who snap at the bait for the reason that they are hungry for glory. But the gold—a medal to hang around your neck, if you win—does not necessarily glitter, and the big parties and fun usually are merely yawning sessions of utter boredom. When reality finally does strike home, the exploited athlete discovers that he has been had and that he is the victim of a ruthless mob of paunchy, egotistical Olympic committee politicians who control his destiny with despotic fervor.

Has anyone ever heard of an Olympic committee member being chastised and penalized before the world for his indiscretions, his collusive deals with commercial interests or under-the-table pacts guaranteed to benefit his own selfish interests?

It hasn't yet happened, has it?

On the other hand, athletes have suffered punitive action for failing to stand at attention during ceremonies, for breaking the curfew rule, for exhibiting a raised fist, for speaking truthfully when it is contrary to the arbitrary philosophy of the committee.

It is unfortunate that both the International Olympic Committee and the United States Olympic Committee are composed of bitter old men who have failed to keep pace with the times. The IOC, for example, banished for life Vince Matthews and Wayne Collett of the U.S. team. They finished one-two in the 400 meters and then committed the "unpardonable sin" of chatting and fidgeting on the victors' stand as the Star-Spangled Banner was played. This, said the IOC, was a demonstration of gross disrespect.

The two athletes claimed that they could not concentrate on the ceremony because the situation did not ring true to them. "We weren't protesting," said Collett. "We were merely going about our business. Which is what Whites do, go about their business without thinking of Blacks."

But the IOC banished them from Olympic competition forever, with hardly a defensive whisper in behalf of the American athletes from the U.S. committee.

There were similar attitudes demonstrated by Black athletes four years previously in Mexico. The raised-fist incident, symbolic of Black power, stunned Olympic officials, but no such drastic action was taken as in Munich.

It is highly significant, however, that every American team has shown similar and official disrespect to Olympic host nations since 1908. But the IOC would not dare banish the United States team, even though it has embarrassed kings, queens, presidents and even dictators at each Olympic ceremony.

It is traditional for each nation to salute the host dignitary sitting in the stands at the opening ceremony by dipping its flag during the march into the arena or stadium. This is a gesture of courtesy and goodwill. However, the flag-bearers for the U.S. team have refused to dip the American stars and stripes. This year Olga Connolly was the U.S. flag-bearer. She led the American team into the stadium, proudly marching to the strains of "When the Saints Go Marching In." And, as had the bearers before her, Olga Connolly carried the American flag past President Gustav Heinemann of Germany without so much as a hint of a dip, striding past him as though he were not present.

This international insult has been perpetuated since 1908 with the unofficial sanction of the U.S. Olympic Committee. No individual has ever been reprimanded for this posture. If two athletes can be banished from the Games for fidgeting under their own flag, why is it that no action has been taken for an insult of international proportions by an entire team?

The USOC has not taken some kind of action because, obviously, it has approved such blatant behavior. American officials were "shocked" over the blasé actions of Collett and Matthews on the victors' stand but have remained calm, cool and undisturbed as America's flag-bearers and marchers have insulted the leaders of every host nation for 65 years. So why get excited and shocked then when our own athletes have, from time-to-time, elected to quietly cast a reflection on some of the inequities and humiliations they are subjected to at home?

The "shock" experienced when Black athletes indicate their dissatisfaction exposes a pricked conscience and evokes screams of indignation. The image of goodness the official committee seeks to portray to the rest of the world is exposed. The retaliation is in the form of punishment and the USOC snaps the whip.

The lack of propriety and respect for the 11 Israelis who were kidnapped in the Olympic village and assassinated was dramatically illustrated when Avery Brundage, the American president of the IOC, insisted that the Games continue the day following the tragedy. While many people recoiled at the prospects of sports as usual, Brundage called upon his archaic old men's club to give the resumption of the Games their blessings.

The service for the dead was transformed into an unsettling rally with 80,000 spectators encouraged to approve Brundage's declaration that the Games "must go on."

And in his speech Brundage had the audacity to equate the massacre of the Israeli's with his own setback concerning the Rhodesian team's ouster from the Games because of that country's vicious racial policies. Brundage called the Rhodesia incident "political blackmail." He said the Olympics had been subjected to "two savage attacks." He was bitter because racist Rhodesia had been barred (against his wish to have it participate) and riled because the assassinations had marred the alleged "purity" of the Olympics.

The raw insensitivity of Brundage and other officials ruined the XX Olympiad. The callousness seeped on down through the ranks of the athletes and created incidents and wounds that will never heal.

This was particularly true as far as the Americans were concerned. Not one American athlete came away from the Games satisfied that he had participated in an immaculate event, one which he could refer to in later years with pride. Not even Mark Spitz, who won seven gold medals in swimming. The assassinations sent him scurrying home with a bitter taste. Blood had tarnished his medals and his memories.

The administration of the American teams by its irresponsible chaperon and supervisor staff was disgraceful.

Two U.S. athletes were banished from the Olympics for their alleged bad manners, another had his medal taken away because a U.S. team physician didn't bother to file papers on this athlete's use, for chronic asthma condition, of a "banned" medication. The top two U.S. sprinters were late to the mark and automatically disqualified because of an error by their coach. The reaction of the U.S. Olympic guardians and supervisors over these disasters and reversals was so unsportsmanlike that other nations viewed the Americans as grotesque, whimpering crybabies. So much so, in fact, that when the American team had legitimate protests, like in the case of the much-publicized basketball incident, they found no sympathy, no friends to defend them.

Even our own athletes responded with disdain. Commenting on the inefficiency of the U.S. officials, one American athlete protested, "When you wanted a manager or trainer, you couldn't find them. Their services were just not available. They left us completely on our own. We had to make our own arrangements. When you needed them they were gone somewhere."

These are facts the U.S. public should be aware of, because it was the American public who dug deep into their pockets to raise the $10 million necessary to send the athletes, coaches, trainers and managers to Munich. The U.S. party included 168 coaches, trainers and managers. They were in charge of 447 athletes. That would seem staff enough to do the job properly. It wasn't, however, because so many of the supervisory staff shunned their responsibilities.

The most graphic example, of course, of utter procrastination on the part of an American who failed in his duties was that of track coach Stan Wright, a sincere and dedicated man, but one who lost the right time.

Wright misinformed sprinters Eddie Hart, Ray Robinson and Robert Taylor of the starting time for the semi-final heat of the 100-meter dash. Considered among the top three favorites to win the event, Hart and Robinson, the co-world record holders, were automatically disqualified because of their tardiness (Taylor barely showed up in time to qualify), and watched from the stands as Russia's Valery Borzov won the gold medal.

Stan Wright's main responsibility was to get the athletes to the track on time. That's what he was paid for. He was duly censored and severely criticized for his transgression, thrashed in the press and virtually crucified by American athletes and officials.

The most vicious lashing, however, was administered by ABC-TV's super egotist, Howard Cosell, the pompous ex-lawyer who resorted to the most shameful tactics imaginable during his relentless grilling of the defenseless, embarrassed coach of the U.S. sprinters.

Cosell had no official connection with the U.S. team but, nevertheless, he took it upon himself to whiplash Wright with a cross-examination comparable to that reserved for the worst of felons and notorious criminals. Cosell was rude, brazen and unmerciful in his attack, badgering Wright with incriminating questions, even after the coach had admitted that he had made a horrifying and unforgivable mistake. It is doubtful that anyone in sports history has been subjected to such a demeaning interrogation.

ABC-TV spent a total of $23 million covering the Olympics. Cosell performed as though he were privileged to cajole, harangue and harass Wright before a world-wide audience of millions for that reason.

Cosell's insolence was exceeded only by his bad manners and deportment. He prides himself on his habit of applying the "shock treatment" with his grating nasal voice and brash technique. In this instance, he must have walked away from the microphone extremely proud of the way he crushed Wright, a man who obviously was unaccustomed to such derogatory treatment.

Cosell was equally obnoxious in his comments on the judging of the boxing matches. This was especially true when a U.S. boxer lost a close decision. He took it upon himself to judge the judges. Having coasted to a degree of fame on the coattails of Muhammad Ali, the former heavyweight champion, Cosell now considers himself the world's most authoritative boxing expert.

The truth of the matter is that there were some very bad boxing decisions, but Americans also won some that they should have lost, as well as vice-versa.

By his actions Cosell added to the illusion that Americans are crybabies and poor sportsmen. As Robert Markus pointed out in the *Chicago Tribune* afterward: "If we are going to compete in the community of nations we are going to have to learn to accept the bad calls with the good. Or maybe the alternative of not competing at all might be considered." America's greatest debacle and disappointment in the Olympics was its loss in the basketball competition. The American team was defeated by the Russians by the score of 51–50. The victory was achieved by the Russians in the "official" final three seconds—or, ostensibly, after the game was over. There was a wild mix-up at the conclusion.

The Americans thought they had won, 50–49. The officials said, "No." Our team was forced to play another three seconds, and the Russians scored the final, winning basket during that time.

There were wild protests after the controversial conclusion, and the USOC protested to the IOC in vain. Thus, they lost the basketball championship for the first time. The defeat brought an end to America's streak of 63 consecutive Olympic victories and seven straight gold medals.

Yet, once again, this disappointment was the result of poor administration.

The fact of the matter is that the American team was poorly coached by the veteran Henry Iba. There were available to Iba expert scouting reports, compiled over the past four years. Iba should have, but did not, heed the advice of the scouting sheets which he supposedly read and reread for weeks before the Olympics.

The scouting reports revealed that the Russians had a veteran team (most of the Russians had played together for eight years), and that the way to beat them was to run them into the ground with a fast attack.

"The Russians have a strong defense," said one report, "but it can be penetrated effectively if the U.S. team attacks continuously. We cannot play control ball and win. The Americans must capitalize on their superior speed and shooting ability."

But for some unexplainable reason Iba insisted on ball control against the Russians, which was playing right into the Soviets' hands. They fell back on defense as the Americans played a deliberate, regimented brand of basketball. They waited until the U.S. team had to rid itself of the ball in the final seconds of the compulsory 30-second rule and then closed in with a pressing defense. This forced the Americans to shoot hurriedly and inaccurately.

The Americans played poorly. They refused to intimidate the opposition, while the Russians resorted to an aggressive defense. The U.S. team's deliberate style produced only 21 points in the first half simply because they did not attack with all possible speed.

"We should have been ahead of them by 10 or 15 points," said an American assistant coach. "But we laid back and waited for their defense to smother us on offense, and consequently our shooting was horrendous."

If Iba had followed the scouting instructions ("the Russians are extremely slow getting back on defense," the reports said) and sent the U.S. team out with an aggressive, fast-breaking attack, there would have been no reason for the wild confusion at the end. Our players would have been so far ahead of the Russians that the last three minutes, let alone three seconds, would merely have been routing. The U.S. team should have coasted home with room to spare.

But Iba stubbornly refused to heed the advice passed on to him by the best scouting staff in the world. "I followed the Russians all over the world for four years," said one scout, "and turned in reports that a child could understand. I also lectured to the American team numerous times before they met the Russians, even demonstrating their weaknesses on a blackboard. Those reports were ignored, however, in that final and most important contest."

Afterwards, once again our Olympic representatives displayed their inability to take defeat gracefully. Right or wrong, our team should have reacted to the decision of the appeals committee with some show of character.

Instead, Iba flew home to Oklahoma without waiting for the result, and his players refused to take the stand to receive their second-place silver medals. Russia and Cuba, which finished third, lined up behind the No. 1 and No. 3 steps of the podium. The U.S. players refused to appear.

Once again America's "good sportsmanship" image was smeared before the world. The "we-was-robbed" screams of the Americans still echo across the housetops of Munich and above the big bowl where the Olympic flame once blazed.

In the aftermath of all the confusion and controversy, the question arises: Should the Olympic Games be continued?

The XX Olympiad is gone, leaving only bitterness, murder, hate and bigotry. It was staged under the cloak of good sportsmanship and man's love and respect for his fellow man. But actually it was one nation pitted ruthlessly against another under regulations more often associated with war. It was an affair that was supposed to bring men closer together, but one which served largely to drive them farther apart.

In an editorial on the Olympic farce, the *Sporting News* observed:

"Perhaps the best that can be said of the 1972 Olympics is that they have ended. Stalked by tragedy and ripped by bickering, official bungling and political infighting, the Games are suffering from a bad case of disillusionment and bitterness. If the athletes' performances, by and large, were superior, the post-victory conduct (of a few) was hardly exemplary. And the coterie of Olympic administrators succeeded only in muddying already troubled waters.

"Overshadowing all, the slaughter of 11 members of the Israeli delegation by Arab killers shook the world. One might have assumed that this carnage would have turned the Games into a sober, reflective camp, minus the customary scrapping over judges' decisions and other paltry issues. But after a memorial in which Avery Brundage managed to lament the ouster of Rhodesia almost as much as the Israeli tragedy, the resumption of the Games revealed nothing had changed.

"If anything, the yelping attained a new shrillness. It must be said, too, that the ineptness of those conducting the show grew even more obvious.

"Where do the Olympics go from here? Perhaps to oblivion unless the hysteria and passions can be tempered. The record isn't encouraging. For some governments involved, it's not fun and games. It's win at any price. Utopia and the Olympic ideal still are a long way from reality."

There is no better time than now to change the archaic system under which the Olympic Games have been staged. Lord Killanin is succeeding the obstinate Avery Brundage as president of the International Olympic Committee. He has inherited a giant headache. And if he can't cope with it, the Games should be abolished.

He says he is more liberal than Brundage. He has been president of Ireland's Olympic Committee for 22 years. He indicates he is in favor of a broad restructuring.

It is better that the Olympics be banished than to continue the bickering. Hostilities must be ended. It is doubtful that this will happen.

The ingrown Olympic bureaucracy is not about to disband itself. *Life* magazine probably viewed it properly, saying: "Unless Killanin can convince the 74-man IOC of the need for reform—an unlikely prospect—and unless the various national Olympic committees reshape their organizations and their thinking, the Olympics will continue to lurch along as a flag-waving, medal-counting, money-making [*ABC paid more than $13 million for TV rights*] world's fair, trading on the athletes but keeping them silent and powerless."

If nothing else, the United States should refrain from participating if its Olympic officials cannot accept defeat gracefully or treat its athletes fairly and courteously. We should either accept the rules of the game ... or take our bat and ball and go home. The world is sick of U.S. wailing and whimpering.

*This magazine piece appeared posthumously. Wendell's target was hypocrisy, both that of the USOC and the IOC. It is not surprising that*

Smith was not a fan of Howard Cosell. They practiced different styles of journalism. Smith reported on stories; Cosell became the story.

Note that Wendell describes the protest as being in support of Black Power. Tommie Smith writes in his autobiography, Silent Gesture, that the raised fist was not intended as a symbol of Black Power (see pages 16, 22, and 161). Whether or not it was in support of Black Power, Wendell supported the right of the individual to perform the protest act (we will see that clearly in the position he takes on Jim "Mudcat" Grant). Wendell did not support the Black Power Movement, the Black Panther Party, or the Nation of Islam. He was consistently a non-violent integrationist in the spirit of Dr. King. Wendell did, however, support an individual's right to protest during the playing of the national anthem and to become a member of the Nation of Islam, Black Panther Party, etc. I attempted to discover who owns the rights to Tuesday at Home magazine to obtain permission to use this article but was unsuccessful.

# 5

# Confronting Racism

*The individuals who confronted racism employed a variety of techniques. Some confronted racism directly while others operated behind the scenes. Racism occurred where it might be expected, but also in some surprising places. It could be overt; it could be covert.*

*Wendell attempted to be fair when determining if racism was in play. He tended to give an individual the benefit of the doubt. He was not quick to blame racism for failure. But when he found it, he fought it. Hard.*

## December 10, 1938

### Smitty's Sport Spurts, *Pittsburgh Courier*, p. 16

Sometime during the minor league convention in New Orleans next week, we expect to read in the papers that the leaders of the great American sport have sent a formal protest to Mr. Adolf Hitler, demanding he quit calling helpless Jews out before they even get to the plate.

We doubt however that they'll say anything real mean to Adolf, because they realize he could retaliate with some very embarrassing fast ones. For instance, he might ask them why they don't quit talking about stopping the New York Yankees with all the white teams. Then too, he might even ask the Detroit Tigers why "inthehell" they don't get Josh Gibson to catch for them. They keep shouting for a good catcher, but can't seem to find one. He might ask Pittsburgh why they didn't hire Ray Brown of the Homestead Grays last season when they needed a pitcher to carry them through in that last month. He might ask a hundred other questions that would make their faces turn red with democratic, American fair play!

*Same as Hitler*

Being an American institution, designed to promote fair play, democratic ideals and the theory that all men are equal, it will be the duty of this organization to send a protest to Hitler. But they'll feel mighty sheepish about it. They play the same game as Hitler. They discriminate, segregate and hold down a minor race, just as he does. While Hitler cripples the Jews, the great leaders of our national pastime refuse to recognize our black ball players.

We must hand it to Adolf for one thing. He comes right out and tells why he objects to Jews. He is wrong, of course, but he doesn't think he is. And, he doesn't hide or refuse to answer when asked about it.

## Hitler and Landis

But you take "Hitler" Landis, for instance. He, nor any of his aides, have the courage of Adolf. When asked about the inclusion of the black "jews" into baseball they beat around the bush ... and then swing out on something else. Of course, they are Americans, men who believe in freedom and all that other bunk Mr. Roosevelt tried to hand Adolf. Incidentally, Mr. Roosevelt would have to scramble some if Adolf asked him why black Americans must ride in jim crow cars and the like, in this land of the brave and free!

## Adolf Laughs

Mr. Adolf Hitler probably receives all these messages from the great land of America and laughs like everything. For he is no fool. He knows that right here in this great land of ours, Jews do the very same thing to black folks that he is doing to them over there. He's just carrying out the lessons he learned from the likes of Mr. Roosevelt, Mr. Landis, whom he must admire, and some of our Jewish friends.

We think that the major leagues should just let Mr. Hitler alone. They have a bit of justice to deal out themselves. Perhaps it would be better if they received a letter from Adolf and let him tell them what to do before they started on him.

While the baseball session is going on next week, we would like to see a number of our black baseball fans send Mr. "Hitler" Landis and his Storm Troopers a few messages about the injustices they support and cater to. It won't do any good, perhaps, as far as the plight of the Negro ball player is concerned, but it might remind them to keep their unjust traps shut.

*It was common knowledge in 1938 that Hitler was a bully and a racist. The Final Solution, the death camps, and the Holocaust were not. Wendell is accusing Landis of being a bully and a racist, not a genocidal maniac. This piece was written early in Wendell's career. He remained willing to confront racism directly but toned down his language. Perhaps he was maturing. He was also meeting some white individuals who were as committed to change as he was. He did not have an epiphany like Malcolm X had at Mecca, but like Malcolm, Wendell was a thoughtful individual who modified his views when presented with facts that contradicted his opinion.*

## November 9, 1940

### Smitty's Sport Spurts,
### *Pittsburgh Courier*, p. 18

*Bates and N.Y.U.*

The shadow of prejudice and un–Americanism once again falls across the supposedly liberal portal of New York University. Last week, President Harry W. Chase and Coach Mal Stevens showed that they approve of racial segregation and all the rest of the principals that Adolf Hitler is advocating by refusing to permit Leonard Bates, Negro halfback, to play against the University of Missouri.

New York University is an institution supported for the people and by the people. New York University, situated in the heart of America's most cosmopolitan city, is an edifice of learning supposedly dedicated to the cause of democracy and the future of this nation. But the Violet of NYU is crushed and bent this week, and droops its once proud head shamefully earthward as the true colors of the men who guide that institution are brought to light in bold relief.

*They Kicked Democracy*

NYU kicked democracy smack in the face when it submitted to the demands of the rebel University of Missouri. Perhaps President Chase and Coach Stevens thought they were winning the favor of Missouri by keeping Leonard Bates at home. But Missouri probably thinks less of NYU now than it did before. At least Missouri is frank enough to admit that Negroes are not wanted there and should keep away. But NYU operates under a cloak of deceit and superficial sincerity. NYU will accept Negroes, then lynch them and flay them with a democratic rope and whip.

The Violet of NYU is purple. But the will of its executives is weak and the color of their spines is a ghastly yellow. They flaunt the flag of democracy and then smear that flag with a brush comparable to the one Hitler is using to smear the life of Europe.

Leonard Bates is a fine, clean-cut young American. He went, like thousands of other young Americans, to NYU to secure an education so that he might become a better American, if that is possible. But he now knows that NYU lacks whatever he thought it had. He knows now that

NYU lacks the guts of Wisconsin and Notre Dame, because they refused to compete against Missouri last year when the Crackers tried to draw the color line on a black-faced boy who was a member of the Wisconsin track team. Wisconsin refused to submit to Missouri's demands and Notre Dame suddenly announced that it would be impossible for them to make the trip to Missouri. The meet was called off.

## Ignored Protests

The students of NYU are shining examples of American manhood and womanhood. They protested vigorously against the demands of Missouri. But NYU's Chase and Stevens ignored those protests. After all, who are the students? They simply play on the team, support the team, cheer for the team and make it possible for NYU to haul down thousands of dollars a year with that team.

Leonard Bates should turn in his uniform. He should quit NYU just as NYU quit him. Leonard Bates went to NYU to secure an education, and he is getting one. He is getting the kind they teach in Germany and Italy these days. He is being taught by Messrs. Chase and Stevens that he is inferior. He is being taught that NYU's way is the American way and that there is no place for the black man in the American scheme of things.

Of course, the things he is being taught are lies. They are NYU lies. There is a place in this American scheme for a black man. Leonard Bates should leave NYU before Messrs. Chase and Stevens poison him with Hitlerism.

Leonard Bates should quit NYU and prove that "it can't happen here!"

*Wendell is concerned with three parties in this piece. Leonard Bates is advised to leave NYU and find an academic institution that will provide him with a better education. The University of Missouri is behaving terribly, but what else was expected? NYU is the problem. There is the hypocrisy. There is an entry in Chapter 7 that describes how Southern Methodist University handled this issue. Surprisingly, the Southern school got it right in 1938 while the Northern school got it wrong in 1940. Wendell does not hesitate to praise the former and condemn the latter. He has the courage to go where the truth takes him.*

# February 23, 1946

## Sports Beat, *Pittsburgh Courier*, p. 12

*All Sportswriters Aren't Liberal or Fair...*

There is a widespread opinion among the public that sportswriters on daily newspapers are the most liberal and broadminded chroniclers of news in journalism. And, there is a very definite reason for this belief. On the whole, sportswriters have been most liberal spreading favorable adjectives around about prominent Negro athletes. Joe Louis, for example, has had "good press" ever since the day he started fighting. Henry Armstrong, Satchel Paige, Josh Gibson and countless others have enjoyed the favoritism of the influential sports scribes. All athletes, and others in public life, welcome a favorable press. Writers mold public opinion and if an athlete or an actor is to attain success, the attitude of the general public must be for, and not against, him.

There is one particular segment within the sports-writing fraternity, however, that isn't as broadminded on racial equality in sports as it could be. That group is known as the baseball writers. Most of the recognized baseball writers with whom I have talked, have a passive attitude toward the fight for Negro players in the majors. Many of them, for obvious commercial reasons, have called upon Organized Baseball to open its doors. They write that kind of stuff because it is in "good taste." They can't justifiably denounce such a campaign, so they put their tongues in their cheeks and write something that appears to be in support of the effort.

But a perfect example of the hypocrisy that lies between the lines they write was clearly evident two weeks ago when the New York chapter of the baseball writers' organization put on its annual banquet. They put on a "show" for their invited guests, many of whom were owners of major league teams, in which they went out of the way to belittle Branch Rickey, the Brooklyn owner, and heap insults upon Jackie Robinson. Here, for example is an excerpt from their script:

The scene is cast in a Southern setting. A Negro butler (Jackie Robinson) is dusting a table with his back to the audience. He turns slowly, disclosing the upper part of a Montreal uniform. He peers into the wings and says, "Looks lak de massa will be late dis evening."

Later a character supposed to be Commissioner Chandler appears and after making a speech, claps his hands and calls, "Robbieeeee!"

> **BUTLER:** "Yassah, Massa. Here Ah is!"
>
> **CHANDLER:** "Ah! There you are, Jackie. Jackie, you ole wooly-headed rascal, how long have you been in the family?"
>
> **BUTLER:** "Long time, Kun'l. Marty long time. Evver since Massa Rickey done bo't me from de Kansas City Monarchs."

That is a sample of the stuff the so-called liberal New York baseball writers heaped on their guests in that "burlesque." It is clearly obvious that they were taking well-aimed pot shots at both Rickey and Robinson. They are not all for equality in sports and they gave vent to their feelings in this vicious manner. They weren't courageous or brave enough to express their feelings in their respective newspapers (that might affect circulation), so they put on this dastardly act behind closed doors. The parts were played by well-known writers of the New York chapter of the association, but their names were not made public for fear of being reprimanded. Therefore, the entire blame for that "Nazi Opera" must be heaped upon the entire body.

Thus, the next time you read a story in the *New York Times, Post, News, Mirror, Journal, Herald-Tribune*, or any other "highly regarded" New York publication, dealing with racial equality in baseball, just remember that it will probably come from the pen of a writer who was a part of that "act" they pulled on Robinson and Rickey. And, above all, when you start classifying liberals and fair-minded organizations in the world of sports, be sure to cross off the New York Chapter of the Baseball Writers Association.

*Imagine Wendell having to sit in the press box with these men. There were white baseball writers who were members of this organization who were not racist. But Wendell had to be careful in discerning between false friends, overt enemies, and sincere allies. It was often difficult differentiating between these groups because individuals behave inconsistently. Some of the individuals who participated in this event made contributions to integrating baseball. The skit is inexcusable. Wendell had to remain resilient and move forward.*

*The Baseball Writers Association of America required members to write for daily papers. Conveniently for the BBWAA, but not necessarily coincidently, Black papers tended to be weekly papers. Sam Lacy of the* Afro-American *in Baltimore and Washington and Wendell became, respectively, the first and second Black members of the BBWAA. Disparate impact is a legal standard that emerged from the civil rights movement (see* Griggs v Duke Power*). It holds that a law or rule can be deemed discriminatory on the basis of outcome; a prosecutor need not prove intent to discriminate. The BBWAA rule on surface seems race neutral. However, given that Black papers were weekly, it had the impact of keeping Black sportswriters out of the organization. Wendell entertained the idea of organizing a Black version of the BBWAA.*

## January 26, 1952

### Sports Beat, *Pittsburgh Courier*, p. 14

*Louis Has Always Been a Fighter for Equality...*

It has been written elsewhere that Joe Louis, currently waging a one-man war against discrimination in golf, has always avoided entanglements on racial questions.

That is why, perhaps, the writers from the other side of the tracks expressed great surprise when he took such a militant position on the San Diego incident and socked the PGA with a barrage of verbal blows.

To the contrary, Louis has never avoided racial entanglements. Whenever confronted with a discriminatory problem, he has never failed to take a definite position. He has never failed to let it be known that he does not believe in discrimination or segregation.

He has always been a fighter for racial equality. He has always been an ardent advocate for equal rights in this country. The ex-champion has never gone around looking for "Incidents" but whenever or wherever he has found them, Louis has put up his dukes and fought back in no uncertain manner.

His fights in the racial ring haven't been as spectacular, perhaps, as in the boxing ring, but the results have been just as effective. He has scored a lot of knockouts down through the years in his battles with prejudice and hypocrisy. He has won most of those fights, too, but there has been little publicity about them. He'd rather have it that way. The PGA situation is one of the few the general public has been told about.

## He Once Defied an Army General...

When Louis was in the Army, he became involved in numerous fights concerning discrimination and segregation. There was the time in England, for instance, when he was on tour, giving boxing exhibitions at various camps.

The story, as told to us, goes something like this:

He was scheduled to box an exhibition one day and arrived at the stadium approximately an hour before he was to enter the ring. He sensed something was wrong when he saw hundreds of white soldiers entering the stadium and a group of forlorn Negro servicemen standing outside. He asked the Negro servicemen why they were standing around outside. He asked them if they had tickets.

"We can't go in," one of them said. "This is supposed to be off limits for Negro soldiers. We were just standing here so we could get a look at you when you arrived."

Louis told the barred Negro soldiers not to go away. Then he entered the stadium. When the time finally came for him to enter the ring, he failed to appear. After waiting for at least a half hour, the soldiers inside the stadium grew impatient.

They demanded his appearance by clapping and shouting "We want Louis, we want Louis."

Meantime, Louis was sitting in his dressing room. He was still attired in his regular Army uniform. A special services officer came rushing in, obviously excited. "Come on, Joe," he said, "get dressed, it's time for you to go on."

Louis informed the officer he would not box until the Negro soldiers outside were admitted. In desperation, the officer left, only to return soon with the commanding officer, a general. The general pleaded with Louis to go through with the exhibition, but it was all in vain. "I won't box until you let those Negro soldiers in," Louis said. The general then told Louis, who was a sergeant, that he was ordering him to go through with the exhibition. Louis ignored the order.

Convinced that Joe was determined, the general issued an order to admit the Negro soldiers. Louis then put on his boxing togs and went through the exhibition. Although he entered the ring an hour late, the soldiers gave him a rousing ovation when he appeared.

Afterwards, the general thanked Louis and congratulated him for the position he took in regard to the Negro soldiers. "If I can do anything for you, Joe," the general said, "to show my appreciation for the fine exhibition you put on, just tell me. If you hadn't fought here tonight we might have had a military riot. If there is anything you want, just let me know what it is."

"'There is only one thing I want, General,' said Sergeant Louis, 'and you have it.'" The general asked him what it was.

"I'd like to have a fatigue jacket like the one you are wearing," Louis told him.

The general immediately took off the jacket and gave it to Louis, adding: "I'm glad to give it to such a fine soldier, Joe. I want you to know, also, that Negro soldiers will be admitted to our sports events in the future."

## Schmeling Sealed His Own Doom...

Everyone recalls, of course, the way he annihilated Max Schmeling in their second fight. In 1936 Schmeling knocked him out and returned to Germany where he was hailed by Hitler and the Nazis. Schmeling boasted that no Negro would ever be able to beat him, especially Louis. He belittled Joe and the Negro race. He said Negroes were ignorant and uncivilized. He urged that they all be placed in concentration camps "as soon as Germany achieves the goal of world domination." Louis read about Schmeling's disparaging remarks and vowed to make him eat his own words. Joe went on to win the heavyweight championship from Jim Braddock and afterward said:

"I won't be satisfied until I fight Schmeling. I want to get even with him for the things he said about me and about my race."

On the night of June 22, 1938, Louis got his revenge. He knocked Schmeling out in the first round. The fight lasted exactly 2 minutes and 4 seconds. The idol of Germany's "Master Race" had been destroyed.

Throughout his career Louis has fought people and institutions responsible for racial bias and discrimination.

On his recent trip to Japan, for instance, he received an invitation to visit Formosa and meet Madame Chiang Kai-shek, the mouthpiece of the Chinese Nationalists. He refused because "the Madame" has exhibited her dislike for Negroes many, many times while visiting the United States.

Louis despises prejudiced politicians. On the day the funeral for Senator Bilbo of Mississippi was held, one of Joe's friends asked him if he knew about it.

"No," he said, without cracking a smile, "but I'm certainly in favor of it."

*Max Schmeling and Joe Louis would become friends. The Nazi press mischaracterized Schmeling's beliefs to enhance the Nazi Party. This fact was not widely known in 1952. The primary point of this piece is that Louis fought racism aggressively but in his own way. Neither Jackie Robinson nor Joe Louis tolerated it.*

## November 9, 1957

### Sports Beat, *Pittsburgh Courier*, p. 24

The latest subterfuge being employed by the Anarchists of America (those who would overthrow the Government with "gentle" violence) to keep all Americans from enjoying the advantage of all America is a viciously plotted and carefully planned, campaign to discredit and vilify the concerted efforts of the NAACP to compel America, and the South in particular, to practice what it preaches to the rest of the turbulent world.

On one side of the podium, American whites rant fanatically: "We believe everyone is equal. We are all brothers under the skin. We must fight to retain the free world."

On the other side, however, there are Senators, Governors and smug diplomats who admit that when they talk about the so-called free world, they aren't advocating the elimination of jim-crow schools, the poll tax or the despicable pattern of segregated sections of the nation. They seem to be in the majority these crucial days.

"Ignore those conditions; We're talking about the rest of the world."

Amid all this, the NAACP is legally and courageously fighting back, resorting only to the courts of the land, adhering only to the precepts of the constitution. In so doing, the organization (poor enough, Lord knows) has continued to win legal cases nationwide by insisting that white

Americans "practice here what they preach over there." "Here," of course, is the United States ... and "there" is Europe, Russia and the Middle East.

The anti–NAACP campaign has been so effective lately that there are many of all races, colors and religions who have come to look upon it rather suspiciously. Laws have been devised against it in Little Rock and elsewhere; forthright members have been ostracized, and solely because the organization insists that Americans adhere to their credo, it has been called "a Communist-dominated organization."

That's the pitch now. If you belong to the NAACP, you're a "red." You're plotting, they lie, for the "Violent overthrow of the Government."

But nothing is farther from the truth. The NAACP is in no way as dangerous as the countless White Citizens Councils, or the KKK, or any of the other flag-waving, race-baiting organizations now in existence.

If it were, then there wouldn't be such illustrious Americans as Jackie Robinson, Dr. Benjamin Mays, Daisy Lampkin, Kivie Kaplan, Oscar Hammerstein, Dr. C.B. Powell, Hon. Bessie Buchanan, Lena Horne, Hon. Archibald Carey, Sammy Davis, Jr., the Rev. Martin Luther King, Earl Dickerson, Walter Reuther and the others identified with the Duke Ellington–Branch Rickey testimonial dinner for the benefit of the 1957 Freedom Fund dinner at the Hotel Roosevelt in New York on Nov. 22.

Nor would such stirring athletes as Brooklyn's (Los Angeles now) Don Newcombe and Jim (Junior) Gilliam, the White Sox Larry Doby, or the New York Giants, Willie Mays (San Francisco now) go all-out to help make this unprecedented affair a success.

All those named above belong to the NAACP. They are successful in their chosen fields. Certainly they'd shun any organization whose purpose it was, or is, designed to snuff out the system which has brought them fame and also financial fortune.

Of all the people associated with this testimonial dinner for Mr. Rickey and Mr. Ellington Nov 22 in New York, there is no doubt that Jackie Robinson, general chairman, wants it to be an overwhelming success.

And why shouldn't he? Rickey is one of the great humanitarians of our time. Ellington is one of the geniuses of our time.

There is a significant connotation between Robinson and Rickey. Mr. Rickey made it possible for Robinson to exhibit his skills in a field where hundreds, even thousands, of Jackie's color had been denied before—the Major Leagues.

Mr. Rickey defied all unwritten laws, all social patterns, all bigots, as well as all owners of baseball teams—to do what he believed was innately right ... allow Negroes to play in the Major Leagues.

Therefore, it behooves everyone who is remotely connected with what is going on now in this country to support this dinner.

This banquet is not only for Branch Rickey, Duke Ellington, but, also Jackie Robinson and his committee, the NAACP, and all America.

If you don't support it, then don't squawk if the anarchists and bigots triumph. It'll be too late to beef then.

*When all else fails, call 'em Commies. The NAACP, Commies. Advocates for the integration of MLB, Commies. Martin Luther King, Commie. Wendell does what a good journalist should do here. He presents the facts and counts on his readers to recognize the truth.*

## September 24, 1960

### Sports Beat, *Pittsburgh Courier*, p. 25

Well, Now!

How could Manager Jimmy Dykes of Cleveland suspend Jim (Mudcat) Grant for the rest of the season just because he wasn't in tune when the national anthem was played?

It seems that Grant became involved in a controversy in the bullpen with Coach Ted Wilks during the rendition of the national song.

Grant, who has stayed in the majors by beating—of all people—the Washington Senators, is alleged to have said: "This land is not so free. I can't even go to Mississippi."

That comment apparently started the argument. But what "Mudcat" said is absolutely true and ball players can be suspended and fined through the years, from now on, and it won't make any difference.

Dykes said: "There is no excuse for what he did." There is an excuse for what he did, and perhaps it would be better for all concerned if there were more Negro players like Jim Grant.

Perhaps it would be better if some other players, like Willie Mays and Ernie Banks, to name a few, would rise up and rebel.

It is true that this land is not so free, where Negroes are concerned, and Grant's observation is not in any way a shocking contrast to the general trend of things. Grant cannot go to Mississippi a free man. A Russian Communist will receive much better treatment there, as we all know. So why should Wilks get so upset over "Mudcat's" comment?

Perhaps if a few of the established players, like Mays, Banks, and even intellectuals such as George Crowe of Cincinnati took the same position as Grant, some progress would be made.

You cannot hide all things by completely trying to ignore them. What Grant said is the truth. Dykes said: "It seems that Grant made some remark about what a lousy country this is while the national anthem was being played. Wilks answered him back and Grant said: "I don't have to take that from anybody; and took off."

"I suspended him because he didn't report to me."

Then Dykes reportedly said: "There is no excuse for what he did."

Well, there is news here for Dykes. There is an excuse for what Grant did ... and a good one.

Perhaps this one, lone pitcher finally got tired of being pushed around ... got tired of singing the national anthem, which says so much and offers so little. Let's stop pretending.

Isn't it about time, for example, that major league clubs, in all areas of sports, stop separating their players when they travel below the Mason-Dixon Line?

Why should Negro ball players be left on the wayside? Why should the New York Yankees force Elston Howard and Hector Lopez to stay in hovels while the rest of the members of the team wallow in luxury?

Why should Al Smith and Minnie Minoso be compelled to get off the ball club bus and be confined to a restricted area while the rawest white rookie enjoys the most lush conveniences?

There is no logical reason for it. Grant's attitude and reaction is not strange, just shockingly true. If this is the "land of the brave and home of the free," why don't they do something about situations like that?

Why do they, instead, try to pretend that Jim (Mudcat) Grant is wrong and Mississippi right?

*Throughout this book I refrain from speculating on what opinion Wendell might have held regarding a current issue. Based on this article we can conclude, however, that Wendell would not oppose an athlete kneeling or in some way protesting during the playing of the national anthem. That is different from saying that he would have supported the cause or that he would have perceived it to be the best way of making the point. In this instance, he not only supported Grant's right to make the protest but he also agreed with the point Grant was making. He is again calling out some of his friends, the Black stars of the game, to be more assertive.*

# January 28, 1961

## Pittsburgh Courier, p. 37

*Time for Diamond Stars to Follow in Footsteps
of Patterson's Fight Against Bigotry*

Floyd Patterson's stirring stand against segregated seating for his third encounter with Ingemar Johansson at Miami Beach, Fla., in March, is of historical significance.

No Negro athlete of prominence has ever before laid the issue on the line as forthrightly, nor as bluntly, as did Patterson in this instance.

When he signed for the bout last week, Patterson demanded that an agreement be included in the contract whereby the promoter, namely, Feature Sports, Inc., had to post a $10,000 bond guaranteeing that there will be no seating segregating Negroes and whites at the fight.

The agreement had been reached orally beforehand, but Patterson apparently did not trust the Miami Beach city officials. He insisted that a cash guarantee be put up, thereby assuring him that none of his people will be humiliated at the fight.

He is to be the sole judge of the seating arrangement. He said his decision will be based upon "any complaints" made to him. He added:

"Always when I get in the ring I look over the crowd and I can tell then if there's any segregation."

If there is segregation in this instance, of course, the promoter will have to cough up ten grand. Consequently, it is not likely that there will be any intentional separate seating on the basis of color at this championship fight.

All of which brings up a very interesting point:

Why don't Negro baseball players take a similar position on the segregation and humiliation they suffer during spring training every year?

Why won't some of the many brilliant Negro players come forth and protest the racial restrictions to which they are subjected in Florida and elsewhere each spring?

Only they can answer those questions. Maybe they don't want to become involved in such a controversy because they are what is known as "Fat Cats." They are making big money and therefore, refuse to become involved in an issue that will be solved eventually.

Why should a Negro baseball star making a salary of $50,000 per year submit to conditions which a white rookie making $7,000 would not stand for?

There is no justifiable answer to that question. The truth of the matter is that there are a number of "Uncle Tom's" among Negro major leaguers who would rather "leave well enough alone," and accept the degrading conditions under which they exist during spring training than take a position such as Patterson did, with respect to his fight with Johansson.

This is not an indictment of all Negro major leaguers. There are a number who are willing to go to bat against spring segregation. There are many more, however, willing to accept anything rather than jeopardize their "lofty" positions.

There are Negro major leaguers who do not even want to discuss their deplorable training camp plight, lest they "cause trouble." There are others who only want to talk about it "off the record." What they say is this:

"No, I don't like living apart from the ball club during spring training, but don't say so because the front office will think I'm trying to make trouble."

It has been 14 years since Jackie Robinson first crashed the major leagues. That is a long time and Negro players have now proven themselves, insofar as ability is concerned.

Most of them are enjoying a life of security, living easily and in luxury. Many are so well established that the clubs they play for cannot do without them. All are enjoying the type of life that Robinson made possible.

Is it not time, then, that some of these stars step forward and make a determined effort to improve the conditions of those who will follow them?

Yes, it is time.

Why should Negro ball players continue going on, year after year, bowing to racial segregation? Why can't they reach a "no segregation" pact with the owners of their teams for which they play?

Why can't they follow the example of the courageous sit-ins from Negro colleges and the stand taken by Floyd Patterson?

We leave the answers to those questions to the Negro players in the major league.

*Wendell took different approaches when advocating for MLB integration and the end of Spring Training segregation. Brown v Board had much to do with the change. Wendell spent most of the first 10 years of his career supporting the end of the color line in MLB. He thought it would happen but knew it was a marathon. He returned to the theme regularly, but not constantly ... column after column. It was not realistic to take that approach for a change that took a decade of Wendell's career to accomplish. Brown v Board put Spring Training segregation on the wrong side of the law. Wendell did not have to convince owners to adopt the change. Segregation could be challenged in the courts. But Wendell was not even advocating that. If the Black baseball stars aggressively pushed for the end to segregation of Spring Training facilities, he thought it would crumble. It frustrated him that they would not do it. "Fat Cats" and "Uncle Tom's" were not terms Wendell used lightly. He did not name names, but he was writing about Willie Mays, Ernie Banks, Hank Aaron, and others who he knew and liked. However, Wendell could not bring himself to specifically call any of those Black players "Fat Cats" or "Uncle Tom's." He knew they did not deserve that label. He was angry and frustrated. Ironically, it is Floyd Patterson who is the hero in this column, an athlete Wendell harshly criticized in other columns.*

*Wendell eventually lost patience waiting for the players to take the lead and he did write column after column, week after week, advocating for the end of segregation during Spring Training. It would be a stretch to say that he did it single-handedly. But it was close enough for some to argue (see Chapter 1) that Wendell deserved a Pulitzer Prize for his efforts. Wendell is best known for traveling with Jackie Robinson, but he had a supporting role in that event. He played the leading role in integrating Spring Training. And* Brown v Board *put him on the right side of the law. He no longer had to plead for a favor. The Supreme Court had rendered its decision. Integrating Spring Training was simply implementing the decision.*

## April 15, 1961

### Sports Beat, *Pittsburgh Courier,* p. 38

Sarasota, Fla—The loneliest couple in this picturesque town of 45,000 people is Mr. and Mrs. Edward Wachtel. They are the proprietors of the DeSoto Motel, the four-unit establishment where the Negro members of the Chicago White Sox lived during spring training. The official headquarters for the club was the Sarasota Terrace Hotel, which refused to accept the Negro members of the squad, Minnie Minoso, Al Smith, Juan Pizzaro, Stan Johnson, Floyd Robinson, Winston Brown and Frank Barnes. Mr. and Mrs. Wachtel came to their rescue when President Bill Veeck and Secretary Ed Short of the White Sox were frantically searching for suitable quarters to house the seven players.

Firmly opposed to any form of segregation or discrimination, the Wachtels volunteered to take in the rejected players. They are paying a heavy penalty for their benevolence and courageous stand against the bigotry which exists in this West Coast Florida community. As soon as it was learned that the Wachtels had consented to accept the Negro players, the proponents of segregation here launched an attack of harassment upon the kindly couple.

The motel is situated in the heart of a white neighborhood. It is a neat, rambling green and white construction, located on Route 301, Sarasota's main thoroughfare. Ed Wachtel purchased the establishment when he moved here with his wife, Lillian, five years ago for $90,000. He was a prosperous realtor in New York before he retired and came to Sarasota to live what he expected to be a life of quiet contentment. His decision to accept the Negro members of the Chicago team, however, created a turbulence which has made him the most despised individual in the community.

Scorned and ostracized by their immediate neighbors, as well as some of the civic leaders, the Wachtels are still living a lonely and desolate life. They are paying an exorbitant price for living in their motel with the seven

Negro players in a middle-class neighborhood which was tightly restricted previously. However, the 60-year old Jewish motel owner shrugs off the penalties he and his wife have suffered with a benign indifference.

"I accepted these young men," he says, "because I do not believe in segregation. I am fighting it here in Sarasota in my own quiet way. I have lost some of my most intimate friends, but that is the price a man must pay sometimes for doing what he believes is right. The ball players were perfect gentlemen and I was honored to have them as tenants. There isn't a neighbor around here who can point an accusing finger at them."

Those who objected to the presence of Negroes in the motel threatened Wachtel and his wife with bodily harm.

"When it was first discovered that we were going to accept the Negro members of the White Sox," Mrs. Wachtel said, "people called us all hours of the day and night and demanded that we refuse them. They said that if we didn't, they would bomb us out. We also received calls from men who said they were members of the Ku Klux Klan and that they were going to kill us."

Mr. Wachtel and his wife are stubborn, fearless people. They refused to bow to bigotry.

"Naturally, my wife and I were frightened," he said, "especially when they told us they were going to bomb the motel. But we decided that we would take the chance. I informed the sheriff of the threats and for the first week the police kept a close watch on the place. However, I think the community finally accepted the fact that it wasn't such a bad thing, after all. I only receive one or two daily threats now and the police no longer consider it necessary to guard the motel around the clock."

"I have been told too that the management of the Sarasota Terrace Hotel has decided to accept all White Sox players next spring, regardless of race. If that is true, then I am happy. If the policy is changed, then I will have the satisfaction of knowing that I contributed something in my small way toward the betterment of mankind."

Mr. and Mrs. Wachtel lived an isolated life with Minnie Minoso, Al Smith and the other Negroes on the White Sox team. The club has gone North but the Wachtels have not. They're still at the mercy of Sarasota's hostile, anti–Negro zealots. But they are not yielding in their determination to make Sarasota a better city for all people, regardless of race or color. "I'm not afraid," says Mr. Wachtel. "I know what I have done has been right. My wife and I are all alone, but the contentment in our hearts is company enough."

*They did not have to do it. The Wachtels could have quietly declined to house the players ... nobody would have known. Their lives became complex and dangerous. Wendell simply tells the story. He senses that is all he need do. The Wachtels played only a supporting role in this drama. There were many Wachtels in the civil rights movement. Oscars are given for supporting roles.*

## January 6, 1962

### Sports Beat, *Pittsburgh Courier*, p. 32

"The Comiskey baseball dynasty has ended and therewith one of the grand eras of the sport has come to a close."

Thus wrote one sportswriter after Charles Comiskey, grandson of the founder of the Chicago White Sox, Charles A. (The Old Roman) Comiskey, sold his interest in the club for an estimated three million dollars.

It truly was the end of an era, but just how "grand" it was is a matter of conjecture. During the 62 years the Comiskey family belonged to the game's hierarchy baseball grew from a mere sport to a business of tremendous financial stature. Major League franchises blossomed in value from a pittance to enormously valuable properties, so much so, in fact, that the last Comiskey associated with the White Sox demanded some three million dollars for his minority interest in the club and got it.

Financially it was a booming, lush era. But from a humanitarian standpoint, it was the "Dark Ages." The game was controlled by some of the most reactionary individuals in this country's business and sports history.

Until the young Comiskey signed Minnie Minoso in 1951, his father and grandfather before him enthusiastically helped to perpetuate baseball's rigid and unswerving barrier against the employment of Negro players.

They were hardy and active members of that powerful and arrogant major league hierarchy which included such other "aristocratic" baseball families as Washington's Clark C. Griffith, Boston's Robert Quinn, Philadelphia's Connie Mack, New York's Jacob Ruppert, Detroit's Frank J. Navin, the Giants' Charles A. Stoneham, Pittsburgh's Barney Dreyfuss and William E. Benswanger and others.

Those people, as well as some others, shaped the destiny of the major leagues and, therefore, are often affectionately referred to as the game's "grand old families."

But when you look back on their records and see how they maintained the color-line in the national pastime for more than 50 years, you realize they weren't so grand after all.

They perpetuated a vicious "white only" system: refused to open the game up to hundreds of skillful performers solely because those players were Negroes. They denied employment to great hitters, brilliant pitchers, sensational outfielders and magnificent infielders because they were black men.

*The primary point here is that the "grand old families" pursued a racist policy and denied Black players the opportunity to compete in MLB. Wendell is a bit harsh, but these men gave him the run-around for the first 10 years of his career. His attitude is understandable. A lesser point, but one I think still needs to be made because I am a baseball fan, is that the policy severely damaged the game and its history. Can you imagine not seeing Willie Mays, Roberto Clemente, Ernie Banks, Jackie Robinson, Hank Aaron, Frank Robinson, Roy Campanella, etc.? Major League Baseball missed players every bit as great who played in the Negro Leagues prior to integration. Those players lost more than the fans did, but we all share a grievance with those "grand old families."*

## August 15, 1964

### Sports Beat, *Pittsburgh Courier*, p. 14

*One Man's Opinion: Stan Isaacs Didn't Misquote*
*Louisiana's Alvin Dark*

The term—"misquote"—is the most frequently used plea in sports and politics.

Every time someone gets into difficulty, every time someone "pops off" and expresses an unpopular view, and the statement bounces back in print, the "victim" screams—"mis-quote."

This cry always, of course, reflects on the integrity of the writer. The implication is that the writer is trying to put something into the mouth of the person who made the statement that the person really didn't say.

But that is not always true. And it is the impression here that Alvin Dark, the manager of the San Francisco Giants, resorted to this technique when he declared last week that what he allegedly said about the mental deficiencies of Negro and Latin American ballplayers was intentionally distorted.

In all such cases you have to consider the source. The source in this instance is not infallible, but it is a reliable and respected one.

The source is Stan Isaacs, the baseball writer for *News Day*, a newspaper in the Long Island, N.Y., area. Although few people outside of New York know about it, this particular paper is a large one. It is, in fact, one of

the largest in the country. One of the reasons that it is so large and successful is because it employs competent and dedicated writers. Stan Isaacs is
one of them, a good newspaperman who writes a good baseball story.

Isaacs wrote a story in which he quoted the manager of the Giants as
saying the following:

"We, the Giants, have trouble because we have so many Negro and
Spanish speaking players on the team.

"They are just not able to perform up to the white ball players on this
team. They are just not able to perform up to the white ball players when it
comes to mental alertness."

Dark, reportedly, made that statement in San Francisco. Afterwards,
the story was carried by the wire services and naturally, the "back lash"
was thunderous.

So much so, in fact, that Alvin went running to Ford Frick, the commissioner of baseball, to explain his position. Frick told him not to worry,
that everything would be all right.

Alvin called it—"a misinterpretation." He declared that he didn't
have to defend himself. "My record speaks for itself," the Giants manager
asserted. "Color, race or nationality never made any difference to me. I am
only interested in performance.

"We have six Negro and Spanish speaking players on the regular team
and I think he [Isaacs] just took for granted I said those things because I
am a Southerner and they are Negroes."

That's Dark's defense. Willie Mays dutifully, came to his defense two
days later. But it makes no difference who rallied behind Alvin. The question—a logical one—is this:

What did Alvin Dark really say to this reputable newspaperman?

Knowing Stan Issacs, this reporter must believe that he wrote exactly
what he heard, that he did not fabricate any part of that story. Also, that
after it created such a furor, Isaacs, a gentleman, tried to get the Giants'
manager off the hook.

In analyzing the story, one cannot forget that not too long ago a writer
asked Dark what he thought about civil rights and racial discrimination.
He said, reportedly:

"I think Negroes are pushing too hard. I think they are rushing
things."

That statement in itself branded Dark. He is from Louisiana, and
proud of his Southern heritage. There is nothing wrong with that. But the
fact remains that Alvin still thinks, apparently, like a man from the deep
South. He just can't shake it off. Therefore, it is conceivable to us that he
could have said what he allegedly said as Isaacs reported. It may not have
been intended maliciously, but it is conceivable that he said it.

After all the excitement, Dark told the Associated Press:

"If you are going to make such statements, you've got to be either stupid or ready to quit baseball."

We would prefer to think that he is ready to quit. How could Alvin Dark be so stupid?

## *August 4, 1970*

### "Dark still bothered by racist charge,"
### *Chicago Sun-Times*, p. 75

There is the sound of the bayou in Alvin Dark's soft Louisiana voice.

If you close your eyes while he's talking you'll detect echoes of the Confederacy and plantation life, and Jeff Davis, secession and the blare of Appomattox.

In voice and demeanor he epitomizes the essence of southern aristocracy. He is a gentleman first, then the manager of the Cleveland Indians. There is a strong rumor that owner John Allyn has offered him the White Sox chief executive position.

Alvin Dark possesses all the required credentials. He has managed the Giants, Kansas City and Cleveland and spent a year as a coach with the Cubs. He is regarded as a baseball brain.

If there is anything at all peculiar in Dark's dossier it is the brand of bigotry that a Long Island, N.Y. baseball writer stamped on him six years ago. He has not been able to remove it. Most Negro players, including Willie Mays, suspect [respect] him. The blemish has remained because, perhaps, there is so much of the solid South in Dark's voice and manners.

"I am not a bigot," he said Sunday at Sox Park, "but it is hard to shake that reputation because of my southern background and heritage. That writer who said I made uncomplimentary remarks about Negro and Puerto Rican players in 1964 was out to get me. He made me a racist in his paper. I have found it impossible to erase that charge, even though a number of Negro players have vouched for me. Luke Easter, the old Cleveland first baseman is one of them." In late July 1964, the Long Island paper, *Newsday*, published a two-part series in which Dark is alleged to have said:

"We have trouble because we have so many Negro and Spanish-speaking players on the team. They are just not able to perform up to the white ballplayer when it comes to mental alertness.

"One of the biggest things is that you can't make them subordinate themselves to the best interests of the team. You don't find the pride in them that you get in the white player."

Needless to say, those remarks, allegedly made by the manager of a team dominated by Negro and Puerto Rican players, created all kinds of havoc within the Giants' team, as well as in baseball's administrative offices.

"I didn't say what he wrote," Dark said Sunday while sitting in the Cleveland dugout. "That writer purposely misinterpreted a discussion we had about ballplayers in general.

"I said that some players were selfish and lacked pride. I said that some players weren't mentally alert. I did not refer to race or the language they spoke.

"When I was playing with the Giants, stars like Monte Irvin, Hank Thompson, Willie Mays and other were my teammates. There was never a cross word between us. As a manager, I have always handled my players fairly. If a player produces, he plays. If a player refuses to hustle, he does not play. That's all that matters to me."

The *Newsday* story has stayed with Alvin Dark for six years. At the end of the 1964 season, Horace Stoneham fired him as manager of the Giants. He believes he was fired because of that story. "It had to be," he said, "because we certainly had a good season that year. We were knocked out of the pennant race one day before the end of the season.

"Just before the last game of the season, Stoneham came to me and said, 'Al, I'm going to hire another manager for next season.' That was all he said. I said, 'Okay, Horace, it's your ball club.'"

Since that time Alvin Dark has been around. He has managed two other teams and maintained his reputation as a sound field leader. The rap they put on him as a racist is the only smudge on an otherwise impeccable record. He'd like to get that blotch wiped off.

Maybe he can someday.... Perhaps when he rids himself of that Louisiana drawl things will get better.

*Wendell has two problems with Dark's comments. If Dark was accurately quoted, Wendell is offended as a Black man. But Wendell is also a journalist who takes exception to athletes saying something foolish and then claiming to be misquoted. Jackie Robinson had a habit of claiming he was misquoted, and Smith did not accept that from Jackie either. If Dark attributed lack of intelligence and effort to the accused player's race, that is racist. Willie Mays defended Dark in 1964. But Mays was the team leader, and the Giants were in a pennant race. He had a vested interest in smoothing relations between players and manager. Jackie Robinson also defended Dark, and Jackie had no love for the Giants despite having long since retired from baseball. I spoke with Billy Williams and Ken Holtzman who played for Dark in Oakland. Williams also was Dark's teammate with the Cubs.*

*Both men clearly stated that Dark treated all players the same on the field. Holtzman did add that Dark seemed interested in converting him from Judaism to Christianity. Inappropriate, but not necessarily racist. If Dark attempted to convert atheists and Muslims as well, it was not the Jewish race he had an issue with. It would be the non-believers in Christianity regardless of race. It would still be inappropriate behavior for a manager to attempt to change a player's religion.*

*In Chapter 10, Wendell assesses Commissioner Landis' legacy. Wendell acknowledges that Landis said the right things about integration but did nothing to advance it. Smith argues that actions mean more than words. Fair enough. In the case of Al Dark, we have a guy who denies saying something a journalist alleges Dark said. Those who played for and with Dark testify that he treated all players the same. Based on Wendell's preference for actions over words, Dark deserves the benefit of the doubt. When Wendell revisits Dark in 1970, he seems willing to grant that to Dark. But then there is this from Dark's contribution to Jackie Robinson's book* Baseball Has Done It: *"In fact, I felt that because I was from the South—and we from the South actually take care of the colored people, I think, better than they're taken care of in the North—I felt when I was playing with them it was a responsibility for me. I liked the idea that I was pushed to take care of them and make them feel at home and to help them out any way possible that I could in playing baseball the way that you can win pennants."*

*That reads more like a reason one adopts a homeless dog. If Dark were only saying that he felt good about helping Negro ball players feel comfortable in the big leagues and become better baseball players, fine. He has a point in the first half of the statement. Black families that moved from the South to the North left one form of racism and discovered another. They were not and could not have been "taken care of" in the Christian sense in the segregated South. Dark might have been unable to see that because he did feel Christian goodwill toward the Black race. However, people who are perceived to need to be "taken care of" because they are members of a race perceived to be inferior are experiencing racism. The race that perceives itself to be superior is practicing racism. Whether the "superior" race has benign or malignant intent is not relevant. This is dangerous ground. I recommend that the reader obtain a copy of the Robinson book and read Dark's entire essay. Dark's behavior was not racist. Dark's heart was not racist. But somewhere in Dark's philosophy there lurks a racist presumption.*

*Wendell reports that Dark is charged with saying, "I think Negroes are pushing too hard. I think they are rushing things." If Dark meant that Black people were not yet civilized enough to handle it, that is racist. If he meant that the folks he knew back home were having a difficult time adjusting, he was correct. If he thought Black individuals were civilized but needed to go slower for the benefit of the folks who found it difficult to adjust to integra-tion, he was wrong, not racist. I am not certain what he meant. His behav-ior during his playing, managing and coaching career demonstrated that he was comfortable with an integrated society. Wendell seemed uncertain but was attempting to be fair. Perhaps restricting the conversation to two possibilities, racist or perfectly color blind, prevents us from understand-ing each other. If we dig deep enough, most of us probably have some racist belief or premise. We fall somewhere on the continuum between Adolf Hitler and Martin Luther King (closer to MLK than to Hitler). It is as much about where we want to go as it is about where we are at any given time. We think we know ourselves and each other, but perhaps we do not. Al Dark clearly wanted to be more like King. Wendell wanted to give him that opportunity. Wendell thought he knew Dark in 1964. By 1970, he was not certain.*

*Al Dark and Wendell Smith were imperfect but good men trying to understand and be understood by one another. We need more of that. That is why I have spent so many words on this matter. I appreciate the reader's indulgence.*

## October 31, 1964

### Sports Beat, *Pittsburgh Courier*, p. 15

*Aaron to Seek Facts on Atlanta's Bias*

[EDITOR'S NOTE: The U.S. Supreme Court is currently considering the plea, made by an anti–Negro restaurant owner, that the public accommodations section of the recently passed Civil Rights Law is unconstitutional. No major league city can afford to be "bush league" in civility.]

The directors of the Milwaukee Braves took a quick vote in Chica-go's Racquet Club, and ultra-exclusive emporium which bars newsmen, Negroes and Jews, and decided to move the team, lock, stock and barrel, to Atlanta, Ga.

After making that momentous decision, the directors then slipped out a side door and took to the hills. Ernie Johnson, a former Brave pitcher, who now works as the team's public relations director, was designated as the directors' spokesman.

He obviously didn't like the assignment any better than the elusive directors. But the job was his and he did his duty.

"The Milwaukee Braves have decided to move to Atlanta, Ga., for the 1965 season," he announced. "The decision was made today at a board meeting, etc.…."

Then he went on to explain that the fans in Milwaukee had not responded in sufficient numbers to "warrant the team staying in the town." There were available figures to contradict that statement, but Johnson, left on the hot seat by the fleeing directors, did not attempt to refute them. He was cool and calculating when confronted with such figures.

He lost his composure, however, when one of the gentlemen of the press shocked him with this question:

"Hank Aaron, the Braves' outstanding player, and other Negro stars on the team, contend they don't want to move to Atlanta because of possible racial problems; they say they don't want to move their families there; did the board of directors take that fact into consideration before making their decision?

"The previous day, Aaron had rebelled against the move, along with thousands of Milwaukee fans. 'I don't want to live in the deep South again,' he said. 'I want my children to attend integrated schools, as they are now doing. I have lived in the South. I was born in the deep South, and I don't think it is a good place to raise children.'"

Ernie Johnson, the man the Braves' executives put on the spot, tried to soften Hank's protest.

"I think Aaron's statement was misinterpreted," he said, squirming. "He really doesn't mean that he doesn't want to play in Atlanta. What he really means, as I understand it, is that he does not want to live there the year around."

What Hank said, of course, was not something that had to be interpreted. What he said was that he does not want to live in Atlanta at any time, during the season or off-season. It was Johnson who was trying to bring in an interpretation, not the newspapermen. In trying to do so, he sounded like one of Barry Goldwater's excuse-men. Johnson didn't do a very good job. Like Goldwater's interpreters, he was caught in a state of complete frustration.

"If you don't understand what I'm saying," the former pitcher said, "then ask Aaron just what he meant."

So ... one enterprising newsman did. He contacted Aaron soon after, and this is what the best player in Milwaukee's turbulent major league history said:

"I'm going to make my own investigation of the playing conditions for Negro players in Atlanta. If I find that they are as bad as I understand they are, I'll probably ask the club to trade me.

"I certainly don't like the idea of playing in Atlanta and I have no intention of taking my family there."

In all fairness to Atlanta, it must be said that there has been some revolutionary racial changes in that bustling Southern city. More racial progress has been achieved there than in any metropolitan city below the Mason-Dixon line, thanks to such spirited white citizens as Ralph McGill, the famous editor, and others. But apparently Aaron is not aware of those changes. Nobody has so informed him, and that's not his fault. The fact is that he does not want to move there.

"Baseball," Hank said, "has helped better race relations in the South. I can see some improvement in Houston. But I don't know how it will be in Georgia." Lee Maye, who with Rico Carty, provides the Braves with an all-Negro outfield agreed with Aaron.

"I expect that there's going to be a lot of humiliation for me there," Maye said glumly.

It is obvious that the Braves' board of directors never discussed the move to Atlanta with Aaron, nor with other Negro players on the team. All the directors want is—"out!"

That is just one of the many things that is wrong with the whole proposition. It also is one of the many things that might be wrong with the Braves next season. Morale, at the moment, is very low ... and could continue to be so during the coming season.

*The problem is less Atlanta and more the way the move was handled. But Atlanta is not irrelevant. Had the move been from Milwaukee to Buffalo without consulting the Black players it would not have been a concern. Wendell is fair to Atlanta and acknowledges that the city is relatively progressive. He concedes that Aaron might not be aware of that fact. But clearly, there exists an insensitivity here to the Black players' concerns that is disturbing. Why would the Braves not at least notify the Black players on the team that this move to a Southern city was being considered?*

## March 13, 1965

### Sports Beat, *Pittsburgh Courier*, p. 15

*A Guy Who "Knows" About Prejudice*

This was before the big fight in Chicago last week and Julie Isaacson, who is almost as tall, and considerably heavier, than his 6-6 200-pound heavyweight, Ernie Terrell, was talking about life and things in general.

They call him "Big Julie." He's a compulsive talker from Brooklyn. He loves horse racing, baseball, boxing, Roger Maris of the Yankees and Joe Louis. He also loves New York City ("In comparison, all other cities are Bushville"), and Miami's balmy weather at this time of the year ("You can sit on a bench at the track and sleep all day in the sun").

Big Julie does not love everything, nor everybody, however. Among his hates is racial prejudice. "I don't know too much about the fight game," he was saying to the sportswriters gathered around him in the press room at the Sheraton-Chicago Hotel. "All I do is protect my fighter, make sure he gets everything he needs and that nobody takes advantage of him. And, above all, I ain't gonna let any of those bigots push him to the back of the bus.

"I'm a Jew, and I know what prejudice is. So I watch out for it when I'm with Terrell. I ain't gonna let anybody insult him, or segregate him, or try to discriminate him. If they try it, I'll belt them right in the mouth."

Big Julie is president of a toy-makers' union in New York. He screams and whispers when he talks, and he spouts the words around the big, long cigar that's always in his mouth. He's a Damon Runyon character, alive and walking around.

"Do you know about prejudice?" sneered Big Julie. "Listen to this.... I'm down in Ft. Lauderdale, Fla., a few years ago. The Yankees are training there and I'm with my man, Roger.

"It's my birthday, so Roger says 'Make a reservation for five tonight; the dinner's on me. It's your birthday, so I'll pop. Call that restaurant and get a table. I'll meet you there after we workout.'"

Big Julie leaned back in his chair and continued: "There are more liberal places in this country than Ft. Lauderdale, and there are more liberal restaurants than this one I'm calling. I said to the guy on the other end of the line, 'I want a reservation for five.'

"The guy says, 'What's your name?'

"Julie Isaacson.

"There is a long pause, and then says, 'Spell it.'

"J-u-l-i-e.

"'No,' he says, 'the last name.' So I spell it for him.

"'I'm sorry,' he says, 'We don't have any reservations left.'

"So, I say 'Okay.' Then I go to Roger and tell him what happened. He knew what was going on. So, he calls the restaurant and says, 'This is Roger Maris. I want a reservation for five.'

"'Oh, Mr. Maris of the Yankees!' says the restaurant guy. 'Sure, anything you want.' We went over to the restaurant and the guy greets us like we're kings. The table for five is all set up, but before we can sit down, he wants to take us on a tour of the place. So, he shows us the whole establishment. He's as nice as can be.

"Now the time comes for us to sit down and eat. Maris says to him: 'I don't think we want the reservation, after all. I've changed my mind.'

"The guy is all upset. 'Is there anything wrong, Mr. Maris?' he asks.

"'Just forget it,' Roger tells him.

"So, we walk out the door. But just before we depart, I turn to this guy and I say to him—'I'm Julie Isaacson, the person who called for the reservation about a half hour ago. You told me you didn't have any. You're a liar!'

"Then I took a deep breath and spit right in his eye.

"When we walked out, he was trying to keep from drowning."

That's Julie Isaacson, the manager of Ernie Terrell.

*Good for you, Roger Maris!*

## February 3, 1970

### "Ashe is caught in South Africa dilemma," *Chicago Sun-Times*, p. 80

When Arthur Ashe, now 26 years old, was a small boy in Richmond, Va., his father, a disciplinarian, told the future tennis star, "You don't get anywhere making enemies. You gain by helping others."

Arthur, tall and lithe now, probably is the best tennis player in the world. He definitely has the greatest assortment of shots in the game, and he is without a doubt the most famous member of the United States Davis Cup team.

And at the moment he is in a dilemma because, contrary to his father's advice, he has made enemies in some areas. He has elected to fight apartheid as it is related to South Africa and tennis. He believes that by doing so he is helping others, somehow. On the other hand, he may be hurting more than helping.

Because he is black, the South African government has refused to issue him a visa to play tennis there. He cannot play as an individual but would be granted entry as a member of the U.S. Davis Cup team. That's weird, of course, but so is South Africa.

### Won't Join Team

"I wouldn't go as a member of the Davis Cup team," bespectacled Arthur Ashe said. "If I'm not acceptable as an individual, as a human being, then I'm not acceptable under any other circumstances or conditions."

Arthur Ashe is a highly articulate man. He is a graduate of UCLA. He is not a militant on matters of race. He speaks of the South African ban dispassionately, without bitterness. He was in town over the weekend for the Sporting Goods show.

"Actually it doesn't matter to me if I play there," he said. "It in no way affects my tennis life. All I'm trying to do is to help in some small way the 13 million blacks who live in South Africa. Also, incidentally I'd like to help the other non-whites who are suffering there. Besides those 13 million black Africans, there are two other racial groups who suffer because of their pigmentation. There are 1,500,000 mulattoes, people of white and black parentage; and there are the 2,000,000 Asians, who are either Indian or Chinese. They suffer, too, because of their skin color."

### Atrocities Tragic

The atrocities inflicted upon those races by the ruling 3,000,000 whites are tragic, to say the least. Arthur Ashe's dilemma is that his stand against South Africa's inhumanity may be causing more harm than good.

"Every time I say something against that system in South Africa," he said, softly, "the government gets tougher with the non-whites. Anytime anyone says anything about it, the South African government cracks down on the blacks, browns and reds. As a result, I've tried to be careful as to what I've said in this visa-tennis dispute.

"But there are times when you just can't help saying harsh things. Do you realize that native blacks have to carry passports in South Africa?

"It's all so ridiculous, so utterly incongruous; the Japanese, for example, do not have to adhere to the racial laws there. They are yellow, but they are treated the same as whites because Japan does millions of dollars worth of business with South Africa annually. The almighty dollar is the difference."

### Doesn't Blame Players

South Africa has virtually isolated itself from the world of sports because of its racial policies. It was barred from the last Olympics in Mexico and now it appears it will be ousted from Davis Cup and other major world tennis matches.

"It's too bad, in a way," Ashe said. "I know that the South African tennis players want to compete against the best players in the world but won't be able to now. I also know that some of them did what little they could to help me get a visa to play there. This thing is all involved in politics and that's unfortunate. Athletes don't think like politicians.

"The South African athletes don't dare say anything or they, too, will suffer. When Gary Player, the great golfer, is asked about this type of thing, he say, 'I have no comment. I am a golfer, not a politician.'

"I don't blame him for saying that. If he said anything critical of apartheid they might take his citizenship away from him. That goes for all South Africans. Too bad."

*Wendell gives Ashe the forum to state the problem. He does not tell us what Ashe thinks. He allows Ashe to inform the reader. While interviewing a man as articulate and intelligent as Arthur Ashe, let him talk directly to the reader. Wendell should be commended for what he did not do here. He did not get in the way.*

# 6

# Friendly Fire

*Wendell criticized individuals he liked and respected. Branch Rickey, Sugar Ray Robinson, Jim Brown, and Ernie Banks are subject to friendly fire in this chapter. Four of the entries address Negro League team owners. Wendell had a love/hate relationship with them. He respected their entrepreneurship and that they provided Black players with the opportunity to display their talents. But they refused to adopt sound business practices despite Wendell's warnings. Wendell loved the Negro Leagues for what they were; he hated the reason the Negro Leagues existed. He would have liked to see them continue in some capacity as a professional baseball league. But they could not survive MLB integration. He sadly watched them die. Ironically, he made a significant contribution to their demise.*

## May 14, 1938

### Smitty's Sport Spurts, *Pittsburgh Courier*, p. 17

*A Strange Tribe*

Why we continue to flock to major league ball parks, spending and hollering, stamping our feet and clapping our hands, begging and pleading for some white batter to knock some white pitcher's ears off, almost having fits if the home team loses and crying for joy when they win, is a question that probably never will be answered satisfactorily. What in the world are we thinking about anyhow?

The fact that major league baseball refuses to admit Negro players within its folds makes the question just that much more perplexing. Surely it's sufficient reason for us to quit spending our money and time in their ball parks. Major league baseball does not want us. It never has.

Still, we continue to help support this institution that places a bold "Not Welcome" sign over its thriving portal and refuses to patronize the very place that has shown that it is more than welcome to have us. We black folk are a strange tribe!

Negro baseball is still in its infancy. In the last ten years it has come a long, long way. Gone are the days when the players having the most knives and razors won the ball game. Gone are the days when the teams appeared before the public dressed like scarecrows and reminded us of the lost legion. Gone are the days when only one or two good players were on a team. Now their rosters are filled with brilliant, colorful, dazzling players who know the game from top to bottom. Negro teams now have everything the white clubs have. Except of course, the million dollar ball parks to play in; parks that we helped to build with our hard earned dollars. Nevertheless we ignore them and go to see teams play that do not give a hang whether we come or not.

Sounds silly doesn't it? Well—it's true! Despite the fact that we have our own teams and brilliant players, the most colorful in the world, mind you, we go elsewhere and get a kick out of doing it. Suckers! You said it brother!

They're real troopers, these guys who risk their money and devote their lives to Negro baseball. We black folk offer no encouragement and don't seem to care if they make a go of it or not. We literally ignore them completely. With our noses high and our hands deep in our pockets, squeezing the same dollar that we hand out to the white players, we walk past their ball parks and go to the major league game. Nuts—that's what we are. Just plain nuts! Listen! If any one of us wanted to talk to one of the ball players whom we've been spending our hard earned dough on, screaming and hollering, stamping our feet and clapping our hands for, we'd probably be ignored. If he did speak to us it would probably be a disrespectful salutation such as "Hello George," or "What ya' say Sam." Or maybe even worse than that. Oh he wouldn't eh! That's what you think. Don't forget that he comes from Mississippi, Georgia, Texas or any other place you can think of below the Mason-Dixon line. And he's white. He looks upon us as something the cat brought in. Even though he is playing ball in a northern city, making northern money he still looks upon us that way. He's a leopard and you know what they say about their spots. You can't change 'em!

We have been fighting for years in an effort to make owners of major league baseball teams admit Negro players. But they won't do it, probably never will. We keep on crawling, begging, and pleading for recognition just the same. We know that they don't want us but still we keep giving them our money. Keep on going to their ball games and shouting till we are blue in the face. Oh, we're an optimistic, faithful, pride-less lot—we pitiful black folk. Yes sir—we black folk are a strange tribe!

**There are plenty of white people who would appreciate our side of the story ... if they knew it! Pass your *Courier* along to such a friend.**

*This was the first of several columns Wendell addressed to Black sports fans. When Jackie Robinson broke the MLB color line, Wendell reminded Black fans that they too were being evaluated by white fans. He cautioned them to conduct themselves properly when attending games. This column is early in Wendell's career. It is the only example I found of Wendell doubting whether baseball would ever integrate. He is supportive of Negro League owners but will soon begin to have mixed feelings about them. The request to share the* Courier *with a white person that appears after Wendell's column appeared often throughout the paper. White people did read Black newspapers.*

## June 17, 1939

### Smitty's Sport Spurts, *Pittsburgh Courier*, p. 17

Tom Wilson, president of the Negro National League, takes exception to the column we did two weeks ago in regards to this organization. So riled was Mr. Wilson that he promptly sat down and wrote a stiff letter to our Editor-in-Chief, Mr. Robert L. Vann, charging us with everything from perjury to blackmail.

The Negro National League proxy points out that his organization does a huge volume of business every year and infers that it is a real credit to the race. Despite all the faults of the League, Mr. Wilson wants no more such columns appearing in public print. Above all things, he wants us to retract the charge that the League is not run properly.

Now, we realize that the men who invest money in Negro baseball are taking a big gamble. They are liable to lose thousands of dollars a year, and some have even gone broke. We also realize that it is impossible for the N.N.L. to run on the same basis as the majors. Such an effort would require too many green-backs.

### Why Overlook Errors?

But even so, should we overlook the errors of any business, even the N.N.L., just because of large investments? Should we approve of inexcusable negligence on such grounds?

Mr. Wilson and the N.N.L. seem to assume that the public is obligated to them in some way and that the League can make no mistakes. They would have us believe that every team in that organization is living from hand to mouth, that every team is losing money and therefore we should take down our hair and cry for their salvation.

*Players Improved*

Negro baseball has progressed in one way and retrogressed in another. The players have improved in playing ability and mannerisms. They are no more the roughnecks we once were ashamed of, but fine athletes and gentlemen. On the other hand, the bigwigs, the men who run the game from the front office, have failed to keep pace with their employees.

They are gentlemen, yes, but they have failed to handle the business end of the game properly. It is the duty of the N.N.L. to keep the public informed on such things as averages, disputes, scores of games, proper standings, trades, and all the other angles that the average fan wants to know about. After all, it is the public that pays the freight and makes it possible for that business to exist. The League is a big business but not as big as the public. The N.N.L. officials have failed to recognize that fact! Fortunately, the players have.

Regardless of the contentions of Mr. Wilson, we still claim that the Negro National League is sorely in need of a dose of good medicine. We still insist that a club owner has no business as president of the League, or that any other club owner should hold an official office.

*Some Questions*

We will gladly retract these claims if Mr. Wilson will answer a few of the following questions. They are questions which, if answered satisfactorily, will be a revelation to the average fan and uninformed newspaper men throughout the country.

Here, Mr. Wilson, are the questions:

Who are the five leading pitchers?

What are the fielding and batting averages of the teams? Kindly inform us who determines a League game and an exhibition game.

When is that determined and by whom?

When, if such a thing is determined in advance, is the public and press informed?

Who informs the public and press when a player is signed or released?

When a player is traded and ordered to report to another team and refuses to do so, what action is taken by the league officials?

Is he permitted to stay in the league with the same team?

Who assigns the umpires?

Who is the umpire in chief?

Have your umpires ever had a joint meeting to discuss situations that may arise in a ball game?

Last, but not least, Mr. Wilson, what are you, as President of the Negro National League, going to do about Ferrel and Whatly, now of the

Homestead Grays, who were taken from Birmingham of the American League without sanction of the American League officials? Are you going to force the Grays to return them to the American League, or okay it with the excuse that the American League took some players from your league without official sanction? Are you going to say that two wrongs make a right?

If possible, answer those questions Mr. Tom Wilson, and we'll say that the N.N.L. is being run by a group of real business men. If you don't, we'll still say you guys don't know what you're doing!

*It did not take long for Wendell to be frustrated with Negro League owners. Tom Wilson seems to think that a Black sportswriter should not criticize the Negro Leagues. Team owners were constantly stealing players from each other, and the absence of written contracts contributed to that. It is also difficult to fully appreciate the accomplishments of Negro League players because performance statistics were not consistently maintained. If a fan did not see the players play, he had no objective way to evaluate their performances. There was an attempt made to remedy that but to little avail.*

*Tom Wilson owned the Baltimore Elite Giants. J.B. Martin owned the Chicago American Giants. Martin's brothers owned the Memphis Red Sox. The Chicago and Memphis franchises were in the Negro American League. The Baltimore franchise was in the Negro National League. Wilson was the NNL president. Martin was the NAL president. That incestuous arrangement invited trouble.*

## December 18, 1943

### Smitty's Sports Spurts, *Pittsburgh Courier*, p. 14

*Negro Owners Must Prepare for the Future*

I am firmly convinced that the time has come for owners of Negro baseball teams to settle down and start operating on a sound business basis. If there was ever a time for these men to start figuring and planning for the future, it is now. Perhaps they can't see it, but the fact remains that their teams, and especially their players, are potential markets for the big leagues. No one knows when the majors will drop the color barrier and decide to admit Negro players. Perhaps this will never come to pass, but it is more than likely it will happen in the not so distant future. If and when this does happen the Negro players selected will by necessity come from the ranks of organized Negro baseball. Consequently, it seems to me, it would be wise for owners of teams in the Negro American and National leagues to stabilize themselves to the extent that they will be able to realize a financial profit if they are forced to give up some of their players.

Some people in Negro baseball have been arguing that the major leagues will not drop their time-worn barrier. That, however, is a matter of speculation. No one knows what will happen. The draft is taking a terrific toll in the majors and there is the possibility that some of the teams in the big leagues, mainly as a means of self-preservation, will seek to solve the problem by daringly signing up some Negro players. As they operate now, the Negro owners are in no position to bargain with major league teams for their players. The Negro owners will have to accept, whatever they are offered. In fact, the major leagues will be conceding a point if they recognize the claims of owners of Negro teams. I say that because the business methods in the Negro American and National leagues are not up to par and it wouldn't take much arguing on the part of a major league owner to prove that the two Negro leagues aren't really organized.

And, if the Negro leagues aren't organized, then a major league owner is in no way compelled to recognize the contracts and agreements which ordinarily apply to trades and sales of ball players.

That kind of reasoning may seem far-fetched to some Negro owners. They can't, however, escape the fact that they are a potential market for the majors. That fact alone should be enough to inspire them to tighten the business strings within their organizations and prepare for the future.

## Past Season Greatest in History

Even more important than the major league threat is the fact that Negro baseball enjoyed its greatest financial year in 1943. I believe I am safe in saying that every team in organized Negro baseball, with the possible exception of one, realized a profit of at least five thousand dollars in 1943. At least three teams went over the fifteen-thousand-dollar mark. When that kind of profit is realized it automatically becomes a big business issue. There is no doubt about it, Negro baseball has now attained the "big business" classification. It has passed the stage of being merely a sport or a hobby.

On the basis of the money made during the 1943 season, it seems to me that the owners should plan and prepare to protect such a profitable business; that they should concern themselves with a long range program designed to bring them even larger profits in the future. Sound business tactics will assure them of profits in years when the country has returned to normal. These are exceptional times. The public is willing to spend freely now. But this prosperity is not going to last. After the war, when we return to normalcy, it will take shrewd manipulation and sound business to continue operating.

*Should Develop a Post-War Program*

Sunday afternoon in Chicago the Negro American league will hold its annual winter meeting. It would be a wise move, I think, if these owners would turn their attention to a post-war program, designed to protect their interests and investments in the future. The Negro American league is blessed with a corps of men who have the financial means to remain in baseball for many years. None of them, however, is willing to go on forever without getting some of the money back that they have invested. At the present time they are enjoying financial success and realizing a profit. However, I am sure past experience has taught them that baseball is a difficult business to be in when prosperity is at a low ebb.

Dr. J.B. Martin, president of the Negro American League, is a good business man. He also has the help and co-operation of such capable men as Ernest Wright of Cleveland, Dr. B.B. Martin of Memphis, Tom Baird of Kansas City; Abe Saperstein and Tom Hayes of Birmingham and a number of others. It seems to me that such a group of men would have the foresight to look ahead and realize that sound, practical business is the only assurance for a continuation of the success they are now enjoying.

*Wendell is more optimistic that MLB integration will happen. World War II enabled Black baseball fans to earn more money at better-paying jobs and increase their disposable income. Wendell knows this will not go on forever. The good times will eventually end.*

# September 1, 1945

## Sports Beat, *Pittsburgh Courier*, p. 12

*Is Branch Rickey Kidding?*

So many psychopathic cases have developed on the fertile turf of Ebbets Field, home of the Brooklyn Dodgers, down through the years that it is generally accepted that such mental miscues could only happen in that slap-happy borough of New York. The hilarious fans of Brooklyn have seen their idols attempt to catch fly balls with their heads; watched in amazement as one of the Dodger infielders chased the opposition across home plate with the winning run in an effort to make a put-out; and more than once saw two or more Dodgers standing on the same base engaged in heated debate as to who had the priority.

Such incidents became so common that they gave birth to two observations which are now accepted nationally. One inspired the famous nickname, "Bum." The other was "unconditional surrender" on the part of fandom, who reluctantly admitted that "it could only happen in Brooklyn."

And, after reading a statement made by Branch Rickey, the Dodgers' big boss, in the St. Louis *Sporting News* during an interview, I am just about convinced no one can escape that strange malady which seems to grip people associated with baseball in that city where the tree grew, an event so astounding, it seems, that a woman writer won wealth and fame by simply recording the feat in a book. It could only happen in Brooklyn!

Commenting on the possible expansion of the major leagues, the usually sober thinking Rickey said: "It is not exactly a secret that St. Louis cannot support two major league clubs. This has been admitted. And there have been publicly confessed efforts, both by the Cardinals and the Browns, to move into other territory." And then, Mr. Rickey makes this breath-taking statement: "The situation in St. Louis is complicated. There is a vast Negro population there, and it has not yet got into the habit of supporting Major League Baseball."

Then the Brooklyn boss fires a pointed question in desperation. "What is to be done about St. Louis?" he asks seriously.

Is Mr. Rickey kidding? The answer to his question is in the heart of his previous statement. He says St. Louis cannot support two major league clubs. That statement is so true that it is tragic. He infers, however, it might be possible if the management of the Browns and Cardinals could capitalize on that vast Negro population in St. Louis. Negroes in St. Louis, he points out, have not "got into the habit of supporting major league baseball."

"What is to be done about St. Louis?" Rickey asks. He says it's a very complicated situation.

## What Is So Complicated About It?

I'd like to ask Mr. Rickey one question on this matter. The question is this: "What the hell is so complicated about St. Louis?" If the majors want to pull that city out of the financial doldrums, all they have to do is put some Negroes on those clubs. The reason that the vast Negro population there has not yet got into the habit of supporting major league baseball is because they are clearly conscious of the vicious discriminatory policy the two St. Louis clubs, and all others—including Mr. Rickey and his Dodgers—foster against Negro players. The St. Louis clubs have not only been guilty of discriminating against Negro players, but Negro fans as well.

Until a few years ago, Negro fans in St. Louis were forced to sit in a special jim-crow section. Sportsmen's Park was the only major league park in the country that had such a policy. Negro fans were forced to sit where the park wanted them to sit. They were segregated, whether they like it or not.

It is significant, too, that this policy was rigidly enforced while this same Mr. Rickey was bossing the St. Louis Cardinals. Can it be possible that Mr. Rickey used to fret a bit on those dull and dark days when there were more players on the bench than people in the park, and wonder why more of that vast Negro population didn't show up to be jim-crowed?

## Seems to Be Sincere Man

I met Mr. Rickey in his office last spring, when he called a meeting of the press and announced he was unofficially associated with the newly organized United States League, the brainchild of energetic Gus Greenlee. At that time Mr. Rickey seemed to be extremely interested in Negro baseball and the future of the Negro players as related to his advancement into the majors. Mr. Rickey had agreed to give two Negro players a "look over," and he lived up to his agreement. He "looked them over" and then decided they weren't good enough for his Dodgers. Whether they were good enough or not is a matter of opinion. It was his opinion that they were not. And, in view of the fact that his word is final on such matters, we must accept his negative opinion.

The important thing, it seemed to me, was that Rickey did grant those two players—Terris McDuffie of the Newark Eagles, and Dave (Showboat) Thomas of the Cubans—an audience. Even though he turned them down, he did establish himself as a man willing to face the issue. He appeared to be a man with his feet on the ground, and not one trying to evade the issue. I am still inclined to believe that he is sincerely interested in the fate of the Negro player. After talking with him privately for an hour in his office and being exposed to his views and opinions on this question, I have no other alternative. He seems to be a deeply sincere man.

That is one reason why I am taken back a bit by that absurd question he asked about the St. Louis situation.

"What are we going to do about St. Louis?"

The answer is obvious.... Hire Negro ball players!

And that goes for Brooklyn, too, Mr. Rickey!

*Branch Rickey would soon sign Jackie Robinson to a professional base-ball contract. I don't know if Wendell knew of this yet. Perhaps he could sense that Rickey was different. The St. Louis Browns did sign two Black players: Hank Thompson and Wilfred Brown. Still, Negro fans did not support the team. Wendell would write a column critical of those Black fans. Both players were released after a month. Thompson would go on to have a successful career with the New York Giants. Brown would never play in the major leagues again.*

## January 26, 1946

### Sports Beat, *Pittsburgh Courier*, p. 16

*They're Reaping What They've Sown...*

The owners of teams in Negro baseball have suddenly become deeply concerned about the organizational structure of their leagues and are now soliciting the aid and support of baseball's high commissioner, A.B. (Happy) Chandler. It is significant to note, dear readers, that this concern is not motivated by a desire to improve the status of the Negro player, but simply to protect their own selfish interests. These owners—some of whom are white—have rolled along their merry way down through the years, ignoring the common laws of organized baseball and grasping what they could wherever they found it.

Despite the pleadings of the Negro Press and other forces interested in the general welfare of Negro baseball, they have arbitrarily gone overboard in exercising their right of "free enterprise." Generally, the Negro owners have exhibited little or no racial pride, and the white owners in business with them haven't forced the issue in matters designed to improve the status of the game, the player, or the unfavorable impression Negro baseball has created with the public as an institution. The white owners in Negro baseball have very wisely let the issue stand pat, less they become involved in issues with their Negro colleagues relative to racial progress and advancement.

When Branch Rickey signed Jackie Robinson last fall to a Montreal contract, he blew the roof off of Negro baseball. Suddenly there was a great uproar from the officials of Negro baseball. They charged that Rickey was stealing their property and had refused to recognize that they existed as a league. They emphasized that they were in no way anxious to hinder the progress of the Negro player advance, but insisted that they should be compensated for producing him to such men as Branch Rickey. The officials of the Negro American and National Leagues demanded financial consideration on all "future and similar deals."

The truth of the matter is this: Few, if any, of the owners in Negro baseball are sincerely interested in the advancement of the Negro player, or what it means with respect to the Negro race as a whole. They'll deny that of course, and shout to the high heavens that racial progress comes first and baseball next. But actually, the preservation of their shaky, littered, infested segregated baseball domicile comes first, last, and always.

*All They Saw Was Gold...*

Anyone under the impression that the signing of Jackie Robinson was received with joyous acclaim within the portals of Negro baseball is sadly mistaken. While approximately 13 million Negroes and possibly a like number of whites received the announcement with enthusiasm, there was a sullen reaction and frantic scramble to "save everything before the avalanche" inside the house of Negro baseball. So they went whimpering to Chandler, pleading for recognition and no further repetition of the "Robinson case." All they saw was the glittering gold they've been reaping for the past four years; all they envisioned was the crumbling of their bawdy house; all they cared about was the perpetuation of the "slave trade" they had developed via the channels of segregated baseball.

Now, Chandler tells Negro baseball to "get your house in order," and infers that if it does so, Organized Baseball will interest itself in the possibility of admitting Negro baseball. What does that mean? It means that the presidents of the Negro leagues must be removed and men who are not officially affiliated with teams inserted. It means the end of syndicated baseball, the death of the far-flung "booking system." It means the end of make-shift schedules and all the other inconsistencies that have made it a farce. It means the formation of a real, business-like organization.

If those moves are made, you can bet that they will be made with a reluctance. The men who are now in the driver's seat in Negro baseball are in no way anxious to be harnessed or regimented by rules and regulations. They want to continue operating as they have in the past; giving practically nothing and taking almost everything. They still want to schedule games according to their whims and dictate according to their wishes. There are certain officials in Negro baseball who revel and gloat over their positions, and there are others who maintain their lordly posts because it enables them to foster a vicious yet profitable system of exploitation. All this will end if they get their "house in order."

And while they are frantically running around searching for a way to continue their pirate-like methods, their ball players are being left vulnerable to the flattering advances of outside interests.

There is no reason why the appeal to Chandler for recognition by Organized Baseball should not be viewed with suspicion. There is reason to believe, however, that owners of Negro teams hope to put the brakes on the surge of Negro players headed in the direction of the majors. It would not be too fantastic to assume that once they are a part of Organized Baseball they hope to join up with reactionary forces already there. Such an undesirable union could hamper the advancement of the Negro player into the majors considerably. Negro baseball would then be a part, yet not a part, of Organized Baseball. They could possibly operate on this theory: "You leave our players alone, and we'll leave yours alone."

### Why All the Mystery?...

If there is not a subtle plan below the surface, then why all the mystery? Commissioner Chandler said last Sunday that he had met with "officials of the Negro leagues." Such an event must have been a momentous occasion, because there are owners in both Negro and white baseball who did not know of such a meeting. If they met with Chandler, when did they meet, and where? Why was it that the press and general public were not informed? And, who were the officials of the Negro leagues with whom Commissioner Chandler met? Thus far, no one seems willing to answer those questions.

Any apprehension that develops over the relationship between the officials of Organized Baseball and the officials of Negro baseball is only natural. Organized Baseball has practiced a vicious policy of discrimination against Negro players, and in so doing made it possible for the segregated Negro leagues to flourish and prosper. While wallowing in the mire of segregation and discrimination, the owners of Negro baseball were the benefactors of that vicious system, and they benefited greatly. So much so, that the gold blinded them and they are now firmly caught in their own trap.

*Negro League team owners were not angels. Some were involved in nefarious activities like the numbers racket. They were repeatedly warned about what was coming and they ignored it. They did realize large profits in some years. Some of them did lack racial pride as Wendell defines it. But Wendell did not have any of his money invested in the Negro Leagues. Wendell did increase his fame by writing about Negro League baseball. The Negro Leagues provided a forum for Black players to demonstrate their abilities. Wendell is on firm ground when he chastises Negro League owners for their sloppy business practices. He knew many of them personally and might have known their motives. Smith knew that the owners were in a difficult position, but they had ignored warnings. In a sense, they came to the harm. He had limited sympathy for them.*

## January 24, 1948

### Sports Beat, *Pittsburgh Courier*, p. 16

*So, There Was No Contract!*

Proof that most Negro baseball clubs are operated on a slip-shod basis is clearly evident in the case of John Ritchey, 22-year-old catcher of the Chicago American Giants, who has been signed by San Diego of the Pacific Coast League. Ritchey was recently signed by the Coast league club and the announcement of the event set off a growl and roar from the vicinity of Chicago. J.B. Martin, owner of the American Giants, and president of the Negro American League, charged that the San Diego club had stolen Ritchey from him. He immediately dispatched a letter of protest to Commissioner Chandler. He demanded an investigation.

But before Chandler could go to work on the case, he asked Martin to send him a duplicate of Ritchey's contract for the past season. Ritchey had played with the Giants throughout the '47 season and had won the league batting crown. Surely Martin had a contract for this valuable young player.

When Martin searched through his files—or whatever in the world he uses to keep such important documents—there was no contract to be found. He then called in Candy Jim Taylor, manager of the club. "I want Ritchey's contract for last season," he said. "I have to send it to Chandler."

Taylor raised his eyebrows in surprise. "I don't have his contract," he said. "You're the owner and you sign the ball players."

"I thought you had signed him to a contract last spring," Martin said with a low moan. "I was sure you had." Taylor hadn't however.

Martin then had to write Chandler and tell him he could not find Ritchey's contract. "But," he wrote, "he's still my property. He played on my club all last year."

The commissioner must have rolled in the aisle when he learned of this laxity on the part of the president of the Negro American League. Obviously he has been operating his club on an *Amos 'n' Andy* basis.

Chandler then wrote to Martin: "The Executive Council of Baseball would want to handle, with the most careful ethics the cases of organized baseball taking players from the Negro leagues. At present, I am somewhat at a loss to know how we can hold one of our minor league clubs responsible for the violation of an alleged contract when the contract itself cannot be found, and when, apparently, those responsible for obtaining the contract are uncertain whether or not they ever did obtain it."

When Brooklyn signed Jackie Robinson and sent him to Montreal, J.L. Wilkinson of the Kansas City Monarchs hollered "robber," too. But like Martin, he was unable to produce a bona fide contract with Robinson's name on it. That, too, we'll call a slight oversight. In fact, that's all you can call it.

But in each instance that "slight oversight" cost the respective owners many a good dollar. Robinson has turned out to be a $50,000 ball player, and Ritchey goes into the Pacific Coast League an excellent prospect.

*Jackie Robinson is preparing for his third season in professional baseball and the Negro American League president does not have a star player under a written contract.*

*March 12, 1949*

## Sports Beat, *Pittsburgh Courier*, p. 10

*Fight Mob Member Talks to Himself...*

Now ain't this a mell of a hess? This here Joe Louis ups and quits the fight game. He ain't gonna be the Champ enny more. Says he's tired with it all. How can a guy get so tired he don't wanna pick up 500 grand? It is disgusting to say the least, and the next time I see him I'll think twice before I give him a good hello. He's tired!

What about me? I ain't got nobody enny more to mooch off. This here Louis ups and quits without even giving me a chance to get a new angel. They say he's a good guy. Always thinks about his friends first, then hisself. Now, I know that ain't a bit true. Did he think about me when he decided to retire? No! Did he call me in for a conference and say: "Look, Hotnose, I'm giving up the crown, get yourself a new hustle." No! He gives me no consideration whatsoever.

Believe me, when I tell you, I am irritated no little. I am around with this Louis for fourteen years. In all that time I served him faithfully. I travel with him. Eat with him. Sleep with him. I even go to Europe with him, and to South America. I am even considerate enough to take his money from him. Sometimes he doesn't know it. But I always say it is better to have your friends take your money than a stranger. After all, you may never see a stranger again. But this Louis could always depend on seeing me again. In fact, the only time I ever leave him is when he goes off to the war.

*The Very First to Greet Him*

I wouldn't have taken a powder on him then except that I am a guy who advocates peace and do not like to get mixed up with fore-ners. I am particularly glad to ignore fore-ners who go around carrying guns with bullets in them. Hotnose (that's me) is a peace-lovin' man. So I stayed over here and looked after the Champ's business interests. I lived in his apartment, drove his car, ate in his restaurant and danced in the evenings at his night club. Once I even wrote him a letter when he was over there.

And—who was at the boat when he came marching home? Me! Old Hotnose! When they tie up the boat at the dock, I am right there. The Champ comes marching down the gang-plank and who is the first to greet him?

Me! Ole Hotnose! I am the first to shake his hand. I am the first to pat him on the back. I am the first to say he looks fine and ask how the war was. I am also the first to ask him to loan me some money. And I am the first to get it.

That just goes to show you what a good, close friend I am to this 'ere Louis.

I cannot understand how he can do this to me. How he can leave me holding the bag. I do not mind holding bags. But, after all, this one does not have anything in it.

If I do not get a few bobs, I will not be able to eat. And if I do not eat I am sure to lose weight. There is one thing I cannot stand—a man who is so hungry he is losing weight. He gets so skinny! In fact, before Louis comes along I am, very much that way. I was so skinny I used to have to stay inside on windy days. But Louis comes along and I latch on to him, lead him to fame and, of course, fortune. It was then that I began to put on weight and could venture out on windy days.

## That Walcott Fight Was Enough

This is the second time within two years the Champ has put me in an embarrassing position. The first time was when he fought Jersey Joe Walcott at Madison Square Garden and almost lost his title. Walcott knocks him down twice and the fight is closer than 12 o'clock. I am never so embarrassed before in my life. When Louis is on the floor, all my friends at the ringside turn around and look at me. They sneer at me and say that my ride is over; that I'll have to get a new hustle. They seem very glad, too. I, of course, am very worried.

I yell to the Champ and tell him to get up off his pants and go after this Walcott. After all, I do not know this Walcott very well and there is no way that I can latch on to him in case Louis loses the title. Then, too, this Walcott does not have much money to give around. He has a wife and six brats. Louis seldom has a wife. Sometimes he does, then again he doesn't.

Fortunately, Louis gets up off his pants and saves our title. I am very glad because it would have been most embarrassing to me had he lost. What would my intimate friends have said? I told the Champ afterward that I wouldn't tolerate such monkey-shines again.

Now he has gone and done it! He's left me high and dry. I cannot face one friend. My pride is hurt to the quick. Nor, do I have any means of getting any quick money.

The very least he could have done was to have given his crown to me. That would have been a gesture of real, true friendship. There is nothing so valuable as a heavyweight crown. If there had been a warm spot in his heart he would have given it to me—Ole Hotnose.

I could have gotten a good price for it in a pawn shop!

*Wendell does not name names. But he has seen the entourage. Louis was not the only fighter to have one. But Joe Louis is arguably Wendell's favorite athlete and an American icon.*

## *January 12, 1957*

### Sports Beat, *Pittsburgh Courier*, p. 22

New York City—Sugar Ray Robinson, a shell of a champion, was battered from his lofty throne by a sincere, but mediocre, fighter who refused to be awed or impressed by the King's arrogant strut and cheap threats of annihilation.

Robinson was nothing more than a gaudy, cheesecake champion when he climbed into the ring before those 18,000 fans in Madison Square Garden. His primary mission was to collect $138,000. That's what the "Pretender" to the throne taxed his subjects and public for the privilege of watching him flounder and stumble … and fall and fumble … for 15 inglorious rounds.

"His Majesty" is all through as a super fighter and any boxing commission anywhere that permits him to milk the public at top prices again is guilty of collaboration.

His conqueror, Gene Fullmer, is a butcher without a cleaver. He chops away and chops away, but couldn't dent your chin with an axe. The first fighter that comes along with any class at all will beat him. Class is something Robinson once had in the ring … and now he has even lost that completely.

In other years, a bulldozer like Fullmer wouldn't have gotten close enough to him to mess up his "conked" hair. But those greased and straightened strands were all over his battered head when this fight was over.

When His Lordship climbed into the ring, aided and assisted, of course, by what he refers to as his "entourage," one got the impression that he might be saying to himself: "Well, I'm going to give the suckers a break. I'll acknowledge the presence of a few of them." Then he turned to the crowd and with a hypocritical smile on his face greeted some of the ringside celebrities. He was condescending and benevolent, going so far as to give a few special peasants a soft, cute wink.

Meantime, over in the other corner, the one who had come to be assassinated by the vain King, stood calmly, quietly. He had no time for quips or smiles. He had come to fight, not to pose and strut like a clown in a small town burlesque show.

Then the bell rang, Fullmer went out and gave His Majesty a sound thrashing, bulling him all around the ring, knocking him down and cutting him up so that the blood from his slashed left eye splashed on some of the screaming ringside peons. But they didn't mind. After all it was "royal" blood, which is something you can't get every day for the small sum of $30.

The best thing to do against a crude fighter like Fullmer is to dance away and try to box him. Retreating is the better part of valor in a case like that. That should have been easy for the "mighty" champion because once upon a time he had the gall to glide out on the stage and offer the public his version of the old soft shoe and some other steps that only the dutiful members of his "entourage" had been permitted to witness. In those days he wore a top hat and tails instead of trunks. But he had that same beautiful smile on his face and it illuminated the entire theatrical world, as well as the peasants sitting in the pews below him.

But for some reason His Highness didn't slay 'em in St. Joe or Keokuk, or Chicago, Detroit, Wilkes Barre or Rochester. Actually, the peasants stayed away in droves. So he decided to go back to the good thing—boxing. He did, and here he was now trying again in trunks to dance away from the ever-charging Fullmer. But he couldn't do it. The old soft shoe routine wasn't any good in the ring, either. And Fullmer, who can't dance a lick, stayed with him and went on to take the title. He wasn't even breathing hard when it was over.

But His Lordship was. He was weary, battered and beaten ... down to the point that he was too exhausted in the dressing room to flash that internationally famous smile. He just looked down at the peasants and admitted that he had lost.

And ... they looked back at him and asked: "Where now, mighty King, where now?"

Naturally, he couldn't answer them.

*Wendell was correct. Robinson's boxing skills were substantially diminished. However, he would defeat Fullmer four months later to regain the middleweight title. Then he would lose the title to Carmen Basilio later that same year. But he was not quite finished. He defeated Basilio in 1958 to win back the title for the last time. He permanently retired after his last fight in 1965.*

## July 18, 1959

### Sports Beat, *Pittsburgh Courier*, p. 25

Why is it so many fighters, especially those who hit the top, wind up destitute and broke?

That question is forever on the horizon and one nobody can adequately answer apparently. It is interesting to note, however, that very few former fighters from the preliminary ranks ever get caught in the breadline.

Yet over the years thousands of undistinguished fighters come and go without having to depend upon charity when they finally realize they are sub-par performers and wasting time in the ring.

What happens to those fighters? They never had a bank account, never made enough in one bout to buy a home, a big car or open a glittering night club. Many others on top have only to lose their investments for one reason or another.

The simple answer to that question may be this: The fighters who never were good enough to crash the select circle of champions, or near champions, were always conscious of the fact that someday they'd eventually have to call it quits and go get a job. Few preliminary fighters have become emotionally upset or frustrated over the prospect of becoming an ordinary guy carrying a lunch box to work every day.

Some people argue that the former champions and topnotch challengers go astray and eventually become public wards because of great pride. When their glory days are over, such people reason, they can't stand the ordinary humdrum of everyday life, the monotonous task of pulling their bones out of bed every morning and hitting the pavement with the rest of the working world.

But that, it seems here, is a ridiculous excuse for the former blue ribbon boys. The truth probably is that they abhor work and prefer to live on past achievements. It is acknowledged that many were duped out of fortunes by conniving, slippery managers and when they realized it, turned bitter against all forms of legitimate work.

The fact remains, however, that none, if any, was swindled out of his physical resources. All were, ostensibly, healthy and strong enough to join the nation's working forces and become acceptable, ordinary citizens.

All of this came to mind recently when a customer walked into Sugar Ray Robinson's barber shop and encountered a former middleweight fighter by the name of Danny (Bang Bang) Womber.

Womber is now probably 30 years old. He was an energetic, spirited middleweight who showed flashes of skill on occasions but never was good enough to hit the big time.

In the main, he was a preliminary fighter appearing on the cards that featured the magnificent Sugar Ray. Womber fought in the big cities, Detroit, Chicago, New York and Los Angeles, because he happened to be one of Ray's sparring partners. He realized early in his career that he lacked championship qualifications. Unlike many champions, Womber had his eyes on the future, on the day when he'd have to bow out even as a preliminary fighter.

Wisely, he went to barber's school and learned the trade. Now he works in Sugar Ray's well patronized and highly successful shop.

"I knew I had to learn a trade of some kind," Womber said, "because eventually I'd have to get out and look for a job. So I went to barber school. I also had a few side jobs. I'd work during the day and train at night.

"The only interruptions I had was when Sugar Ray needed me at one of his training camps. All the time I was fighting, I was also learning this trade. Now, I'm happy that I did. I do real good here as a barber, and it is dignified work. I'm not ashamed to walk out and face the people who once paid money to see me fight. And, I get the impression that those people like me just as much now as they did then, maybe more. I think people respect me."

Danny (Bang Bang) Womber is a working man today ... a good barber and in no need of financial help from others.

There's a man with pride, we'd say! Ex-champs, please note.

*Wendell had covered boxing long enough to see that fistic success in the ring did not guarantee financial success outside it. Joe Louis and Sugar Ray Robinson turned to show business to earn a living after their boxing careers had ended (Sugar Ray made a comeback after show business). Sugar Ray's heart seemed to be in the show biz circuit, but Louis was just going through the motions. Robinson negotiated his own contracts. Louis left that to others. Ray was moody. Louis was amiable. They took different paths but ended up in the same financial situation. Danny Womber was no match for Robinson or Louis in the ring, but outside of boxing, he did all right.*

## December 7, 1963

### Sports Beat, *Pittsburgh Courier*, p. 15

*There is a misprint in the paragraph beginning "The actions of the administrators..." I don't know how it is supposed to read; therefore, I did not make any corrections.*

*Smitty Takes Blast at Negro Colleges Who Played
Games Following JFK Death*

Of all the incredible events that transpired over the horrifying weekend of President Kennedy's assassination, the revolting decision of certain Negro colleges to play football in that hour of international bereavement must be recorded among the most shocking and disrespectful.

While the world grieved, no less than ten Negro college administrations sanctioned football and played games that meant absolutely nothing. The hypocritical administrators of those colleges sent immature young men out to play ... to run and cavort in the shadow of John F. Kennedy's bier.

Is there any wonder that the youth of this nation—particularly Negro youth—face the challenge of adulthood and the future with apprehension and a high degree of bitterness?

Put the names of those administrators down in the history books of American infamy, in indelible ink. They should never be forgotten. For it was those men who encouraged mere boys to romp and grapple joyously in the nation's saddest hour.

Do not blame the boys.

They had no voice, no choice, in the matter.

They were victimized by those who parade sanctimoniously before the public as the molders of tomorrow's men, this nation's future leaders.

The boys were sent out to play games by educators who are pledged to set examples. No President ever risked more—nor lost more—than did John F. Kennedy on behalf of Negroes.

It is not necessary to record here what the late President attempted to do for this nation's Negro community. If there are those who are not aware of President Kennedy's relentless and unswerving devotion to the Negro cause—we can only suggest that they climb the hill in Arlington Cemetery where his body is embalmed.

Look at his grave.

Look at the lonely grave of John F. Kennedy.

Elsewhere around the nation, it was an interval for weeping.

The action of the administrators who blew whistles to play in such an hour of shame and mourning is almost beyond comprehension. For, with the possible exception of Abraham Lincoln, no American ruthless mob of hypocrites and desecrate the immaculate dignity of an honorable man and President. In essence, they spat upon his coffin and honored him with a wreath of thorns.

They will deny this, of course. Mobsters always rise in protest and plead innocence when hit on the head by the gavel of decency and respect. But the record speaks for itself. They cannot deny that they played with an ardent fervor and without shame, while the chimes of death tolled universally for Mr. Kennedy.

No less than one hundred administrators of other colleges agreed on that tragic weekend that the boys and girls in their schools should refrain from participating in athletics. They, out of respect, canceled or postponed football games and other athletic events.

The Negro colleges of which we write harbored no such respect.

The names of the administrators of those Negro colleges are not worthy of mention here, or elsewhere. However, there is no reason not to list the games that they permitted to be played. Here they are:

Fisk vs. Morehouse
Florida A&M vs. Bethune-Cookman
J. C. Smith vs. Fayetteville State
Prairie View vs. Southern Louisiana
Winston-Salem Teachers vs. St. Paul

We may have missed a few other games, but it does not matter. The fact remains that those games mentioned above were between schools considered leading Negro institutions of learning. Nor are the results of those games worthy of mention. Under the circumstances … nobody won.

*Wendell is no less angry here than he was when writing about the worst of discrimination against Black athletes. Early in his career Wendell covered Black college football. He had a sentimental attachment to it. To see it sullied in this way was more than he could tolerate. The prior week he had written one of his saddest columns. (See Chapter 10.) This week he was fuming.*

## October 3, 1964

### Sports Beat, *Pittsburgh Courier*, p. 14

The hysterical response by the nation's daily press to Jimmy Brown's comment relative to the veiled affinity between America's Negroes and the Black Muslims was as hilariously ridiculous as the statement itself.

In a story in the current issue of *Look* magazine, the Cleveland Browns' mighty fullback declared that the "Black Muslim's basic attitude toward whites is shared by almost 99 per cent of the Negro population."

Jimmy is, perhaps, the greatest fullback in football, but it is hardly conceivable that he will ever be employed as a bank teller or auditor. He obviously can't figure percentages. It is safe to estimate that he overshot the percentage mark by no less than 90 per cent.

The daily press, however, accepted his figure as gospel and splashed his estimate all over the sports pages. It is amazing, indeed, how the daily media reacts at times on racial matters. It has a fantastic aptitude for quoting unqualified "experts" on racial subjects which should be left solely to qualified experts. If such esteemed gentlemen as Ralph Bunche, Roy Wilkins, Whitney Young, or the Rev. Martin Luther King had made the comment, there would have been justification for press hysteria.

But not when Jimmy Brown, a football player, makes such a statement. No more so than if Y.A. Tittle or Paul Hornung, also football players, should say that 99 per cent of the nation's white population is dedicated to the principles of the Ku Klux Klan. The daily press certainly would view such a statement by either as maniacal or idiotic.

Brown's comments about football and his Cleveland Browns' career were much more authoritative and interesting to us than his Black Muslims-Negro population reference. He is an expert on football; on Muslims and 99 per cent of the Negro population, he is not.

He answers many questions in the Look Article, for example, that have never been answered before, most of them relating to the dissension which developed on the Browns team in the latter stages of Coach Paul Brown's reign.

"In 1962, I told Cleveland club owner Art Modell that if Paul Brown remained as head coach in '63 I wanted out," Jimmy reveals in the *Look* magazine article. "Trade me, I told Modell, or I'll quit. I was not the only player to make such a threat."

That revelation by Jimmy Brown is intriguing. It exposes a form of mutiny on the part of the Cleveland players. Many suspected that a wholesale rebellion caused Coach Brown's dismissal. Jimmy's story confirms it.

Commenting further on Coach Brown, Jimmy says that the players had the feeling at the end that their coach no longer was obsessed with winning the championship, but merely with having a good season; one that did not disgrace his name.

"Morale was shot," Jimmy reveals. "Thus Paul was fired—not because I and other players demanded to be rid of him, but because Art Modell simply moved to protect his investment."

Jimmy sounds a little ambiguous on that point, of course. There is no doubt whatsoever that Paul Brown was kicked out because he could neither handle, nor regiment, his players any longer. The coach lost his touch ... and when that happens to any coach, he has to go. "Although I was billed as Paul's star performer," Jimmy says candidly, "I had no relationship with him. I wanted to, but his aloofness put him beyond approach. Yet, curiously, during my rookie season I thought Paul was a great guy. Paul dazzled me with compliments and solicitude. I led the league in rushing that year with 942 yards, and we won the Eastern Division title.

"I had every reason to expect that I would always be happy working for Paul. But I didn't realize at the time that Paul followed a pattern in his handling of men—a pattern in which, at an almost predictable moment, he would turn off his amiability as decisively as a plumber turns off the warm water with a twist of his wrench."

Those are just some of the exciting incidents and experiences

Jimmy Brown reveals in the *Look* article. It's exceptionally good reading, probably the best story on the "inside pro football" ever exposed to the public.

Only his estimate of the Muslims and their influence over 99 per cent of the Negro population can be considered an offside play.

*Wendell demonstrates his ability to dissect an issue as finely as need be to analyze it objectively from different perspectives. He respects Jim Brown's intelligence but calls him out when Brown makes a ridiculous statement. And Wendell criticized the press for not challenging Brown.*

# 7

# Progress

*Wendell was a bridge between the white and Black communities. He fought racism and acknowledged progress in race relations. He believed that things could get better and enjoyed writing about it. Chapter 6, "Friendly Fire," begins with an entry written in May 1938 that is negative. The first piece in this chapter is written five months later and the reader can see a change in Wendell's tone. He was meeting white people, some of them Southerners, with surprisingly progressive attitudes regarding race relations. Wendell experienced much disappointment during his career, but he never lost faith in America's capacity to improve. Nor did he cease insisting that America fulfill its promise to Black citizens. There was too much that could be done to be too negative. There was too much that needed to be done to be sanguine.*

## October 29, 1938

### Pittsburgh Courier, p. 17

*Matty Bell Tells of Team Vote Which Erased Color Line*

Famed Coach of S.M.U., Who at One Time Played Professional Football with Robeson, Pollard and Slater, Thinks Negroes Will Eventually Star on Big White Southern Teams—Players Rate Kenny "One of Greatest."

*Rates Texas College on a Par with S.M.U.; Lauds Anderson*

They're Mustangs ... but they're tamed and civilized!

That was the impression we received after having a heart to heart talk with Coach Matty Bell and members of his razzle-dazzle Southern Methodist University football team, from Dallas, Texas, Saturday afternoon just before they tried to lariat the Pitt Panther in the University of Pittsburgh Stadium.

Through the kindness of Garrett Turner, the Colored trainer, who has been with S.M.U. ever since the school started 23 years ago, we had the pleasure of talking with the man and the team that last year disregarded southern tradition and custom, and made a progressive step up the ladder of racial understanding, by agreeing to play against Kenny Washington and Woodrow Wilson Strode, the two Colored football stars of the University of California at Los Angeles.

Last season, before the S.M.U. game, authorities of the California school informed Coach Bell that they would keep their two Colored stars, Washington and Strode, on the bench when their teams played if he wanted them to. But the fair-minded Texans refused to let U.C.L.A., a northern institution of higher learning (?), "sell-out" the two Colored stars by replying that they would gladly play against them.

As a result, Strode and Washington played in the game against the southerners. Despite the brilliant playing of the two Negro Stars, the broad-minded Mustangs walloped "those yankees" 26 to 13 in a rip-snortin' game that had approximately 50,000 football fans delirious before it was over. But neither the score or brilliant playing of the two teams was nearly as significant as was the fact that for the first time in Southwestern history, a southern college willingly pushed aside petty prejudices and principles and refused to draw the color-line where Negro football players were concerned.

Coach Madison "Matty" Bell has been in the coaching business for the past eighteen years. A typical Texan, tall and lanky, he knows football inside and out. His was the first Southwest Conference team to play in California's famed Rose Bowl, and the first to place two players on an All-American team in the same year. In 1916, along with "Bo" McMillan, he played on the famous Centre College team that gained national fame by walloping some of the biggest and best teams in the country.

After graduation, Bell cast his lot in professional football. One of the best teams, he says, he ever played on was in Milwaukee, Wisconsin. On that team were such gridiron immortals as Fritz Pollard, Paul Robeson and Duke Slater, all of whom made All-American teams during their college careers.

As soon as we met the famous Southern Methodist mentor, we hopped on the question concerning Negro players on northern college teams playing against southern white college teams.

"Do you think," we asked, "will there ever be a time when southern schools will play northern schools who have Colored players, without demanding that the color-line be drawn?"

"I certainly do," he answered sincerely, "the time is bound to come and I hope that it will be soon. Southern colleges must realize that they cannot keep on making such demands. It not only weakens teams when they must bench these Colored stars, but also creates a lot of ill feeling."

Coach Bell talks with that slow drawl characteristic of southerners, but he holds nothing back and says exactly what he thinks. "I don't believe in drawing the color-line in sports," he confessed, "because when you do it takes something out of it. I think that every boy should have his chance to participate regardless of his color."

The Southern Methodist Coach was simply stating the ideals and sportsmanship he displayed last year when he refused to insist that U.C.L.A. bench Kenny Washington and Woodrow Wilson Strode. We finally found an opening for the question we wanted answered the most and shot it to the genial Texan full blast.

"Just what is your candid opinion of Kenny Washington and Woodrow Strode of U.C.L.A.," was our query.

## Washington One of Best

"Kenny Washington is one of the best football players I have ever seen," he replied, looking off in the distance as though he were visualizing the day last year when the sensational Colored star almost beat his great team single handed.

"Why that guy can do everything," he exclaimed. "He passes, runs, kicks and is a great defensive man. He sure had us worried in that game.

"And that Strode," he added, "played a great game, too. He's a sweet end. He wasn't as great as Kenny, but believe me he's a wonderful player."

Changing the subject, we asked the Southern Methodist leader if he thought that someday Negro students will be admitted to the white colleges in Texas.

"I certainly do," he answered quickly, "and although it will be quite some time from now, I am sure it will happen."

"The south," he added, "is changing. The people are becoming more broad minded and the new generation is much more liberal than their ancestors were."

"Just how do you think this change will come about," we questioned.

"Well," he said slowly, "education will be the most motivating force. In time people will see that many of our ideas today are wrong and they'll change things, especially in the south. Some day," he predicted, "a Colored boy will make a good record in athletics in high school and some southern white school is going to take him in. Of course he'll have to be a mighty level headed kid and a darn good student," he added.

Throughout the interview the Southern Methodist coach spoke the attitude of the educated southern man in the south today. He proved to us that he is one of the squarest and most sincere coaches in the country. It is easy to see now why it is that his teams are so good year after year.

Just before he left to attend his boys, he indicated that he was impressed with a number of Colored players he had seen in the south. Just before leaving Dallas for Pittsburgh he attended the game between Texas College and Kentucky State. The well-coached teams and the excellent playing of Myles Anderson, Texas' great halfback, brought forth volumes of praise from the famed coach. Texas beat Kentucky, 33 to 6.

"Why that boy Myles Anderson is a great player," he told us in excited tones. "He is better than any backfield man I have here with me today."

"Would you like to have Anderson on your team?" we asked.

"I sure would," was his answer, before departing to give his pass-throwing Mustangs their last minute instructions.

Although Matty Bell has compiled a great record as a coach, his record speaks for itself: 74 wins, 43 losses, and 10 ties, and he is known as one of the fairest and squarest coaches in the game, we learned it was not that which made him so cock-sure and confident of himself. The fact that his grandfather fought with the Confederacy in the Civil War, is much more consoling to him, from all indications, than his fine achievements in the grid game. After such an interesting grid round-up with Mustang Matty Bell, we immediately sought out other persons connected with the team. Fortunately we ran into the school's Athletic Director, Jimmie Stewart.

Like Coach Bell, the soft-spoken Mr. Stewart favored Colored boys playing in games against Southern schools.

"We have been trying to get U.C.L.A. to play us down in Dallas," he informed us, "and if they could have made the trip this year, Kenny Washington and Strode would have played right there with them."

After our conversation with liberal-minded Jimmie Stewart, we cornered the team's captain, Charlie Sprague, the fourth and last son of a famed family who have written pages of football glory at S.M.U., and whose father is the Mayor of Dallas, Tex.

"Captain Sprague," we asked. "What kind of a player is Kenny Washington?"

"Boy, 'O Boy," said the friendly captain, who in three years has played three different positions for S.M.U. First he was a center, then a tackle and now a pass snaring end, "Washington is the best back I have ever played against. He is a treat to watch. But," he added, "a terror to play against."

Captain Sprague also favored permitting sepia footballers to play against Southern white colleges.

## No Color Question

"Why," he said, "our boys didn't think anything about it. We figured we wouldn't get much credit for beating U.C.L.A. without Washington and

Strode. They are the best men they have, so we voted unanimously that they be permitted to play in the game." The next person we talked to was Nolan Jackson, one of the team's quarterbacks.

"Kenny Washington is the best back I've ever played against," he told us. "We played plenty hard in that game and banged Washington up a lot, too."

## Tough Game

"You see," he explained, "Wash carries the ball on almost every other play, and in that game against us he played 42 minutes. He was all over the field and when we weren't tackling him, he was tackling us."

"Was the game very rough," we asked the hefty Quarterback.

"Yes," he replied. "It was a rough game, but it was very, very clean. We played hard and so did they."

Before leaving we had another talk with Garrett Turner, the gray-haired, distinguished Colored trainer for the Mustangs.

"I have been with S.M.U. for 23 years," Mr. Turner said, "and they have always treated me fine. I do most anything I want to do, and Coach Bell treats me just like he treats the boys."

Turner thinks that Jimmie Stewart and all are just about the swellest men on earth.

"Mr. Stewart," said Turner, "has been good to me for so long that I don't know what I'd do if he ever left S.M.U."

The quiet spoken trainer is S.M.U.'s number one rooter. He travels all over the country with the team, and doesn't think any team can beat 'em except when they have an off day. But even closer to his heart than the S.M.U. Mustangs, is his eighteen-year-old daughter, who is studying music at Bishop College. He says that someday she'll be famous in the music world.

Although Southern Methodist lost the game to Pitt, they made a host of friends here in Pittsburgh. And one thing is certain, they can come back any time they want to, if they bring that 73-piece swing band, that had the Pitt jitterbugs shoutin', "glory-glory" and dancing in the aisles Saturday!

*This is one of the longer pieces Wendell wrote for the* Courier. *It is also one of the most important. Bell was a white Texan who embraced integration. And his players shared his attitude. Wendell was finding allies in places he least expected. He recognized it. He embraced it. He was a young journalist meeting individuals who challenged his way of thinking. He was also a thoughtful young man who was willing to think and reconsider.*

*August 19, 1939*

## "'Owners Will Admit Negro Players If Fans Demand Them'—Cards' Pilot," *Pittsburgh Courier*, p. 16

The fighting Cardinals of St. Louis hail from a town that was considered an important stronghold in the bitterly fought war of 1861. A town that hoisted Confederate flags and sent its young men to fight "Yankee oppression" under Lee, Johnston and Stonewall Jackson.

St. Louis is strictly a metropolis of Dixie, a town that lives by southern tradition. The great Mississippi caresses its banks and seals its connection with the South and all that section stands for.

St. Louis is the only town which has a team in the major leagues that compels Negroes to sit separated from the whites. Sixteen teams make up the two major leagues and this is the only city where the Jim Crow law exists in the big league parks.

In the past five years, however, there has been evidence of the new "Reconstruction" period taking place in St. Louis. Slowly, but surely, St. Louis is leaning toward the more genial side. The sports world is without doubt, playing the leading role in this change.

The law which prohibited Negroes and whites from meeting in the prize fight ring was changed recently. Henry Armstrong took advantage of that kind of new liberalism last winter when he went back to his home town and fought before a crowd that hailed him as a great champion.

St. Louis was proud of Hurricane Henry and showed it!

On August 18 we interviewed the St. Louis Cardinals' manager, Ray Blades, and two of his outstanding players, Pepper Martin and Paul "Daffy" Dean, on the question of Negroes crashing the major leagues. What did these famous ball players think of sepia diamond greats?

Forty-two years old, Ray Blades took over the Gas House Gang when Frankie Frisch was kicked out of the driver's seat. Blades has his team in the thick of the fight for the National League pennant, and before it is over may have them at the top of the heap. "If the baseball fans want Negro players in the big leagues," said Blades when we interviewed him in the lobby of the Schenley hotel, "the owners will have to sign them. There is no doubt," he continued, "that there are plenty of Negro players capable of playing major league ball. And a number of them would be outstanding stars. But, as yet, the owners have not seen fit to put any of them on their teams."

Ray Blades, like the seven other managers we interviewed on this vital question, blamed the owners of big league teams and not the managers or players for the exclusion of Negroes. "It is not up to the managers or players," said the Cardinals pilot, "but up to the men who pay out the salaries. We are hired to play ball and win a pennant. That is not a problem for us to decide on."

Blades said he had seen a number of Negro players capable of playing in the majors. "I think Satchel Paige, Josh Gibson and Oscar Charleston are the best Negro players I have seen," said Blades when we asked him to name the best sepia players he had seen. "Paige is one of the best pitchers I have seen anywhere," he said, "and very few pitchers have ever been able to throw a ball faster than he throws one. I am sure that he could make the grade if given a chance in the majors. He has all the polish and ability of a big league pitcher."

What did the St. Louis manager think about Josh Gibson, the sensational catcher of the Homestead Grays? "I think he could make the major leagues with ease," Blades answered, "and right now we have some mighty good receivers. Gibson has power, can hit like everything and is fast for a catcher," Blades pointed out. "There are a number of managers who could use a catcher like Gibson right now," Blades said.

The Red Bird pilot seemed to be impressed with the playing of Oscar Charleston, now manager of the Toledo Crawfords. "Charleston was one of the best ball players I have ever seen," said Blades, "and I am sure he could have made the grade in the big leagues. He could hit and field with the best of them. I played against him in a number of exhibition games and declared right then that he was good enough."

After listening to Blades laud these sepia diamond aces, we asked him when he thought Negro players would be accepted in the big leagues. "I cannot venture to say," he said, "because I don't know how the owners look upon the question. Right now, I would say that the chances are very slim. In fact, I might even say that they might never be admitted. However," he continues, "the owners might change their minds tomorrow and give Negro players a chance.

"You know," Blades pointed out, "prejudice and other social problems must be overcome before Negro players are admitted. In St. Louis for instance, it might be a difficult problem right now," he said, "because it is a southern town and, although the times seem to be changing slowly, I don't think they are ready for Negro players. Another thing, baseball has existed one hundred years without the Negro player, and that alone may convince the owners that it is not necessary to hire him."

We pointed out that big league baseball had survived something like ninety-seven years without night games, but that now it is important and even essential in some cities. Blades agreed with us when we pointed out St. Louis as a town that could use a stimulant of some kind to attract more fans. St. Louis is not large enough for two major league teams, and as a result both the Cardinals and Browns suffer. They have the lowest attendance figures in the majors.

There is a story going around that insists that a fan, after seeing a game in which the Cards played in St. Louis, said: "It was a mighty good game, but everybody there could have sat down on the bench with the Cardinals, including the ticket-takers." Which is just another way of showing how bad the attendance is in St. Louis. "Well," said Blades, "before Negro players are admitted I think that the social prejudice that exists right now will have to be broken down."

After getting Manager Blades' response on the question we cornered John Leonard "Pepper" Martin, the roughest, toughest, devil-may-care ball player in the big leagues. Pepper Martin was born in Temple, OK, and although he's lost some of the fire and dash he had several years ago, he's still an important cog in the Cardinal's machine.

"I have played against some of the best Negro ball players that ever lived," said Pepper, "and many of them could easily make the major leagues. I think that Satchel Paige is one of the greatest pitchers that ever threw a ball. A few years ago," Pepper continued, "I played with Diz Dean and some other big leaguers against the Kansas City Monarchs. I'm telling you they really had a team. I saw at least five guys on that team good enough for big league baseball."

Here for the first time, Pepper revealed to us the secret of his escapades in the world series of 1931, in which he ran wild on the base paths and practically stole Mickey Cochrane's glove. "For the latter part of 1930 I was playing with a group of All Stars which included Diz Dean, Paul Dean and a number of big leaguers, and we had exhibitions with the Kansas City Monarchs," Pepper told us with a twinkle in his eyes and a big smile.

"We were winning the game 4–1 in the last of the ninth. The colored team came to bat three runs behind and we were sure of victory. However, the first man up got a hit, and then it was on. The man on first streaked for second just as our pitcher threw to the batter. The batter laid one down the first baseline and beat it out. The man who had streaked for second, went all the way to third. From that time on," said Pepper, "they drove us nuts. Every man that got on ran like they were wild around the bases, and they finally won, 5 to 4. That aggressive type of ball, the type that Ty Cobb always advocated," said the Cardinal captain, "impressed me and I made up my mind right then that I would play that type of ball in the majors. I did it all that next season and throughout the world series against the Athletics," said Martin with pride.

And that is the story behind Pepper Martin's sensational play in that famous series in which Pepper reached his greatest heights.

When asked whether or not he thought Negro players would ever crash the majors, Pepper said he could not say. "However," he added, "a number of Negro athletes such as Joe Louis, John Henry Lewis and Henry Armstrong have done much toward enlightening the public and made the road easier for colored ball players. Joe Louis has done a great deal toward easing the Negro athlete's burden," said Martin, "and has won the admiration of millions of white people.

"Jack Johnson did a great deal of harm to the Negro race by not doing what was expected of him," Martin pointed out, "but Joe has been a gentleman and has not tried to take advantage of his position, thereby breeding ill feeling between the races. Louis, Armstrong and John Henry are real gentlemen and all of the big league ball players regard them highly.

"Negroes have been admitted to every other branch of sport," said Martin returning to the subject of the interview, "and I think that in time they will be included in big league baseball. "Just how long it will be, I cannot say. But I am sure that in the future we will have Negro players up here in the big leagues. There are plenty of them good enough and it is only a matter of time before they are admitted. Some of the big league players would object," said Pepper when we asked him if some of the white players would resent a Negro teammate, "but on the whole I think they would be accepted right along with the others. After all, we're playing this game to make a living and just as long as the money keeps rolling in twice a month that's all that matters." The veteran Cardinal outfielder lauded the playing of Satchel Paige, "Cool Papa" Bell, Josh Gibson and Willie Wells. "I have played against them in exhibition games," said Pepper, "and I rate them big leaguers."

After talking to Pepper Martin we placed Paul "Daffy" Dean on the stand and questioned him on the Negro ball player and his possibility of crashing the major leagues. Daffy Dean is the brother of the famous "Dizzy" Dean and until he hurt his arm two seasons ago, was one of the greatest pitchers in the history of baseball. He hails from Holdenville, Okla., and is 27 years old. Last year he pitched in the Texas League and won 16 out of 24 games.

It may be significant to note at this time, that Paul was very liberal when we questioned him on the Negro ball player. But—he did not submit to our questioning willingly and graciously as did the rest of the big leaguers we questioned for this series of articles. We approached "Daffy" in the lobby of the Schenley hotel on the same morning we interviewed Ray Blades and Pepper Martin. His big 6-foot frame was draped across a comfortable chair and he was talking with a number of teammates. It was approximately 12 o'clock in the day and they were just sitting around waiting until it was time to leave for the ball park. We introduced ourselves and told Daffy that we would like to ask him a few questions whenever he had time. He stared at us for a moment, ignoring our offer to shake hands and said rather curtly, "Naw, I don't wanna talk to ya!'" We were more than surprised by this rude rejection. We said nothing, just stared back.

As we turned to go, Pepper Martin, who was sitting nearby and witnessed Paul's attitude, jumped up from his seat and rushed over to the indignant Daffy. They conversed in whispers for a moment and then Martin turned to us suddenly and said, "Come on over, he'll talk to you now."

So we went over and talked to the only player out of forty interviewed who acted as though he didn't care to talk ... eccentric Daffy Dean! This time Daffy seemed more willing to talk to us. Perhaps Captain Pepper Martin was responsible for the sudden change. We asked Daffy a number of questions and weighed everything he said carefully.

"Yes," said Paul, "I have played against a number of Negro ball players whom I thought were good enough to play in the majors. I think that Satchel Paige is one of the best pitchers I ever saw, and Gibson is a mighty good catcher."

"'Would you object,' we asked, 'if a colored player was signed by the Cardinals?'"

"No, I would not care, all I want is my money," was his answer.

We thanked Daffy for the interview and left.

Oh, yes, we shook hands before saying good-bye!

*During the 1939 MLB season Wendell interviewed players and coaches from each of the eight National League teams. He had tired of going in circles dealing with team owners who argued that while they personally had no problem with integration, their players and coaches would not accept it. Wendell did what a good journalist should do: He went to the source.*

*He could not interview the players at Forbes Field; Black journalists were not welcome there. Instead, he interviewed them in the lobby of the Schenley Hotel in Pittsburgh. Visualize this: Here is this 25-year-old Black sportswriter, a stranger to these white players, two years out of college, wanting their opinion on MLB integration. Seventy-five percent of the respondents were comfortable with MLB integration. One of the friendlier interviewees in this piece is Pepper Martin. Daffy Dean eventually warms up to Wendell. Martin was from Oklahoma while Dean hailed from Arkansas. Each of the eight reports is longer than most of the pieces Wendell wrote for the* Courier.

*Note the use of the word "sepia" to describe skin color. It is typically used in reference to photographs. Wendell used the word often early in his career.*

## December 7, 1940

### Smitty's Sport Spurts, *Pittsburgh Courier*, p. 17

Chicago—Nov. 29—The pupil beat the teacher here tonight in Chicago Stadium when the College All-Stars defeated the Harlem Globe Trotters, 44 to 42, in one of the greatest games of basketball we have ever witnessed.... Like the All-Star football game, this classic is expected to determine whether or not college basketball is as good as professional. Judging from tonight's presentation, they are on about par. True, the College All-Stars won ... but the two-point advantage they held is not enough to determine which of the two groups play the best ball, college or professional.

The setting here tonight was stupendous.... All the color and splendor of a ten-ring circus.... And when John Pane-Gasser gave his stirring rendition of "The Star-Spangled Banner," with twenty-two thousand standing there, forming a silhouette in the shadows of the giant spotlight ... and Old Glory unfolding gracefully as his beautiful voice filled the stadium ... a guy couldn't help feeling that ... "It's great to be an American!"

A few breaks one way or the other and the Globe Trotters would have won the game.... But regardless of the results, they are a great team and Manager Abe Saperstein can take them to the four corners of the earth without a bit of fear.... This team, I believe, is the first Negro quintet in years that has enough to challenge the great record of the New York Renaissance. One thing, it is a young team set now for a brilliant future.

There are no "tramp" athletes on this ball club, either. Every one of the players impresses you with his carriage, poise and intelligent conversation. After you've been around them for a while you suddenly realize that basketball is now a big business. This club is run by Abe Saperstein on a strict business basis. All the players are on a monthly salary. And a good monthly salary. They play at least seven games a week. At the same time, Mr. Saperstein is directing the Savoy Big Five, which is designated as his minor league team. When he runs across a good prospect, Saperstein sends the player to the Savoy club for training. If during the course of the season one of the Globe Trotters is released or injured all Saperstein has to do is send a telegram to Chicago for the understudy playing with the Savoy quintet. Inside of twenty-four hours, the vacancy will be filled. The Globe Trotter office on Clark street in downtown Chicago, is a three-room establishment. And from 9 o'clock in the morning until late at night it is bustling with activity.... Yes sir, basketball is becoming a big business.

The *Chicago Herald-American* rates plenty of credit for the way the All-Star game was presented. There wasn't the slightest mix-up in any way.

The entire setup was handled smoothly and successfully. The fact that it drew the largest crowd in basketball history speaks for itself. But it doesn't reveal all the work that was behind it. Sports Editor Edward Cochrane, Leo Fischer and the rest of the sports staff deserve a world of credit. We doff our caps to them. It was, gentlemen, terrific!

*This feature appeared six years before MLB integration. Every issue of the* Courier *carried stories of racism throughout the United States. How could Wendell possibly have felt proud to be an American during the playing of the national anthem? Because it was a big step toward America making good on its promise of racial equality. This game was played between a Black professional team and a college all-star team comprised of white players. Wendell knew that fighting racism was a marathon. He had to pace himself. Acknowledging and celebrating progress was essential to pacing. It did not hurt that Wendell loved basketball and this proved to be a great game. He was a sports fan too.*

## February 9, 1946

### Sports Beat, *Pittsburgh Courier*, p. 16

*Northerners Dominate National League...*

There has been a popular belief down through the years that the majority of the ball players in the majors hail from the Southland. Those who have been opposed to the entry of the Negro player in the majors have used that belief consistently. "Southerners dominate the big leagues," they have pointed out, "and therefore, Negro ball players would never get along on major league teams."

After thumbing through the newest edition of the National League "Green Book," a statistical booklet edited by Charles Segar for the benefit of sportswriters, I have found that the Southern player is in the minority in that league. Jackie Robinson and John Wright, both of whom will be with Montreal in 1946, are potential members of the Brooklyn Dodgers, a National League club. The facts revealed in the "Green Book" indicate that Robinson and Wright will come in contact with more players from the North than the South in the National loop. For the sake of argument, we will have to assume, of course, that the Northern player will be more tolerant than those from across the Mason-Dixon Line. If such is the case, then the two Negro players have at least one important condition in their favor already.

The Brooklyn Dodgers have forty-seven players named on their active list in the "Green Book." Of this number, thirty-three are residents of the

North and fourteen of the South. In other words, the percentage of Northern players on the Brooklyn team is 70.2 as against 29.8 for the South. In the entire National League there are 386 players on the active list for 1946. Of this number, 264 are residents of the North and 122 hail from Dixie. The total percentage of Northern players is 67.8 and the percentage of Southern players is 32.2.

## Five Managers from North...

The North also has the edge when it comes to the geographical locations of managers in the National League. Five live above the Mason-Dixon Line and three are from "rebel country." Brooklyn's chief, Leo Durocher, is from liberal New York City; Bill McKechnie of the Cincinnati Reds is a resident of Wilkinsburg, Pa; Charley Grimm, pilot of the Chicago Cubs, is a Chicagoan; Franklin Frisch boss of the Pittsburgh Pirates, hails from New Rochelle, N.Y., and Billy Southworth, the leader of the Boston Braves, lives in Columbus, Ohio. The Southern managers are: Ben Chapman, Philadelphia Phillies, Montgomery, Ala.; Eddie Dyer, St. Louis Cardinals, Dallas, Texas and Mel Ott of the New York Giants, who lives in Metairie, La.

Here is a geographical chart of the rosters of the eight clubs in the National League:

| Team | Manager | Players | North | South | %North | %South |
|------|---------|---------|-------|-------|--------|--------|
| Brooklyn | North | 47 | 33 | 14 | 70.2 | 29.8 |
| Boston | North | 51 | 33 | 18 | 60.5 | 39.5 |
| Chicago | North | 45 | 35 | 10 | 77.7 | 22.3 |
| Cincinnati | North | 50 | 38 | 12 | 76.0 | 24.0 |
| Pittsburgh | North | 46 | 32 | 14 | 69.6 | 30.4 |
| Philadelphia | South | 50 | 33 | 17 | 66.0 | 34.0 |
| New York | South | 51 | 37 | 14 | 72.5 | 27.5 |
| St. Louis | South | 46 | 23 | 23 | 50.0 | 50.0 |
| Totals | | 386 | 264 | 122 | 67.8 | 32.2 |

It is significant that in each instance, with the exception of St. Louis, players from the North are in the majority. And, even on the St. Louis team, they are equally divided. If this chart reveals anything at all, it disproves the popular belief that the South sends more players to the majors than the North. While the above figures are strictly based on the rosters of National League teams, you'll probably find approximately the same condition in the American League. We selected the National League simply because Robinson and Wright are potentially future members of it. If they are lucky enough to break into the senior loop in 1946, they'll find that the atmosphere there is decidedly Northern and not Southern as many people have believed for a long time.

*Wendell again demonstrates strong journalistic skills. He checks out the story for himself and discovers a math error that had perpetuated a lie.*

## October 4, 1947

### Sports Beat,
### "The Series Takes The Town...,"
### *Pittsburgh Courier,* p. 13

New York City—The Big Town's all dressed up in its finest.... It's World Series time again.... From the top of the Empire State Building to the lowest level of the subway, they're talking about the battle between the Yanks and the Dodgers.... The bars and taverns are jammed with television spectators and the voice of Red Barber echoes across the skyline as he describes the thrills of the October Classic.

No better place could have been selected for this big series.... New York, the biggest town of 'em all.... New York with its teeming millions and big time atmosphere.... New York where everybody gets excited about everything and where Wall Street closes up so the bankers and bondsmen and financial wizards of the country can take it all in.

There are newspaper reporters here from all over the world.... Most are members of the colorful sports writing fraternity, but there are some who have come just to see who is here and what the dolls and phillys are wearing.... The photographers must be having a convention because flash bulbs are going off every place you turn.... The big boys, the name fellows of the sports and entertainment world are here in clusters.... There's Bob Hope, Mickey Cochrane, Bill Robinson, Ray (Sugar) Robinson, Leo Durocher, Jack Dempsey, Alex Pompez and a host of others of various degrees of fame. Then, too, there are the ticket speculators.... The guys who sneak up when you're not looking and whisper: "Would ya' like two for the third game! It's bound to be a pip." You ask how much he wants for them. "Give me $60," he says. "I can't afford it, but for you I'll take a slight loss"... You tell 'em you're going to inform Happy Chandler about such goings-on at the World Series, and the guy goes slinking off and gets lost in the crowd.

The hotels are jammed and packed.... The walls are bulging and the bell hops cleaning up, and the liquor control authorities apparently throw up their hands and say: "What do you expect bell hops to do at such a time as this? Pardon us, we're on our way to Ebbets Field."... Then, there's Brooklyn.... Ah, good old Brooklyn, where we meet such characters as Hilda Chester, the fat lady with the cow bell who rings it all year at the Dodgers' home games because Branch Rickey gives her a season pass.... As usual, he's made a good deal. Hilda can holler louder and longer and with more feeling than any butcher you ever heard.... Hilda's always near her beloved bums.... When they came stalking out of the dressing room, she's standing there, giving them encouragement.

"Come on, youse guys," Hilda urges, "let's go get them Yanks today. Let's git them bums from across the river. Yez' got the best b-a-a-a-ll club in the holle world"... Pee Wee Reese goes by, his spikes clicking a song of some sort on the cement that leads down to the runway and under the stands ... "Hey," Hilda roars above the screams of the fanatics who love the Dodgers so much that they watch them leave the dressing room on the way to the dugout, and then run like mad up in the stands to watch them work-out before the game starts. "There's the best shortstop in baseball history. There isn't a better player between Greenpernt and Alaska." Reese smiles, waves a hello to Hilda and disappears.... Out comes Edwards, Walker, Stanky and Hermanski.... The fanatics roar and give them the ole "come on, you wonderful Bums, let's win dis one, too."

Carl Furillo comes clattering out and right behind him Jackie Robinson!

Hilda Chester's at her best now.... She rings the cow bell and is the whoopiest of a whoopy crowd. "Hey, Carl.... Hey, Jackie," she bellows, "we got to knock 'em down today. Now's the time to do it." Hilda Chester is a bulky lady and she uses her weight to push back the mob that threatens to close in on the two players. "Get going now," she orders, ringing the bell furiously, "knock the Yanks cold—them foreigners from the Bronx!"

And so it goes.... It's that way in Brooklyn every day, and the same way across the river.... Everyone's Series crazy and nobody cares what happens from one day to the next.... World Series are always colorful, especially when played in the Big Town.... But this one is especially so because there's a fleet-footed guy by the name of Robinson playing first base for Brooklyn.... Everyone in the stands gets tense when the coffee-colored kid from Pasadena steps to the plate.... His reputation is established.... He's a speedster.... Watch him bunt that ball!... Watch him run!... No!... He didn't bunt.... He swung away and now he's off for second.... The ball's coming in!... Did he beat it?... How that DiMaggio can throw!...How that Robinson can slide!

The air is crisp and the roar of the fanatics goes hurtling over the top of the flag-bedecked grandstand and heads across the city.... That's what electrifies one and makes you sit on the edge of your seat.... That's what makes the Series a classic; what makes guys pay ten times face for a ticket…. That's what causes people to come thousands of miles, just hoping they can get in…. That's what make bell hops take a risk with a bottle, bankers close their financial dens and the stars of radio, screen and stage are out…. That's what makes people like Hilda Chester ring cow bells and blow their tops. That's what makes us glad we're in the sports writing business!

*The primary point of this piece is that the Negro baseball fan for the first time has a rooting interest in the World Series. The reader can sense the excitement in New York City.*

## December 29, 1951

### Sports Beat, *Pittsburgh Courier*, p. 14

*Mr. Veeck Defends His New Manager*

Just about the time Bill Veeck signed Rogers Hornsby as the new manager of the St. Louis Browns, we took the opportunity to point out that baseball, like politics, sometimes makes strange bedfellows.

Mr. Veeck, we said, has always been a sound, solid person on matters concerning a man's race or the color of his skin. When he was operating as boss of the Cleveland Indians he signed Larry Doby, the first Negro to perform in the American League. He also had more Negro players under contract and distributed throughout the Cleveland farm system than any other owner.

Hornsby, on the other hand, has not been too solid or sound when confronted with this issue. We pointed out a number of things we knew about him. They weren't very complimentary, either. We said, in substance, that Hornsby wouldn't tolerate Negro ball players.

When Bill Veeck read the article he quickly came to Hornsby's defense. This is what he said when we ran into him the other day:

"I don't think Hornsby is as bad as you say he is. I have talked with him on this issue and he assures me that the only thing he is concerned about is whether a guy can play baseball. You know my position on such matters and you would know that I wouldn't sign any manager who would be against Negro players. I intend to build the best team St. Louis has ever had. I don't care what color a player is. If he can play ball, he will be on the St. Louis Browns. Hornsby has the same attitude. He wants players, good players, and I know that he is interested in at least two Negroes he has personally scouted."

*Won't Tolerate a Losing Team...*

"Let's not judge Hornsby too harshly. Perhaps he was against Negro players back in the old days. Frankly, I don't know. I do know, however, that he isn't against them now. That is all I care about. He has asked me to sign two Negro players he saw in the minor leagues. He says they're great players. I'm going to try and get them.

"I can't reveal who they are right now because the price on them will go sky high if I do.

"Hornsby tried to get one of these players last year when he was managing at Seattle. He offered to pay $10,000 for the player. But the club that had him wouldn't give him up at that time. That's why I say he isn't against Negro players. Any time a guy offers to pay $10,000 for a player in the minors, he must want that particular player very much."

Veeck then showed us a list of Negro players that the St. Louis Browns are interested in. It is quite possible they will have five on the team this coming season. Veeck added:

"Now do you think we would even consider signing that many Negro players if Hornsby was against them? He has told me that he wants good players. He would probably sign a polar bear if it could do a good job for him out there on the diamond. Hornsby likes to win too much to let a good player get away. He says the Browns are going to play good ball this year or else. The guys who don't perform like big leaguers won't be around long. He will not tolerate a losing team. I won't either. I am going to get him the best players possible and I want results. We aren't going to be the American League door mat any longer."

*Has One Pitcher Who Can Really Pitch...*

Veeck has been working like a beaver all winter, trying to build the Browns into a formidable club. He thinks the team will surprise a lot of fans next season.

"We haven't a bad ball club," he said. "If these new players we have signed come through like I think they will we could be in the thick of the pennant race."

"Veeck says he has one pitcher he won't have to worry about. "I won't have to worry about Satchel Paige," he said. "There's a guy who is a big leaguer all the way. I don't know how old Satch is, and I don't care. As long as he can throw that ball up to the plate, I'm going to have him around.

"There isn't a better relief pitcher in baseball than Satchel. He knows how to pitch. That's the kind of pitcher to have around when the other team starts a rally.

"Satchel can come into a game and cool off a hot team in less than a minute. Yes sir, Satchel Paige will be with the St. Louis Browns next season, you can bet on that."

Returning to Hornsby, Veeck said: "I honestly don't think Hornsby is as bad as you pictured him. All I can go by is the fact that he has been pleading with me to get those two Negro players he saw in the minor leagues. Give him a chance. Let's see how he'll be this coming season. I'm sure he'll be a good manager in every respect." Hornsby couldn't have a better person than Veeck presenting his side of the case. If Veeck says Hornsby's not a bad guy, you can't argue with him. Veeck believers in Rogers Hornsby. We believe in Bill Veeck. So, that's that.

*Rogers Hornsby (this column), Ty Cobb (next column), and Bobby Bragan (later this chapter) demonstrate that individuals can change for the better. Hornsby did not prove to be an effective manager with the St. Louis Browns (not many did), but he would later coach Billy Williams and other talented prospects in the Chicago Cubs organization. Williams did not detect any racism in Hornsby and credits him with making Williams and others better ballplayers.*

*Bill Veeck and Wendell were long term allies in the integration battle. Their widows would remain friends until Wyonella Smith's passing in November 2020.*

## August 8, 1953

### Sports Beat, *Pittsburgh Courier*, p. 14

*Cobb Isn't the Tiger He Used to Be...*

When Ty Cobb was the batting terror of the major leagues there were two things said about him that were apparently, the gospel truth:

1. He could hit any living pitcher.
2. He would hit any living Negro.

There is no dispute about the first claim. His lifetime batting average of .367 is the best in baseball history. No player has ever equaled that mark. He won the American League batting title twelve times, nine in succession.

The second is merely a matter of hearsay. We are inclined, however, to accept the testimony of those who saw him when he was in his prime. They tell us that the "Georgia Peach" more than once became so irritated that he left the playing field, went up into the stands, and demonstrated his fistic prowess on Negro fans. Cobb, they say, despised two things—Negroes and the opposition.

But he gives no indication today of intolerance. Perhaps he has mellowed with the years and wealth. He is now 66 years old and his investments have made him independently rich. Those two things, no doubt, have tempered his views, racially at least.

That is the impression he conveys, anyway. His conversation today belies the attitude he allegedly nursed in the days when he was a two-fisted, bruising, battling ball player, when he would do anything to steal a base, or get a hit to win a ball game.

Tyrus Raymond Cobb of Augusta, Ga., a baseball immortal and a member of the Hall of Fame, was one of the 10,000 spectators at Wrigley Field last week when we took the opportunity to corner him.

### Campanella Rates with the All-Time Greats...

The Dodgers were playing the Cubs and, of course, the Dodgers were winning. The final score was 6 to 5, in favor of Brooklyn. Cobb was sitting in a first-row box seat with his attractive, youthful-looking wife.

He was wearing sun glasses and an egg-colored suit. There was no hat on his head, which is almost bald. His speech was typically Southern. He spoke with a slow, easy drawl.

Which player on the field, he was asked impressed him the most?

"Why that catcher there," he said, pointing to Roy Campanella. "He's the best ball player I've seen in many a year."

Campanella, the Dodgers' stocky catcher, was squatting behind the plate, receiving the pitches of Russ Meyer flawlessly. Last year in a magazine article, Cobb said that Stan Musial and Phil Rizzuto were the only modern players who could compare with the stars of his day.

But now he was praising Campanella for his adroitness, his way of handling pitchers, his great throwing arm and his power at the plate. Obviously, he was sold on the bulky receiver, generally recognized as the best catcher in baseball today. He was fascinated by Campanella's workmanlike manner.

"That fella's a great catcher," he volunteered. "The very best in the game. He reminds me a little of Roger Bresnehan. If he can stick around for five or six more years they'll have to put him along side of the game's all-time catchers."

He looked at his wife, who nodded her approval, and continued: "See the way he works a pitcher. He's in the ball game all the time. If a pitcher can't pitch to that fella, he just can't pitch. He gives 'em a full target. He gives a pitcher confidence, makes him believe he can throw, even if he can't. It's worth the price of admission just to see that fella squat down behind the hitter."

*You Don't See Many Like Roy Any More...*

"The biggest thing they got to worry about in this fella's case," said Cobb, "is his weight. He has a tendency to take on pounds. If he gets too heavy, he won't be much good. A guy can't play ball if he's fat. He's gotta be careful what he does at the table. He can eat himself right out of baseball."

An usher came up and tapped the ex–Detroit Tiger on the shoulder. "There's a colored man here," the usher said, "who says he used to chauffeur for you. Says he worked for you down in Augusta."

Cobb looked around and viewed the visitor. He didn't recognize the man. "I don't know," he said, puzzled, "send him down anyway."

The man came down and shook Cobb's hand. "I don't think you remember me," he said. "But I used to drive for you now and then down in Augusta. Anyway, it's good to see you again." Then he left. Cobb smiled. "I don't remember him," he confessed. "You meet so many people down through the years." The man said his name was Willie. Cobb scratched his head. He couldn't remember the fellow. He was still trying to remember when Campanella waddled to the plate. "Now watch him," Cobb said, adjusting his sun glasses. "This fella can hit, too. He's got power, plenty of power." Campanella made Cobb look good. He promptly doubled to left. "See," said the old ball player, "the fella's got it. He's got class. He's tough. You don't see many like him anymore. Players like that come along once in a lifetime."

What did he think of Jackie Robinson?

"Oh," he said, with a shrug, "he's just a good all-around ball player. He's got it too. He's my kind of ball player."

What about the new players, the young fellows?

"I've seen a few who look good," Cobb said. "That fella out there on second, Junior Gilliam, looks like he'll make good. He's a good, little second baseman. He is just what this club needed. He can hit, run and has a fairly good arm. In fact, this Brooklyn club should coast in. They're strong all the way around. Can't see how they can miss."

Then Ty Cobb turned to his wife. "That fellow," he recalled, "said his name was Willie. I think I remember him now. Sure I do. He chauffeured a little for me down in Augusta. Been a long time, but I remember him now." He took out a large white handkerchief and wiped his perspiring brow. "Nice fella," he said. "Sorry I couldn't remember him when he came down here and spoke to me. But you know how it is, you meet so many people."

*Cobb's encounter with Willie tells us as much about him as his thoughts on Campanella. Wendell's focus is on the present and future. Regardless of who Hornsby and Cobb might have been, Wendell is interested in who they are now. Wendell is not demanding apologies; he is demanding change. If Ty Cobb can change, anyone can.*

*July 3, 1954*

## Sports Beat, *Pittsburgh Courier*, p. 14

*A Base Hit for the Supreme Court...*

Durham, N.C.—When the Supreme Court decided recently it is presumptuous to assume that the majority will voluntarily provide equal, but separate facilities for the minority, it hit the nail smack on the head.

You cannot expect the "haves" to do but so much for the "have-nots." Throughout the South the record shows that. The figures, compiled by such tenacious and exacting people as Alex Rivers for the *Courier* and Charley Ray, the statistically minded public relations expert of North Carolina College, bluntly refute the "traitors" who have crawled and cringed before partial, klanish investigators and sworn sheepishly that "we are satisfied with conditions here as they are."

Such vows are not true. They are the cries of the people who are intellectually inferior ... the whimperings of those who have thrived and prospered on the inequities of educationally starved Negroes who have been compelled to live all these years as second-class citizens.

All you have to do is walk down the country lanes, traverse the bypasses and winding roads of "God's country," and those you meet will tell you this: "We haven't been getting a portion of the democracy they've been talking about. We don't have the schools, the privileges ... the common dignity that the Constitution pledges and guarantees. Everything we receive is strictly 'second-hand.'"

Yet, the taxes are the same, the penal penalties the same and the sacrifices the same. When they draft men for military duty—to fight communism and the Russian threat to the "Free World"—all able-bodied men are eligible, whether they hail from the jagged, rock-bound coast of Maine, or the hot cotton lands of backward Mississippi. Then ... all men are the same.... All blood flows through veins of a common destiny—America!

*They'll Be Playing All Over...*

But, as the Supreme Court pointed out, glaringly, right shall prevail. The South cannot bolt, nor reject the dictates of the world's great democracy. Even in an insignificant area as the world of sports ... that must be acknowledged.

There will be, in the not-too-distant future, Negro athletes participating on college teams all over the country, especially the South. That is an accepted fact ... a condition that all clear-thinking people accept.

Harry Jefferson, the very able and intelligent coach of Hampton

Institute, for example recognizes the inevitable. During a long-distance telephone conversation from the lair of the Pirates, he said:

"As you know, West Virginia has opened all its colleges. So, I think there will be white students at West Virginia and Bluefield in the near future. It will happen elsewhere, too.

"Here at Hampton, for example, we have a bi-racial policy. This is a private institution and we've never been affected by state law. We have a private charter."

Insofar as athletics are concerned what does the Supreme Court decision mean? Will an outstanding Negro high school athlete go to the University of Virginia, rather than matriculate at Hampton?

"I think," said the astute Hampton coach, "that it's going to mean we are going to have more competition for material. It doesn't necessarily mean, however, that we're going to drop by the wayside. We'll be competing with the white schools for top-notch athletes."

How long will it be before Negro colleges will encounter this competition for outstanding Negro athletes?

### It's Settled, Just a Matter of Time...

"I think it will be some time," Coach Jefferson said. "But it will eventually come about. It is something we must face."

What about the future schedules? Will white colleges in the South play Negro schools on the field of athletics? Jefferson answered:

"It will be some time before the Southern Conference or Atlantic Conference will take in Negro schools. That will be, more or less, a matter of economics with them. After all, at the present time our athletics are set up on a small college basis."

What about Negro college presidents? Will they be against interracial sports competition?

"No, I don't think so. The presidents of state schools, I think, will be guided by the way the authorities feel. They are not going to make any effort to run contrary to the policies of the administration. In Virginia, for example, the state's fighting the Supreme Court decision. So, I don't think Virginia State is going out and try to get white athletes or schedule games with white schools. Not, at least, until it's settled."

It is, of course, settled.... No matter what Talmadge or the other leaders of states in the deep South say to the contrary. They swear they won't stand for educational equality ... but you can bet they won't secede, start another Civil War. They lost the last one ... they'll lose again.

And swirling around all this controversy, there is an amusing angle, too. Schools like the University of Illinois won't be able to lure swift-footed, swivel-hipped halfbacks like J.C. Caroline away from a state like South

Carolina. They'll keep gazelles like him … and, believe it or not, let him carry the ball. Even Jeff—a real diplomat—agrees with that observation.

*It is fitting that this column was published the day before Independence Day 1954. Wendell did not live in the South, but he had been there with Jackie Robinson and Wyonella's family lived in Durham, North Carolina. He was a sportswriter in the narrow sense, but in a broader sense he was a journalist with the largest Black newspaper in the country. He understood what the* Brown *decision meant: The law is on the side of integration. Still, he had to wonder if* Brown *would be to Black college athletics what integration was to the Negro Leagues.*

## June 22, 1957

### Sports Beat, *Pittsburgh Courier,* p. 25

That riotous and exciting knuckle-throwing contest staged at Comiskey Park in Chicago the other day between the White Sox and Yankees was the best seen on that particular battle field since the balmy night in 1937 when young Joe Louis flattened James J. Braddock and won the heavyweight title.

Larry Doby, the trigger-tempered Sox' outfielder, scored the knockout this time … and he did it in much quicker time than it took Louis to demolish Braddock.

Art Ditmar, the big Yankee pitcher, threw a bullet at Doby's scalp, and Larry executed the fastest exit seen around Chicago since Dillinger, the slippery bandit, was on the loose.

After that, Ditmar and Doby, both weighing 185 pounds, shouted some contemptuous epithets at each other which were in no way complimentary to their respective families.

As it developed, Doby automatically had the last word in the sizzling debate. Ditmar tried to but only got as far as, "Go to ---," and then there was a very large, bronze fist massaging Art's teeth, which heretofore had been about as perfect as pitcher's teeth get these days.

The punch was a whistling left hook and when it landed an excited spectator asked:

"When did the White Sox sign Sugar Ray Robinson? He's the only one we've ever seen throw a punch like that."

The blow was reminiscent of the one with which Sugar Ray destroyed Gene Fullmer on May 1 just a few miles away from the site of this battle. It was short and loaded with power, knocking the stunned Yankee pitcher on the back of his lap.

Ditmar's sudden collapse ignited the subsequent battle royal. In a flash the two dugouts were empty and baseball players were slugging and gouging, scratching and swinging all over the place.

There was a big pile up and a traffic jam between home and first, where it all started. Doby was on top of Ditmar, trying to extract a few more of the Yankee pitcher's teeth ... and Bill Skowron, the Yankee first baseman, was on Doby's back, gingerly trying to embrace Larry around the neck ... and Walt Dropo was riding Skowron side-saddle, like Wyatt Erp ... and Enos Slaughter was astride Dropo, scratching the big fellow's back like a wildcat ... and pugnacious Billy Martin was trying to burrow under the pile, like a frantic mole, and come up with a few solid bites.

Elsewhere, players were scrambling and wrestling, attempting to keep each other from joining the original pile.... And managers Al Lopez and Casey Stengel were doing some excellent roadwork, running hither and yon, back and forth between the startled helpless umpires and the combatants.

After Doby decided he'd had enough sparring with Ditmar, he accepted a challenge issued by Martin, the café champion, who apparently didn't get enough fighting at the Copacabana in New York recently. However, this was only a brief skirmish, a dull preliminary bout in comparison to the main event.

When peace was finally restored, Doby, Dropo, Slaughter, Martin and Whitey Ford were told they couldn't play ball with the other boys any more that afternoon. So, the little urchins went sauntering, and sulking, off to their respective clubhouses (ushered by the police of course) where they soothed their wounds. Now, there is one highly significant aspect about all this that commands mention, and cannot be stressed too emphatically. At no time during, before, nor after the brawling did any player on their team resort to specialized name-calling or racial slander.

There was a voluminous amount of profanity, of course, and the legitimacy of many relatives questioned—but racial hatred had no part in this wonderful, free-swinging melee.

Ditmar did not refer to Doby's racial ancestry when they started barking at each other. Nor did anyone else among the 50 some players involved.

This was a team battle and an integrated one, if you please.... Doby vs. Ditmar.... Howard vs. Minnie Minoso.... Dropo vs. Slaughter, etc.

On both sides, it was one for all and all for one. In every sense of the word it was a brotherhood fight. The only distinction in this rollicking conflict was the color of the uniform, not the face.

Even though it was through a mild form of violence ... the White Sox and Yankees exemplified on this occasion what all Americans should be when a crisis arises—for each other.

Thanks, boys … it was a delightful afternoon.
*Wendell is employing humor here, but there is a serious point to be taken. It did represent progress.*

## August 2, 1958

### Sports Beat, *Pittsburgh Courier*, p. 25

*Close Call for the Champion...*

Houston, Tex.—That was a close call Joe Brown had here the other night. It was too close for comfort, in fact. He managed to hang onto his lightweight crown, beating Kenny Lane in a sparkling, 15-round battle before a record-breaking Texas crowd.

Lane, a sturdy farmer out of Muskegon, Mich., put up a surprisingly good fight, much better than anticipated by anyone, including Brown.

At the first bell, Joe was a 2½ to 1 favorite to triumph. But it was obvious by the end of the fourth round that Lane, a left-hander, had been grossly underrated. He fought the aging champion on even terms most of the way and was on his feet at the end, almost as fresh and strong as when the fight started.

Brown, on the other hand, was weary from the grueling ordeal and in no way certain that he was still the world lightweight champion. Lane had refused to roll over for dead, like many thought he would. Throughout he was a rugged competitor, taking all Brown had to offer and repeatedly coming back for more. Kenny's sharp right jab and well-timed left hooks kept him in the running all the way.

*Slim Margin for Joe Brown...*

Fortunately for Brown, the officials voted him the winner by the slimmest of margins. All three cast their ballots for him and in so doing enabled Joe to remain champion.

The unanimous vote in Brown's favor surprised many. It was that close a fight. There were many in the overflow crowd of 10,000 plus who thought Lane won.

It was a just and fair decision, however. Brown won it on his do-or-die rally in the 15th and final round. During the last three minutes, the champion pulled victory out of the fire when he unleashed an attack that almost overwhelmed the plucky challenger.

Afterward, many observers duffed their caps to the three officials— Judge Bill Cornelius, Judge Jimmy Webb and Referee Ernest Taylor.

There was reason, perhaps, to suspect that the officials would lean to Lane in a close fight. After all, this is Texas and the deep South. Here was a Negro champion defending against a popular white challenger. It figured then that the latter would have more going for him in this area for obvious reasons.

The general consensus beforehand was that Lane could very easily win the decision if he managed to be on his feet at the end.

### *Officials Given High Praise…*

"All he has to do," said one critic before the fight, "is stay upright, and they'll give it to Lane on that achievement alone. Everything is to his advantage if he stays upright and makes any kind of showing at all."

Well, as it developed, Lane did make a good showing and was very much erect at the finish. He made such a determined stand, in fact, that few, if any, left the arena before the official decision was rendered.

The three officials, however, gave a just decision. They were not swayed by the color of skin, nor did they bow to prejudice, which they could have done easily under the circumstances.

Instead, they called it right and voted a "true bill" for Brown. It took a lot of courage because Lane was the sentimental favorite, and many an official in the past has been influenced by the roars and cheers of a partisan crowd.

Out of all of this, considerable progress was made. Ten years ago it is likely that under similar conditions Brown would have lost his title if he had fought Lane, or any other white fighter, in a fight as close as this one was.

### *"People in Texas Are Growing Up…"*

A New York writer, saluting the officials for their honesty and fair decision, best described the reaction and sentiment of most fans when he said:

"The people in Texas are growing up. The votes of the three officials prove that conclusively."

He was absolutely right. Texas justice in this instance was fair indeed. The better man won the fight and that's the way the verdict was handed down. Progress may be slow in some parts of the South, but it is making strides.

Joe Brown, still the lightweight champion, will probably put his personal "amen" on that observation.

*This Brown decision did not have the impact of the* Brown *decision discussed a few columns prior. But, to Wendell, it too was worth celebrating.*

*September 17, 1960*

## Sports Beat, *Pittsburgh Courier,* p. 52

Looking back over the past 30 years of the *Pittsburgh Courier's* existence, a man who has been privileged to cover the sports beat must, unless he is ungrateful or unimaginative, admit he is truly one of the chosen few.

There was first, Ira F. Lewis, and then Bill Nunn, Sr., and Chester L. Washington, Jr., followed by this observer, and now Bill Junior, the son who is stalking his father's illustrious footsteps.

The older guys—from Lewis through Nunn Sr.—saw, and fought for, what has come to pass ... big leaguers making as much as $80,000 or more a season, like Willie Mays; and football players worth nine men for one, such as Ollie Matson; and basketball players like Wilt (The Stilt) Chamberlain, who hauls down an astronomical figure; and boxers, and tennis players, and now even golfers competing in areas no one ever thought Negroes would ever reach.

This has been a life of splendor and excitement—baseball training camps, fight camps, the Olympics—and other arenas of excitement for the younger ones that the older ones, by their dedication and perseverance made possible.

Thus those who sit in the press box at the World Series, or ringside at the big fights, or in "typewriter row" at similar classics, should remember that they are there because of the ceaseless campaigns waged by those before them, particularly by those representing this newspaper. If the editors of this publication permit a bit of crowing in this particular issue its audience should be tolerant, for this is a newspaper that has something of which to be proud ... such as the "discovery" of Joe Louis, when he was a mere neophyte, and Jackie Robinson, and Henry Armstrong; and many more trail-blazers, including Dorie Miller and the "Double V" campaign during World War II, to make a few contributions outside the field of sports.

Over the span of the past 25 years this publication has been an intricate and articulate part of all that has happened from the Negro's standing of progress and advancement.

Its impact in the field of sports has been particularly significant and worthy.

Of all the discoveries insofar as individuals are concerned, Joe Louis, the former heavyweight champion, is probably the most important.

Louis was "adopted" long before he ever won the title and presented to the world as a symbol. He came on from a raw, untutored Golden Gloves fighter to the heavyweight championship, defending that title twice as many times as any other titleholder in history.

But he was, during the years of World War II, more than just a boxing champion. He was an inspiration to all Americans, regardless of race, creed or color.

He, by his excellent conduct, set the stage for others to follow ... in baseball, football, golf, tennis, boxing, etc.

There would have been no Jackie Robinson in 1947, nor the Willie Mayses, Roy Campanellas, Althea Gibsons, etc., had not Louis paved the way.

The point is, of course, that those who stand and cheer the exploits of Negro athletes in these days and times should never forget the contribution made by Louis, who set the stage for all that has happened. Had he made one major mistake, uttered one thoughtless comment, failed to stand up under pressure (like the second Max Schmeling fight) there would not have followed the Robinsons, Gibsons, etc., for many years.

Not even the child-like Floyd Patterson would be bouncing around from pillar to post as heavyweight champion of the world had it not been for Louis.

It was Louis alone who set the stage for all the glory that these eyes have seen over the past 20 years.

So, this is a salute to Ira Lewis and Nunn Sr., and "Ches" Washington Jr.

They found the man who paved the way ... for the sports editors who followed them on this paper ... and the spectacular band of athletes now accepted so enthusiastically from coast to coast.

*We need not speculate about who Wendell thought was "The Guy." Joe Louis was the most significant Black athlete Wendell covered. Joe Louis did not make Jackie Robinson a better ball player. He did, however, accelerate the timing of the opportunity. If MLB integrated a few years later, Jackie Robinson would have been considered too old to be the first. Wendell also took pride that the* Courier *reported on Louis from the beginning of Joe's career. In Wendell's eyes, Joe Louis was the definitive heavyweight champion of the world.*

## December 8, 1962

### Sports Beat, *Pittsburgh Courier*, p. 18

Maury Wills of the Los Angeles Dodgers has been amply rewarded for grand larceny ... and the word—"grand"—is very appropriate in this instance.

The durable little shortstop slid right into the Most Valuable Player award honor with a total of 104 base thefts. That record exceeds all others, including the immortal Ty Cobb's.

Maury's grand achievement in grand larceny certainly must have been gratifying to Bobby Bragan, who recently was appointed manager of the Milwaukee Braves.

When the MVP was placed on Maury's head, there is no doubt that Bragan smiled and probably said to himself: "Well, the kid finally made it, as I knew he would."

Then his thoughts probably drifted back to the day when Maurice Morning Wills of Washington, D.C., reported to him at Spokane in 1958. Bragan was managing the Dodger's farm club and Wills reported as an infielder who had been traveling around the minors from one town to the other like a circus barker.

"He was so small and frail," Bragan told us during spring training at Vero Beach last March, "that I didn't think he had the stamina to play every day. But I had an infield full of holes, so I kept him. He played third, shortstop and second for us. He was a right-handed hitter but couldn't connect with a curve ball if you rolled it to him. So I turned him around against right-handed pitching and he finished with a respectable .253 batting average."

The rest is history, of course. In 1959, Maury was a standout in the World Series. In 1960, he batted .295, a surprising figure on the basis of his past record, and since then has consistently stayed in above .280. Last season he was one point below the .300 mark.

"Nobody was interested in him," Bragan remembered, "because he was so weak at the plate. But when we converted him to a switch-hitter at Spokane, he started getting results."

When Wills was promoted to the Dodgers in '59, it was a desperation move. Los Angeles was in dire need of a shortstop. Bragan told the front office: "I have a kid who will play shortstop for you for years, if you give him the chance." So they brought 5-10, 160-pound Wills up to the majors. He isn't going back any time soon.

It took a lot of doing for the little man to win the MVP award. He had to use all his amazing skills during his race to the honor to beat out the equally amazing Willie Mays.

Equally as interesting is the fact that Wills continued the domination of Negro performers in the National League with respect to the coveted prize. During the past 14 years, the MVP award has been won 11 times by Negroes.

Jackie Robinson won it first in 1949. Roy Campanella gained it three times, Ernie Banks, twice, Mays, Frank Robinson, Aaron and Don Newcombe also won it.

Newcombe won it as a pitcher, all the others with the exception of Maury, copped it with their hitting and fielding. Wills is unique in that he accomplished the feat with his feet—running the bases.

He revived a lost art and in so doing became the most exciting personality in the sport last season. C.C. Johnson Spink, writing in baseball's bible, *The Sporting News*, said: "His base-stealing pyrotechnics stand out above everything else that happened during the season. The Dodgers' shortstop, who spent years in the minors and was almost bypassed, stole 104 bases in 165 contests. At the 156-game mark, he topped Ty Cobb's modern record of 96. In the final weeks of the season, crowds flocked out to watch the little guy run."

Thus, Maury Wills will go down in history with baseball's greatest. He raced to the MVP award ... and if he keeps going the next few seasons may run through the front door that leads to the Hall of Fame.

*Bobby Bragan was a man who held racist views when Jackie Robinson broke the color barrier. Branch Rickey gave Bobby Bragan the opportunity to change his racial views and make a positive contribution to race relations and MLB. Bragan seized it and Maury Wills was one of the results. Could Rickey have done that today? Or would public outcry have prohibited Bragan from coaching in professional baseball? Bragan might have been ostracized long before he met Maury Wills. Branch Rickey did not tolerate racism. He did not compromise with racism. He did however prefer that an individual who held racist views be given the opportunity to change. What do we want?*

## March 26, 1966

### Sports Beat, *Pittsburgh Courier*, p. 11

*A.L. Deserved Accolades for Calling Umpire Emmett Ashford*

The pitch, thrown by Ken Holtzman of the Chicago Cubs was high ... it sailed behind the hitter, Willie Smith of the California Angels.

It was only an exhibition game but, nevertheless, hitters resent being thrown at in any kind of contest. So Willie Smith started out to the mound, bat in hand, to square things with the pitcher.

His journey was interrupted, however, by Emmett Ashford, the five-foot, ten-inch, 185-pound umpire, the first Negro ball-and-strike man in major league history.

"Take it easy, Willie," he said, stepping in front of Smith, "there'll be no fighting here today."

This was in Palm Springs, Cal., and marked the first time Ashford had umpired a game between major league teams since Joe Cronin, president of the American League, promoted him to the big leagues last October.

Thus, a brawl was averted and peace was restored by the colorful arbiter in blue behind the plate. Thousands of fans will see Ashford calling 'em as he sees 'em in American League games this summer. There probably will be similar incidents such as the one described above but nobody is worried because Ashford is the kind of cop who knows what to do when trouble erupts. He has been umpiring for 25 years, the last 12 in the Pacific Coast League. At the age of 47, he has come to the majors comparatively late but, nevertheless, his eyes are good and he can call out balls and strikes with the authority of a supreme court justice.

Ashford, who is a showman on the field, loves his work. He is a dramatic, arm-flinging umpire. He calls out his decisions hard and clear.

"He creates excitement," said Joe Cronin when he appointed Emmett. "He adds something to the game. The fans will surely like him when they see him in action."

A native of Los Angeles, Ashford is a graduate of nearby Chapman College, where he played second base and centerfield. He broke into organized baseball as a Southwest International League umpire on July 4, 1951. He advanced through the Arizona-Texas League, the Western International League and the Pacific Coast League, where he was umpire-in-chief the past three seasons.

In all his years as an umpire Ashford has had only one major conflict with a player and, ironically, his assailant was a Negro. It happened two winters ago in the Dominican Republic's winter league. The hitter was Julian Javier, a journeyman second baseman with major league experience. Emmett called a strike to which Javier objected strenuously.

"Get back in the batter's box," Ashford warned, "or I'll call the next pitch a strike, no matter where it is." Javier refused to do as ordered. The next pitch was 10 feet from the plate, "St-ee-rike three," shouted Ashford, "you're out."

Javier, enraged by the call, stepped around the catcher and planted a sharp left hook on Ashford's cheek-bone. The blow staggered the umpire, but he refused to go down. Instead, he struck back with his mask.

The Latin-American Baseball Federation suspended Javier for three days. It was Ashford's justifiable opinion that the sentence wasn't severe enough. He argued that the player should have been benched for at least a year, if not for life. So, he packed his mask and said goodbye to everybody in the Dominican Republic.

There'll be no such problems in the major leagues, of course. They just don't go around belting umpires in the big leagues.

"I expect the players to question some of my decisions," Ashford said recently, "but there'll be no violence, I'm sure. Players in the majors know how far they can go with an umpire."

Major league fans will watch Ashford's work with interest this season. They'll be wondering, naturally, just how far the players will go when he renders a decision they don't like.

This much is certain—they'll go as far as the showers if they protest too much.

*Bill Haller was an American League umpire when Ashford became the first Black MLB umpire. He thought Ashford was a good umpire but was called up after his prime. Many Negro League players were denied the opportunity to play MLB for that reason. The window was a bit wider for umpires than players.*

*I mentioned this column to Ken Holtzman. He remembered the incident. He was quick to point out that he hit Smith with a slow curveball and they later became friends (and teammates). Furthermore, Holtzman was later in that game thrown at by one of the pitchers on Smith's team. Ball players just don't forget.*

## February 27, 1971

### We Believe... by C.C. Johnson Spink, Editor and Publisher, *The Sporting News*, pp. 17, 30

*Integration in Hall of Fame*

St. Louis, Mo.—The fact that Jackie Robinson and Roy Campanella are in the Hall of Fame speaks for itself in refuting charges of "segregation" by critics of the new honors being conferred at Cooperstown on the star players of the former Negro baseball leagues.

Satchel Paige, the first to be selected—and deservedly so—will be represented by a plaque in a special section of the baseball shrine, apart from the regular Hall of Fame. No segregation by color is intended. The only line being drawn is between those who starred in the major leagues and those who played in the Negro leagues.

Two of the most prominent Negro sportswriters in the country, both members of the selection committee for the Negro players, agree with us.

Sam Lacy of the Baltimore *Afro-American* told us, "Critics of the manner in which the early Negro players are being recognized want to disregard the fixed rules governing admittance to the Hall of Fame. These include a period of required major league participation and statistics to attest to their right of entry into the shrine."

*White Stars Stopped at Door*

"Unlike restrictive covenants, the Hall of Fame rules make no mention of color. As evidence of the strict adherence to the rules, there are many great white players who have not been admitted, like Lefty O'Doul and Addie Joss, just to cite two whose records are familiar.

"While the greatness of Satchel Paige is generally acknowledged, nobody can say how many games he won during his career or how many homers were hit by Josh Gibson or how many hits sprang off the bats of Cool Papa Bell, Oscar Charleston, Bizz Mackey and Jud Wilson. Every player whose plaque is in the Hall of Fame has witness to his right of residency.

"For 10 years, members of our committee fought for recognition of the Negro league stars, and none of today's critics wrote a single word in support of the campaign. But now they're expressing dissatisfaction with the results. It is my feeling that nothing can be gained by refusing the honor for Paige and the other Negro stars who will follow."

Wendell Smith, Chicago sportswriter and broadcaster, said the establishment of the special category for players who performed in the Negro leagues before 1947, the year Robinson joined the Dodgers, has "many controversial implications," but he added:

"The fact remains that baseball's intentions are sincere and good. It also is a fact that baseball is trying to atone for its past sins when black players were barred from the majors solely on the basis of color.

"All of the members of the committee which is helping in the selection of the black players are aware that these men are of official Hall of Fame caliber and it would be ideal if they were enshrined there.

"But there are technicalities and regulations which must be revised before that ideal is attained. Neither the commissioner nor the special selection committee has the authority to change the Hall of Fame rules. Only the Hall of Fame officials can bring about such a readjustment.

"Whether that will be done remains to be seen. It is quite possible that eventually this special category for Negro players will be eliminated and Paige and other black players will be moved into the official Hall of Fame.

"In the meantime, this special category in the museum is one giant step in that direction. Applying a cliché it seems appropriate to point out that there are times when you have to crawl before you can walk."

Another well-known Negro sportswriter, A.S. (Doc) Young of Los Angeles, was much more critical. Young, who is the author of a book, *Great Negro Baseball Stars*, published in 1953, described the special section for black players as a gimmicky sort of arrangement with Madison Avenueish packaging.

He went on to say, "My sentiments were expressed perfectly by the *Los Angeles Times* cartoonist, Conrad, who depicted a Caucasian figure shaking hands with a Negro and saying, 'Congratulations. I hope you won't mind sitting in the back of the dugout.'"

Nevertheless, Young conceded there was "some logic" to Commissioner Bowie Kuhn's explanation of why the Negro league players were not being admitted to the regular Hall of Fame, but he added: "As far as I'm concerned, the overriding factor is this: The oldtime Negro league greats were ready, willing, able and anxious to play Organized Ball, but they were barred for reasons of race and color. The least they should receive now is full-fledged honors." While unhappy with the present arrangement, Young said, "Its salvation is the spirit of good intentions," but he declared there should be a simultaneous, mass induction of all eligible old-time Negro greatest—or "this thing could drag on for 50 years."

## Foster's Rule Cited

Young was especially disturbed because no provision had been made to honor Negro commissioners, owners and managers. He said the special section would be "a farce" without Andrew (Rube) Foster, whom he described as "a great manager and a commissioner so outstanding that Bowie Kuhn would have admired him, had he known him." Foster died in 1930.

We believe Satchel Paige's own words fit the situation. If you remember, one of his rules for staying young was: "And don't look back. Someone might be gaining on you."

While you can lament the years of discrimination against Negro players, you can't rewrite the pages of history. You can't put players in the major leagues who were never there, as great as they might have been.

You can't "look back"—all you can do is look ahead to the days when Willie Mays, Hank Aaron, Ernie Banks and other great Negro stars will join Robinson and Campanella at Cooperstown to add further proof to the fact that the Hall of Fame is not segregated.

*Controversy surrounded the Hall of Fame's decision concerning how to include Negro League players in the Hall. I included this article because it represents progress and it demonstrates how individuals can differ civilly. Legitimate points made by one side are acknowledged by the other. The disagreement doesn't get personal. Both sides seem to appreciate that they want to get to the same place. They disagreed civilly.*

# 8

# Women!

*There was no WNBA in Wendell's era. Women did not box or play ice hockey. He did not ignore female athletes. There were few about which he could write. Had Wendell lived fifty years later, he would have been able to write about the Williams sisters in tennis, any number of Black women who participate as players and coaches in women's professional and college basketball, and Laila Ali in boxing, to name a few. He would still be searching for a high-profile Black woman on the LPGA tour, though.*

*While Wendell believed there was a place for women in sport, he retained the traditional view of women shared by most sportswriters of his era. Exceptional women played sports. They did not become sportswriters or broadcasters. Eventually they would want to marry and have children like "normal" women. Most of the women Wendell interacted with in sports were the wives of male athletes.*

## May 15, 1948

### "Now the 'New Look' Is in the Fight Game," *Pittsburgh Courier*, p. 14

*Chicago Fight Mob Startled When Attractive Young Woman Barges Into Gymnasium as Trainer of Fighters and Proves She Knows What It's All About*

Chicago—They say there is no place in the manly art of self-defense for feminine pulchritude because a woman can't bear the flow of crimson or tolerate the many breeches of etiquette which the fight mob accepts as dignified and appropriate.

That's why eyebrows at the Ringside Gymnasium soared to a new high last week when curvaceous, charming Priscilla Anderson walked in with young Floyd Williams, a middleweight who is turning professional under her guidance. At first, the Ringside tenants were suspicious of the attractive woman trainer and they let it be known in no uncertain terms. "This is no place for a doll," they said. But it didn't take them long to learn that this was no gag. Obviously, the "doll" knew what she was doing as she put Williams through his paces. She had a stopwatch and she timed him when he skipped rope. When his timing was off punching the bag, Priscilla ordered the fighter to stop and she explained what was wrong.

## A Real Trainer

When she said to a friend standing nearby, "We'll do about two miles on the road in the morning and then he'll be ready," Priscilla declared herself "in" because that is the mark of a real trainer—getting up and running with a fighter in the early morn.

Priscilla may be a innovation as far as the local fight fraternity is concerned, but she's well known in other localities. She has a trainer's license in Ohio, Indiana and Washington, D.C.

Despite the fact that she is a native Chicagoan and lives at 9348 Wentworth, the 25-year-old trainer with the "new look" does not have a license to work in Illinois. The Illinois Commission is now considering her application, however, and before long she'll be seen working in the corner with fighters here.

## She Loves Boxing

"I've been interested in fighters ever since I was five years old," Priscilla explained. Her father, Spencer Anderson has managed fighters for years. "I've been around them all my life," she said, "and I guess if I'd been a boy I would have been a fighter."

Priscilla and her father form a family team. He manages the fighters and she trains them. One of the battlers in the Anderson stable is Willie Cheatum, a veteran lightweight. He vows that Priscilla knows as much about fighters as any trainer in the business. Last Monday night he lost a close decision to Talmadge Bussey at Marigold Gardens.

"If she'd been in my corner," he said, "I would never have lost that fight. She would have told me just how to beat that guy. But she didn't have an Illinois license and they wouldn't let her work in my corner."

Priscilla agreed. "He lost the fight in the last round," she said. "They should have sent him out swinging away. If he had forced the fighting in that last round Willie would have won. I would have made him fight that way."

## Husband a Scout

Priscilla uses her maiden name for business purposes. Her married name is Mrs. L.E. Fulbright and her better half works on the railroad. He has no objection to her being mixed up in the fight game. "In fact," she said, "my husband helps us. He acts as a scout. If he sees a good fighter during his travels he signs him up and sends him to us."

Like all trainers, her greatest ambition is to develop a champion. "I want to be the trainer of a world champion some day," she said as she watched young Williams with hopeful eyes. "I don't know when I'll uncover one, but I'm going to keep trying."

Priscilla's been married five years. She adores children but the stork has never stopped at her house.

"I haven't any children to train," she said, "so I satisfy my motherly instinct by training fighters."

*Wendell treats Ms. Anderson with the respect she deserves. I do not know if Wendell would have been comfortable with women boxing, but he obviously is comfortable with them training men. His perspective is relatively progressive. Still, he thinks it necessary to comment on her appearance. His comments regarding her appearance are positive, and he would be surprised to find anyone who might have a problem with that. In fairness, I came across articles in the* Courier *written by women about women and they too would be complimentary of a woman's appearance. And when Wendell wrote about male trainers, he would usually describe their physical appearance. He would often describe them humorously, however. When writing about a male athlete, Wendell did not comment on the athlete's sex appeal. There is gender bias in Wendell's writing about women. But to a degree, some of what might appear as bias is the difference in etiquette at the time. Wendell is following social convention when he describes Ms. Anderson's physical appearance in a positive way. The reader should also note that Wendell reveals her address. Different era.*

## September 18, 1948

### Sports Beat, *Pittsburgh Courier*, p. 22

*Baseball's Glamour Girl Bows Out...*

Effa Manley, the beauteous boss of the Newark Eagles is divorcing baseball because of "mental cruelty and indignities." It seems that only small crowds have been turning out to see her team play, upsetting her mental tranquility quite some. The indignities she has suffered have been caused, no doubt, by cold-hearted newspapermen who refuse to let her operate both the Newark Eagles and their respective newspapers. The writers contend that such a dual role is against union rules, plus the fact that she knows nothing about the newspaper business.

There are many of us, however, who will miss the "Queen of Newark" because despite the fact that she tried to tell us how and what to write, she was always good copy. That was especially true at the infrequent meetings of the two leagues. There was never a dull moment when she attended and we always knew who would start those confabs popping.

Despite her riotous threats and growling when things didn't go her way, Mrs. Manley was every inch a fine, dignified lady and extremely emotional. In fact, she was never known to miss the opportunity to cry at one of those brawling sessions and at times it was so touching the sympathetic members of the press would pat her with platonic affection and suggest that she get out of baseball and go home to her kitchen and streamlined mop.

Her weepings always gave those meetings an atmosphere of moistness, whereas before her arrival on the baseball scene it was always dry as an African desert. The gentlemen of the press would sit around listening to the executives double-talk each other and play tit-tat-toe while the schedules were being drawn.

## She "Loved" the Working Press!

But when the Fair Lady from Jersey stepped into the picture things picked up and the scribes always kept pencils in hand, ready for action. Invariably Mrs. Manley would become involved in an argument with one of her colleagues over which team her club would play on such profitable days as Easter Sunday, Decoration Day, Fourth of July and other holidays. If she didn't get what she wanted, Mrs. Manley would wrinkle up her pretty face and turn on the sprinkling system. She didn't always win using this feminine attack but the flowers on the table over which she stood did.

One thing the press learned about Mrs. Manley early was that she was a fickle woman. She would cater to them in their presence, assure them that they were the back bone of Negro baseball, praise them openly and lavishly about their deathly prose and reveal little inside secrets which the other owners didn't want them to know. On the other hand, however, she always lost her affection, it seems, when closeted with the moguls. It was then that she opened up and fired broadsides at the writers. She charged violently that they had forsaken Negro baseball for major league ball; that they were literally "selling" promising young Negro players to the majors and intentionally trying to kill her Newark Eagles and all other teams in Negro baseball.

Such charges were unfair, of course, but hell's fury can in no way compete with a woman's scorn. Mrs. Manley was definitely a woman. We never have believed that she meant all the mad things she said about the press. It was just that times were changing and so was the entire structure of Negro baseball. Mrs. Manley knew it but refused to believe it.

She was trying to fight off the inevitable and cling to the great days when Negro baseball—the offspring of big league baseball's discriminatory policy—thrived because Negro players had no place else to go. In her rantings she blamed everyone for the demise of her dream world from Branch Rickey down to the press.

During these furious bleats, she refused to recognize the fact that nothing was killing Negro baseball but Democracy. The big league doors were suddenly opened one day and when Negro players walked in, Negro baseball walked out. When men like Rickey and Veeck decided to put some Democracy in baseball, it meant that the lush days for owners of Negro teams were over. When we say lush days, we mean when owners of Negro teams made as high as $50,000 a year profit from their segregated baby. They made that money without too much effort, incidentally. They rented the big ball parks, formed makeshift leagues with irregular schedules, elected puppet presidents and put on shows at excessive prices. The best that can be said for these exhibitions is that they were interesting.

### Good Old Days Are Gone

But the time has come now when Negro baseball will by necessity return to its level. It is doubtful that the owners will ever have such a vulnerable audience or discriminatory paradise from which to pluck a bouquet of crisp, green dollars. Instead, Negro baseball is going to be in the same category as Class "B" minor league teams. It will exist. In fact, it must exist. But the big money days are gone. The overflow crowds are gone. Yet, it still has a place in the baseball picture. There is still a desire on the part of the fans to see Negro players and teams. But not at the same prices or under the same conditions as before. They have a reason to go to big league parks now and see their stars in action. They didn't have that privilege when Mrs. Manley and her Eagles were flying high.

Mrs. Manley always said she'd stay in baseball and take the hard knocks with the good. She said somebody had to keep Negro baseball going, keep it alive. That was back in the war days when her Eagles were out-drawing the white team that owned the park she rented. That was back in the days when discriminatory baseball was a profitable venture; back in the days when such greats as Satchel Paige and Josh Gibson were mighty drawing cards and were the "sweethearts" of the owners.

But now that's all over. The well has run dry. It's a new day and an entirely new structure has to be built around Negro baseball. It must be sound, practical and in no way lavish.

The old days have gone.

So has gracious, charming, eccentric Effa Manley. The boys in the press box are gonna' miss her—tears and all!

*Effa Manley might not have been willing to accept her share (as a team owner) of the responsibility for the Negro Leagues' demise, but she knew when to get out. Wendell better understood that the owners' business practices contributed to the demise, but he incorrectly thought the Negro Leagues could survive MLB integration. Wendell uses sexist language in this column, but he clearly has a degree of respect for Manley. He jests about her eccentricities but recognizes that she was formidable. She was a force in Negro league baseball. "Beauteous boss" is pushing alliteration to the extreme, but that was Wendell's style.*

## July 29, 1950

### Sports Beat, *Pittsburgh Courier*, p. 22

*Thar's Gold in Them Thar' Forest Hills...*

The lady who answered the door said Miss Althea Gibson, the best Negro woman tennis player in the entire world, was having dinner. She said Miss Gibson would see us in a minute.

Miss Gibson must have a great propensity for food because it took her much longer than that. But she finally appeared, wearing what we deciphered was a summer smock. It was short and sleeveless and dangled from her trim body in a casual sort of way.

She is tall and lithe and has that relaxed appearance all good athletes seem to own. She is 5 feet 9½ inches tall, 22 years old and weighs a well-proportioned 130 pounds. Her marvelously efficient arms are a smooth bronze color and slightly muscular. Her legs are like two columns of polished mahogany. Miss Gibson is a handsome woman with an abundance of personal charm.

Around her at the present time swirls the biggest controversy in tennis. Everyone is waiting to see if the smug United States Lawn Tennis Association will invite her to play in the Nationals at Forest Hills next month.

"I don't know whether they will bar me because I am a Negro or not," she said. "In the first place, I must reach the qualifying stages. If I do good in my next two tournaments then I will be satisfied that I rate consideration."

The Nationals are the world series of tennis. The player who finally comes through on top can turn professional and get rich. There's a pot of gold at the end of the Forest Hills rainbow and anyone with enough coordination to bounce a tennis ball knows it.

### *She's Moved Up Fast in Three Years...*

Miss Gibson was a good tennis player four years ago but it wasn't until she went to the finals of the National Indoor Tournament in New York that she became nationally prominent. Before that she had run the gauntlet of various Negro tournaments, winning the national singles title three times and triumphed in the Eastern Indoor championships. Now she's knocking on the famed door of Forest Hills and some day may even bat a few around at Wimbledon in staid old England.

She was born in Sumter, S.C., and reared in New York City. She started playing on the streets of New York at the age of 11.

"We used to play what they call paddle tennis," she explained. "You play it with a rubber ball and wooden paddle. I got to be pretty good at it and then started playing tennis. Then I joined the Cosmopolitan Tennis Club and was tutored by Fred Johnson, the coach there. He taught me a lot of things and pretty soon I was going around playing in different tournaments."

Althea is a freshman at Florida A. and M. College and during the winter months devotes most of her athletic time to basketball.

"I like basketball," she confessed, "and play on the school team. It's a good game and keeps me in condition all winter. I was the team's leading scorer last year."

Even if she should reach Forest Hills and emerge victorious, Miss Gibson isn't sure she would turn professional. "I think that would interfere with my education," she said thoughtfully. "I'd like to finish college. I am a physical education major. Most students taking that course want to teach and coach but I think I'd like to be a policewoman in New York or work with juveniles."

### *Alice Marble Is Fighting for Her...*

The fact no Negro has ever been invited indicates there is a subtle "Ladies and Gentlemen's" agreement in Forest Hills against them. But there is a vanguard of fair-minded influential people fighting for Althea and she may crack the ice.

One of the most militant people fighting for her is Alice Marble, four-time winner of the Nationals at Forest Hills and considered one of the greatest women tennis players of all time.

"I have never even met her," Althea said with a note of emotion in her voice. "Miss Marble has gone to the front for me strictly on her own. She has a great deal of influence. Another person who is making her weight felt in my behalf is Mary Hardwick Hare, the English star. She said I am good enough to play in that tournament and she is doing everything possible to get me in. Not only that, but she is working out things so that I can go to England and play in some tournaments."

She has been appearing in a number of big tournaments this summer, leading the way into tennis retreats no Negro has ever tread before. This week, for instance, she played in the National Clay Court Championships in Chicago. Her next big meet will be the East Orange (New Jersey) Grass Tourney.

## A Dream of Forest Hills and Fame...

When she finished high school in New York, Miss Gibson was well on the way to tennis fame. She had offers to attend five different colleges and she finally selected Florida A and M.

"I went there because they gave me the best offer," she explained. "Mr. William Gray was president there then and he was very nice. He gave me a scholarship and encouraged me to keep playing."

She smiled and said no when we asked if any romance had sneaked into her busy life.

"I haven't had time to think of boys or marriage," she confessed. "All my time has been devoted to tennis. I eat and sleep the game and when I go to bed I dream of playing at Forest Hills. The game of tennis absorbs my very life."

Which is all well and good, as far as we are concerned. But any game that can make a girl as attractive as Althea ignore the birds and bees and starry nights ... must be associated with some kind of racket!

In her case, the word "love" is nothing more than tennis parlance and belongs up on the scoreboard.

*Wendell did not appreciate being kept waiting for this interview and he indirectly notes that at the beginning of the piece. He appreciates Gibson's athletic ability and that she might achieve things other Black athletes had not yet achieved. She would go on to win 11 Grand Slam events including Wimbledon and the U.S. Open. The standards of the day permitted Wendell to comment on her appearance and ask her about prospects for marriage. He did not address those issues when writing about Arthur Ashe.*

*June 20, 1953*

## Sports Beat, *Pittsburgh Courier*, p. 14

*The Lady's Playing a Man's Game*

Maybe the guy was tired of baby-sitting or couldn't find the can opener, but, whatever the reason, he was justified when he cried out:

"A woman's place is in the home!"

That undisputable statement rings particularly true, we think, in the case of a baseball player by the name of Toni Stone. She is the hunk of femininity employed by the Indianapolis Clowns. She is a second baseman (?).

She jumps around the country with this club, owned, operated and exploited by Sid Pollock, the "Tarrytown (N.Y.) Terror." She is a lady making a living in a profession designed strictly for men. It is a profession in which only the hale, hearty and strong are likely to succeed, certainly not one in which gentility and refinement are the prerequisites for success.

It is indeed, unfortunate that Negro baseball has collapsed to the extent it must tie itself to a woman's apron strings in order to survive. Mrs. Stone does not, of course, wear an apron. She wears a regular baseball uniform.

The young lady's baseball talents have been publicized considerably since the season started. Mr. Pollock is trying to convince us that she plays second base like Jackie Robinson. The latest averages show that she is hitting .217. That's not much of an average to write home about but you'll have to admit it's not bad for a dame.

It is, however, a reflection on the caliber of ball they now play in the Negro American League. What kind of pitchers do they have in that circuit these days? Any time a doll can hit .217, it means they don't have anything on the ball but the cover. Here is Mrs. Stone's record:

| G | AB | R | H | 2B | 3B | HR | SH | SB | RBI | Pct. |
|----|----|---|---|----|----|----|----|----|-----|------|
| 15 | 23 | 0 | 5 | 0  | 0  | 0  | 0  | 0  | 1   | .217 |

*The Scorers Must Give Her a Break...*

No less than 22 other players are sporting averages below that of Mrs. Stone. What kind of hitters are they! Any guy who can't out-hit a fräulein shouldn't be permitted to play in the Little League, which is an organization for tykes and midgets.

Perhaps the fact that Mrs. Stone is a lady prompts the scorers in the league to be more liberal when it comes to distinguishing between a base hit and an error.

When a question arises they probably say: "She's a cute little thing, let's call it a hit." Or, they might say: "That's a hit, Sweet Thing, Sweet Thing, Sweet Thing."

Wonder what the trend of conversation between Mrs. Stone and her faithful husband is when the little woman comes home from a hard day's work on the baseball field? It probably runs something like this:

HUSBAND: How did things go at work today, Honey?

MRS. STONE: Oh, pretty good. Got a double and single. I should have had 3 for 4 but their centerfielder robbed me.

HUSBAND: Did you get any runs?

MRS. STONE: No, thank goodness…. These woolen socks we wear are very good. They must be 75 gauge.

HUSBAND: How are you in the field?

MRS. STONE: Well, I didn't see anyone in the stands today who looked better than I did. I powdered between innings just to make sure.

HUSBAND: How did the pitcher on the other team look today?

MRS. STONE: I'm telling you that guy's just about as handsome as they come. When that big, strong beast looked down at me when I was batting, I got so excited I didn't know what to do. I won't ever get a hit off him. I get so weak when he looks at me, I can't generate enough strength to bunt. What curves he has!

HUSBAND: I hope none of those guys fall for you.

MRS. STONE: Well, frankly, one did today. But I tagged him out when he came sliding in to second.

HUSBAND: They tell me the manager bawled you out today.

MRS. STONE: He sure did. He blamed me for not getting a pop-up that dropped between the shortstop and me.

HUSBAND: What did you tell him?

MRS. STONE: I told him it is a lady's privilege to change her mind, even on a fly ball. Personally, I think that manager's a foul ball himself.

HUSBAND: Honey, I'm sorry dinner isn't ready yet.

MRS. STONE: What! Not ready yet? What's going on around this house, anyway? If you think I'm going to be standing over a hot second base all day while you loaf around the house, you've got another thought coming.

HUSBAND: But you must remember that I had to dust.

MRS. STONE: That's no excuse. I get dusted every day.

HUSBAND: Some bills came today and one of them is for $350.

MRS. STONE: Yes, I know…. I went downtown yesterday and purchased a new glove.

HUSBAND: Isn't that an awful lot of money for a glove?

MRS. STONE: Not for a silver mink glove. It's really something. I'm the envy of every woman in the stands on Ladies Day.

HUSBAND: Are you going shopping tomorrow?

**MRS. STONE:** I certainly am. There's a big sale on. I'm going to be the first one in the store when the doors open. Those specially designed Roy Campanella bats that were selling for $3.38 last month are on sale tomorrow for $2.45. They're simply divine.

**HUSBAND:** Are you still angry at me for putting starch in your sliding pads when I washed them?

**MRS. STONE:** No, but don't ever do that again. It felt like I was sliding on cement.

**HUSBAND:** I hope you have a good day at the plate tomorrow, Honey.

**MRS. STONE:** I hope you'll have something on the plate when I come home after the game, too.

*The point of this story is to illustrate that the talent level of Negro League baseball had declined substantially. By 1953 most young Black prospects were bypassing the Negro Leagues and entering either the minor leagues or MLB directly. It is easy to miss that given Wendell's use (misuse) of humor in this piece. He is disrespectful of Toni Stone, although he does mention that she does not have the lowest batting average in the league. She is performing better than some men. The attempt at humor is distracting. Wendell is further annoyed because she was playing for the Indianapolis Clowns. Wendell and others did not appreciate the "clowning" element in Negro League baseball. But Toni Stone had the last laugh. In 2019, Lydia Diamond's play* Toni Stone *was performed in theaters across the United States.*

## September 25, 1954

### Sports Beat, *Pittsburgh Courier*, p. 14

*It Happens After Every Fight...*

New York City—It was all over now and here in the visitor's dressing room of Yankee Stadium sat the defeated guest, Ezzard Charles.

He was sitting on a long table with his attractive wife, Gladys, beside him. The defeated challenger wore a light blue sports shirt and dark blue slacks. His wife looked like she had just stepped out of *Vogue* or *Harper's Bazaar,* wearing a bluish-gray mink stole that matched her expressive eyes.

It was rather strange, however, to see her there, sitting beside her beaten husband. Marva was never around like this when Joe Louis was in his prime, nor was Edna Mae when Sugar Ray Robinson was bowling 'em over.

Anyway, Charles was flanked by his wife and surrounded by camera men, television men, radio men and newspaper men. They were firing questions and he was trying to answer them, being most cooperative and, of course, logical, despite the fact that only minutes before his mind and body had been numbed by Rocky Marciano's powerful fists.

Marciano had knocked him out, swarmed over him like a saloon fighter, even clouted him a couple times after the bell. Charles had gallantly weathered the storm for seven rounds, then succumbed when caught by a cyclone of lefts and rights. Before the fight Joe Louis had said Marciano was a dirty fighter. They wanted to know now if Charles agreed.

### *He Didn't Look as Bad This Time...*

Charles weighed the question carefully and then commented, "I wouldn't say that, exactly.

"He's just a rough and tumble guy. He swings all the time and sometimes his punches are off the line. He's crude, I'd say ... just plain crude."

His wife looked at him as though she were surprised. "His low punches and blows after the bell weren't intentional, eh?" she asked, with fire in her eyes.

"Well, how is it that it happens in all his fights? It would be different if it only happened in one or two, maybe three, of his fights, but it has happened in all his fights."

Charles looked at her affectionately but didn't try to answer the question. He understood ... his wife was trying to defend him.

"He's a good, rough, tough fighter," Charles went on. "He punches hard and constantly."

"You don't look bad," his wife assured him. "He didn't hit you like before, like in June."

Charles agreed. He rubbed his bearded face like a man who had been lost in the wilderness and then found suddenly by a rescue party.

"No," he said, "it wasn't as bad this time as the last. It was an easier fight, even though he knocked me out tonight and before I went the distance. I should have beaten him tonight because, really, he wasn't the fighter he was before. And I figure I would have won if the fight had gone about two more rounds. He was bleeding, cut and bashed up pretty good.

"Just two more rounds and I would have won. They would have had to stop it."

Charles shook his head like a man does when he had missed a great opportunity. His wife patted him on the back. "You don't have to be ashamed," she assured him.

"It's just that I know I can beat him," Ezzard said. "When will we fight again?" Someone said it would probably be a long time before Ezzard would get another crack at the crown he once owned. He shrugged his broad shoulders.

"Well," he said, "I'm not going to quit just because I lost tonight. I am going to keep on fighting, I'm not through yet. Somehow, some day, I'll get another chance."

His wife didn't say anything to that but there was a "why does he want to keep on fighting" look in her bluish-gray eyes.

Charles went on answering questions. No, he wasn't hurt in the second round, just surprised when he got hit and went down. No, Marciano was not a great fighter, but a good one in a crude way. No, he never lost the count. In fact, he thought he was up before the referee counted ten. Yes, he was ready to continue when it was stopped.

Finally, the interviewing ended and Charles prepared to leave. The cops cleared a path for him and his wife and they walked slowly out of the dressing room.

After they had gone, someone asked: "What was she doing here in the dressing room? In the past, this has been forbidden territory for women."

"She was here," someone answered, "to console her husband. What better time for a wife to be beside her husband when he's been in trouble and escaped? Maybe she's in love with the guy."

"Yeh," the other agreed, "I never thought about it that way. You know how it is.… You never figure someone cares about the loser."

*It might seem strange to include a column discussing the Charles v Marciano fight in this chapter. Wendell wrote in an era in which the sportswriter respected the private lives of the athletes he covered. He knew that Joe Louis had marital problems with his first wife Marva. And he knew that Sugar Ray Robinson and Edna Mae had issues. He did not want to write about the problems in those marriages, but he did want to make it known that he perceived Gladys Charles to be different. Ezzard Charles would die a slow and degrading death from Amyotrophic Lateral Sclerosis. Gladys Charles remained by his side until he died. Wendell answers the question as to why Gladys was in the locker room with the suggestion "maybe she's in love with the guy." That might have been a subtle jab (pun intended) at some of the other boxers' wives he knew.*

## August 24, 1957

## Sports Beat, *Pittsburgh Courier*, p. 25

This is written for the feminine members of the Lonely Hearts Club. Its purpose is to revive the hopes and marital aspirations of old maids, spinsters, divorcees, widows and sweet young maidens yet untouched.

If you're married, Lady ... then don't read this. Just stay home and fix the Old Man's meals. Otherwise, this data on unmarried, unattached ballplayers may give you ideas.

And, such ideas will simply inspire your devoted, hard-working spouse to wind-up like a big league pitcher and belt you right on the snoot.

If, however, you're single and on the prowl.... If you're seeking a dashing prince astride a snow-white steed ... the following information on baseball bachelors is offered free of charge.

Realizing such sacred information is likely to precipitate a battle-royal, the following advice is hereby given ambitious female contenders:

1. As soon as the bell rings, come out fighting. Score your knockout as quickly as possible.

2. Pay no attention to the rules. Come out kicking, scratching, clawing, screaming.

3. If you floor your opponent, don't let her up. Ignore the compulsory eight-count. Kick her right in the teeth.

4. Forget the no-foul rule. If you can foul her up in any way, don't hesitate to do so.

5. If you are inclined to be fat, refuse to weigh in. They may discover you're over the weight-limit and disqualify you. (If you're over 167 pounds, it is recommended that you rush to an established training camp, like Greenwood Lake, N.Y., or Pompton Lakes, N.J., and run on the road every morning until you drop dead.)

6. Whatever you do, be in GOOD SHAPE when you go into this fight.

7. Finally, be clever. When they give the last-minute instructions and tell you "to come out fightin,'" wait until your opponent turns her back ... then let her have it—WHAM-O!

Now that you've been thoroughly briefed on the womanly art of mayhem, you're ready for all available information on these bronze Adonises in the majors eligible to be lured, baited and, of course, solidly hooked. In all, there are 10 of these elusive, prosperous, fun-loving fugitives, five in each league. Significantly, seven hail from Spanish-speaking countries and only three from the United States. (What's that they say about those so-called sultry senoritas?)

As a special service, we present the following scratch sheet through the courtesy of the internationally famous "Snatch 'Em Quick and Don't Let 'Em Go Club, Inc."

## American League

| Player | Team | Age | Hair | Eyes | Hgt. | Wgt. | Ancestry | Salary* |
|--------|------|-----|------|------|------|------|----------|---------|
| Durham | Baltimore | 24 | Black | Brown | 6:01 | 186 | American | $7,000 |
| #Minoso | Chicago | 33 | Black | Brown | 5:10 | 175 | Cuban | 32,000 |
| Lopez | Kansas City | 24 | Black | Brown | 6:00 | 168 | Panamanian | 15,000 |
| Power | Kansas City | 25 | Black | Black | 6:00 | 190 | Panamanian | 18,000 |
| Becquer | Washington | 24 | Black | Black | 6:00 | 162 | Cuban | 10,000 |

## National League

| | | | | | | | | |
|--------|------|-----|------|------|------|------|----------|---------|
| Amoros | Brooklyn | 25 | Black | Brown | 5:07 | 163 | Cuban | 15,000 |
| Robinson | Cincinnati | 21 | Black | Brown | 6:01 | 190 | American | 17,000 |
| &Fernandez | Phila | 25 | Black | Brown | 6:00 | 167 | Cuban | 8,000 |
| Clemente | Pittsburgh | 22 | Black | Brown | 5:11 | 175 | Puer Rican | 10,000 |
| $Alston | St. Louis | 27 | Black | Brown | 6:05 | 195 | American | 8,000 |

*Estimated
#Best Catch
&Most Handsome
$He's a Big One

So there they are, girls. Select the one you want, then go to your respective corners and come out fighting.

Those of you who are married should go home and mind your own business. It's not our fault if you had your chance … and blew it.

*Doubtful this one would make it in to print today. Even by 1957 standards it is a bit much. But Wendell obviously thought it was clever and no one at the* Courier *stopped it. In another piece Wendell is walking the streets with Teddy Horne (Lena Horne's father) after a boxing match. They encounter a man and a woman fighting. The woman is holding her own for a while, but the man connects with a solid punch and down she goes. Wendell made light of the event. He was not a misogynist. He was a man living in a different era.*

# 9

# Muhammad Ali

*When Wendell began his career in 1937 Joe Louis was the heavyweight champion of the world and the title meant something not only in the sports world but also the world. And the champion was expected to hold the title with dignity. Joe Louis, Ezzard Charles, Jersey Joe Walcott and Rocky Marciano behaved the way Wendell thought champions should behave. After Marciano retired, however, the champions did not measure up to Wendell's expectations. Then, along came Cassius Clay.*

*While as a journalist Wendell appreciated Clay as good copy, Smith did not think much of Clay as a boxer or potential champion. This would change. Wendell developed respect for Ali as a fighter and an individual. Ali respected Wendell in return. I find it surprising that Wendell, who would always view Joe Louis as The Champ, could appreciate Ali's very different qualities. I also find it surprising that the young brash champion who seemed to respect no one respected Wendell.*

*Joe Barrow, Jr., reports that Louis and Ali had respect for each other as well. They were different people but did share a common experience. A war cost each of them several years of his boxing career. Joe Louis served in World War II. Muhammad Ali refused to serve in Vietnam. Louis was not permitted to defend his title; Ali's title was taken from him.*

## August 3, 1963

### Sports Beat, *Pittsburgh Courier*, p. 15

*Clay Is Next in Line to Feel Wrath of Champ Sonny Liston*

Now that heavyweight champion Sonny Liston has disposed of Floyd Patterson, the strange, introvert and frail-hearted ex-titleholder, he now turns his attention to the "Filibuster Fighter," Cassius Clay. If nothing else, Clay has added color to what has been a dull heavyweight picture.

Patterson was too sanctimonious to be interesting ... and all the other heavyweights, with the exception of Clay, are still undistinguished.

Cassius is, of course, a delightful relief in these days of uncolorful warriors. He is an extrovert with an imagination and charm. He is flippant, gregarious and excitingly articulate. Clay has arrogantly declared that Liston "is a disgrace as a fighter" to the boxing business; that Sonny is "uglier than a bear drinking hot vinegar"... and that he'll knock the champion out in short order.

"If Liston doesn't stop his jive," declared Cassius after last week's fight in Las Vegas, "I'll kayo him in five."

Eventually, of course, Cassius must put up or shut up. Negotiations are under way for a Liston-Clay fight in September. Tax complications may delay the engagement until next year, but whenever the fight does come off, the undefeated Louisville Lip must do something besides talk. Perhaps before he risks his health against the cruel but efficient champion, Cassius should have a long talk with Two-Ton Tony Galento, the portly heavyweight who once attracted world-wide attention by boasting that he would "knock Joe Louis flatter than a two-day-old glass of beer."

Louis, never one to talk back, listened intently, and then one night caught Tony with a left hook, under official circumstances, and proceeded to annihilate him. Galento hasn't been heard from since. Clay's chatter is amusing and intriguing to millions upon millions of people. His rantings and ravings have stimulating impact and arouse the curiosity of the most blasé individuals.

"Maybe this 21-year-old kid can do what he says," declare many people hopefully. "Maybe he can beat Liston and become the heavyweight champion."

Liston, meantime, is still carrying his past on his powerful back. He is a victim of intolerance. He finds it almost impossible to shake off the mistakes he made during his juvenile years. People, he has learned, are unforgiving.

"Even if people don't like me," he said after the Patterson farce, "they may as well get used to me as heavyweight champion. They're going to have to tolerate me for a long time."

The legions of anti–Liston people don't like that prediction, but if they are realists, and impressed at all by sheer facts, they may as well adjust themselves to the champion's superiority over the class of mediocre challengers standing in line. There is no one around at the moment good enough to extend Liston. He is head and shoulders above all he surveys and rules in the heavyweight division. That goes for Cassius Clay too. There is reason to believe that Cassius is more aware of that fact than the majority of people who are trying to "wish" him upon the heavyweight throne.

As everyone knows, talk is cheap. On the other hand, ability is not come by easily. Either you have it, or you don't. Patterson didn't have it, although there was once a time many thought he did.

Cassius doesn't have it either—although there are some trying to impose it upon him. Cassius is lean, young, and hungry. People of that breed and circumstance start revolutions without considering the consequences. Obviously, Clay isn't considering the consequences. He's talking up a big gate and a severe beating.

Whether a full pot is more vital than good health is a matter of conjecture in this particular instance. To most sensible people, health takes precedence over anything else. Apparently Cassius Clay is too healthy for his own good.

The fact of the matter is that Clay is a second-rate fighter. Some day he may develop into a top-ranking battler. At the moment, however, he is as green as the big money he is seeking.

A veteran fight trainer gave this appraisal of Clay after he was promised that he would not be identified here:

"Clay doesn't know how to fight," the man declared. "He can't punch to the body, he stands up too straight and he has no defense. He refuses to keep his hands up, and as far as I can determine, he hasn't learned anything much since he fought in the Olympics."

That is the opinion of most seasoned fight men. They say with authority that Clay can't fight. They mean of course, that he can't fight the likes of Sonny Liston and escape disaster. In other words, no one should get excited about Clay's chances against the champion. He doesn't have any.

*Not only did Wendell expect Liston to defeat Clay, but he also thought the reigning champion might seriously hurt the challenger. Wendell was in the majority. Many in Wendell's "fight mob" did not think Clay was a great fighter and gave him no chance against Liston. The reader might also note that Wendell is sympathetic to Liston. That would change.*

# January 16, 1965

## Sports Beat, *Pittsburgh Courier,* p. 15

*Clay Is Still Champion Until Someone Beats Him*

The campaign launched by the World Boxing Association to "get" Cassius Clay and erase his image as the heavyweight champion of the world is now officially under way.

The WBA, which claims 48 of the 50 states in the Union as bona fide members, has ceremoniously sanctioned a bout between Ernest Terrell and Eddie Machen as a "fight for the heavyweight championship." The winner of the contest, which will be staged in Chicago on March 5 will be the "new heavyweight champion," insofar as the WBA is concerned.

That means, of course, that the eccentric Clay, who has been recognized universally as heavyweight champion, will be acceptable as titleholder in only two states, New York and Massachusetts. Those two states do not belong to the WBA.

The WBA, which is a politically controlled body, operates on the ridiculous theory that the heavyweight championship is vacant. It refuses to recognize Cassius The Pop-off as the titleholder. According to its ratings, the WBA says Terrell is the No. 1 contender, followed by Floyd Patterson, George Chuvalo, Machen and Zora Folley.

Neither Cassius nor Sonny Liston rate so much as a nod from the WBA. On the other hand, the ratings offered by the highly respected Ring magazine recognize Cassius as the champion and Liston as the No. 1 contender. Ring rates Patterson second, followed by Terrell, Cleveland Williams and Chuvalo.

The WBA officially ignores Clay and Liston because it claims they "concocted" a return bout after Cassius took the title from Sonny last year in Miami. The WBA was opposed to a return match, claiming, with some justification, that other contenders should receive consideration before Liston. Sonny surrendered the title while sitting on his stool.

The proposed Clay-Liston rematch never came off. Cassius was stricken with a hernia complication on the eve of the bout, which was scheduled for Boston.

The WBA then wanted an elimination tournament held, featuring Terrell, Patterson, Chuvalo and Williams. Liston might have been included but he, running true to form, became involved in an incident with the police in Denver and eliminated himself. Williams suffered similar embarrassment when a policeman shot him in Houston, Tex.

Meanwhile, Patterson and Chuvalo signed to fight in New York and the WBA promptly rubbed them out because the Empire state is not a member of the association.

Thus, the WBA's two "good guys"—Terrel and Machen—will fight for the "vacant" title on March 5.

If all this sounds confusing, it's understandable. But that's the way the heavyweight situation is today and it is going to take some time to straighten it out.

The blame for the confusion must be heaped upon the shoulders of the recognized champion, Clay, and his incorrigible No. 1 contender, Liston.

The WBA wants to eliminate Clay because it claims he has not only violated the no-return bout clause, but, also, failed to conduct himself with the dignity expected of a heavyweight champion. Unfortunately, however, the WBA's motives, or attitude, in this area are suspect. It is our belief that the WBA disapproves of Clay's honeymoon with the Black Muslims to such a degree that it wants to execute him as champion. This attitude might be construed by some as "religious persecution."

We agree that Clay's conduct has been highly unwarranted, but not because of his association with the controversial Muslims. Rather, it has been his childish, absurd rantings and ravings in public with respect to his fighting ability. He shouts to the house tops that he's the greatest, ignoring the fact that modesty is the mark of a champion and that public esteem is a desirable goal for all athletes. On the other hand, you can't consciously dethrone a champion because he has a big mouth.

If you don't like him, you should find a fighter who belts him in the mouth hard enough, and often enough, to take the title. Championships are won in the ring ... not outside of it.

As far as most recognized boxing authorities are concerned, the Terrell-Machen winner will be a synthetic champion, the WBA to the contrary. Cassius will be accepted as the real champion until some capable challenger hits him in his big mouth and scatters his teeth. And even that feat must be achieved inside the ring.

*Wendell makes a principled defense of Clay. He doesn't like Clay's antics. He is not a fan of the Black Muslims. But neither Clay's antics nor his religion is relevant to the title. The title goes to the best boxer, so argues Wendell.*

## December 11, 1965

### Sports Beat, *Pittsburgh Courier*, p. 15

*Muhammad No Longer a Laughing Matter*

They're beginning to take Cassius Clay or Muhammad Ali seriously...

He has said all along that he's the greatest of all time. Now the skeptics who laughed at him originally are wondering if they made a mistake. He isn't, of course, the greatest ever but at the moment he's the most competent fighter in the ring and is going to be the heavyweight champion for a long time.

"I'll be the champion for at least two more years," he predicted the other day before a curious audience. "I'm going to fight Ernie Terrell next and then I'll take on a couple of other contenders, beat them, and go into retirement undefeated."

Nobody laughed at the prediction. There was a time when they looked upon him as a clown, but not anymore. Not after the way he toyed with Floyd Patterson. He humiliated Patterson.

"I didn't go near him in the first round." Clay explained. "I'll tell you why:

"I arrived at the arena late. I didn't have time to warm up in my dressing room. So when I went into the ring I decided to take the first round as an exercise period. That's what I did. I cooled it for the first three minutes. That made Patterson look bad, of course, because he couldn't catch up with me. I moved too fast for him. That also made the experts look bad because they've always said that Patterson was so fast on his feet that nobody could keep away from him.

"Patterson had no business in the ring with me. All he had was a big heart. I tried to knock him out in the fifth round and again in the sixth. He took a terrible beating but stayed on his feet. I admired him for that, and let up on him."

Patterson surrendered in the 12th round, claiming he had injured his back. Many of the people who are beginning to take Clay seriously are sports writers. They abused Cassius after the fight. They said he was cruel, sadistic.

"I can't do anything right for them." Cassius said, laughing. "They don't like me because I talk so much and am right so often.

"If I had knocked Patterson out in the first or second round they would have rapped me for taking advantage of him. So I let him go. I was nice to him in that I didn't put him in the deep freeze early.

"I looked out at the crowd and saw a lot of people at ringside from all over the country. Some of them came from Los Angeles, others from as far away as New York. I decided to give them a little show for their money. I said to myself, 'They'll feel cheated if I knock him out early. After all, they came to see a show and I'm going to give them one.'"

Clay carried Patterson. He could have knocked Floyd out any time he wanted to.

"He should count his money and call it quits." Cassius said "Floyd can't fight any more. He's all washed up. He should retire before someone hurts him permanently."

Clay was too strong too tall and too smart for Patterson. Floyd was inept from the very start. There were times during the bout when he didn't know where he was. "I kept bopping him with my left," Clay explained. "He couldn't get close to me. In fact he really didn't want to get close to me. All he wanted to do was to stay on his feet."

Cassius, always the showman, demonstrated how he whipped Patterson. Dancing gracefully up and down the room, he jabbed at an imaginary Floyd Patterson. He feinted, jabbed a long left and then threw a short right hand to the jaw.

Early in the real fight the referee warned Cassius for talking to Patterson. "I kept saying to him," Clay explained, "come on, Sucker, get past that left hand if you can. I said all kinds of things to him. He never said anything to me, he was too busy trying to stay alive. The referee kept telling me to shut up. What I can't understand is why I couldn't talk. Do you know of any rule that says one fighter can't talk to another? I've never heard of it."

There is no such rule in the book. The referee obviously felt sorry for Patterson. "I did too," said Cassius. "That's why I didn't knock him out."

*Wendell is aware that Clay is now Ali, but he continues to refer to him as Cassius Clay.*

## January 20, 1970

### "Foggy future keeps Cassius on the move," *Chicago Sun-Times*, p. 73

His name is Muhammad Ali. It once was Cassius Clay but he discarded it when someone, probably Malcolm X, the deceased Muslim prophet, told him that it was his "slave name."

Muhammad Ali was once recognized as the heavyweight champion of the world (and still is in many areas) but they stripped him of his crown because he was one of the first to announce his opposition to the war in Vietnam. He said unequivocally that he would not fight against people "who haven't done anything to me."

He refused to be drafted and that disobedience has been costly. He not only lost his means of livelihood and the heavyweight title, but also millions of dollars and the right to leave the continental limits of the United States.

And ... he may yet have to pay a heavy fine and serve five years in a federal penitentiary if found guilty of evading the Selective Service Act.

Not only is Muhammad Ali in trouble with his country, he also is in trouble with his religious brethren. He has been cast aside by the Muslims because he insisted on fighting in the boxing ring after he had been consecrated a minister of that faith.

Muhammad Ali talked briefly of his five years of troubles during luncheon at Fritzel's, and also urged everyone to see his Tuesday night computerized fight with the late Rocky Marciano at selected theaters in the Chicago area.

## Future Foggy

Tall and handsome at 28 years of age, he looks ahead to a future that is foggy, almost obliterated with uncertainty. As a consequence, he is a man rushing many places in many directions, all at the same time.

"I'm going to colleges around the country and talking to students," he said rapidly, "and they listen to what I have to say and they like me. I have had to turn down many offers to speak because I am about to move into a new home in Philadelphia.

"It's a big estate on the outskirts of Philadelphia with plenty of running room for the children and a big swimming pool. It's nice and quiet. We'll have plenty of privacy. There are good schools there, too."

After he gets his family settled in the new home, he will start working on his autobiography. "I have a good writer working with me," he said. "He is Richard Durham, who wrote 'Bird of the Iron Feather,' television's first black soap opera. The publisher has received orders from all over the world." He estimates that the book will net approximately $500,000, and a similar amount will be realized from movie rights.

If all should happen to go right for him in court, and he escapes the military draft rap, Muhammad Ali could very well become one of the country's most prosperous young men.

## Winner a Mystery

For the computerized fight he and Marciano fought 75 one-minute rounds in a secret place. They pulled few punches as they battled it out before the cameras. Muhammad says the promoters of the fight have refused to tell him who won the bout. Marciano never knew either. He was killed soon after in a plane crash.

Who would have won an uncomputerized fight between Muhammad Ali and Rocky? Who would have won if they had been matched in a legitimate battle?

"I don't know," said Ali who usually picks himself as the winner. "He was a real tough, hard punching fighter. He was 10 years older than I am and had to knock off fifty pounds for our computerized fight—and even then he gave me a lot of trouble.

"After the first three days of our secret fight, I had to take a few days off because my arms were all black and blue from blocking his punches. They were very sore. On the other hand, he needed the rest, too. I cut him up pretty badly around the face.

"I just can't predict who would have won the real fight. All I know is that he was plenty of trouble."

Trouble, it seems, has been Muhammad Ali's sparring partner for a long, long time....

*Ali shows surprising humility in refusing to say who would have won the Ali v Marciano fight. His career was in flux. We know that his greatest fights were ahead of him. He did not know if he would ever fight again. Oh, in case you are interested, Marciano won the computerized version of the fight.*

## September 23, 1970

### "Long layoff Ali undoing," *Chicago Sun-Times*, p. 87

It appears that Muhammad Ali has legally regained the degree of respectability that is required of fighters who aspire to fight for the heavyweight championship of the world.

The courts have proclaimed that, at least for the time being, he cannot be denied the privilege of pursuing his profession while awaiting a decision of an appeal as a conscientious objector.

So Ali, who is also known as Cassius Clay, is working at his trade again, training strenuously for an Oct. 28th comeback bout with rugged Jerry Quarry in Atlanta. He has not fought since March 1967.

Can a fighter be in drydock that long and come all the way back? Can he beat Quarry, a better than average trial horse, and then regain the title by beating Joe Frazier?

"I don't know if I can do all that," he said the other day while training in Miami. "All I know is that I have to get in shape for Quarry and then I have to beat him before I can even start thinking about Frazier.

"If I lose to Quarry there won't be any need for me thinking about a title fight with Frazier."

### Layoff Hurt Louis

It is not going to be easy for the ex-champion to regain the marvelous skills he possessed three years ago. Perhaps he has the same desire and enthusiasm for fighting, but whether he can regain the timing and co-ordination that enabled him to beat all challengers who once came his way remains to be seen.

Joe Louis was not as good after taking time off for World War II, nor have been other fighters who were forced, for one reason or another, to stay out of the ring over an extended period of time. They all lost something while they were away from the boxing wars.

At the moment, Muhammad is a reasonable physical facsimile of his former self. He weighs a fleshy 225 pound, which is 15 more than he weighed in his last encounter three years ago.

His trainer, Angelo Dundee, says Ali should have little trouble knocking off ten pounds for the Quarry fight. After watching the fighter train for a week, Dundee was pleased with what he saw.

"He's still fast as lightning," Dundee said, "and he still has that hard, accurate jab. He hasn't lost the will to fight and as soon as his timing returns he'll be as good a fighter as he ever was."

Dundee says Ali's greatest asset is his tremendous pride. Muhammad has never been beaten professionally and, Dundee says, that fact alone will compel him to fight with his old zest and skill.

"He believes he still is the greatest fighter there ever was in the ring," Dundee explained, "and he is determined to prove it all over again."

Muhammad is also aware of the fact that there is only one way to make money in the boxing racket. You must win to get those big, big purses. He has been guaranteed $200,000 for the Quarry fight. Before he was grounded, he collected many purses in excess of that amount, but during the past three years his income has been paltry in comparison. So he wants to hear the jingle of those big purses again.

## He Needs the Money

Ali is very concerned about money, which is not exactly an unforgivable sin. He made a lot of it and there are intimate friends who say he gave most of it away to his religious colleagues.

Muhammad denies this, however. He contends that Uncle Sam took most of his money in the form of taxes. In fact, he was shouting about that as far back as 1965.

The day after he knocked out Floyd Patterson in Las Vegas (2:18 of the 12th round) he was holding court for the press. Patterson said he was disappointed in the outcome because he was "fighting to retain the title for his country." Ali had threatened before the bout that he was going to take the crown to another country and "live in peace."

"Who was I fighting for?" Clay demanded. "Who gets 75 percent of all my money? If you think about it, you'll realize that I was fighting for all of you!"

So, on the basis of that comment and what lies ahead for him, Muhammad Ali apparently wants to start fighting for "all of you" again…

*Smith refrains from defending or criticizing Ali's anti-war stance. Wendell has seen what a long layoff did to Joe Louis' skills and has perspective on this issue.*

## November 17, 1970

### "Chamberlain vs. Clay? It's a good idea," *Chicago Sun-Times*, p. 80

There is all this talk about Joe Frazier vs. Muhammad Ali and a $10 million gate, the greatest ever in boxing history. Assuming that Muhammad, or Cassius Clay, if you please, wins that fight, what would Muhammad vs. Wilt Chamberlain draw in a heavyweight title bout?

"With me in there with him it would draw a zillion!" predicted Wilt Chamberlain, smiling coyly behind his immaculately trimmed beard. He stretched his enormous 7-3 body over the 6-foot hotel bed, his size 14 shoe extending far beyond it, pointed toward the ceiling like a pair of leather skis. "I honestly believe I am the only man big enough to handle Cassius," he said. "It's going to take a really big man to beat him. There isn't anyone in the ring today big enough to do it, including Frazier."

This was the giant of all current athletes talking a few days ago while relaxing in his hotel room a few hours before a basketball game at the Chicago Stadium. He is so large he is awesome and so strong that practically every player in pro basketball scampers in the opposite direction when he comes charging down the court.

### An Impressive Figure

Wilt Chamberlain weighs 290 pounds and not an ounce of it is fat; it's all muscle. And it is coordinated muscle. He's not a big, awkward stumbling goon. He moves with long, fluid strides and when he leaves the floor and soars toward the basket, he dunks the ball with almost effortless grace.

He is so strong and irrepressible on the court most guards are certain that if they grab the ball when Wilt is going up for a shot he could, if he desired, stuff the ball through the hoop with them still attached.

"I saw Cassius not long ago," he said, holding his head up off the pillow so he could see over his huge chest, "and told him to get ready for me. He said he thought it was a good idea and that he'd be willing to fight me. He said it shouldn't take me long to become a fighter because I'm a natural athlete. Cassius said we'll make a zillion if we ever fight."

Chamberlain gives you the impression that he has grown weary of playing basketball, despite the fact that his $200,000-plus salary is tops for professional athletes in this country. He has achieved more than most men playing round ball and is looking for new worlds to conquer. That's why, probably, he seriously considered becoming an end for the Kansas City Chiefs and also talked about becoming a fighter when Floyd Patterson was heavyweight champion.

## Getting More Serious

"I am more serious about it now," he said, "than I was when Floyd was the champion. My basketball contract will be out at the end of this season and this time next year I'll be free to do anything I want."

Chamberlain is as fearless as he is huge and, as a result, commands enormous respect wherever he goes. He has always been large and there was a time that he would turn vicious if somebody made fun of his height. There's the story, for example, about the man who was 6-7 who walked up to the towering Los Angeles Lakers' star in a New York hotel and said, "Well, well, here's the world's most famous midget in town again. How many appearances are you making at the circus today!"

Chamberlain didn't relish that type of humor. He grabbed his antagonist by both shoulders, lifted him off the floor and said, "Now, you're going to be a nice fellow, aren't you—and shut up!" The helpless 6-7 comedian was awe-stricken. He had never been handled like a baby before. "Yes, sir," he whimpered, "yes, sir."

Chamberlain dropped him. "Well then," he said, "be nice!" Then Wilt walked away before the man's bulging eyes.

## Fight No Fantasy

"I guess people will laugh when they hear that I want to fight Cassius," said the giant from Los Angeles, "but I don't think this is a fantasy. I believe I can move as quickly as Clay and I know that I could keep him away from me with my left jab, which would be much longer than his.

"If I can develop a good right-hand punch and learn how to defend myself, I think I would have a good chance to beat him."

In these days of mediocre and unexciting fighters, the boxing world might welcome such an attraction as Wilt Chamberlain. Nobody can say the man isn't colorful and there is no doubt whatsoever that he's a legitimate heavyweight.

His ability as a basketball player is universally known and acclaimed. Whether he can dunk anybody with a pair of boxing gloves on is another matter. Maybe we'll find out some day.

*It would have been an interesting fight. As Wendell makes clear,*

*Chamberlain was an outstanding athlete who could have and did succeed in sports other than basketball.*

## March 9, 1971

### "'I Ain't No Champ,' Moans Once Invincible Ex-Champ," *Chicago Sun-Times*, p. 28

New York—They led the once invincible Muhammad Ali out of the ring and down the steps and escorted him to dressing room No. 6. They stretched him out on a long table and he rolled over on his left side, felt his swollen right jaw tenderly and grimaced. The swelling distorted his handsome face. His personal physician, Dr. Ferdie Pacheci, examined him and said, "You'd better go to the hospital and haver this X-rayed."

There were about 20 other people in the room, including Ali's mother and one reporter. This was the first wake in the ex-champion's brilliant career. People spoke in whispers and Muhammad now knew the sting and pain of defeat for the first time.

His mother, Mrs. Odessa Clay, sat to one side, on a long wooden bench. She was attired in a blue lace dress and wearing silver shoes. "He'll be all right," she kept saying over and over, as though to reassure herself that her son was not seriously injured. "He'll be all right, I'm sure."

Ali said nothing. They stripped him of his fighting togs and now he had only a white towel draped across [his] otherwise bare body. He lay there like a corpse, body utterly motionless, eyes closed. He kept his hand on his swollen jaw and his trainer, Angelo Dundee, kept walking around the room, seeming confused.

Somebody asked his mother how she felt about all this and she answered:

"I feel good about it, really good. I think he fought a very good fight for a fellow who had been inactive for three years." This was her son's third fight since he had been stripped of his title in 1964 after he refused to be drafted by the U.S. Army.

The door opened now and in walked Diana Ross, the famous singer. She was Mod-dressed, wearing a black big-apple hat, white sweater with love beads around her neck, black hotpants and high matching boots. Ali, who had a string of 31 straight victories, including 25 knockouts, until this disastrous Monday night, saw her and came back to life. He sat up on the long table and invited her to sit next to him. Diana Ross, the singer, sat beside him, kissed him and took his left hand in hers. "Hi, champ," she said, smiling.

"I ain't no champ," Ali said with remorse. He shook his perspiring head as though he couldn't believe he had been beaten by Joe Frazier, now the undisputed champion of the world.

DR. PACHECO came over and said, "You'd better get ready to go to the hospital."

"MOMMA, are you going to the hospital?" Ali asked, holding his jaw.

"Yes," she replied, "I'll go."

The fighter got up off the long table, buttoning his collar as he walked into the adjoining room. He looked into the mirror and examined his jaw. It was swollen all out of proportion now and, as he studied it in the glass, he shook his head disconsolately.

Dr. Pacheco and Angelo Dundee looked at the swollen reflection in the mirror. "I don't know if it's fractured," the doctor said. "We won't know until we see the X-rays."

*Wendell Smith was the only journalist Ali permitted in the locker room that evening. He noted that there was one reporter in the room. He did not bring attention to himself.*

## *June 22, 1971*

## "A new Ali faces uncertain future," *Chicago Sun-Times*, p. 81

Muhammad Ali, the former heavyweight champion, came stalking into the Fire Department gymnasium for his daily workout with the usual array of hangers-on walking in his footsteps.

You would have thought that he was still the champion, his handsome head erect, eyes bright and a confident smile on his lips. His hangers-on shuffled behind him closely, calling him "champ" and waving to the crowd on hand to watch him go through his paces for his July 26 fistfight with Jimmy Ellis.

Somebody mentioned that maybe the fight would not draw a big crowd down in Houston because Ellis was once Ali's sparring partner. "He was like your batting practice pitcher," the guy pointed out.

"But," said the former champion quickly, "he's a good fighter and he proved it in the fight he had with Joe Frazier. Jimmy was ahead until Frazier knocked him out."

"What does Ellis have that could trouble you in this fight?" the guy asked, pessimistically.

"Well," replied Ali, running the question over in his mind before continuing, "he has a quick left hook. It's a good one. Not as good as Frazier's, of course, but a good one."

## Memory of a Hook

The mention of a left hook brought back memories. That's the punch with which Frazier floored Muhammad in the 15th round last November. It was the most decisive punch of the fight and clinched the title for Frazier in the minds of the officials judging the bout in Madison Square Garden.

"Were you surprised when that left hook knocked you down?" someone asked.

"Sure was," said Ali, rubbing the suet around his stomach with his right hand. "Sure was. It packed more power than I ever imagined. It was a stunning punch."

Once upon a time Muhammad Ali was a man of many quips and much exuberance. He was a braggart and super egotist. He humiliated people he fought with his brash comments and belittled their talents with a fearless arrogance.

His loss to Joe Frazier seems to have changed his personality. This is a new Muhammad Ali working out at the Fire House. He gives credit to Frazier and says he has nothing but the highest respect for his old sparring partner, Ellis.

He declares that he lost a little of his speed during his three-year layoff and that he just may not be the fighter he was before his encounter with the man who took his title.

Then, too, there are some heavy items on the 29-year-old ex-champ's mind. In the first place, there is a Supreme Court decision coming up very soon relative to his status as draft evader. That has to bother him, just a little. Also, there is Ellis. Ali has to be concerned about this bout, if for no other reason than that he does not know for sure how much talent he lost over the three-year span he didn't fight because of his draft problems.

## Hard Question

What about his endurance and stamina? What about his punching power? Has he lost his keen marksmanship with the left hand? Can he slip punches as he once did? Can he stand persistent pressure, the kind Frazier exposed him to for 15 rounds?

Those are the questions that have to be going through Muhammad's mind. If he looks back to the Frazier fight, the answers may frighten him because he was not proficient in any of those categories.

The truth of the matter is that nobody knows now how well Muhammad Ali can fight. Nobody has been able to determine since Joe Frazier whether he has disintegrated to the extent that he can't even cope with a fighter of Jimmy Ellis' suspected talent. Perhaps Muhammad Ali has lost it all, suddenly and unexplainably.

Whether he is fighting his sparring partner, or his mother, there is the distinct possibility that the new Muhammad Ali is nothing like the old Cassius Clay.

*Wendell describes a different Ali. Smith had fewer than 18 months to live and did not see the rematch with Frazier nor the third Ali v Frazier fight. It might have surprised Wendell to learn that Ali would fight for another decade ... although probably not. Wendell was familiar with boxers hanging on long past their prime because they needed the money. He would have recognized it: Joe Louis, Sugar Ray Robinson, and a host of other ex-champions fighting well past their primes.*

# 10

# Loss

*Wendell died relatively young and many of the people he bids fare-*
*well to in this chapter did as well. Causes of death include suicide, military*
*accident, boxing head injury, various health conditions and assassination.*
*The columns are primarily tributes, but some are not flattering to the dece-*
*dent. Like Wendell, many of the subjects accomplished something signifi-*
*cant despite the relatively few years afforded them.*

*The reader can see changes in Wendell's writing style throughout this*
*collection by comparing the columns he wrote in the late 1930s to those he*
*was writing in the 1950s. When Wendell started his career writers such as*
*Grantland Rice who wrote in a dramatic style were in vogue. As his career*
*progressed, Wendell began to trust the drama of the circumstance and tone*
*down his writing style. I found his tributes to John F. Kennedy and Ernie*
*Davis particularly moving.*

## *May 15, 1943*

### Smitty's Sports Spurts, *Pittsburgh Courier*, p. 18

I hope I am not writing Lt. Wilmeth Sidat-Singh a eulogy. *[Wendell*
*misspelled Sadat.]* He is missing somewhere in the vicinity of Oscoda,
Mich., where it is alleged that he was forced to leap from his plane when
motor trouble developed. The War Department has announced that the
plane was found, but at the time of this writing Sidat-Singh was missing.

One week ago Sidat-Singh visited this office. He was on his way to
Oscoda then for advanced training. He was wearing his "wings" and, naturally, was proud of them. Three of his flying mates were with him. They
had their pictures taken, and answered the questions of a host of admirers
who followed them wherever they went.

I guess I am the last sportswriter to have interviewed Lt. Wilmeth
Sidat-Singh before he disappeared. He was a great athlete at Syracuse

University. He starred in football and basketball. After his college days, he played a year with the New York Renaissance and Washington Bears and then went to Tuskegee. It is easy to understand why Sidat-Singh wanted to fly. He was the personification of speed, both on the football field and hardwood. He had courage, heart, and would gamble when the stakes were highest. It was only natural, I guess, that he should have chosen the Air Force. During the interview last week, Sidat-Singh said: "We know we have a great big job on our shoulders. We are among the first Negro flyers, and we have to make good. This is a war and we are ready for anything … come hell or high water."

Come hell or high water … that was Sidat-Singh. He played football and basketball that way. The bigger and tougher they came the better he liked it. He was a rugged, handsome guy, who had an infectious smile and a winning way about him. He won friends … he won ball games … and he won his "wings" at Tuskegee the way he lived … simply by being himself … modest, sincere and considerate.

Sidat-Singh is the first of our famous Negro athletes to encounter real trouble in this war. Like Michigan's great Tom Harmon, Sidat-Singh's been "forced down." I hope he'll come tramping back like Tom did through the wilds and wastes of upper Michigan … so we can all stand up and cheer him once again.

*Sadat-Singh was planning to attend medical school. He was a gifted athlete and an intelligent young man with great promise. Wendell expected to write about his life's achievements, not his sudden death. Welcome to World War II.*

## December 2, 1944

### Smitty's Sports Spurts, *Pittsburgh Courier*, p. 12

*Landis Is Gone, But Not Forgotten…*

Kenesaw Mountain Landis is dead. For 25 years he ruled big league baseball with an iron hand. And for 25 years Negroes tried to influence Mr. Landis to take as firm a step on the question of Negroes in the majors as he did on everything else associated with the game. Landis freed baseball "slaves." Landis cracked down on gamblers. Landis barred respectable men, Bing Crosby, for instance, from becoming owners of big league clubs if they were associated with horse racing. He held himself up as a symbol of honesty and courage before the entire sports world. He was against anything that even tended to cast a bad reflection on baseball.

Perhaps he was exactly what he appeared to be—a Gibraltar of Honesty.

But I cannot help feel that Mr. Landis never set his teeth into the question of Negroes in the majors with the same zest that he did other problems which came under his jurisdiction. True, he did give a representative group of Negroes an opportunity to formally appeal to the owners at a meeting in New York one year ago this month. And, he always insisted that there was no rule, "written or otherwise," against Negroes in the majors. But the fact remains he never used his wide and unquestionable powers to do anything about the problem. Landis played a subtle "fence game" on this question. It was the one problem he preferred to let ride. It was the one problem he never faced with the courage and exactness that he faced others. He created the impression in many quarters that he did not favor the ban against Negro players. But he didn't create that impression in all circles. I have yet to meet a newspaperman, white or Negro, who believed Landis meant what he said on that question. And, in reviewing his great career, it is the one big flaw I find. Perhaps I have misjudged Mr. Landis. Perhaps he did mean what he said.

However, deeds, not just mere words, prove the things a man stands for. Mr. Landis had 25 years to prove that he wanted to see negroes in the majors.

Yet they buried him this week and we are still fighting for Negroes in the majors.

*Wendell knows he does not have the evidence to convict. There is reasonable doubt. But the circumstantial evidence is overwhelming that Landis did not want MLB to integrate. In a sense, Landis was a victim of his own success. He had effectively controlled many aspects of MLB during his tenure, and Wendell knows that if Landis wanted MLB integrated, MLB would have been integrated. Smith treats Landis fairly, particularly considering Landis' lack of support, or direct opposition to, a cause to which Wendell was dedicated.*

## November 20, 1948

### Sports Beat, *Pittsburgh Courier,* p. 10

*Jake Powell Finally Called Out...*

I don't suppose there were many among us who shed tears the other day when we read that Jake Powell, once of the Washington Senators and

New York Yankees, had plugged himself with a bullet and blown himself out of this world.

True enough, it was a tragic thing. Suicide is always tragic. But Jake was a gentleman of tragedy. He was always a problem child, always in trouble and always on the go because nobody could get along with him. He rode the baseball rods from Chattanooga to New Haven, Springfield to Wilkes-Barre, Albany to Harrisburg, Dayton back to Albany, Washington to New York, New York back to Washington and from Washington to death!

On Aug. 4, 1938, Alvin (Jake) Powell, then an outfielder for the New York Yankees, was interviewed during a radio broadcast over WGN in Chicago. Asked what he did during the winter months, Jake, talking extemporaneously, said he worked as a policeman in Dayton, Ohio. Then, after a few more questions, Powell was asked if he had any hobbies. He replied that he derived considerable fun out of his job especially when it came to "cracking n-----rs over the head."

That remark created an explosion. The radio station immediately went off the air. Protests poured in from thousands of people. The Yankee ball club was urged to get rid of Powell. The avalanche was so tremendous that Commissioner Landis suspended Powell for ten days. Landis issued the following statement: "Over the radio in his so-called dugout interview, before Friday's game, player Powell made an uncomplimentary reference to a portion of the population. Powell has been suspended for ten days."

So Powell was suspended and much of the tension was eased. If Negroes in New York had been as vigorous as those in Chicago, Powell would probably have been sold or sent to the minors. But the blasé, cool, staid New Yorkers said nothing and Jake lingered for a while longer.

Last week they trapped him. He was passing phony checks. The cops nabbed him and he finished it. He blew his brains out in the police station.

Jake's gone. We feel just like the man, who when asked if he were going to Huey Long's funeral, said: "No, but I'm in favor of it."

So long, Jake.

*In fairness to Dayton, Ohio, Jake applied to be on the police force in that city but was not accepted. Perhaps Wendell should not have written a column like this after Powell had committed suicide. Wendell was not a mean individual. That he would write this column under these circumstances gives the reader an idea of how much anger Wendell choked back during his career. This is one of the rare instances in which he vented it.*

*July 19, 1952*

## Sports Beat, *Pittsburgh Courier,* p. 14

*Gus Greenlee Was One in a Million...*

We knew that Gus Greenlee, the big, robust, dynamic man of Pittsburgh was ill. But we didn't think he would die. Somehow, you just assume that men like him never get that sick, never succumb to the ravages of time or disease. Men like him, you figure, never have time to stop breathing ... there's too much for them to do.

But he did die, and the flowers they placed on his grave at the final rites last week are already withering away. He has gone, but you can't forget him.

He was, indeed, one of the great men of our time. Had he not passed this way, there probably wouldn't be a Negro player in the big leagues today.

He had as much to do with that "great experiment" as anyone we know, including Branch Rickey. It was Greenlee, in fact, whom Rickey called upon when he first started thinking about signing Negro players.

That was around 1944 and Gus, having been thrown out of Negro baseball by the envious and ruthless men who were running it, was fighting back. He was in the process of organizing the United States League, a circuit that never bloomed profusely but did turn out to be the avenue which led Jackie Robison, Roy Campanella and the others to the majors.

Greenlee had been negotiating with the Brooklyn ball club for the use of Ebbets Field. He intended to put one of the franchises of his new league there. He had selected Pittsburgh, Detroit and Cleveland as the other towns around which to build the league.

*He Took the Big Gamble...*

He had tackled an almost impossible job because the owners in the Negro National and American Leagues were blocking everything he was attempting to do. They wanted to keep him out of baseball because he was the type of man who would dominate any organization with which he was associated.

When he tried to lease Ebbets Field, for instance, this vile group of operators in the two established Negro leagues went to Rickey and warned him not to do business with the genial Pittsburgher. They told the Brooklyn owner that Greenlee was a shyster, a phony, a man not to be trusted.

They did all that, despite the fact that Greenlee had, as president of the Negro National League, made Negro baseball a going concern. He was the originator of the famous Pittsburgh Crawfords. He was the man who discovered Negro baseball's greatest attraction Leroy (Satchel) Paige. After he secured Paige, Greenlee brought in Josh Gibson and thereby united the greatest Negro battery of all time.

He organized the East-West game and started four team doubleheaders. He took the big gamble all the other owners of Negro teams were afraid of when he started promoting "classics" in major league ball parks. Before he came along, few owners wanted to risk their money renting big league parks.

But Greenlee went ahead. He was a gambler. He also had faith and believed the game could be sold to the public on a big time basis.

The result was that Negro baseball reached its greatest heights under his direction. Crowds numbering as high as 50,000 turned out for the games. The owners made more than they had ever dreamed of making.

## They Turned Their Backs on Him...

Those big crowds attracted the attention of major league owners. Rickey, for instance, was especially impressed. The daily papers started devoting considerable space to Negro baseball. Consequently, the ban against Negro players in organized baseball was projected with great force before the public. Baseball fans started asking why players like Paige, Gibson, Willie Wells, Buck Leonard and all the other great Negro stars weren't in the majors. The big league owners never had the courage to tell why, but they were embarrassed constantly.

Financial setbacks, some of which were caused by his willingness to take great risks in the promotion held, finally forced Greenlee to take his Pittsburgh club out of the Negro National League. When he tried to get back after a span of approximately three years, the men who had profited by his genius turned their backs on him. As a result, he went about organizing the United States League.

That was when Rickey came into the picture. He encouraged Greenlee to the extent that he offered him Ebbets Field rent free until such time as the team Gus planned to place there was a profit-making venture.

The league never did prosper, due to many circumstances beyond Greenlee's control. But all the time it was operating on a flimsy basis, Greenlee was drilling into Rickey the necessity of signing Negro players.

Finally, one day in 1945, Rickey said to him:

"If you think you can find me a player good enough to play in the majors get him for me." He then made Greenlee swear to secrecy. Rickey told him that no one must know about the plan. Later, Rickey gave him permission to discuss the plan with a few intimate friends. We happened to be one of the few he told. In fact, we spent many hours going over the list of prospects with him. Jackie Robinson's name eventually came out on top.

## Forgot All About Negro Baseball...

Greenlee knew that whenever a major league club signed Negro players, it would sound the death knell of Negro baseball. He knew, too, it meant that his proposed United States League would die.

But, unlike other promoters in Negro baseball, he did not care. He said:

"I don't care if I never own another Negro team or promote another game. I want to see Negro players in the major leagues. I know that all other Negroes do too."

When it finally did happen, he was happy. The men in Negro baseball who had fought him so viciously cringed and cursed the day that Rickey signed Robinson. They realized that the "gravy train" had come to the end of the line.

Greenlee, like millions of other Negroes, blessed that historic day. He never thought about Negro baseball any longer. He was not the type of man who would perpetuate segregation or profit off it at the expense of his people. He was a man with a great racial pride.

That's why, no doubt, Rickey had great respect for him. He could see through the other promoters of Negro baseball. They were only interested in money, nothing more.

Greenlee was interested in fostering the advancement of Negro players, no matter what it cost him personally. He was a big man physically and spiritually.... He was the kind of man you should never forget.

*Gus Greenlee did things no other team owner attempted. He built a stadium. And they came ... for a while. But his Pittsburgh Crawfords were funded by his Crawford Grille and numbers operations. When the numbers business met hard times, Gus could not afford to retain the talent that made the Crawfords "must see." Then the stadium burned down. He attempted to bring the Crawfords back into the Negro Leagues, but the other team owners kept him out.*

*Wendell perceived Greenlee to be different from the other owners. Gus wanted to see Black ball players in Major League Baseball and Wendell appreciated that Greenlee seemed to put the interests of his race before his financial interests. As Smith tells it, Greenlee had a hand in helping Branch Rickey bring Jackie Robinson to Brooklyn. Wendell never forgot that.*

*There is a touch of melodrama to Wendell's writing in this piece that harks back to early in his career. He had known Greenlee for a long time. Also note that when he refers to himself he uses "we."*

*December 25, 1954*

## Sports Beat, *Pittsburgh Courier*, pp. 1, 4

*German Boxer Starts Fund with $500 for Ed Sanders' Widow*

Perhaps Ezzard Charles, Johnny Saxton, Archie Moore, Sandy Saddler and Others Will Help Family of Fallen Fighter.

It doesn't take long to know and like a nice fellow ... even if you don't speak the same language.

You don't have to be a linguist or an interpreter. The guy is either okay, or he isn't.

That's the way it was between Peter Muller, the German middleweight, and Ed Sanders, the Negro heavyweight. There was a language barrier between them, but they overcame it.... Got to know each other and liked each other immensely.

Muller was talking about their friendship the other night ... telling how he met big Ed in Boston.... How they ran on the road together every morning.... How they worked out at the same time in the gym ... and how each was pulling for the other to win their respective fights.

Muller won his fight with ridiculous ease. Sanders lost his. Muller lived to tell the story. Sanders died.

"He was a wonderful fellow," Muller said softly. "He was one of the finest fellows I've ever met." His American representative, Fred Sommers, served as the interpreter. "We got to be very good friends. We trained together in Boston, ran on the road and ate together.

"After the workouts, he'd come to my room in the hotel, or I'd go to his. We'd show each other different ways to punch or how to duck certain punches. We had fun, and we learned a lot together, although we didn't speak the same language."

Sommers confirmed what the German fighter was saying. "They were always together," he said. "They were pals from the very start. That is understandable, too. Anyone who knew Ed Sanders just had to like him, he was that kind of person, a big lovable guy with a great future."

*Sanders Promised to Come Back Soon...*

"I'll never forget the look on his wife's face," said Muller, "when they told her that Ed was dying. I've never seen such a lonesome face before. I wanted to cry, but I couldn't ... not then, anyway."

Big Ed Sanders was 25 years old, tall, handsome and genial. Maybe he should never have been a fighter. He was too nice, perhaps. The 1952

Olympic champion, Ed was knocked out forever by Willie James in the eleventh round in Boston two weeks ago.

"I haven't been fighting in this country long enough to make any real money," Muller explained. "But, nevertheless, I'm going to donate $500 to Ed's wife. I want to help out in some way. I'm only sorry that I can't give more."

Muller and Sanders fought on the same card that night. "We were in the same dressing room," the German fighter said. "We wished each other the best of luck. When it was time for him to fight, I said, 'Hurry back , Ed.' He laughed and said, 'I will.' When he did come back, he was dead." Muller's $500 donation is significant. Here is a fighter who knew Sanders only a few days. He comes from a foreign country that not too long ago thrived on and boasted of Aryan supremacy, hated Negroes and killed Jews. Hitler is dead and gone, but the seed of hatred he planted is still there. Some of the stench could have rubbed off on Muller. He was too young, of course, to fight for the Nazis. But he wasn't, or isn't too young to remember or recognize Adolf's program of obliteration.

However, the young German fighter apparently has refused to accept it.

*Let's Help His Wife and Infant Son!...*

It is significant, too, that, as far as we know, there has been no offer to match Muller's contribution from any of the many Negro fighters around the country.

They, it seems, should have been the first to come forth and offer to help his wife and year-old baby in some way. To our knowledge, they have offered none whatsoever.

Perhaps they will.... Perhaps fellows like Ezzard Charles, Johnny Saxton, Archie Moore, Sandy Saddler and some of the others will get together and establish some kind of benefit to help Ed Sanders' family. Certainly, they are not going to let Muller, a German immigrant, set the example.

Ed Sanders was a credit to the fight game, to his country and his people. He was an all-around athlete at Jordan High School in Los Angeles, starred at Compton Junior College in football and track. He was also outstanding in both sports at Idaho State College. In October 1951, he enlisted in the Navy. In 1952 he was an Olympic champion. Every one of the fifteen million Negroes in this country should be proud of Ed Sanders, deceased. During the short time he lived, he represented them with honor and distinction. He was an athlete to whom they could point with pride.

Can it be that now that he is dead they are going to forget him? Is it not possible for some of you to come to the aid of his distressed and grieving family in this crisis?

Ed Sanders is dead ... but there is still a young wife and infant son. They need help.

Are they going to get that help from their own people? Pete Muller is not one of those people. He is a German, a foreigner.

Are you willing to contribute to this worthy cause? If so, send your contribution to the Courier, in care of William G. Nunn, Sr., managing editor. The address is 2628 Centre Avenue, Pittsburgh, Pa.

Meantime, here's hoping that the vast army of Negro fighters will get together and do something for Ed Sanders ... gone but not forgotten!

We'd like to wish Mrs. Sanders and her son a merry Christmas ... but we just don't have the heart.

*Wendell understood that death was an ever-present danger in the life of a boxer. But this death was particularly difficult to accept. The* Courier *established a fund for the benefit of the Sanders family. There was no safety net that would provide for these victims of tragedy. It was up to institutions within the Black community to take the initiative to address problems.*

## *November 30, 1963*

### Sports Beat, *Pittsburgh Courier,* p. 15

*JFK Asked to Meet Ernie Davis in '61;*
*Little Realizing a Final '63 Reunion*

The assassination of the President of the United States is a tragedy beyond comprehension ... an act of violence so dastardly that it transcends every conceivable aspect of rationalization.

It is, of course, irreconcilable.

Writing at the time of men who play little games seems almost sacrilege as one contemplates the magnitude of this reprehensible, absolutely unforgivable, deed.

In this hour of sorrow, as well as national disgrace, it is almost dishonorable to mention athletics, or the men who participate in them, because they are so inconsequential and irrelevant.

However, we do not think it inappropriate to recall at this time the untimely death of another young man, who in his comparatively small way, also bore the mark of greatness. He was one of those who played the silly, over-emphasized games of which we write.

He played best the game the President liked the most—football.

He played it better during his time than any of his contemporaries. Like President Kennedy, he exemplified the finest type of human being. And, when death struck—his star was ascending in the heavens.

Even though his combined scholastic and football achievements were in many ways unmatchable, they were not the source of his greatest thrill.

His greatest hour was the day, he often recalled, that he had the honor and privilege of meeting and shaking hands with John F. Kennedy, President of the United States.

His name was Ernie Davis. He died last summer of leukemia.

The significance of the honor was not that Ernie Davis asked to meet John F. Kennedy. It was that the President asked to meet him.

It was on Dec. 6, 1961. Ernie was in New York to receive the Heisman Trophy, the most coveted honor a college athlete can be awarded.

That same day, the great Syracuse performer had been named to the All-American team selected by the nation's football writers and broadcasters.

He amassed a total of 2,946 votes, an avalanche in comparison to the total polled by some of the other players on the same team.

The Chief Executive asked to meet Davis, who also was voted the "outstanding college player of 1961," only a few hours previously. Traffic delays and failure to pass quickly through a police cordon caused Davis to be late for the interview.

He missed the appointment. The President had waited at the Hotel Carlyle as long as he possibly could.

Davis went to the Downtown Athletic Club for lunch, sorely disappointed over his bad luck.

He had just started on his roast chicken at the Athletic Club when word was received that the President would be at the Waldorf-Astoria and expressed a desire to see Ernie at 2 P.M.

This time, Ernie got good blocking on the way to the President's hotel and made it in time. There he had three pictures taken with President Kennedy.

"I talked to the President for about thirty seconds," Davis said proudly afterward. "He asked me about my future and expressed interest in Syracuse, as the university had given him an honorary degree. It was my biggest thrill.

"I never thought for a moment I'd get the honor of shaking hands with him. This is the highlight of my football career. He's such a fine man…"

That night Ernie Davis became the twenty-seventh athlete, and first Negro, to receive the Heisman Trophy. Among those to witness the ceremony was Mrs. Arthur Radford of Elmira, Neb., the mother of the nation's finest football player.

Ernie was 6 feet, 2 inches in height, weighed 212 pounds. During his career at Syracuse, he gained 2,386 yards rushing. That achievement broke the mark set by Jimmy Brown, 2,091. He also broke Jimmy's records for total yards gained (3,414), scoring (220 points) and touchdowns (35). Brown now plays for the Cleveland Browns.

At the time that Ernie met President Kennedy, the writers took liberties and wrote such amusing leads as:

"The nation's most famous touch football player met the country's best college football player here today, etc..."

As everyone knows, President Kennedy was an ardent football fan and also himself, enjoyed playing touch-football.

Ernie subsequently was drafted by the Washington Redskins, the first Negro ever selected in the draft by that team. He later was sent to the Cleveland Browns in a trade for Bobby Mitchell, who still is with Washington.

As fate would have it, Ernie never had an opportunity to play with Cleveland. Last summer, on the eve of the annual All-Star game in Chicago, he was fatally stricken. He survived longer than expected but finally succumbed, on May 18, 1963.

Fortunately, he lived long enough to experience his greatest thrill.... He shook hands with the man who was assassinated last Friday.

Both are gone now.

End of story....

*Linking the passing of Ernie Davis and John F. Kennedy is effective. Wendell is writing from the heart. There is no melodrama.*

## *August 5, 1964*

### Sports Beat, *Chicago Daily Defender*, pp. 22, 28

They say that professional football teams are only motivated by hard, cold cash. Take away the fat salary checks, say the detractors of the pros, and there is nothing to the game. There is an essence of truth to the charge, of course, because the men who play professional football are depending on it for a livelihood. If they don't get paid, they don't play. The majority of the pros have homes and families they must sustain. They are tough men in a bruising business. It is not fun, in the sense that college football is, to play this game for a living. It is a serious business, a profession in which a man's security is dependent upon his ability to run, pass, tackle and block. The old college try and rah-rah spirit is irrelevant on the professional battle field. Yet, there are motivations which transcend finances in professional football. They may only be temporary, but on rare occasions money actually becomes secondary, and the will and desire to win is generated by a factor over which no one has any control. For the want of a word let's call it—inspiration.

Friday night Coach Otto Graham's College All-Stars will find themselves entangled with such a team, the Chicago Bears. The motivation in this instance is not money nor pride. Instead, it is death and sorrow, tragedy and dedication. The world champion Bears have pledged the 1964 season to Willie Galimore and John Farrington, their teammates who were killed in an auto crash July 26.

Owner-coach George Halas has called upon his team to dedicate each game to its former comrades, Galimore and Farrington. The Bears are responding in a manner which is above and beyond financial consideration. All of which means, of course, that the All-Stars not only find themselves confronted by the best team in professional football, but, also, a squad of grim, dedicated men with more than the fire of victory in their eyes. Tears of sorrow also are in those eyes.

Graham has a squad of talented players at his disposal for this annual classic. There are such fine ball carriers as Willie Brown of the University of Southern California, Willie Crenshaw of Kansas State, and Matt Snell of Ohio State. He is fortified with such accurate-throwing quarterbacks as Pete Beathard of USC, George Mira of Miami and Jack Concannon of Boston College. In the line are such sturdy musclemen as Scott Appleton, Texas, George Bednar, Notre Dame; Hal Bedsole, USC, Mel Profit, UCLA and Carl Eller of Minnesota. But, with all that ammunition, it is not enough to conquer the Bears this time. Last year the All-Stars beat the Green Bay Packers, then the champions, and the team from the northland never recovered completely from the shock. They subsequently lost the championship to the Bears.

Now the All-Stars are facing another shocked team. Death has shocked the Bears, not defeat. It has inspired them, shaken them from any lethargy, or over-confidence, which could have betrayed them as the Packers were last year. The Bears will win this one for Galimore and Farrington—35–7.

*The Chicago Bears defeated the College All Stars 28–17 as Wendell expected. However, the Bears followed up their 1963 championship season with a 5–9 record in 1964. It was a bad year to be a Bears fan. And things would not get much better for a while.*

*I know of four columns Wendell wrote for the* Chicago Defender. *He was writing for the* Pittsburgh Courier *as well. Both columns were called "Sports Beat," but the content was different. It is remarkable that Smith would have columns with two rival Black newspapers. It appears the experiment lasted for only one month.*

*November 27, 1965*

## Sports Beat, *Pittsburgh Courier,* p. 15

*Baseball Can't Forget Branch Rickey*

Branch Rickey will go down in baseball history as the executive with the most original mind, the game's best organizer and the greatest judge of raw talent the game ever knew.

He'll also be revered as the man who defied a vicious tradition and opened the door to the major leagues for all Negro players who had the ability to make the grade. That contribution was the finest of many he gave to the national pastime.

He developed and inspired such imperishable performers as Jackie Robinson, Roy Campanella, Don Newcombe, George Sisler, Pepper Martin, Dizzy Dean, Joe Medwick, Rogers Hornsby, Stan Musial and countless others.

Wesley Branch Rickey ... a name to be remembered forever, not only in baseball history but in American history. A God-fearing, checker-playing, horse-trading, cigar-smoking, double-talking, non-alcoholic sharpshooter with a mind so agile that it ran ahead of his facile tongue. Rickey was baseball's great emancipator long before he freed Negro players from the bondage of discrimination and segregation. He was the first to develop the farm system and provide opportunities for hundreds of youngsters who otherwise never would have reached the major leagues. He did that when he was in St. Louis winning six National League pennants (before Rickey, they had never won a pennant) and four world championships in 25 exciting years.

Rickey was considered a great con man when it came to finances. He had a fearsome reputation as a bargainer and down-beater of prices. The sportswriters complained that he paid coolie wages. But that reputation was not necessarily true.

Rickey had tremendous respect and admiration for Jackie Robinson, but it was Roy Campanella who won his undying affection. He threw his pocketbook wide open to Campanella, a gesture which proved that he wasn't a skinflint. After the 1949 season, Rickey called Campanella to discuss the next season's contract.

"Roy, you're a fine catcher," he said, "and have a good bargaining position."

"Thanks, Mr. Rickey," said Roy. "What kind of salary are you offering me for 1950?"

Rickey handed his bulky catcher a slip of paper. "Write down the salary you think you ought to have." Campanella was stunned. "Remember," Ricky reminded him, "you're the best catcher in the National League."

Campanella grinned, grabbed a pen from Rickey's desk and wrote out a figure on the paper. "Now fold it," Rickey said. Campanella folded it. Rickey took it, put it in his pocket.

"All right, Roy," he said, "that's your salary for 1950."

Campanella blinked. "Mr. Rickey, I put a big figure down there. Don't you want to look at it.?"

Rickey smiled. "Whatever you put down, Roy, I got the biggest bargain in baseball." They shook hands. At the door, Campanella turned, still puzzled. "Mr. Rickey," he said, "won't you just take a peek at that figure? I tell you, I wrote big."

"That's your salary, Roy," said Rickey. "we'll sign the contract in a few days." Rickey never sought special attention or credit for breaking baseballs color line.

Commenting on that historic contribution and the part Jackie Robinson played in it, he once said:

"Some honors have been tendered, some honorary degrees offered because of my part in bringing Jackie Robinson into the major leagues. I have declined them all. To accept honors, public applause for signing a superlative ballplayer to a contract? I would be ashamed!"

*In the story of MLB integration, Branch Rickey is the emancipator and Commissioner Landis the plantation owner. But the roles were reversed here.*

*MLB clubs could sign a player who was good enough to play in the major leagues but keep him in the minor leagues if they were already sufficiently manned at that position. At least that prevented other teams from getting the player. That is "covering up" the player. It is obviously advantageous to the team with the player. But it hurts the player and reduces the overall talent level of MLB. Wendell's teammate on his American Legion team, Mike Tresh, was covered up by the Tigers for a while. Wendell wrote a column about covering up players and used Mike Tresh as an example. Commissioner Landis ruled against the Tigers, freeing players like Tresh to sign with other teams. Branch Rickey created an extensive network of minor league teams while with the Cardinals. It did create an opportunity for many young players to enter professional baseball. However, Rickey also used that minor league network to cover up some of the players he signed but could not yet use with the Cardinals. Wendell knew about covering up. I do not know if he realized that Rickey was the architect of it. He clearly knew, and wrote, that Landis acted aggressively to end it.*

*April 2, 1966*

## Sports Beat, *Pittsburgh Courier*, p. 15

*Saperstein Dedicated Career to Display of Talented Tan Athletes*

The world of sports lost one of its most colorful and imaginative personalities when Abe Saperstein, originator of the Harlem Globetrotters, passed away recently.

Saperstein, a little man with big ideas, took a team of basketball players off Chicago's South Side, 40 years ago, and through perseverance and promotional genius developed that quintet into the most famous aggregation of Negro athletes in the world.

But he did not confine his activities only to basketball. He also was a person of considerable influence in the baseball world 20 years ago. He did as much as anyone we know to break down the barrier against the Negro in major league baseball.

He was not a crusader in the accepted sense of the word. He didn't jump up on soap boxes back in those days and chastise the major league owners for ignoring Negro players. Instead, he promoted games between Negro teams and insisted that those promotions be staged with dignity and in big league style.

Even though those promotions were exceedingly profitable to him over the years, he never hesitated to relate to the major league owners with whom he did business the virtues of Negro players. He knew that the day Negroes entered the majors that particular aspect of his business was doomed. Yet Abe wanted to see those players compete in the big leagues.

The day that Jackie Robinson entered the majors as a member of the Brooklyn Dodgers in 1947, he was elated.

"I've been praying for this day," he said, "even though I know it means the end of Negro baseball as we have known it down through the years. But, nevertheless, justice has finally been done and now the Negro player will really come into his own."

At that time Abe was acting-agent for the most colorful player in the game, outside the major leagues—Leroy (Satchel) Paige. He immediately started negotiating for Paige's entrance into the majors. He wanted no compensation for his efforts, just an opportunity for Satchel.

One day in 1948, when the Cleveland Indians were wavering and slipping in the thick of the pennant race because of a sagging bullpen, he called Bill Veeck, then owner of the club.

"I have just the pitcher to stabilize your bullpen," Abe told his good friend. "If you sign this guy, you can't miss winning the pennant."

"Who is he?" Veeck asked, excitedly. "We're really in trouble in that department."

"Leroy (Satchel) Paige," said Abe. "He can do the job for you."

Veeck heaved a disappointing sigh. "Oh, come on," he said to Abe, "quit kidding. I need a pitcher who can come in and get the other team out; Satch' is older than the hills."

"I'll tell you what I'll do," said Abe, "I'll bring him over to Cleveland and let you and Lou Boudreau take a look at him. If he can't make your club, I'll pay all the expenses for the trip, it won't cost you a thing."

Abe talked so sincerely and convincingly that Veeck didn't have the heart to turn him down. "Okay, Abe," Bill said. "Bring him over and we'll take a look at him."

Satchel was barnstorming in some isolated place in the west with a team of semi-pros. Abe spent considerable money on long distance calls trying to locate him.

"You gotta be kidding," Satchel said. "I'll never get a chance to pitch in the majors." Paige was then well into his late forties. He had lost all hope of ever being a major league pitcher. He thought Saperstein was pulling a joke on him. Satch' hung up, and Abe frantically called him back.

A few days later, Satchel, accompanied by Abe, his long-time friend, was in Cleveland working out under the critical eyes of Boudreau. Abe and Veeck sat in the stands. Satch' was on the mound and Boudreau behind the plate to inspect his pitches. This was the supreme test, despite the fact that there wasn't a hitter in the batters' box. It was early in the morning and they were the only people in the spacious park. Satchel threw approximately 100 pitches to Boudreau, the manager. No less than 90 of those pitches were strikes. Lou, who originally thought that the idea was a Veeck-Saperstein gag, now was convinced that Paige could do the job for him.

"He'll do," Boudreau told Veeck, "he can get the ball over the plate with something on it. I can use him." So, Satchel Paige finally made it to the majors. He won, or saved, six crucial games that season and Cleveland went on to win the pennant and beat the Braves in the World Series.

Abe Saperstein will be missed … especially by Satchel Paige and Bill Veeck, and all the others who knew and admired him. And I among them.

*Abe Saperstein is a controversial figure. Saperstein not only created and owned the Harlem Globetrotters but was a promoter of Negro League games and partial owner of a Negro League team. Wendell viewed Saperstein as one who provided Black athletes an opportunity to travel the world and earn a good salary. Some argued Saperstein exploited Black athletes and offered nothing more than the traveling minstrel show. Wendell's wife, Wyonella, was employed by Saperstein as an office employee. That could be viewed as a conflict of interest. Could Wendell objectively evaluate his wife's employer? But Wendell had already determined that Saperstein was a good guy before Wyonella was hired. Had he harbored concerns, it is doubtful that Wyonella would have wanted to work there or that Saperstein would have wanted to employ her. Wendell had known Rickey and Saperstein for more than twenty years at the time of their respective deaths. He had worked closely with both on integration. He trusted them and with good reason.*

# Bibliography

Alexander, Charles C. *Rogers Hornsby: A Biography*. New York: Henry Holt, 1995.

Altman, George, with Lew Freedman. *George Altman: My Baseball Journey from the Negro Leagues to the Majors and Beyond*. Jefferson, NC: McFarland, 2013.

Bak, Richard. *Joe Louis: The Great Black Hope*. Dallas: Taylor, 1996.

Banks, Ernie, and Jim Enright. *Mr. Cub*. Chicago: Follett, 1971.

Bass, Jack. *Taming the Storm: The Life and Times of Judge Frank M. Johnson, Jr., and the South's Fight Over Civil Rights*. New York: Doubleday, 1993.

Boyd, Herb, with Ray Robinson II. *Pound for Pound: A Biography of Sugar Ray Robinson*. New York: HarperCollins, 2005.

Brashler, William. *The Story of Negro League Baseball*. New York: Ticknor & Fields, 1994.

Dettloff, William. *Ezzard Charles: A Boxing Life*. Jefferson, NC: McFarland, 2015.

Dwyre, Bill, ed. *The Roger Kahn Reader: Six Decades of Sportswriting*. Lincoln: University of Nebraska Press, 2018.

Edmondson, Jacqueline. *Jesse Owens: A Biography*. Westport, CT: Greenwood Press, 2007

Erskine, Carl, with Burton Rocks. *What I Learned from Jackie Robinson: A Teammate's Reflections on and off the Field*. New York: McGraw-Hill, 2005.

Eskenazi, Gerald. *The Lip: A Biography of Leo Durocher*. New York: William Morrow, 1993.

Grant, Jim "Mudcat," with Tom Sabellico and Pat O'Brien. *The Black Aces: Baseball's Only African American Twenty-Game Winners*. Farmingdale, NY: The Black Aces, 2006.

Harkness, Jerry, with Dan O'Brien *Connections: A Memoir*. Ramsey, MN: Smith Printing, 2018.

Holtzman, Jerome. *No Cheering in the Press Box*. New York: Henry Holt, 1995.

Kahn, Roger. *The Boys of Summer*. New York: Harper & Row, 1971.

Lacy, Sam, with Moses J. Newson. *Fighting for Fairness: The Life Story of Hall of Fame Sportswriter Sam Lacy*. Centreville, MD: Tidewater, 1998.

Lamb, Chris. *Conspiracy of Silence: Sportswriters and the Long Campaign to Desegregate Baseball*. Lincoln: University of Nebraska Press, 2012

Lanctot, Neil. *Campy: The Two Lives of Roy Campanella*. New York: Simon & Schuster, 2011.

Lanctot, Neil. *Negro League Baseball: The Rise and Ruin of a Black Institution*. Philadelphia: University of Pennsylvania Press, 2004.

Leonard, Buck, with James A. Riley. *Buck Leonard: The Black Lou Gehrig: An Autobiography*. New York: Carroll & Graf, 1995.

Lester, Larry, and Sammy J. Miller. *Black America Series: Black Baseball in Pittsburgh*. Charleston, SC: Arcadia /Tempus, 2001.

Libby, Bill, and Vida Blue. *Vida: His Own Story*. Englewood Cliffs, NJ: Prentice-Hall, 1972.

McMurry, Linda O. *To Keep the Waters Troubled: The Life of Ida B. Wells*. New York: Oxford University Press, 1998.

Murray, Jim. *The Jim Murray Reader*. Lincoln: University of Nebraska Press, 1988.

Peterson, Robert. *Only the Ball Was White: A History of Legendary Black Players* and All-Black Professional Teams. New York: Gramercy Books, 1970.

Rapoport, Ron. *Let's Play Two: The Legend of Mr. Cub, the Life of Ernie Banks.* New York: Hachette, 2019.

Reisler, Jim. *Black Writers/Black Baseball: An Anthology of Articles from Black Sportswriters Who Covered the Negro Leagues.* Jefferson, NC: McFarland, 1994.

Ribowsky, Mark. *The Power and the Darkness: The Life of Josh Gibson in the Shadows of the Game.* New York: Simon & Schuster, 1996.

Robinson, Jackie. *Baseball Has Done It.* Philadelphia: J.B. Lippincott, 1964.

Schneider, Russell J. *Frank Robinson: The Making of a Manager.* New York: Coward, McCann & Geoghegan, 1976.

Schulian, John, ed. *The John Lardner Reader: A Press Box Legend's Classic Sportswriting.* Lincoln: University of Nebraska Press, 2010.

Schuyler, George S. *Black and Conservative: The Autobiography of George S. Schuyler.* New Rochelle, NY: Arlington House, 1966.

Smith, Tommie, with David Steele. *Silent Gesture: The Autobiography of Tommie Smith.* Philadelphia: Temple University Press, 2007.

Spink, J.G. Taylor. *Judge Landis and 25 Years of Baseball.* New York: Thomas Y. Crowell, 1947.

Talley, Rick. *The Cubs of '69: Recollections of the Team That Should Have Been.* Chicago: Contemporary Books, 1989.

Tunis, John R. *All-American.* New York: Harcourt, Brace, 1942.

Tygiel, Jules. *Baseball's Great Experiment: Jackie Robinson and His Legacy.* New York: Oxford University Press, 1983.

Tygiel, Jules, ed. *The Jackie Robinson Reader: Perspectives on an American Hero.* New York: Penguin, 1997.

Whitaker, Mark. *Smoketown: The Untold Story of the Other Great Black Renaissance.* New York: Simon & Schuster, 2018.

White, G. Edward. *Creating the National Pastime: Baseball Transforms Itself (1903–1953).* Princeton: Princeton University Press, 1996.

Wiggins, David K. *Glory Bound: Black Athletes in a White America.* Syracuse: Syracuse University Press, 1997.

# Index